Smugglers, Secessionists
& Loyal Citizens
on the Ghana–Togo Frontier

Western African Studies

* forthcoming

Smugglers, Secessionists & Loyal Citizens on the Ghana–Togo Frontier

The Lie of the Borderlands
Since 1914

PAUL NUGENT

Senior Lecturer in African History
Edinburgh University

Ohio University Press
ATHENS

James Currey
OXFORD

Sub-Saharan Publishers
LEGON

James Currey
73 Botley Road
Oxford OX2 0BS

Ohio University Press
Scott Quadrangle
Athens, Ohio 45701

Sub-Saharan Publishers
P.O. Box 358
Legon, Ghana

British Library Cataloguing in Publication Data
Nugent, Paul
  Smugglers, secessionists & loyal citizens on the Ghana-Togo
  frontier : the lie of the borderlands since 1914. –
  (Western African studies)
  1. Smuggling – Ghana – History – 20th century 2. Smuggling –
  Togo – History – 20th century 3. Ghana – History 4. Togo –
  History 5. Ghana – Boundaries – Togo 6. Togo – Boundaries – Ghana
  I. Title
  966.7'03

        ISBN 0-85255-473-7 (James Currey cloth)
        ISBN 0-85255-472-9 (James Currey paper)

Library of Congress Cataloging-in-Publication Data
available on request

      ISBN 0-8214-1481-X (Ohio University Press cloth)
      ISBN 0-8214-1482-8 (Ohio University Press paper)

Typeset in 10½/11½ pt Monotype Ehrhardt
by Long House Publishing Services, Cumbria, UK
Printed in Great Britain
by Woolnough, Irthlingborough

For Eliane
Me kwal wè vuvu

Contents

Maps, Photographs & Tables

Acknowledgements

This book has its distant origins in a doctoral thesis written for the School of Oriental and African Studies, London. I am grateful to my supervisors, Richard Jeffries and Donal Cruise O'Brien, and to my external examiner, Richard Crook, for comments made at the time. These led me to embark on fresh paroxysms of research and ultimately to divide the original project into two unequal halves. My first book, *Big Men, Small Boys and Politics in Ghana: Power, Ideology and the Burden of History, 1982–1994* (Frances Pinter, 1995), built on the smaller part of the thesis. The second monograph is more thematically tied to the original, but by virtue of a considerable amount of new research it bears only a passing resemblance to it.

I am extremely grateful to the following bodies for the funding that has enabled me to return to Ghana and Togo to pursue additional archival and field research: the Nuffield Foundation (Small Grant No. SOC/100 (99)), the Carnegie Trust for the Universities of Scotland (in 1994 and 1996) and the Hayter Travel Fund of the University of Edinburgh. The first draft of this book was admittedly unwieldy, and I would like to thank Lynne Brydon for insisting on surgical cuts. I am equally indebted to Richard Rathbone for taking the time to give a second opinion, and for urging me to be wary about cutting too deeply. I trust I have found a happy medium. I would also like to acknowledge the assistance rendered by staff at the Ghana National Archives (Accra), where Frank Ablorh, Edith Wood and Joseph Anim-Asante went out of their way to help; the Togolese National Archives in Lomé, which was a pleasure to work in; the regional branch of the Ghana Archives in Ho; and Rhodes House Library in Oxford. In relation to the latter, I am grateful to Bodleian Library, University of Oxford, for reproduction of the following photographs MSS. Brit.Emp. S. 528, pp. 216 (top), 216 (bottom), 217 (top), 218 (top), 218 (bottom), MSS. Afr. S. 934, Papers of S. Sandford (photo of court case). I am also indebted to Anona Lyons for production of the maps.

When I first took up residence in Likpe-Mate at the end of 1985, little did I realize how much this locality would shape my perceptions of Ghana and life in general – and little did the good citizens of that place realize how much I was going to become a recurrent fixture, returning periodically to quiz them on one subject or

Acknowledgements

another. It is with deference to them that I added 'loyal citizens' to the title of this book, for the fact of the matter is that the Bakpele and their neighbours generally resent being typecast as smugglers and/or secessionists. The late Nana Soglo Allo III generously provided me with accommodation in his home during the initial 15 months and on subsequent return visits. His generosity will remain with me always. The same is true of the late Jacob Torddey, who took me to each town in Likpe and further afield over 1985/86. Jacob had a genuine fascination with the history and cultures of the Volta Region. He also happened to be a formidable linguist and seemed to know just about every valuable informant in the northern half of the Volta Region. I only regret that Jacob did not live to read the final product. The most prolific informant of them all has been Emilson Kwashie, who has been incredibly generous with his time as well as with his private records. He embodies all of the best attributes of the Convention People's Party tradition and serves as a veritable memory-bank of local history. I should also make special mention of my best Mate friends: 'Don't Mind', Ben and Dan, who have kept me going with *fufu*, palm-wine and laughs over the years.

When I started out, the timing could hardly have been worse. While the Ministry of the Interior was led to believe I was a South African spy, the regional administration suspected me of being a CIA agent! I am eternally in the debt of Harry Asimah who, while working for the Committees for the Defence of the Revolution in Ho, saved me from the clutches of the Bureau of National Investigation – at some risk to himself. I was also greatly assisted by the Department of Political Science at the University of Ghana, and in particular by Professor Kwame Ninsin. The department remains my first port of call, and for hospitality in less fraught times I especially thank Professor Joseph Ayee, Dr A. Essuman-Johnson, Professor Emmanuel Gyimah-Boadi, Professor Mike Oquaye and Dr Amos Anyimadu. I would also like to acknowledge the efforts of Mrs Valery Sackey of the Castle Information Bureau in reassuring officialdom that national security was not under threat. In Accra, I am especially grateful to Mrs Emily Asiedu ('Auntie') for enabling me to join the list of regular visitors to her home. The 'Asiedu Institute' has generated an academic output that would certainly score a starred 5 in any British Research Assessment Exercise. I would also like specially to acknowledge the friendship and practical assistance across the board of Alhaji Mohammed Abukari and Kwami Tay, which in each case dates all the way back to 1985. There is also a special thank you due to Nana Soglo Allo IV who has kept me abreast of recent developments in Likpe and been an invaluable informant in his own right.

Fellow researchers and friends who have fed me with juicy titbits over the years are Tony Asiwaju, Gareth Austin, Lynne Brydon, Jan-Georg Deutsch, Hastings Donnan, Neil Ford, David Killingray, Carola Lentz, Birgit Meyer, Richard Rathbone and Peter Yearwood. In Edinburgh, I would like to thank Paul Bailey, Crispin Bates, Ian Duffield and Steve Kerr for buying me beer in Maxie's and keeping the topic of conversation off the dreaded Ghana–Togo border. Equally, I would like to thank Graeme Small (he of the broken beds), Bill McQueen, Pip and Gareth Austin, Christopher Fyfe, Martin Dent, Mariclaire Langstaff, Ken and Pravina King as well as my sister and brother-in-law, Diddy and Marc Skinner, for reminding me of the uncompleted task from time to time. I would also like to acknowledge Fergus and San

Acknowledgements

Nugent for the financial help which initially set me on my way. If one could play a book backwards to reveal its hidden message, like those 1970s records, then Rahsaan Roland Kirk would surely have a lot to say for himself. Every word in this book has been typed as a keyboard accompaniment to his great works – so if there are passages that make no apparent sense I blame his ghost. Finally, this book is dedicated to the incomparable Eliane Ngoué, who is by far the best research discovery I have ever made.

Paul Nugent
Edinburgh

Abbreviations

AEC	All-Ewe Conference
ARPS	Aborigines' Rights Protection Society
BMT	British Mandated Togoland
CCC	Chief Commissioner of the Colony
CDO	Civil Defence Organization
CDR	Committee for the Defence of the Revolution
CEP	Commissioner of the Eastern Province
CEPS	Customs, Excise and Preventive Service
CFA	Communauté Financière d'Afrique
CMB	Cocoa Marketing Board
COC	Comptroller of Customs
CPP	Convention People's Party
CPS	Customs Preventive Service
CSA	Colonial, Secretary, Accra
CSD	Cocoa Services Division
CUT	Comité de l'Unité Togolaise
DC	District Commissioner
DTG	Deutsche Togo Gesellschaft
ECC	Enlarged Consultative Commission
ECOWAS	Economic Community of West African States
EPC	Ewe Presbyterian Church
ERP	Economic Recovery Programme
GNAA	Ghana National Archives, Accra
GNAH	Ghana National Archives, Ho
JHP	John Holt Papers
JPC	Joint Provincial Council of Chiefs
NA	Native Authority
NAL	National Alliance of Liberals
NCBWA	National Congress of British West Africa
NLC	National Liberation Council
NLM	National Liberation Movement
NPP	Northern People's Party
NRC	National Redemption Council
OAU	Organization of African Unity
OCBF	Officer Commanding British Forces (Togoland)
PDC	People's Defence Committee
PMC	Permanent Mandates Commission (League of Nations)
PNDC	Provisional National Defence Council
PRO	Public Record Office
PP	Progress Party

Abbreviations

PTP	Parti Togolais du Progrès
RC	Regional Commissioner
SCC	Standing Consultative Commission
SEFPS	South Eastern Frontier Preventive Service
SMC	Supreme Military Council
SNA	Secretary of Native Affairs
TC	Togoland Congress
TNAL	Togolese National Archives, Lomé
TNFU	Togoland National Farmers Union
TOLIMO	National Liberation Movement for Western Togoland
TU	Togoland Union
TVT	Trans-Volta Togoland
TYM	Togoland Youth Movement
UAC	United Africa Company
UCPN	Union des Chefs et Populations du Nord-Togo
UGCC	United Gold Coast Convention
UN	United Nations
UP	United Party
VODYA	Volta Development and Youth Association
VORDA	Volta Region Development Association
VOYA	Volta Youth Association
V/TDC	Village and Town Development Committee
VYA	Volta Youth Association

1 *Customs Preventive Service post at Aflao, 1920s* (MSS. Brit. Emp. S.528, Bodleian Library)

2 *Customs Preventive Service post at Buem–Baglo, 1926* (MSS. Brit. Emp. S.528, Bodleian Library)

3 *Cocoa lorries leaving Leklebi-Dafo in British Togoland, 1920s* (MSS. Brit. Emp. S.528, Bodleian Library)

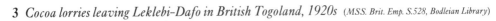

4 *Smugglers apprehended by the Customs Preventive Service, Noepe, 1929*
(*MSS. Brit. Emp. S.528, Bodleian Library*)

5 *A typical haul of contraband goods: American tobacco, Dutch gin, gunpowder, percussion caps, lead pellets and lead bars, Noepe, 1929* (*MSS. Brit. Emp. S.528, Bodleian Library*)

6 *A smuggling case before the court, probably Leklebi-Dafo, undated*
(MSS. Afr. S.934, Sandford Papers, Bodleian Library)

7 *Sarakope, to the south of Agotime-Kpetoe, where only a road surface separates Ghana from Togo. The bar is located in Togo, the taxi in Ghana* (Photo: Paul Nugent)

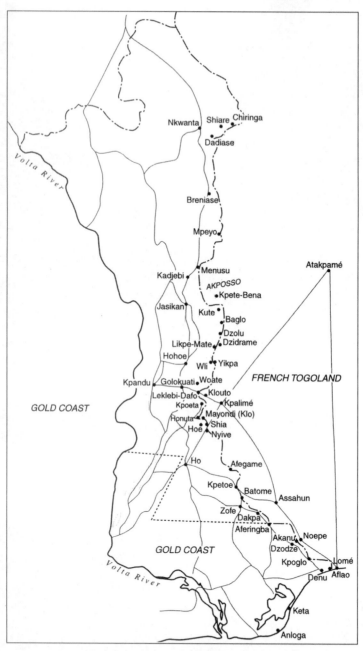

Map 1 The Ghana—Togo borderlands

Introduction

The Lie of the Borderlands

The Ghana–Togo borderlands in comparative perspective

Once upon a time, Europeans ruled over Africans and deemed that it was good. Although that assessment was never entirely overturned, doubts slowly intruded, and there came a point for each of the colonial powers when a withdrawal seemed to be for the best. This much is a matter of historical record, but academic opinion is still divided as to how profound the impact of colonialism really was. One view is that European rule left an overwhelming and lasting impression upon African societies – remoulding economies to suit external needs, restructuring indigenous political hierarchies and forging new mentalities in a refracted European image.[1] In the judgement of many, the colonial legacy is also very much a living one, and lurks behind much of the contemporary malaise on the continent.[2] Other commentators have been rather more circumspect about the claims advanced in respect of the colonial project. Sceptics point out that colonial states were typically anaemic creatures that were able to assert themselves when it mattered, but were never really able to get inside African societies. As far back as 1969, the doyen of Nigerian historians,

[1] This kind of assessment, with an emphasis on the deleterious economic side-effects, is exemplified by Walter Rodney in *How Europe Underdeveloped Africa* (Nairobi: East African Educational Publishers, 1972). Another older work, Michael Crowder's *West Africa Under Colonial Rule* (London: Hutchinson, 1968), paid greater attention to the impact of colonialism upon chiefly authority. This theme has recently been taken up, with a different emphasis, by Mahmood Mamdani in *Citizen and Subject: Contemporary Africa and the Legacy of Late Colonialism* (Kampala, Cape Town & London: Fountain, David Philip & James Currey, 1996), chs 2–5. See also Crawford Young, *The African State in Comparative Perspective* (New Haven & London: Yale University Press, 1994) chs 4–5. There is an equally substantial literature on the impact of the interwoven influences of Christianity, cash cropping and education. A good example is Jean and John Comaroff, *Of Revelation and Revolution: Christianity, Colonialism and Consciousness in South Africa, Volume One* (Chicago & London: University of Chicago Press, 1991); and John L. Comaroff and Jean Comaroff, *Of Revelation and Revolution: The Dialectics of Modernity on a South African Frontier, Volume Two* (Chicago & London: University of Chicago Press, 1997).

[2] Most recently, Basil Davidson, *The Black Man's Burden: Africa and the Curse of the Nation-State* (London: James Currey, 1992); and Mamdani, *Citizen and Subject.*

1

Introduction: the lie of the borderlands

J.F.A. Ajayi, depicted colonialism as a mere 'episode' in the grand sweep of African history, remarking that '[w]hile the lives of some communities were profoundly affected, others had hardly become aware of the Europeans' presence before they began to leave'.[3] The manpower statistics produced by A.H.M. Kirk-Greene, which reveal how pitifully few European administrators were on the ground at any given time – especially in West Africa – are suggestive of why this should have been the case.[4] In consequence, serious doubts have been expressed as to the capacity of the colonial states to effect much transformation of any kind.[5] Indeed, more recent events have raised questions of whether the European conception of modernity was itself ever firmly rooted in African soil.[6]

Although there are substantive differences of interpretation surrounding the colonial question as a whole, there is a surprising degree of consensus about at least one aspect of the European legacy: namely, the enduring impact of the territorial partition of Africa. Africanists who subscribe to variants of what one might call a 'fatal impact' thesis are inclined to highlight the manner in which colonial boundaries scythed their way across pre-colonial trade routes, cultural complexes and political sovereignties. The Nigerian novelist Wole Soyinka has summed up this assessment of the partition, invoking typically colourful imagery:

> One hundred years ago, at the Berlin Conference, the colonial powers that ruled Africa met to divvy up their interests into states, lumping various peoples and tribes together in some places, or slicing them apart in others like some demented tailor who paid no attention to the fabric, colour or pattern of the quilt he was patching together. One of the biggest disappointments of the Organization of African Unity when it came into being more than 20 years ago was that it failed to address the issue ... [We] should sit down with square rule and compass and redesign the boundaries of African nations.[7]

Even the sceptics have been inclined to concede that colonial boundaries were one European legacy that mattered profoundly in the long run. Hence, in the article referred to, Ajayi could write that:

> The new boundaries, once the Europeans were agreed on them, were intended to be permanent and no longer to expand or recede at the will of Africans. They were also meant to become lines of human divide, with utter disregard for the historical destinies of hitherto contiguous and sometimes even closely related communities. For a long time, and even now with the exception of a few, notably in the mandated territories, these boundaries have been regarded as not even

---

[3] J.F.A. Ajayi, 'Colonialism: an episode in African history', in L.H. Gann and Peter Duignan (eds), *Colonialism in Africa 1870–1960 – Volume 1: The History and Politics of Colonialism 1870–1914* (Cambridge: Cambridge University Press, 1969), p. 504.

[4] A.H.M. Kirk-Greene, 'The thin white line: the size of the British colonial service in Africa', *African Affairs*, 79, 1980.

[5] Goran Hyden has argued, in very elegant terms, that African peasants in places like colonial Tanganyika were for the most part 'uncaptured' and have remained so since independence. See *Beyond Ujamaa in Tanzania: Underdevelopment and an Uncaptured Peasantry* (London: Heinemann, 1980) and *No Shortcuts to Progress: African Development Management in Perspective* (London: Heinemann, 1983).

[6] Patrick Chabal and Jean-Pascal Daloz, *Africa Works: Disorder as Political Instrument* (Oxford, Bloomington & Indianapolis: James Currey & Indiana University Press, 1999), pp. 45–7.

[7] Interview with Wole Soyinka, 'Bloodsoaked quilt of Africa', *The Guardian* [London], 17 May 1994.

negotiable. To that extent, at least, the European intervention has so far had something of the finality with which [Harry] Johnston credited it.[8]

This assessment comes very close to the evaluation, offered some three decades later, by Basil Davidson.[9] And although their own agenda is a very different one, Patrick Chabal and Jean-Pascal Daloz have themselves suggested that 'the apparent arbitrariness in the permeability of those borders' is precisely what has lent them great practical significance in the instrumentalization of disorder.[10] Their reference to the proliferation of illicit trade and the manner in which violence spills across – and is almost attracted towards – frontier zones is reflected in a great deal of contemporary research.[11] Although modern African boundaries might not quite function as intended, historians and political scientists seem to agree that the partition was both decisive and enduring. To anyone who cares to listen, the map of Africa appears to speak in no uncertain terms: it says 'Europeans were here' while 'Africans are here and there'.

This monograph seeks to provide the first rounded history of one particular African border zone, namely, the one that presently separates the contemporary West African states of Ghana and Togo. On the face of things, this a border that bears many of the hallmarks of its African prototype. To start with, it represents the handiwork of a complex cast of European actors – British, German and French – spanning a period of some five decades.[12] In Africa, the process by which borderlines were arrived at differed not just from what had gone before, but also from the classic European and American models.[13] Prior to the twentieth century – when, as Ali Mazrui shrewdly observes, the African experience was exported back to Europe – rough spheres of influence between neighbouring centres of power gradually solidified as the formal state borders of Europe.[14] The making of the Franco-Spanish border in the Pyrenees, which has been so skilfully written up by Peter Sahlins, is a case in point.[15] By contrast, the American model was one in which settler populations repeatedly spilled across the borders that colonial governments and newly independent states sought to fix, thereby necessitating the demarcation of fresh sets of

[8] Ajayi, 'Colonialism', p. 504.

[9] Davidson, *The Black Man's Burden.*

[10] Chabal and Daloz, *Africa Works*, pp. xix, 88.

[11] I follow the standard distinction between boundaries and frontiers. The former represent lines of separation, whereas the latter represent the zones located on either side of those lines. The term 'border' may be used in a more abstract sense than 'boundary', but here I will deploy them more or less interchangeably. On these distinctions, see J.R.V. Prescott, *Political Boundaries and Frontiers* (London: Allen & Unwin, 1987), chs 1–2.

[12] The British first defined their south-eastern border in 1874. The arrival of the Germans in 1884 necessitated a formal partition of the interior over the following decade. The expulsion of the Germans after the First World War was then followed by a further division of territory between the British and the French in 1919. Towards the end of the following decade, this border was finally fixed on the ground.

[13] I have paid some attention to the question of pre-colonial frontiers in 'Arbitrary lines and the people's minds: a dissenting view on colonial boundaries in West Africa', in Paul Nugent and A.I. Asiwaju (eds) *African Boundaries: Barriers, Conduits and Opportunities* (London & New York: Frances Pinter, 1996), pp. 36–41. See also Verkijika G. Fanso, 'Traditional and colonial African boundaries: concepts and functions in inter-group relations', *Présence Africaine*, 137/138, 1986.

[14] Ali Mazrui, *The Africans: A Triple Heritage* (London: BBC Publications, 1986), pp. 276–7.

[15] Peter Sahlins, *Boundaries: The Making of France and Spain in the Pyrenees* (Berkeley: University of California Press, 1989).

boundaries. Across most of Africa, boundaries were not an organic development, but neither were they the product of rolling frontiers of colonial settlement. Instead, they arose out discrete decisions on the part of the European powers to divide African space between themselves. The Germano-British agreements to partition the trans-Volta in the later nineteenth century, and the subsequent repartition of German Togoland between Britain and France after the First World War, were not even made on African soil.

Secondly, this border was arrived at by means of an interplay between the standard European cartographical conventions and a series of local interventions.[16] The normal pattern was for verbal agreements to be followed by the production of maps purporting to represent African spatial realities. The lines that were delineated had subsequently to be demarcated on the ground, usually through resort to a boundary commission.[17] Because cartographic symbolism and mother nature did not always see eye to eye, the maps had frequently to be modified in the light of conditions in the field. Although in this particular case there was a greater resort to rivers and watersheds than in some other parts of Africa, where astronomical lines were preferred, the process of arriving at boundaries was a broadly familiar one. Moreover, at the conclusion of the process, the Ghana–Togo border was scarcely visible to the naked eye, even after a string of pillars and cairns had been physically erected.[18] Although the Togolese authorities have since fenced a section of the border in Lomé, there is still no physical barrier separating the two countries.[19]

Thirdly, this boundary might be considered fairly typical in that it cuts through what A.I. Asiwaju calls common 'culture areas' – a term that is intended to be broader than that of 'tribes' or ethnic groups. In his continental checklist, Asiwaju lists the Ewe, Akposso, Konkomba, Anufo and Moba as cultures divided by this particular line.[20] Although one may quibble about the contents of the list, the salient point is that the Ghana–Togo border appears to segment a greater number of 'culture areas' than many others. Finally, the carryover of boundaries into the independence era, which has been much lamented by Soyinka and others, is very obvious in respect of this particular region. To all intents and purposes, the present borderline is the same as that which was demarcated by the Franco-British Boundary Commission of 1927–29.

---

[16] There is a very substantial literature on the power of the map. The concerns of this study lie elsewhere, but I have been influenced by my reading of some of this literature. See Matthew Edney, *Mapping an Empire: The Geographical Construction of British India 1765–1843* (Chicago: University of Chicago Press, 1990); Jeremy Black, *Maps and History: Constructing Images of the Past* (New Haven & London: Yale University Press, 1997); Jeffrey C. Stone, *A Short History of the Cartography of Africa* (Lewiston, Queenston & Lampeter: Edwin Mellen Press, 1995); also Peter Yearwood, 'From lines on maps to national boundaries: the case of Northern Nigeria and Cameroun', in J. Stone (ed.), *Maps and Africa* (1994), and '"In a casual way with a blue pencil": British policy and the partition of Kamerun, 1914–1919', *Canadian Journal of African Studies*, 27, 2, 1993.

[17] In distinguishing between delimitation and demarcation, I am again following orthodox terminology. On this point, see Prescott, *Political Boundaries and Frontiers*, p. 11.

[18] This is a typical pattern. See Ieuan Griffiths, 'Permeable boundaries in Africa', in Nugent and Asiwaju, *African Boundaries*.

[19] The Togolese erected a fence along the most sensitive part of the border in 1996.

[20] A.I. Asiwaju, 'Partitioned culture areas: a checklist', in A.I. Asiwaju (ed.), *Partitioned Africans: Ethnic Relations Across Africa's International Boundaries 1884–1984* (London & Lagos: Christopher Hurst and University of Lagos Press, 1984), p. 257.

Although the governments of Ghana and Togo have periodically convened their own joint boundary commissions to clear up lingering uncertainties – and at other times have bemoaned the fact that there was any partition at all – the line itself is deeply etched into the political landscape.

For all of these reasons, therefore the Ghana–Togo border appears to provide the ideal site for the borderlands scholar in search of a case-study. In what follows, however, I wish to contest much of the conventional wisdom about African boundaries on four grounds: firstly, that European constructions owed more than is commonly thought to indigenous precedents; secondly, and more importantly, that the act of creating a paper border set in motion a local dynamic in which populations became actively engaged in the inscription of the contours on the ground; thirdly, that ethnic identities were actually the product of the border – rather than existing prior to the partition – but also that they proved far less salient than local and indeed territorial identities; and finally, that far from being marginal, border communities have been active participants in the shaping of national cultures and indeed the contours of the state itself. My task is therefore an ambitious one, namely, to demonstrate that most of the expectations about the impact of colonial boundaries upon African peoples are confounded in this instance. Although this constitutes a single case-study, I believe that its findings carry important implications for our understanding of other border regions. It would be helpful to give the reader some sense of the route which was taken in order to arrive at this unexpected destination. This inevitably involves an element of personal biography, not for reasons of academic self-indulgence dressed up as 'self-reflexivity', but because the final product genuinely has resulted from a dynamic interaction between the researcher and the subject of enquiry.

Focus of the study

By comparison with some regions of the world, African boundary studies are still in their relative infancy. However, a reasonably substantial body of theses, monographs and articles has appeared over the last three decades – some of it informed by a reading of the comparative literature – that has been of assistance in framing relevant questions for research.[21] African boundary studies fall into two broad categories. The first is made up of research that has taken the state, and associated issues of territorial sovereignty, as its primary focus. Within this corpus, there is a further distinction to be made between those studies that have a legalistic focus and others whose concerns are primarily political. The former deal mostly with the definition of boundaries, associated disputes and mechanisms for their resolution.[22] The second

---

[21] A.I. Asiwaju has led the way in seeking to break down the insularity of Africanists, by drawing attention to the similarities (and differences) between African borderlands and those of other parts of the globe. See, for example, his 'Borderlands in Africa: a comparative research perspective with particular reference to Western Europe', in Nugent and Asiwaju, *African Boundaries*.

[22] See, for example, Ian Brownlie, *African Boundaries: A Legal and Diplomatic Encyclopaedia* (London: Christopher Hurst/Royal Institute of International Affairs, 1979); S. Pierre Petrides, *The Boundary Question Between Ethiopia and Somalia: A Legal and Diplomatic Survey with 20 Maps* (New Delhi: People's Publishing House, undated); and the contributions to Carl Gösta Widstrand (ed.), *African Boundary Problems* (Uppsala: Scandinavian Institute of African Studies, 1969).

sub-category is more interested in the political phenomena that arise out of the existence of international boundaries, such as irredentism, separatism, regionalism and the problem of refugees.[23] The second broad category comprises research that is primarily local in scope. Its practitioners are less interested in state institutions than in the experiences of border communities themselves. Some historical studies, most notably the monographs of A.I. Asiwaju and William Miles, have considered the divergence of administrative practices, especially chieftaincy, on either side of a boundary line.[24] Other research carried out by historians, geographers and anthropologists has focused on local experiences and uses of the border. This includes studies of community, migration, refugee flows and international smuggling networks.[25]

The two broad clusters of research have therefore addressed themselves to different kinds of issues, each offering something that is missing from the other. Hence the first body of writing pays serious attention to the linkages between border regions and their hinterlands, whereas the second has a tendency to depict border communities in a more disembodied fashion. On the other hand, the second body of literature makes up for the rather abstracted coverage of borders in much of the state-centred literature. In this book, I seek to mine some of the advantages of both approaches. I endeavour to make sense of everyday interactions across the line, but also to examine how border communities have become participants in the shaping of national

---

[23] See, for example, Saadia Touval, *The Boundary Politics of Independent Africa* (Cambridge, Mass.: Harvard University Press, 1972); Christopher Clapham, 'Boundaries and states in the new African order' and other contributions to Daniel Bach (ed.) *Regionalisation in Africa: Integration and Disintegration* (Indianapolis & Oxford: Indiana University Press & James Currey, 1999); and David McDermott Hughes, 'Refugees and squatters: immigration and the politics of territory on the Zimbabwe–Mozambique border', *Journal of Southern African Studies*, 25, 4, 1999. For a revisionist account of how hard boundaries have helped to configure power relations within African states, see Jeffrey Herbst, *States and Power in Africa: Comparative Lessons in Authority and Control* (Princeton: Princeton University Press, 2000).

[24] A.I. Asiwaju, *Western Yorubaland Under European Rule: A Comparative Analysis of French and British Colonialism* (London: Longman, 1976), and William F.S. Miles, *Hausaland Divided: Colonialism and Independence in Nigeria and Niger* (Ithaca & London: Cornell University Press, 1994).

[25] A.I. Asiwaju, 'Migrations as revolt: the example of the Ivory Coast and the Upper Volta before 1945', *Journal of African History*, 17, 4, 1976 and 'Law in African borderlands: the lived experience of the Yoruba astride the Nigeria–Dahomey border', in Kristin Mann and Richard Roberts (eds), *Law in Colonial Africa* (Portsmouth, NH & London: Heinemann & James Currey, 1991). Also S.H. Phiri, 'National integration, rural development and frontier communities: the case of the Chewa and the Ngoni astride Zambian boundaries with Malawi and Mozambique'; Bawuro Barkindo, 'The Mandara astride the Nigeria–Cameroon boundary'; and David Collins, 'Partitioned culture areas and smuggling: the Hausa and groundnut trade across the Nigeria– Niger boundary up to the 1970s', all in Asiwaju, *Partitioned Africans;* and Janet MacGaffey, *The Real Economy of Zaire: The Contribution of Smuggling to National Wealth* (London: James Currey, 1991). See also D.J. Thom, *The Nigeria-Niger Boundary, 1890–1906: A Study of Ethnic Frontiers and a Colonial Boundary*, Africa Series, 23, Athens: Ohio University Centre for International Studies, 1975; Wilberforce L. Hinjari, 'The impact of an international boundary on the political, social and economic relations of border communities: a case study of the Kano/Katsina states of Nigeria and Niger Republic', in A.I. Asiwaju and B.M. Barkindo (eds), *The Nigeria-Niger Transborder Co-operation* (Lagos & Oxford: Malthouse Press, 1993); and Vincent B. Thompson, 'The phenomenon of shifting frontiers: the Kenya–Somalia case in the Horn of Africa', *Journal of Asian and African Studies*, 30, 1–2, 1995. For a comparative overview, with African examples, see Hastings Donnan and Thomas M. Wilson, *Borders: Frontiers of Nation and State* (Oxford & New York: Berg, 1999).

cultures. In that sense, I have come to think of this project as a hybrid between the insights of an Asiwaju and a Peel.[26]

In truth, this is not how I initially conceived of the research. When I first embarked for the field in the latter part of 1985, it was very much with a view to conducting detailed local research that would address the question of what borders have meant to the Ewe and other divided peoples. Under the influence of some political science literature that suggested that the Ghanaian state was in retreat, I fully expected to encounter communities whose frame of reference lay across a nominal boundary line rather than with their more distant national hinterlands.[27] I was particularly interested in the phenomenon of smuggling, because I expected it to shed light both on the strength of cross-border affiliations and the process of disengagement from the state. After some months of interviewing in Likpe, it dawned upon me that my starting assumptions were out of kilter with the perceptions of my informants. I became conscious of the fact that while villagers made frequent journeys across the borderline, they nevertheless regarded Togo as a foreign land where unpredictable (and often unpalatable) things were likely to happen. I was also struck by the fact that my informants identified strenuously with something called Ghana, and were often more familiar with the geography of Central Region than, say, with the Atakpamé area that was considerably closer. Of course, I had read enough about fieldwork methodology to be alert to the possibility that my informants were telling me what they thought I wanted to hear. However, after 15 months of local research and a number of follow-up visits, the consistency of responses during formal interviews and more informal interactions – carried out in people's homes, on the road and in local bars – convinced me that my starting assumptions had indeed been misplaced and that the border did constitute a mental barrier of sorts.

It eventually dawned on me that it might be impossible to divorce the macro-question of why colonial boundaries persisted from the micro-question of how border people made use of them. I therefore began to explore the possibility that border communities had helped to give practical effect to the paper partition. As I delved more deeply into land cases during subsequent research visits, I was struck by the frequency with which litigants invoked the partition in order to disqualify rival claimants from the other side of the line. This confirmed that border peoples were not just victims of arbitrary European decisions, but were significant contributors to these arrangements in their own right. I was also intrigued to discover that some smugglers had opposed Ewe unification because of the apprehension that it would endanger their livelihoods. The oft-repeated claim that it was a resolution of the OAU that has led to the perpetuation of African borders after independence had always seemed distinctly implausible. It seemed more likely that these borders were grounded in everyday local practices. I have ended up being convinced that the contraband trade has helped to render the border more legitimate and not less so.

---

[26] An Asiwaju in the sense of a shared concern with border locations, and a Peel in terms of the emphasis upon the incorporation of border communities into a national space. See J.D.Y. Peel, *Ijeshas and Nigerians: The Incorporation of a Yoruba Kingdom, 1890s–1970s* (Cambridge: Cambridge University Press, 1983).

[27] I subsequently went on to critique this literature in my Ph.D thesis, entitled 'National integration and the vicissitudes of state power in Ghana: the political incorporation of Likpe, a border community, 1945–1986', University of London, 1991, ch. 6.

7

Introduction: the lie of the borderlands

Nevertheless, a purely instrumental explanation is not adequate in itself. Whereas I initially suspected that patriotism was a convenient cover behind which all manner of illicit activity might be lurking, I gradually woke up to the possibility that there might also be a delicious paradox at work: namely, that the very act of smuggling made border peoples more aware of what made them Ghanaian rather than Togolese. The more I pondered on this paradox, the more the reactions of my informants seemed to make sense.

The point in all of this is not to resurrect some romanticized notion of African 'agency', which has been the target of much criticism in the past. In fact, the implication is actually a rather hard-nosed one: namely, that indigenous agency might be as disabling as much as empowering. However, even this would be to somewhat misplace the emphasis. What I have been tacking towards is an appreciation of the ways in which ordinary peoples have constructed the world in which they live – in the sense both of creating and interpreting it. One can readily see that border peoples have created an enabling environment for themselves, but it also has to be recognized that the existence of a border has brought constraints in its train. I am therefore attracted to a quasi-Foucauldian conception of power – although I have no desire to anchor myself to Foucault's problematic – because it embraces the possibility that ordinary people may participate in shaping the very ideas and practices that place limits upon their behaviour.[28] If the border may be regarded as a site of power, encrusted with its own specific forms of knowledge, then it has to be seen as one that bears a dual aspect. Opportunity and constraints are part of a single package, which is precisely what makes border zones such sites of ambivalence and ambiguity – and, of course, such fascinating research sites.[29]

In the field, I was further struck by the fact that state agencies appeared on the scene as purposeful actors. I became increasingly uncomfortable with the insinuation that border communities were somehow divorced from the structures of the state, when all the evidence before me seemed to demonstrate the opposite. In 1985, when Ghana was only just emerging from the most acute crisis in its history, there was nothing to indicate that the writ of the state had ever ceased to run at the local level. I therefore began to take seriously the possibility that the state was a significant factor in the local equation, and that its assistance might even be actively invoked by border peoples. At the same time, I have set out to demonstrate how the ideologies and practices of the Ghanaian state have themselves been shaped through a dynamic interaction with border communities. Border regions are often considered as marginal in a political as well as a spatial sense. This is especially true of Ghana where there is a deeply-engrained perception that the country has been constructed around its Akan heartlands. Part of my objective is to establish that the character of the post-colonial state has been moulded through its unfolding interactions with border populations. While the latter may be territorially peripheral, they have played at least as great a part in the making of modern Ghana as the notional core. Hence the irony of the portrayal of the peoples of the Volta Region as not quite Ghanaian by the least temperate spokesmen of the Busia–Danquah tradition.

---

[28] Michel Foucault, *The History of Sexuality: An Introduction* (London: Penguin, 1978), pp. 92–102.

[29] I differ with the otherwise instructive account of Hughes, 'Refugees and squatters', in that I don't perceive any necessary contradiction between the two.

Inevitably, as I was sucked into examining the relationship between border communities and the Gold Coast/Ghanaian state, something else had to give. Whereas the research of Asiwaju and Miles genuinely straddles their chosen boundaries, I have only been able to do so only to a limited extent. The reader will find that some chapters deal in detail with cross-border relations, whereas others scarcely touch on them. The reason is that this study is primarily concerned with communities living on the Ghanaian side of the international line. These are made up of people who often smuggle and have kin in Togo, but it is important to emphasize that the same individuals are likely to have even more family members living in Accra, to listen regularly to the Ghana Broadcasting Corporation and to belong to a branch of a mainstream or charismatic Ghanaian church. The history of the last fifty years, in particular, has been one of the embedding of institutions and *mentalités* that are quintessentially Ghanaian. Although I do not explore the relationships between Togolese border communities and their own hinterland, I would expect the findings of any such research to be commensurate. Although my approach has its obvious disadvantages, I believe I am being faithful to local realities in portraying communities that face both ways, but which lean more towards their national centres.

The scope of the research

This study addresses itself to the eastern marches of what was once known as British Southern Togoland, an area that is somewhat smaller than the contemporary Volta Region of Ghana (see Map 1). Although the internal boundaries and the nomenclature have shifted over time, the research area spans what has at various times been called the Ho, Kpandu and Buem-Krachi Districts. Some reference will also be made to the southern border, which used to divide the Gold Coast proper from German and later French Togoland, and somewhat fewer to the borderlands north of Nkwanta.

The research began in the mid-1980s as an in-depth study of one border community, that of Likpe, most of which lies within within a 20 km radius east of Hohoe. It was during this phase that I carried out the bulk of my fieldwork interviews and came to an appreciation of the local meanings that were invested in the border. It was in Likpe that I came face to face with smugglers, border officials, chiefs and one-time supporters of political organizations that had favoured either the confirmation or the repositioning of the border. Many of my examples are drawn from Likpe, and my fieldwork experiences suffuse the entire text. I make no excuse for this because some of the most fruitful research on Ghana and other parts of Africa has been informed by an appreciation of local dynamics. Some might argue that it is dangerous to extrapolate from local studies, but then it is extremely difficult to make sense of the whole unless one has understood the inner workings of some of the constituent parts – especially when the researcher is an outsider. It is arguably also much easier to work outwards from a local study than in the opposite direction. Although the doctoral thesis was centred on Likpe, I later made a conscious effort to widen the field of vision, both conducting interviews in other localities (over 1992, 1994, 1996 and 1997) and thoroughly mining the archival record in Ghana, Togo and Britain. When it comes to land disputes and smuggling cases, both of which loom large in this text, much of the richest material comes from communities that lay outside of my original fieldwork area.

As any contemporary historian of Ghana will know, the official record becomes noticeably balder the closer one comes to the present day. I have been fortunate in being able to tap some sources that have not been available to other researchers – such as current files of the Ministry of Agriculture, the Stool Lands Boundaries Settlement Commission and the Public Tribunals. But I was also able to gain access to the substantial archive of the late Nana Soglo Allo III of Likpe. When I first arrived in Likpe-Mate in late 1985, and took up residence in his home, I quickly became aware of the fact that he was harbouring a large body of official correspondence, some of which had begun to assume a second life as toilet paper. I salvaged what I could and asked Nana Soglo if I might be granted access to the original documents. Although he selected certain correspondence for me to look at, he held back most of what might be considered contentious – although some continued to turn up in its other incarnation. However, by the time I returned in the 1990s I had demonstrated my credentials, and over subsequent visits I was able to pore over the contents of his complete archive. As I expected, the files contained a good deal of fascinating correspondence on chieftaincy politics, but there was also a substantial body of material relating to smuggling, the conduct of border officials and the activities of the People's Defence Committees (PDCs), the Committees for the Defence of the Revolution (CDRs) and the People's Militia. There was also some highly revealing correspondence in Ewe between the Likpe chiefs and their counterparts located on the Togo side of the border. Taken together, this documentation furnished a working map of everyday interactions with governmental authorities – at the district, regional and national levels – and with neighbouring communities just across the border. Virtually none of this information would become available by immersing oneself in an official archive, and I like to think that this neatly demonstrates the virtues of grounding one's research in a specific locality.

The structure of the book

Finally, it remains to explain how the text is arranged and to alert the reader to some of the signposts along the way. The book follows a straightforward chronological format, which is the basis for the grouping of the chapters into parts, but it does treat a number of divergent themes. This means that there is sometimes a switch of register from one chapter to the next. I have sought to signal these transitions at the commencement of each new theme as an aid to the reader. The greatest disjuncture comes with Chapters 5 and 6 when the focus shifts from social processes to an examination of the politics of unification/integration. I am conscious of the possibility of a jarring effect, and I have therefore sought to use Chapter 4 as a kind of shock-absorber that can smooth the transition. At one point, I considered omitting the politics chapters altogether, but eventually concluded that a history of the border that did not look at the political dimension thereof would be less than satisfactory. I have therefore eschewed literary aesthetics in favour of academic functionality.

Introduction: the lie of the borderlands

The chapters themselves are grouped into three parts. The first addresses the making of the Togoland border by a diverse range of actors. Chapter 1 locates the European partition in a deeper historical time-frame, arguing that it derived much of its character from the fact that the trans-Volta region already bore many of the hallmarks of a classic frontier zone. It then examines successive attempts to order African space, culminating in the repartition of Togoland between Britain and France after the First World War. Chapter 2 considers the impact of cocoa on the mental geography of Togolanders as well as on the practicalities of land use. Through a detailed analysis of two particular land disputes, I show how litigants sought to deploy the border as a weapon to nullify the competing claims of their rivals. This chapter, which emphasizes African agency, therefore provides a counterweight to Chapter 1. This leads into a detailed exploration of the phenomenon of smuggling in Chapter 3. Here, I chart the evolution of a dynamic relationship between the Customs Preventive Service (CPS) and communities living on the Togoland border. I look not just at the role of the CPS in making the border a reality, but also at the contribution of smuggling itself to etching in the contours of separation.

Part Two takes up the history of the Ewe and Togoland unification movements that directly challenged the terms of the European partition. In Chapter 4, I set the scene through an examination of the impact of Christianity, migrancy and chieftaincy policies on identities at the local level. Chapter 5 then offers a reappraisal of the Ewe/Togoland unification phenomenon from the early 1920s down to the mid-1950s. I argue that the initial challenge took the form of a territorially based nationalism, that coherent expressions of Ewe solidarity followed somewhat later and withered on the vine surprisingly quickly, and finally that a rejuvenated Togoland unification movement was signally incapable of sustaining a constituency in the face of appeals to a greater Gold Coast.

Part Three addresses the history of the Ghana–Togo border since independence. Chapter 6 completes the political analysis, with a detailed account of how the Convention People's Party uprooted unificationist networks and set a lasting seal on integration with Ghana. It also considers why secessionist appeals failed to secure a popular constituency in later years, despite the severe and multi-headed crisis that came to engulf Ghana. Chapter 7 returns to the land question and to smuggling, and illustrates how the two have helped to entrench the border since independence. A brief conclusion draws together the main threads of the argument and relates them to some recent research on borderlands in other parts of Africa.

Part One

Drawing Lines
The Construction of the Togoland Border

1

Tar-Baby Imperialism
The Making & Shaping of the Togoland Frontier

Introduction

The notion that African boundaries were drawn in a haphazard manner and arbitrarily enforced is deeply embedded in perceptions of the colonial past and is often construed as the underlying cause for the troubled state of the continent today. It is distinctive in being shared by laymen and by informed commentators alike. It is, however, a commonplace that at once says too much and too little – too much because it underestimates the extent to which European boundary-makers were guided by indigenous precedents, and too little because it obscures the reality that the practical significance of colonial boundaries varied over time. In this opening chapter, the objective is to revise a diverse stock of conventional wisdom and to offer a more nuanced account of the Togoland frontier as a long-standing zone of engagement.

Although their special status as League of Nations Mandated territories meant that the two halves of Togoland were never formally colonial possessions, for most practical purposes they were treated as if they were.[1] One is therefore dealing with boundaries that functioned very like those that were drawn across Africa from the latter decades of the nineteenth century.[2] As always, it was Europeans who decided where the lines should be drawn and what practical significance would formally be invested in them. It is fitting, therefore, that this account should begin with a close examination of the influences that bore upon colonial decision-making in respect of the Togoland frontier. The crucial role played by Africans in shaping the outcome will receive detailed consideration in the chapters that follow.

During the inter-war years, British policy was overtly imperialist, in the sense that it ultimately worked towards the absorption of the western half of Togoland into the Gold Coast. 'Imperialism' is a concept that bears more than its fair share of theoretical baggage, and so it needs to be appropriated selectively lest it weigh this

---

[1] The two Togolands were placed under 'B' Mandates. A text of the Mandate agreement may be found at PRO CO 724/1.

[2] For a recent overview of the partition, see H.L. Wesseling, *Divide and Rule: The Partition of Africa, 1880–1914* (translated by Arnold J. Pomerans) (Westport & London: Praeger, 1996).

expedition down completely. On the one hand, one needs to be wary of any simple assumption that policy on the ground was the outcome of elaborate blueprints conceived in the corridors of metropolitan power. While the larger political aim was incorporation, border policy itself evolved incrementally as the administration responded to a cycle of practical dilemmas. Typically, attempts to resolve a particular problem gave rise to unforeseen consequences. The net effect was to force the authorities to intervene across an ever-widening field. On the other hand, while economic considerations were certainly never absent from official calculations, it would take some ingenuity to sustain an argument to the effect that the British expected massive economic gains to follow the takeover of western Togoland. In essence, they hoped to clear up certain territorial anomalies deriving from the nineteenth-century partition and to safeguard trade from the south-eastern quadrant of the Gold Coast. Once installed, their behaviour was rooted in their own self-image as the bearers of sound administrative practice. If there was a constant, it was the obsession with symmetry and sound public finance – one not normally considered a British cultural trait, the other almost representing a national obsession. These two priorities helped to confer a certain logic – however warped on occasions and amusing in retrospect – upon British actions in the field. It is this idiosyncratic package that I have chosen to label as 'tar-baby imperialism' – more for heuristic reasons, it should be stressed, than as a theoretical statement.

The political topography of the eastern marches

The popular belief that Europeans, armed with the maxim gun and guided by the compass, rode roughshod across the African landscape owes more to contemporary imperial conceits than is commonly acknowledged. The participants in the partition of Africa at the end of the nineteenth century found it convenient to depict the colonial conquest as a radical rupture – a grandiose act of the imperial will – glossing over the many grey areas of compromise and continuity. Modern critics, in search of the original sin of colonialism, have mostly been content to recycle this image. However, much as historians of slavery have exposed the hangover of pre-colonial practice into the colonial era, I wish to begin by proposing that colonial boundary formation owed more than is commonly thought to historic patterns of trade and politics.

In broadly comparable ways, Igor Kopytoff and Joe Miller have suggested that pre-colonial African societies evinced an in-built tendency towards political segmentation.[3] That is, there was a recurrent cycle of fission – as sections broke away for political and other reasons – followed by fusion as people abandoned more marginal lands at times of ecological crisis. As this cycle repeated itself, social hierarchies were repeatedly rescrambled, with claims to political precedence often resting on assertions that a given section of a community were the 'firstcomers'. The Kopytoff model has a particular resonance in the oral traditions of the various peoples who form the

---

[3] Igor Kopytoff, 'The internal African frontier: the making of African political culture', in Igor Kopytoff (ed.), *The African Frontier: The Reproduction of Traditional African Societies* (Bloomington & Indianapolis: Indiana University Press, 1987), pp. 3–84; and Joe Miller, 'Lineages, ideology and the history of slavery in Western Central Africa', in Paul Lovejoy (ed.), *The Ideology of Slavery in Africa* (Beverly Hills: Sage, 1981), p. 51.

subject of this study. The Volta Region of modern Ghana, a thin strip of land sand-
wiched for much of its length between the Volta Lake and the Togoland hills, is very
obviously a border region today. What is sometimes forgotten is that there are much
older precedents. Historically, this area constituted a meeting point for peoples
migrating from both the east and the west, whether in search of security or access to
well-watered land and other scarce resources such as iron.[4] From the east came Ewe-
speaking peoples, whose oral traditions typically refer to a mass exodus from Notsie
(or Nuatja, located in modern Togo), probably before the seventeenth century, and a
more distant migration from Tado and Ketu (in modern Benin).[5] The northern
branch of the Ewe, referred to as Krepi in nineteenth- and early twentieth-century
sources, divided into a series of small polities (singular *dukɔ*, plural *dukɔwo*), typically
consisting of no more than a cluster of villages loosely bound together.[6] From the
south and west came other peoples, such as the Nkonya, Avatime, Agotime and
Kwahu Dukoman, seeking to escape subordination to an ascendant Akwamu kingdom in the seventeenth century.[7] The decisive defeat of the Akwamu kingdom in

---

[4] For more on the peopling of this area, see M.B.K. Darkoh, 'A note on the peopling of the forest hills of the
Volta Region of Ghana', *Ghana Notes and Queries* 11, June 1970; and Paul Nugent, *Myths of Origin and the
Origin of Myth: Local Politics and the Uses of History in Ghana's Volta Region*, Working Papers on African
Societies, no. 22 (Berlin: Das Arabische Buch, 1997). The iron-working tradition of Akpafu is common
knowledge, but has not received detailed treatment, although there are references to a trade in iron and other
goods (including cotton) in Peter Buhler, 'The Volta Region of Ghana: economic change in Togoland,
1850–1914', Ph.D thesis, University of California, 1975, ch. 2.

[5] These traditions are likely to conflate what may have been a more protracted process of migration. Moreover,
as Law suggests, the genealogies of the polities that were established are likely to have been foreshortened.
D.E.K. Amenumey, *The Ewe in Pre-Colonial Times* (Accra: Sedco, 1986), pp. 1–11, refers to the Ewe tradition
of having originated from Ketu, followed by a movement of some segments to Tado. The emphasis on Notsie
is borne out by the traditions collected in 1915 by Captain R.S. Rattray, which may be found at GNAA ADM
39/5/73. Robin Law attributes greater significance to Tado as a place of origin and suggests that settlements
are probably older than Amenumey posited. See *The Slave Coast of West Africa, 1550–1750: The Impact of the
Atlantic Slave Trade on an African Society* (Oxford: Clarendon Press, 1991), pp. 26, 31; and for a comparable
view, N.L. Gayibor (ed.), *Histoire des Togolais, Volume I: des origines à 1884* (Lomé: Presses de l'Université de
Bénin, 1997), ch. 5. This probably reflects a difference of oral traditions among the Aja/Ewe sub-groupings.
On the Notsie legend, see N.L. Gayibor, 'Le remodelage des traditions historiques: la legende d'Agokoli, roi
de Notse', in Claude-Hélène Perrot (ed.), *Sources orales de l'histoire de l'Afrique* (Paris: CNRS, 1989); and
Nicoué Gayibor, 'Agokoli et la dispersion de Notsé', in François de Medeiros (ed.), *Peuples du Golfe du Bénin*
(Paris: Karthala, 1984).

[6] For a reconstruction of the evolution of a northern Ewe *dukɔ*, with an emphasis upon the decentralization of
power, see Michel Verdon, *The Abutia Ewe of West Africa: A Chiefdom That Never Was* (Berlin, New York &
Amsterdam: Mouton, 1983).

[7] The Avatime people claim to have migrated from the Ahanta area, while the traditions of Nkonya point to a
place of origin at Nyenyam, between Accra and Cape Coast. Both recall having subsumed a pre-existing population at their present location. For a summary of Avatime traditions and history, see Lynne Brydon, 'Status
ambiguity in Amedzofe Avatime: women and men in a changing patrilineal society', unpublished Ph.D.
thesis, Cambridge University, 1976, pp. 18–21; and 'Rice, yams and chiefs in Avatime: speculations on the
development of a social order' *Africa*, 51, 2, 1981. Also 'History of Avatime division', GNAA ADM
39/1/235. On the tangled Nkonya traditions, see C.C. Lilley, 'A short history of the Nkonya division', *Gold
Coast Review*, 1, 1925. The Agotime were an offshoot of the Adangbe. The Kwahu Dukoman were derived
from the main body of Kwahus who became tributary to Akwamu after 1710. See Hans Debrunner, *A Church
Between Colonial Powers: A Study of the Church in Togo* (London: Lutterworth Press, 1965), p. 14.

1733 was followed, significantly enough, by the relocation of its own centre of gravity to the east of the Volta.

In all likelihood, successive waves of in-migration led to a mingling of peoples rather than the preservation of distinct identities and modes of existence. This is best exemplified by the bricolage of peoples, often referred to as 'Togo remnants' or as the 'Central Togo minorities' who are found on either side of the modern border: that is, the Adele, Akpafu, Avatime, Bowiri, Buem-Lefana, Likpe, Logba, Lolobi, Nyangbo, Santrokofi and Tafi located in modern Ghana, and the Ahlo, Akebu, Akposso and the Adele in Togo.[8] Linguistically, these groups are unrelated to their Akan and Ewe neighbours, for which reason they have sometimes been regarded as autochthonous. Yet many of their own traditions allude to phased migrations from either the east or the west – and sometimes both. In the case of Likpe, for example, there are some traditions that refer to a migration from Atebubu to the west and others that repeat the Notsie story. Furthermore, a section of the Likpe community claims originally to have come out of the ground at its present location.[9] Equally, Buem traditions refer to a place of origin in Asante, but also lay claim to a migration from Notsie.[10] Contemporary language maps are potentially misleading, in that some self-professed migrants like the Avatime speak 'Togo remnant' languages, while there are also Ewe-speakers who are perceived as being autochthonous.[11] The safest conclusion to be made is that the mountainous terrain east of the Volta attracted successive waves of migrants and refugees over a period of centuries, helping to forge hybridized societies that are not easily captured by essentialist ethnic categories. In short, this was a quintessential frontier zone in the sense so brilliantly elaborated in the Kopytoff model.

This historic pattern was reinforced in the eighteenth century when the region found itself wedged between competing centres of power in Asante and Dahomey. The rulers of the Asante kingdom came to regard the lands to the east of the Volta as their own sphere of influence in direct succession to Akwamu. Moreover, Dahomey periodically endeavoured to extend its reach along the coastal seaboard, and dabbled in intrigues against Asante for some way beyond the Volta in the 1760s.[12] Failure in this sector encouraged Dahomey to concentrate on other theatres of conquest, such as Atakpamé to the north-west of Abomey.[13] This left Asante free to cement its own

---

[8] It is difficult to be precise about who should be included in these categories because linguistic criteria and oral traditions often pull in different directions. One might include the Nkonya, although their language has conventionally been classified as Guan.

[9] On the diversity of Likpe traditions, see Nugent, *Myths of Origin*.

[10] Entry for Buem in the District Record Book, GNAA ADM 39/5/73.

[11] The incomers often appear to have adopted the languages of the peoples who were already settled in the area, as did the Avatime. An example of an Ewe-speaking people who are allegedly autochthonous is that of Yikpa, on the Togolese side of the border. The people of Likpe-Bakwa and Todome claim to have come out of the ground along with the Yikpa people. On the minority languages, see M.E. Kropp-Dakubu and K.C. Ford, 'The Central-Togo languages', in M.E. Kropp-Dakubu (ed.), *The Languages of Ghana* (London: Kegan Paul International/International Africa Institute, 1988), ch. 6.

[12] Ivor Wilks, *Asante in the Nineteenth Century* (Cambridge: Cambridge University Press, 1975), pp. 53, 320–3; Debrunner, *A Church Between Colonial Powers*, p. 14.

[13] See Robin Law, 'Dahomey and the north-west', in Claude-Hélène Perrot (ed.), *Cahiers du CRA no. 8: Spécial Togo–Bénin* (Paris: Afera Editions, 1994).

authority east of the Volta, which it preferred to effect through local intermediaries rather than by means of direct rule: that is, through the Akwamu and Anlo to the south and the Kwahu Dukoman further to the north.[14] The latter remitted a tribute in slaves to Asante and exercised a harshly exploitative system of rule. The underlying resentment culminated in a co-ordinated revolt by the Krepi *dukɔwo*, led by Kwadjo Dei of Peki, against Akwamu in the 1830s.[15] This occurred at a time when the Akwamus had broken their own ties to Asante and were thus unable to call on the latter's support.[16] Despite military assistance from Anlo, the Akwamus were unable to subdue their northern Ewe subjects who established their effective autonomy in 1833–34. A similar revolt in the north, led by Akpandja of Borada, weakened the position of the Kwahu Dukoman and prepared the way for the subsequent emergence of the Buem state.

Although this turn of events ran directly counter to Asante interests, the latter did not seek to restore their former position until three decades later. In 1868, the Asante launched a concerted military campaign east of the Volta, executed by an estimated 30,000 troops under the command of Adu Bofo.[17] As Marion Johnson has observed, Asante tactics bore all the hallmarks of a scorched-earth policy, in that whole communities were levelled and their people taken back to Kumasi as slaves.[18] Even those groups that agreed to assist the Asante forces, like the Akpafu, found that they were expected to pay a heavy price in human beings.[19] The Asante invasion left a bitter memory, which is deeply etched into the oral traditions of the region today. Many of these traditions recount how a particular people took to the hills to escape the Asante armies. Others are more specific about a wholesale flight of population across the mountains into what is now Togo. There are, for example, accounts of how the Buems were forced to flee to Akposso country, where they were pursued by the Kwahu Dukoman.[20] A recent version of Likpe history recalls that the Bakpele stayed at Akposso for three years and cites this as the basis for a continuing relationship between the two peoples.[21]

Still further to the east, Dahomean military campaigns led to a similar flight of population westwards from Atakpamé into Akposso country. Robin Law has recently directed attention to this comparatively neglected sphere of Dahomean military

---

[14] On the relations between these groups, see Marion Johnson, 'Ashanti east of the Volta', *Transactions of the Historical Society of Ghana*, VIII, 1965, pp. 33–59; and R.A. Kea, 'Akwamu–Anlo relations', *Transactions of the Historical Society of Ghana*, X, 1969, pp. 28–63; Debrunner, *A Church Between Colonial Powers*, pp. 13–19.

[15] On these events, see C.W. Welman, *The Native States of the Gold Coast Part I: Peki* (London: Dawson reprint edn, 1969), pp. 10–12.

[16] Johnson, 'Ashanti east of the Volta', p. 36.

[17] This is the estimate given by the missionary, Ramseyer, who was captured by the Asante forces and taken back to Kumasi. Quoted in Johnson, 'Ashanti east of the Volta', pp. 44–5. For a discussion of Asante military objectives more generally, see D.J.E. Maier, 'Military acquisition of slaves in Asante', in David Henige and T.C. McCaskie (eds), *West African Economic and Social History: Studies in Memory of Marion Johnson* (Wisconsin: Wisconsin University, African Studies Program, 1990).

[18] Johnson, 'Ashanti east of the Volta', p. 48. According to Ramseyer, Adu Bofo paraded 2,000 captives in Kumasi in 1871. Maier, 'Military acquisition', p. 120.

[19] Akpafu traditions in GNAA ADM 39/5/73.

[20] Buem traditions in GNAA ADM 39/5/73; Debrunner, *A Church Between Colonial Powers*, p. 18.

[21] Emmanuel Osibo, 'A short history of Bakpeles (Likpes)' (unpublished manuscript).

operations and concludes that there had been a series of military campaigns to the north and west from the later eighteenth century, even if this did not succeed in cementing actual political control.[22] Most importantly for our purposes, he points to evidence for Dahomean campaigns against Atakpamé from the last decade of the century. Frederick Forbes alluded to one such assault in 1840 (actually 1850). He described how those who could not fight – the old, the young and the women – deserted the town along with everything they could carry.[23] The men who remained engaged the Dahomeans in a fierce battle, but eventually succumbed to superior force. A German official, Lieutenant Plehn, who toured the region in 1896 identified two major episodes in Dahomean aggression against Atakpamé. The first, which he dated very roughly to the turn of the century, apparently led to a decision to relocate the community in mountainous terrain further to the west, where it would be less open to Dahomean attack. On the second occasion, which had taken place in living memory – hence probably a reference to the 1850 campaign – the Dahomeans allegedly massacred a large number of people. Plehn wrote that: 'All the inhabitants who had not been massacred or been captured ran off and hid themselves, some in the nearby bush and others close to the Akpossos who had led them in their flight towards the west.'[24] Although some peoples returned to their homes when the imme-diate crises had passed, others chose to remain in the hills and indeed only ventured down once colonial rule was in place. This evidence would support the impression that the mountain reaches occupied by the Akpossos had come to serve as a place of refuge for peoples from both the west and the east. In that sense, it could be seen as a frontier zone of sanctuary.

In the Asante case, the Adu Bofo campaign formed part of a wider Asante struggle to root out rebellion within its empire. The balance of power was, however, dramati-cally altered when the British actively joined the fray and succeeded in entering and burning Kumasi in 1874. This was followed by the collapse of Asante power east of the Volta, leaving a vacuum which Europeans would ultimately endeavour to fill.[25] The immediate consequence was, however, a state of even greater turbulence as com-munities resorted to settling scores among themselves. Although the Ewe *dukɔwo* were apparently too weakened to deal with Akwamu, the former subjects of the Kwahu Dukoman rallied together and exacted a terrible revenge on their former overlords.[26] The scattering of the Kwahus enabled the Borada chief to consolidate the Buem state, consisting of a diverse collection of Akan, Lefana and other minority

[22] Law, 'Dahomey and the north-west', pp. 149–67.

[23] Frederick Forbes, *Dahomey and the Dahomans*, Vol. 1 (reprint edition by Frank Cass) (London, 1851), pp. 16–17. Law, 'Dahomey and the north-west', p. 156, n. 35, points out that the date of 1840 is a misprint.

[24] Report translated at TNAL Atakpamé 2 APA/2.

[25] Following their defeat, the Asante did seek to revive their fortunes in the east by appointing the French trader, Marie-Joseph Bonnat, as co-governor of the territories beyond the Volta, with rights to a monopoly of com-merce along the Volta River. Having failed on his first attempt, Bonnat visited his notional Ewe domains in 1875, but had given up the enterprise a year later. Wilks, *Asante in the Nineteenth Century*, pp. 608–13; D.J.E. Maier, *Priests and Power: The Case of the Dente Shrine in Nineteenth-Century Ghana* (Bloomington: Indiana University Press, 1983), pp. 91–7.

[26] Debrunner, *A Church Between Colonial Powers*, p. 18, notes that the Kwahu Dukoman survived only in the form of a village at the confluence of the Volta and the Oti rivers. See also Johnson, 'Ashanti east of the Volta', pp. 50–4.

peoples. Those communities that had acted as guides for the Asante forces, such as the Akpafu, equally found themselves on the receiving end of a thirst for vengeance. In some areas, endemic political violence blurred into conditions of generalized banditry. Marion Johnson implies that some areas effectively became depopulated in the latter decades of the nineteenth century as a result of the generalized disorder.[27] At the same time, the importance of the Togoland hills as a place of refuge was further enhanced.

Imperial swapshop: the first cut

As we will now see, this legacy had a direct bearing on the contours followed by the colonial partition itself. After the defeat of Asante, the British found themselves in possession of an expanding sphere of influence east of the Volta. The Danish had already signed over their 'rights' in a treaty of 1850, which the British interpreted as including Peki.[28] On an optimistic reading, the domains of Peki included all those polities which had accepted the leadership of Kwadjo Dei in the revolt of 1833-34. Since even Buem acknowledged paying some tribute to Peki, this could be taken to cover a very wide area indeed.[29] The only potential challenge to this rendition of the facts was posed by Asante, but the latter had momentarily been neutralized in this theatre of operations.

Forced to clarify their intentions in the trans-Volta borderlands, the British found themselves pulled in two directions at once. On the one hand, this area had acquired enhanced commercial significance after the eclipse of Asante. Hitherto, the latter had maintained tight control over the northern and eastern trade routes. The commerce in slaves and salt, between the lower Volta and Salaga, had been supervised and taxed by Asante customs agents posted at riverain towns such as Ahenkro.[30] Moreover, Asante rulers had shrewdly funnelled the northern commerce through the Salaga market in order to maximize the bargaining power of their own state traders.[31] After the defeat of 1874, however, Salaga rapidly lost its former pre-eminence and many of its traders relocated to the south-east. By plying the land routes east of the Volta, Muslim merchants could effectively bypass the riverain Asante customs posts altogether. The Krepi town of Kpandu, which was located on the crossroads of the north–south and east–west trade routes, became the base of many of these merchants. The British were understandably interested in attracting this trade towards the Gold Coast Colony, which had acquired a more definite shape after the

---

[27] Johnson, 'Ashanti east of the Volta', pp. 55–6, notes that a gap between Nkonya and Akroso emerged that was later filled by the establishment of a settlement at Kwamikrom by Abu Karimu, a former employee of the Hausa constabulary.

[28] This was apparently not specified in the treaty itself. See David Brown, 'Anglo–German rivalry and Krepi politics, 1886–1894', *Transactions of the Historical Society of Ghana*, XV, ii, 1974, p. 214, n. 12.

[29] Buem traditions in GNAA ADM 39/5/73.

[30] Johnson, 'Ashanti east of the Volta', p. 34. On the salt trade on the Volta, see Maier, *Priests and Power*, pp. 20–30.

[31] On the tight controls over the kola trade, see Wilks, *Asante in the Nineteenth Century*, pp. 267–71. Gareth Austin has noted that private merchants existed alongside state traders, but nevertheless accepts that the latter were advantaged. Nor does he question the significance of routing trade through Salaga. See '"No elders were present": commoners and private ownership in ownership, 1807–96', *Journal of African History*, 37, 1, 1996.

events of 1874. On the other hand, they were reluctant to become too deeply embroiled in the politics of the region, despite the fact that endemic insecurity posed a threat to the pursuit of commerce itself. In the final event, British policy was generally confined to trying to broker agreements to keep the trade routes open. In the words of Marion Johnson:

> [T]he British, though quite willing to browbeat the smaller states, in the interests of keeping trade routes open, were unwilling to accept responsibility even when directly asked to do so, so long as no other European power was showing interest in the area. Apart from keeping the trade routes open, their sole interest was to prevent the Ashantis from returning to Salaga.[32]

The minimalist policy became increasingly untenable after the German government succumbed to its own domestic pressure for the creation of a trade colony in this part of West Africa in 1884. As both Ivor Wilks and Marion Johnson have observed, the German colony of Togo was inserted into the gap that was opening up between the shrinking imperial domains of Asante and Dahomey.[33] Following the establishment of a coastal base at Lomé, German attention focused on tapping the increasingly important trans-Volta trade routes. By 1886, German officials were active in the area, signing treaties and handing out flags to local rulers. The British, who claimed that that this was already their patch by virtue of the 1850 treaty with Denmark, nevertheless took the precaution of despatching C. Riby Williams to extract treaties of their own. The underlying fear was that if Germany succeeded in advancing her claims, the trans-Volta trade would be diverted away from the Gold Coast. That this was taken seriously is clear from the following warning from Lord Salisbury:

> The importance of Kpandu and Inkunya [sic] to the Gold Coast is very great. The former is a converging point for the trade routes from the interior and the possession of these places would enable the Germans to divert through Lome a very large proportion of the trade which now passes through British territory to the sea coast.[34]

In 1887, the two metropolitan governments signed an agreement that was supposed to divide up their respective spheres of influence. The agreement, which purported to 'leave within the British Protectorate the countries of Aquamoo and Crepee (Peki)', was bedevilled by much the same problems of definition as surfaced in Northern Nigeria a few years later.[35] David Brown points out that the British regarded the agreement as protecting their rights to 'Krepi' as a whole, with 'Peki' merely being added to the text to accommodate German usage. The Germans, on the other hand, regarded the wording as stipulating a limitation of British rights to Peki proper, to the exclusion of the other northern Ewe *dukɔwo*.[36] These contradictory claims remained unreconciled until 1890 when the British government decided to tackle the trans-Volta question as part of a global settlement of imperial claims. Under the Heligoland Treaty

---

[32] Johnson, 'Ashanti east of the Volta', p. 56.

[33] Johnson, *op. cit.*, p. 57; Wilks, *Asante in the Nineteenth Century*, p. 57.

[34] Quoted at Brown, 'Anglo-German rivalry', p. 206.

[35] On the border between Nigeria and what is now Niger, an agreement of 1890, which stipulated that 'all that fairly belongs to the Kingdom of Sokoto' would be left to the Niger Company, ran into similar differences of interpretation. See D.J. Thom, *The Nigeria–Niger Boundary, 1890–1906: A Study of Ethnic Frontiers and a Colonial Boundary* (Athens: Ohio University Centre for International Studies, 1975), pp. 21–2.

[36] Brown, 'Anglo-German rivalry', p. 206.

of that year, Germany assumed rights to the greater part of the disputed area, while the British were confirmed in their possession of Anlo, Akwamu and Peki proper.[37] In consequence, the trans-Volta borderlands north of Peki passed into German hands, in spite of a distinct lack of enthusiasm on the part of the indigenous population.

The southern border between the Gold Coast and German Togoland was drawn according to simple principles. It consisted of a straight line drawn from the coast to the 6° 10' north latitude and then westwards until it struck the left bank of the Aka River. From there an imaginary line pursued the mid-channel of the Aka to the 6° 20' parallel, and then ran westwards to the right bank of the Dschawe and along the bank of that river to the confluence of the Dayi River and the Volta. Finally the line followed the left bank of the Volta up to the so-called 'neutral zone'.[38] The creation of this zone, which had been designed to take the edge off Anglo-German rivalries in the north, was followed by a familiar bout of competitive treaty-signing in that area. But under the Samoa Treaty of 1899, this neutral zone was itself partitioned between the two powers. The boundary line in the north followed the Daka River, from its confluence with the Volta, to 9° north. Beyond that point, the line was to be drawn 'in such a manner that Gambaga and all the territories of Mamprussi shall fall to Great Britain, and that Yendi and all the territories of Chakosi shall fall to Germany'.[39]

The fixing of boundaries on paper was merely the first step in the process of practical boundary-making. An altogether greater challenge was to turn cartographic detail into effective lines of demarcation on the ground. As might have been predicted, German policy was geared towards channelling as much of the caravan trade as possible towards Lomé, which implied a rigid enforcement of border controls. For their part, the Gold Coast authorities sought to suck the caravan trade into their domain, while securing a wider market for their imported goods through Keta. Both sides resorted to the bluntest of administrative instruments to garner what they construed as their own trade. The Germans, for example, stationed customs officials at strategic points along the main east-west trade routes and levied prohibitive duties on caravans heading for British territory.[40] This caused intense annoyance on the part of traders and chiefs alike. In 1897, Heinrich Klose observed that the Kpandu chief, Dagadu, was actively encouraging the contraband trade through the port of Dukludja. This stood to benefit merchants from Britain, which had been placed in possession of the whole river.[41] Whereas the Volta trade had suffered when Hausa merchants adopted the land routes, German customs duties inevitably weakened this

---

[37] The treaty involved a simultaneous settlement of claims in Europe, East Africa and Southern Africa.

[38] The description of the boundary may be found in E. Herslet, *The Map of Africa By Treaty, Volume I* (London: Frank Cass reprint edn, 1967), p. 73. See also Ian Brownlie, *African Boundaries: A Legal and Diplomatic Encyclopaedia* (London: Christopher Hurst/Royal Institute of International Affairs, 1979), p. 251. A dispute over the precise course of the Aka River was never resolved. Arthur J. Knoll, *Togo Under Imperial Germany, 1884–1914: A Case Study in Colonial Rule* (Stanford: Hoover Institution Press, 1978), pp. 34–5.

[39] Martin Staniland, *The Lions of Dagbon: Political Change in Northern Ghana* (Cambridge: Cambridge University Press, 1975), p. 11.

[40] Knoll, *Togo Under Imperial Germany*, pp. 52–3 discusses the controversy surrounding a particularly zealous period of enforcement over 1890–91.

[41] Heinrich Klose, *Le Togo sous drapeau Allemand (1894–1897)*, translation by Philippe David (Lomé: Editions Haho & Karthala, 1992), p. 237.

comparative advantage. For their part, the British authorities sought to discourage salt and kola from being traded into the German sphere.[42]

In the longer term, the manipulation of customs duties proved to be a more subtle and effective weapon in the struggle over commerce. After the incorporation of Anlo into the Gold Coast Colony in 1874, customs duties were introduced into that area.[43] Subsequent increases in the level of import duty led many Anlo traders to relocate their operations to just beyond the British boundary.[44] The establishment of a German colony, centred on Lomé, rendered an escape from colonial taxation imposs-ible for the Anlo merchants, but posed an even greater dilemma for the British. A joint customs agreement between Togo and Dahomey in 1887 established lower rates of duty than prevailed in the Gold Coast, which had the effect of fuelling a contraband trade in liquor and firearms out of Lomé.[45] In 1890, the Gold Coast authorities reduced their duties on the south-eastern border in an attempt to render the Keta trade competitive. Fortuitously, this coincided with a German decision to increase revenue by raising their own customs duties. Four years later, the two administra-tions decided to fully harmonize their respective duties by establishing a common customs zone within the Volta triangle. Under the agreement, specific rates were imposed for alcohol, tobacco and firearms, while a general rate of 4 per cent was set in respect of other imported goods. Arthur Knoll has pointed out that restrictive practices nevertheless continued to operate in respect of the African produce trade.[46] British officials, for example, tried unsuccessfully to prevent German merchants from buying up cocoa from the Peki area.[47] But in respect of the import trade, the formal agreement survived until 1904 and removed most of the financial incentive from smuggling.

It was the Togo administration that ultimately decided to withdraw from the customs agreement, complaining that Keta derived a disproportionate advantage from its application. The German authorities calculated that the key to expanding the overall volume of the produce and import trades lay in making substantial infra-structural improvements within their territory. The first railway line, which was completed in 1905, covered the 27 miles between Lomé and Anecho, and enabled the palm products of eastern Togo to be exported more easily. In 1904, work began on a railway from Lomé to Kpalimé, covering a distance of some 74 miles. The choice of Kpalimé as a terminus was not accidental, but reflected an appreciation of the fact that this town lay on the main overland trade route between Kpandu and the coast. It was also located in a part of the country that was suited to the production of a range of cash crops, including cocoa, cotton, rubber and palm produce. Work on the third railway, covering the 101 miles between Lomé and Atakpamé and designed to

[42] Knoll, *Togo Under Imperial Germany*, p. 54.

[43] On the British takeover of Anlo, see D.E.K. Amenumey, 'The extension of British rule to Anlo (south-east Ghana), 1850–1890', *Journal of African History*, IX, 1, 1968.

[44] Sandra Greene, *Gender, Ethnicity and Social Change on the Upper Slave Coast: A History of the Anlo-Ewe* (London: James Currey, 1996), pp. 140–1.

[45] Knoll, *Togo Under Imperial Germany*, p. 72.

[46] *Ibid.*, pp. 53–4.

[47] The dominance of the German merchants rested on the activities of African buyers. GNAA ADM 11/1/433.

facilitate cotton exports, commenced in 1908 and was completed in 1911. In addition to the three railways and a new wharf at Lomé, the Germans also constructed 760 miles of motorable roads.[48]

Although some imperial funding was provided and the Germans completed much of the work by means of forced labour, substantial capital investments like these necessitated a substantial increase in government revenue.[49] This was effected through a combination of direct taxation and higher rates of customs duty. Hence the general level of duty was hiked from 4 to 10 per cent with effect from 1904, which had the effect of reintroducing an incentive to smuggle. In an attempt to deal with the anticipated side-effects, the German authorities were forced to fortify their border surveillance and to offer financial incentives for the successful apprehension of smugglers.[50] To some extent, the British were also faced by surveillance difficulties. One Gold Coast Customs officer has left a fascinating first-hand account of the thriving contraband trade in gunpowder and spirits across the Volta River into Ashanti.[51] The author recounts an occasion in 1905 when suspicions were raised about the number of coffins being transported across the river for the performance of burial customs on the other side. Having resolved to investigate a particular burial party, the author was initially led by the solemn deportment of the mourners and the smell of decomposing flesh to conclude that the funeral was *bona fide*. But when the coffin was subsequently opened, it was found to contain a quantity of gunpowder and a decomposing lump of 'bushmeat' designed to throw the Preventive men off the trail. This was just one of many ruses which were deployed by border peoples seeking to profit from the existence of the border.

For the most part, British officials felt secure in the knowledge that it was the German authorities who had the greater logistical headache. But if the Gold Coast even appeared to prosper in the short term, it was apparent that the German gamble was paying dividends by 1914. The investment in roads and railways was instrumental in fostering closer integration between the far-flung parts of the colony. According to Donna Maier, the Lomé–Kpalimé railway reduced a journey of 10 days during the dry season, or 15 days during the rains, to a mere two hours.[52] The European plantations were intended to reap many of the anticipated benefits. But as coastal merchants moved inland, peasant producers were able to find a readier market for their agricultural produce and soon acquired a taste for a wider array of imported goods. In the mid-1980s, it was still possible to find informants in Likpe who recalled making the journey across the mountains, via Wli, Fodome, Woate, Kuma-Bala and Kusuntu, to the Kpalimé railhead in order to sell their palm kernels and to buy consumer goods.[53] According to M.B.K. Darkoh, the peoples of Leklebi, Kpoeta and Honuta, which lay in closer proximity to Kpalimé, became so deeply immersed

---

[48] Donna Maier, 'Slave labor and wage labor in German Togo, 1885–1914', in Arthur Knoll and Lewis Gann (eds), *Germans in the Tropics: Essays in German Colonial History* (Westport: Greenwood, 1987), p. 77.

[49] On German colonial finances and forced labour respectively, see Knoll, *Togo Under Imperial Germany*, pp. 79–81, and Maier, 'Slave labor'.

[50] Knoll, *Togo Under Imperial Germany*, p. 73.

[51] See the article 'Gunpowder', in the papers of Howard Ross, Rhodes House Library, Mss. Afr. S.469–75.

[52] Maier, 'Slave labor', p. 78.

[53] Interview with Mensah Ambor, Likpe-Abrani, 14 March 1986.

in the production of palm products that they ceased to pay much attention to food crops.[54] This should not be exaggerated, though, because the coming of the Kpalimé railway also stimulated the production of maize along the line. Indeed, Togo became a net exporter of maize, some of which found its way into the Gold Coast in spite of official controls.[55]

From the perspective of the German administration, the success of the investment programme was proven both by greatly increased levels of exports and by enhanced government revenues.[56] Indeed, the ability of Togo to pay for its own administration earned it the accolade of Germany's model colony. For our purposes, what is more significant is the fact that the Germans were imaginative enough to complete the process of economic restructuring which had begun to unfold in the trans-Volta borderlands after the collapse of the Asante imperial system. A degree of continuity is manifested in the consolidated position of Kpalimé, a commercial town that had acquired some importance in the later nineteenth century. On the surface of things, the German–British boundary affected trade relations between Anlo and Peki, on the one hand, and the areas further to the north on the other. Equally, it rendered east–west commerce across the Volta River more problematic, to the potential detriment of Kpandu.[57] But in each case, smuggling was rife, virtually impossible to control, and financially very lucrative. Where the European partition did not actually follow the grain of an indigenous political economy, it probably did not seriously disrupt it. Indeed, the emergence of new centres of trade, which were associated with the new lines of infrastructure, co-existed with a thriving contraband trade.

The second cut: the partition of German Togoland

The German colonial experiment in this corner of West Africa was abruptly terminated in August 1914 when the Great War broke out. Interestingly, the first shots in this most brutal and costly of conflicts were fired not in one of the infamous theatres of Europe, but actually in Togo. The reason had little to do with the intrinsic value of the colony in the eyes of the combatants, but was rooted above all in global strategy. The Germans had constructed a wireless station at Kamina, north-west of Atakpamé and some 110 miles from the coast, which was reputedly the second most powerful in the world at that time.[58] This communications installation posed an obvious threat to the security of allied shipping in the Atlantic. Spurning German efforts to secure a truce, therefore, French forces invaded from Dahomey on 6 August, followed by the

---

[54] M.B.K. Darkoh, 'An historical geography of the Ho–Kpandu–Buem area of the Volta Region of Ghana: 1884–1956', unpublished M.A. thesis, University of Ghana, 1966, pp. 83–4.

[55] Maier, 'Slave labor', pp. 85–6.

[56] See the tables in Knoll, *Togo Under Imperial Germany*, p. 75.

[57] David Brown, 'Politics in the Kpandu area of Ghana, 1925–1969: a study of the influence of central government and national politics upon local factional competition', unpublished Ph.D thesis, Birmingham University, 1977, p. 9.

[58] This stategic concern is explictly stated in the official history of the war. See F.J. Moberly, *Military Operations: Togoland and the Cameroons* (London: His Majesty's Stationery Office, 1931), p. 4. See also Wm Roger Louis, *Great Britain and Germany's Lost Colonies, 1914–1919* (Oxford: Clarendon Press, 1967), p. 56.

Gold Coast Regiment six days later.[59] The German authorities, cognizant of the superior weight of enemy numbers, retreated from Lomé towards the interior. After some fighting in the Nuatja area, they blew up the Kamina station and surrendered on 26 August. Consequently, the Togoland campaign was wrapped up within a matter of three weeks and a mere four days after the first British shots of the war were fired in Europe. Finding themselves in joint military occupation, the Gold Coast and Dahomean governments agreed to a provisional partition of the territory pending a final settlement after the war. The British took control of the larger western sector, which comprised 'the districts of Lomé-Land, Misahöhe, Kette-Krachi, and the part of the Mangu-Yendi district forming the Dagomba country'. They also assumed responsibility for the railway system and the wharf at Lomé. The French, for their part, took over the eastern sector, which included the important towns of Anecho and Atakpamé.[60]

The British forces were struck by the warmth of the reception that greeted their arrival in towns and villages across Togoland. At Yendi, the capital of the Ya Na, they recorded the joyful greeting that was extended to them and duly noted a formal request to be reunified with the rest of the Dagomba people 'under the British flag and the protection of His Majesty King George V'.[61] Further south, the official history of the campaign contrasted the unpopularity of the Germans with the welcome extended to the occupying army:

> Though in some cases they had been coerced under penalty of instant death to take up arms against us, they took every opportunity to evade such action, to obstruct the Germans and to assist us, while the welcome they extended to Colonel Bryant and his men at every stage of the British advance was most marked and obviously sincere. As a typical instance, Colonel Bryant relates how one old chief came out to meet him bearing a Union Jack which he had kept hidden since 1884.[62]

The significance of producing these flags lay in reminding the British of their much older association with the peoples of the trans-Volta who had initially been courted and had then been abruptly handed over to Germany.[63]

In the Lomé area, the British might almost have been forgiven for thinking they were returning home. The reception here reflected an established tradition of inter-action across the border. Much of the trade of the capital had been conducted with Gold Coast Eweland, and for that reason British West African currency – most notably the shilling piece – had circulated in Togoland despite attempts to establish German coinage.[64] Moreover, the English language had entrenched itself in spite of German efforts to turn back the perceived tide of cultural imperialism. Indeed,

---

[59] Général Maroix, *Le Togo pays d'influence française* (Paris: Larose-Editeurs, 1938), part II, chs 1–3; Byron Farwell, *The Great War in Africa, 1914–1918* (Harmondsworth: Viking, 1987), p. 26.

[60] For details of the agreement, see *Memorandum on Togoland*, Confidential Print, Africa (West), No. 1065, at GNAA ADM 11/1/1620.

[61] Foreign Office, *Togoland* (handbook no. 17) (London, 1919), pp. 22–3; also recalled in Moberly, *Military Operations*, p. 33.

[62] Moberly, *Military Operations*, p. 34.

[63] In subsequent meeting with British officials, the chiefs of the area recalled that it was the British that had delivered them from the Asante. Although there was a strong element of flattery in this, it also happened to be true.

[64] Foreign Office, *Togoland*, p. 49.

English had served as a language of trade not just around Lomé, but as far east as Anecho.[65] Moreover, the missions had responded to popular demand and resisted government pressure in favour of a mixture of German and Ewe, by teaching through an English medium. Furthermore, elite families from Lomé were in the habit of sending their own children to the Gold Coast for an education. One of the most eminent citizens of the capital, Octaviano Olympio, had even attended school in Bristol and Bath.[66] Finally, many ordinary citizens had spent time working across the border, especially on farms along the expanding cocoa frontier of the Eastern Province. In the eyes of many in Lomé, therefore, the British occupation prefigured the return to a more natural order of things.

Further to the north, links with the Gold Coast were more attentuated. Here, the welcome which was extended to the British owed more to dissatisfaction with the strictures of German colonial rule: most notably forced labour, direct taxation and arbitrary punishments. One chief described the experience of the recent past as follows:

> We got much trouble from the Germans and when we were working they flogged us a good deal and we had to work in the rain. When building houses they forced people to carry heavy loads and didn't care if it killed anyone or not. We are tired of the trouble.[67]

Another was more graphic in his denunciation, commenting that '[t]he Germans left no good hair on our heads'.[68] The hardships associated with German rule had together been responsible for a significant haemorrhage of population into the Gold Coast before 1914 – a classic instance of A.I. Asiwaju's 'migration as revolt'.[69] The flight had also alerted people on the other side of the border to the difficulties encountered by their neighbours. Sandra Greene notes that the Awoamefia of Anlo was prepared to offer ten thousand men to assist in Togo, while withholding support for the East African campaign, in order to redress the perceived sufferings of related peoples in the Lomé district.[70] Another factor in the equation was that some peoples who had been partitioned by the Germano-British frontier perceived an opportunity to reunite under the British flag. The best example is the Ya Na, who hoped to regain the adherence of his Dagomba subjects, most of whom had been deposited in the Northern Territories of the Gold Coast.[71] D.E.K. Amenumey may also be correct in suggesting that the Awoamefia really wanted the unity of the 'Awunas', although in this case the agenda could more properly be described as expansionist rather than unificationist.[72]

---

[65] Debrunner, *A Church Between Colonial Powers*, p. 113.

[66] Octaviano Olympio, a descendant of a prominent family of Bahian extraction, was a wealthy planter and trader. See statement of Octaviano Olympio, dated 21 March 1918, at GNAA ADM 11/1/1620.

[67] Statement of chief Anku Sachie of Siafe, GNAA ADM 11/1/1620.

[68] Statement of sub-chief Hongbeto of Agweve, GNAA ADM 11/1/1620.

[69] A.I. Asiwaju, 'Migrations as revolt: the example of the Ivory Coast and the Upper Volta before 1945', *Journal of African History*, 17, 4, 1976.

[70] Greene, *Gender, Ethnicity and Social Change*, p. 142; also David Killingray, 'Military and labour policies in the Gold Coast during the First World War' in Melvin Page (ed.), *Africa and the First World War* (London: Macmillan, 1987), pp. 156–7.

[71] Staniland, *The Lions of Dagbon*, pp. 61–6.

[72] D.E.K. Amenumey, *The Ewe Unification Movement: A Political History* (Accra: Ghana Universities Press, 1989), p. 19. The boundaries of the pre-colonial Anlo state did not extend into what became Togo, although Greene, *Gender, Ethnicity and Social Change*, pp. 139–40, points to the existence of many pre-colonial contacts to the east.

Tar-baby imperialism

British officials on the spot were generally of the persuasion that local opinion ought to be taken into account when it came to devising a more permanent dispensation. As early as 1914, Governor Clifford of the Gold Coast wrote that:

> It should be noted for future reference that any attempt once more to divide the Dagomba country in a manner which is opposed to the ethnological distribution of the native population will be keenly resented by the chiefs and people both in the Northern Territories and in the Sansanne-Mangu district of Togoland. The foregoing applies with equal force to the feelings of the natives in the Peki and Misahohe districts and to the Awuna population of the Keta and Lomeland districts.[73]

Lest more cynical motives be attributed to African opinion, Clifford also made the point that the 'spontaneous expressions of enthusiastic delight' occasioned by the invasion did not merely reflect a distaste for German rule, but embodied a positive desire for ethnic reunification among the Dagombas, Awunas and Pekis.[74] For our purposes, the mention of Peki in this context is particularly significant. As has already been seen, Peki had insisted on its pre-eminence among the Krepi chiefdoms after 1834, and its political claims had been championed by the British as a strategy for protecting their own sphere of influence during the 1880s. This theme was revived after the war, with broadly similar aims in mind. In 1915, Captain R.S. Rattray carried out an ethnographic survey of the Misahöhe district, the underlying purpose of which was evidently political.[75] One of Rattray's objectives was to ascertain how many of the chiefdoms of the district still recognized Peki claims. He recorded that 23 of the chiefdoms in the British zone (and one in the French) still accepted Peki overlordship; nine others (and four in the French zone) had ceased to do so; while 12 (and 13 in French zone) denied the veracity of Peki assertions altogether. On the basis of the Peki claims, the nineteenth-century treaties and many shared traditions, Rattray concluded that the British had a solid basis for planting their rule in the trans-Volta. In his words:

> This completes the evidence which in the words of the preface endeavours to 'prove some connection racially, linguistically, or by reason of conquest or suzerainty, nominal or real, the natives of this part of Togo have with the inhabitants of the Gold Coast Colony.' The case for our right, politically and morally, to take over this part of Togo is in the opinion of the compiler of this short treatise a strong one.

This demonstrates that British officials were, at this juncture, willing to deploy the language of ethnic affinity in pursuit of territorial claims.

If Rattray and his colleagues had been permitted to follow their instincts, all of western Togoland under British military occupation would have been secured after the war. There was, however, a formidable obstacle in the form of countervailing French ambitions. The French authorities coveted Lomé on the grounds that its port facilities were vastly superior to those of Cotonou in neighbouring Dahomey, and

---

[73] Quoted in D.E.K. Amenumey, 'The pre-1947 background to the Ewe unification movement', *Transactions of the Historical Society of Ghana*, X, 1969, p. 70.

[74] Quoted in Amenumey, *Ewe Unification Movement*, p. 10.

[75] A copy of Rattray's report may be located at GNAA ADM 39/5/73. Rattray later went on to write highly influential ethnographies and histories of Asante and the Northern Territories. His spell in the trans-Volta region seems to have been all but forgotten.

that their existing coastline was too narrow. Furthermore, if France was to take possession of Lomé, it made sense that the railways, and the towns connected by them, should be signed over to her as well. Clifford himself recognized, as early as 1914, that the spread of the German communications network greatly complicated any effort to arrive at a equitable division of the former German colony:

> ... no matter how generously each of the two Allied Powers might be disposed to treat the other in the matter of the rectification of frontiers, it is inevitable that whichever of them retains possession of Lomé, and the railway lines which radiate from it, would secure the major part of the advantage, to the exclusion of the other.[76]

Some irony resides in the fact that the very railway and road networks that had helped to foster closer integration within the trans-Volta borderlands now made their segmentation highly likely. If the British conceded Kpalimé, but insisted on retaining the area to the west of the railway line, it was more or less inevitable that the borderlands would have to be divided in two.

The eventual outcome did not depend on the inclinations of British and French officials on the spot – far less on the opinions of Africans – but on the disposition of the metropolitan governments at the end of the war. In January 1918, when it still appeared that a global peace might emerge through something less than an outright allied victory, the Colonial Secretary, Walter Long, had asked the administrators of all the occupied territories to solicit 'native opinion' about their future preferences. The rationale was that this body of evidence, which could be made to suit the rhetoric of self-determination, might furnish useful bargaining counters after the war.[77] J.T. Furley, the Gold Coast Secretary for Native Affairs, dutifully collected statements from the chiefs expressing a desire to remain under British rule. Many, it was noted with some satisfaction, emanated from the 'Krepi' chiefdoms.[78] With outright victory secured in 1919, the British and the French governments subtly switched the premise of their claims from 'native opinion' to rights of conquest. These lay in direct succession to those which had been established during the scramble for Africa. The difference in this case was that the vanquished were obviously German and not African. But this fact, and the role of Africans in securing the result, did not materially affect the equation in the eyes of the victors. Whereas the new map of Europe was thrashed out in the open at the Paris Peace Conference, through resort to a series of territorial commissions, Germany's African colonies were disposed of in secret negotiations between the occupying powers.[79] On the surface of things, the creation of the

---

[76] Quoted in Louis, *Great Britain and Germany's Lost Colonies*, p. 57.

[77] On the expediency attached to 'self-determination' in the occupied German colonies, see Victor Rothwell, *British War Aims and Peace Diplomacy, 1914–1918* (Oxford: Clarendon Press, 1971), pp. 288–91.

[78] For the results of this exercise, see the statements contained in GNAA ADM 11/1/1620 and GNAA ADM 11/1/1622.

[79] In May 1919, the Supreme Allied Council ruled that the British and French governments should make their own arrangements for Togoland. Amenumey, *Ewe Unification Movement*, p. 13. On the territorial consequences of the Paris Peace Conference, see Alan Sharp, *The Versailles Settlement: Peacemaking in Paris, 1919* (Basingstoke: Macmillan, 1991); and Michael D. Callahan, *Mandates and Empire: The League of Nations and Africa, 1914–1931* (Brighton & Portland: Sussex Academic Press, 1999), pp. 28–38. For the African dimension, see Peter J. Yearwood, 'Great Britain and the repartition of Africa, 1914–19', *Journal of Imperial and Commonwealth History*, XVIII, 3, 1990.

Mandates system under League of Nations control was a measured step short of annexation, but the manner in which the African space was haggled over followed a by-now familiar pattern.

From the start of the negotiations in March 1919, the futures of Cameroon and Togoland were considered in tandem. The French Colonial Minister, Henry Simon, was prepared to make territorial concessions in Cameroon, but was found unyielding on the question of Togoland. Simon made it clear that France wanted the whole territory, but that at the very least it insisted on Lomé. Whereas the Foreign Office was inclined to sacrifice Togoland for concessions elsewhere, the Colonial Office had been inclined to bargain hard since the matter was first raised. During the final negotiations, Lord Milner, the Colonial Secretary, was prepared to concede Lomé, but resisted the maximum French demands. This meant that the only practical solution was partition of the former German territory once again.[80] The Milner–Simon agreement of 10 July 1919 provided for a boundary, which conceded around 60 per cent of Togoland to France – including Lomé, Kpalimé, Atakpamé and Anecho – while placing a shrunken western sector – including Dagbon and parts of Eweland – under British administration.[81] The boundary, which mostly followed natural features as identified on Sprigade's *Karte Von Togo* of 1905 (1: 200,000), struck a line through the Togoland hills, thereby dividing the trans-Volta borderlands in two. Although the Ho and Kpandu districts were now placed under the same British administration as Peki and Anlo, and free trade along and across the Volta was restored, Kpalimé was severed from its immediate hinterland and Lomé was once more cut off from Anlo. Milner put a brave face on the outcome, insisting that even if British territorial gains were limited, the final agreement at least offered some scope for reuniting certain 'tribes' that had been divided by the original Anglo-German frontier.[82]

The Togoland settlement evoked considerable dismay in Lomé, on the part of British officialdom and African educated opinion alike. As early as November 1918, Octaviano Olympio had led a delegation to state the case for integration with the Gold Coast, which invoked the historic unity of the 'Awuna' (or Anlo) people. Early in 1919, Olympio and other educated Africans established a 'Committee on Behalf of Togoland Natives', which maintained a steady stream of petitions to the Colonial Secretary and the Allied Powers. Although Governors Clifford and Guggisberg were sympathetic, these expressions of African opinion were studiously ignored in London – as were the considered views of officials on the spot. Following the signature of the Milner–Simon agreement, the Officer Commanding British Forces, Major F.W.F. Jackson, felt impelled to write a lengthy rebuttal of the arguments that had been advanced by the French, in the hope that the agreement might still be amended before it was formally ratified by the newly constituted League of Nations. He contended that Lomé had become an important port not because of any inherent advantages, but chiefly because the Germans had been intent on tapping into the trade of the south-eastern Gold Coast. He also questioned whether it was really of such paramount importance to Dahomey at all, given that Anecho offered better port facilities anyway. Jackson reiterated that African opinion was strongly opposed to any

[80] On these negotiations, see Louis, *Great Britain and Germany's Lost Colonies*, pp. 147–9.

[81] For the text of this agreement, see Brownlie, *African Boundaries*, pp. 254–7.

[82] Louis, *Great Britain and Germany's Lost Colonies*, p. 149.

handover of western Togoland to France, which apart from anything else was incompatible with the vaunted principle of self-determination:

> Since the matter it would appear has to receive the ratification of the Council of the League of Nations, whose avowed object, as I am led to understand, is the protection of small Nations and the principle of self-determination, I venture to think that the first considerations to be met in discussing this question are the wishes of the Natives concerned, as to which Power they desire to administer the Government, in so far, of course as it does not clash with the greater and more important interests of the Powers.[83]

The last qualification did, however, put its finger on the fundamental problem, namely, that the peoples of Togoland represented no more than a very small bargaining chip in a global political settlement. The harsh reality was that neither party was prepared to cede territory without some form of recompense, even if this would have had the effect of satisfying African aspirations. This peculiar form of territorial accounting, in which European powers would haggle over lands that they professed not to want, was nothing new to Africa. It was, after all, the very mentality that had inscribed the Gambian anomaly on the world map. The impassioned arguments of Major Jackson were duly noted and placed on one side. The British administration was instructed to prepare its withdrawal from the territory, including both Lomé and Kpalimé.

As the date of the handover loomed, the administration was besieged by last-minute appeals and protests from a remarkably diverse combination of interests. The most articulate critics of the Milner–Simon agreement, as before, were members of the Lomé intelligentsia, but the latter now found more influential allies. In September 1919, Olympio despatched a further petition through the Liverpool Chamber of Commerce to Milner, for onward transmission to the League of Nations. This petition repeated the charge that the proposed frontier would divide the 'Ewe-speaking tribe' – surely one of the first usages of this term in political discourse – who had been united under the British flag since 1914. It also pointed to the double standards that were applied to European and African boundary questions, stating:

> (14) That the transfer of Togoland against the wishes of the inhabitants will make them feel that their case has been differently treated from that of Alsace and Lorraine.

> (15) That Your Lordships' petitioners will be forced to think that they have been unjustly dealt with because they belong to a subject race and that pledges held out to the World by the Allied Nations in the time of suffering have not been redeemed.[84]

The petition argued, in harmony with Major Jackson, that Lomé was an artificial port that was actually inferior to Anecho. To meet French objections halfway, however, the petitioners promised voluntary labour (from where is unclear) to construct a railway branch line from Nuatja to Anecho which would facilitate the export

---

[83] Jackson to CSA (6 January 1920), PRO CO 724/1.

[84] President of Committee on Behalf of Togoland Natives to Viscount Milner via the Liverpool Chamber of Commerce, dated 16 September 1919, PRO CO 724/1. This point was also taken up by the National Congress of British West Africa at its first conference. See David Kimble, *A Political History of Ghana, 1850–1928* (Oxford: Clarendon Press, 1963), p. 384.

of goods from Atakpamé. Subsequent petitions also emphasized that thriving commercial links between French Togoland and British territory would be adversely affected by the new frontier:

> Lome and Palime are merely centres where the greater portion of food from Keta, Ho and Kpandu districts are brought regularly on market days to be sold. The undue restrictions characteristic of the French Government would render these two important but unproductive centres greatly unpopular and divert these supplies to some other more convenient place inaccessible to us. Many of the inhabitants act as middlemen and derive their income from the produce trade, and therefore anything which tends to resrict its supply is bound to impoverish that particular class of community and more considerably affect the very poor and labouring people.[85]

Finally, the petition alluded to the currency of the English language and the hardships that would be attendant upon the sudden intrusion of an unfamiliar French administration.

The fact that Olympio chose to send this petition through the Liverpool Chamber of Commerce is testimony to the disquiet that was shared by British business interests. Representatives of the Liverpool Chamber met with Milner on at least one occasion and thereafter warned the Colonial Office that they would continue to rail publicly against a grave injustice that was being perpetrated against the native population.[86] The leading British firms in Lomé also submitted their own individual letters of protest. In July 1920, when preparations for the transfer were well in hand, the agent for John Holt warned Major Jackson of the adverse consequences that were likely to follow from any sudden change of administration. The argument was largely of the self-interested kind – for example, that a sudden change of currency would depreciate the assets of British firms overnight. However, the same agent also claimed that local producers and traders, who had become accustomed to dealing with the Gold Coast, would be disorientated by a sudden change of regime.[87] Without a doubt, the most bizarre expression of dissent emanated from certain Orange Lodges based in England. One petition to Lloyd George, sent by a lodge in Edgbaston, contrived to transport the Papist bogey to West African soil.[88] Another petition from an Orange Lodge in Lomé itself, which was sent through a British partner, complained in more conventional terms of 'the separation from our tribe on the adjoining countries of the Gold Coast'.[89] One Colonial Office official wryly minuted that it was doubtful if the petitioners even knew where Ulster was.[90] Whether the Friends of Ulster Loyal Orange Lodge could have found Togoland on the map is an equally moot point.

As we have seen, the most voluble expressions of discontent emanated from the

[85] Petition signed by Octaviano Olympio (12 December 1919), PRO CO 724/1.

[86] J. L. McCarthy to Secretary of State for Colonies (12 January 1920), PRO CO 724/1.

[87] G.R.B. Marcus to OCBF (28 July 1920), enclosure in Guggisberg to Milner (20 August 1920), PRO CO 724/1.

[88] Louis Ewart to Lloyd George (28 May 1920), PRO CO 724/1.

[89] Petition dated 27 May 1920 forwarded by Friends of Ulster Loyal Orange Lodge to Lloyd George, PRO CO 724/1.

[90] The minute noted that the Orange Lodge had originally been founded as a counterblast to a German club that had been geared to creating 'a pro-German lobby among the native clerks etc.'.

vicinity of Lomé. By contrast, the attitudes of the peoples of the interior have not stuck to the archival record in quite the same way. However, it is likely that opinion leaders in the former Misahöhe district understood that certain practical consequences would follow from being cut adrift from Kpalimé. The larger traders of that town worried that commerce would be adversely affected. Hence the French admitted in their internal correspondence that there were strong pro-British sympathies in Kpalimé among the employees of the European firms and other traders – although this was conveniently attributed to their being of Gold Coast origin.[91] Furthermore, those who were about to find themselves on the French side of the line were aware of the possible reintroduction of direct taxation, which had been such an unpopular facet of German rule.

To a limited extent, British and French officials took African feeling into consideration. In some cases, chiefs whose people straddled the Milner–Simon line were canvassed on whether they wished to be placed under one administration or the other. Moreover, communities were informed that they would be be given time to relocate their villages to the other side of the line if they so desired. But this amounted to little more than tinkering with the terms of the Milner–Simon agreement. Any concessions to African opinion had to be squared with the the 'greater interests' of the metropolitan powers. For example, in a detailed memorandum on the implications of the Milner–Simon agreement, the Secretary for Native Affairs, J.T. Furley, observed that if the Agotime people were not handed over to France in their entirety, they would have to be split because of their inconvenient proximity to the Lomé–Kpalimé railway line.[92] The appeals of the Lomé petitioners were given even shorter shrift. In this case, the Colonial Office fell back upon the traditional device, when confronted with unsolicited African opinion, of asserting that the petitioners did not represent the views of ordinary Togolanders. Amenumey has pointed out this was hardly a fair assessment of the situation, given the support for unification on the part of traditional authorities in the south.[93] Besides, the Furley memorandum made it clear where the reason for ignoring Lomé opinion really lay when it baldly stated that '[t]he Awuna claims are not discussed here as the decision to cede the railways will prevent them being adjusted to any extent'.[94] As Amenumey has commented:

> The truth of the matter was that, for reasons of international politics, Britain had decided to accommodate France and was not prepared to jeopardize their relations by any concessions to representations from the Gold Coast and Togo.[95]

After a brief period when the French flag and the Union Jack fluttered alongside one another over Government House, the British formally handed over Lomé and

---

[91] L'Administrateur adjoint Commandant le Cercle de Klouto to Commissaire de la République (8 Février 1921), TNAL Klouto 2/APA 2.

[92] Memorandum entitled 'Togoland boundary: the Anglo-French declaration of 10th July' (dated 29 November 1919), at PRO CO 724/1. This was prefigured in the scenarios that were discussed during the war. See *Memorandum on Togoland*, GNAA ADM 11/1/1620.

[93] Amenumey, *Ewe Unification Movement*, p. 19.

[94] 'Togoland boundary', PRO CO 724/1, 'Division of Togoland'.

[95] Amenumey, *Ewe Unification Movement*, p. 18.

other parts of occupied Togoland in October 1920.[96] The enforced withdrawal was lamented by British officials on the spot, who had been confident of their ability to win a popularity contest against the French. It was regretted even more by the indigenous elites who continued to press their objections long after the battle had been lost, as we shall see in Chapter 5. Once the actual transfer had taken place, the only realistic chance for revision of the Milner–Simon terms lay in specific frontier adjustments at the time of demarcation.

The final cut: the demarcation of the Togoland frontier

As a consequence of the partition, one half of the trans-Volta borderlands was brought back into the spatial orbit of the Gold Coast, while the other half remained separated from it. On the face of things, the Milner–Simon agreement appeared to offer rather limited scope for a rectification of the frontier. It was not predicated on notional 'tribal' or community boundaries, but on geographical features as identified on Sprigade's *Karte Von Togo* of 1905.[97] The agreement did state that the line could be

> slightly modified by mutual agreement between His Majesty's Brittanic Government and the Government of the French Republic where an examination of the localities show that it is undesirable, either in the interests of the inhabitants or by reason of any inaccuracies in the map Sprigade 1: 200,000 annexed to the Declaration, to adhere strictly to the line laid down therein.[98]

But when the agreement provided for a mixed commission to demarcate the border on the ground, it stipulated that it should, 'as far as possible, but without changing the attribution of the villages named in Article 1, lay down the frontier in accordance with natural features (rivers, hills or watersheds)'. The only caveats were that the commissioners would be empowered to make minor modifications in order to prevent villagers from being separated from their lands, and that communities would receive six months after the process of delimitation to relocate across the frontier in either direction.

Initially, the French and British administrations were inclined to be flexible in their interpretation of this agreement in the hope of gaining further territorial concessions from each other. In November 1920, the French Governor, Wöelffel, noted that the Milner–Simon line was unsatisfactory because it divided peoples whose overwhelming desire was to remain united.[99] On the other side, Major Jackson, who had since become the Commissioner of the Eastern Province of the Gold Coast, expressed the hope that these realities would be addressed:

> The Boundary as defined by the Franco-British Declaration of July, 1919, has ruthlessly divided Kith and Kin, therefore, I am assuming the general principle is that the boundary should follow as close as possible the various tribal boundaries as recognised by the natives themselves.[100]

[96] A photograph of this unusual phenomenon may be found in Yves Marguerat, *Lomé: une brève histoire de la capitale du Togo* (Lomé & Paris: Editions Haho & Karthala, 1992), p. 26.

[97] A copy of this map may be found in the map library at the Public Record Office (Kew), at PRO COO 700/66.

[98] A copy of the text may be found in Brownlie, *African Boundaries*, pp. 254–7.

[99] Quoted in Amouzouvi Akakpo, *Les frontières Togolaises: les modifications de 1927–1929* (Lomé: Université du Benin, 1979), p. 2.

[100] 'Memorandum on Anglo-French Togoland Boundary' by Major Jackson, undated, GNAA ADM 39/1/199.

The construction of the Togoland border

Although there was general agreement, that the Milner–Simon agreement needed to be interpreted liberally, the prospect for substantive revisions depended upon the willingness of the two administrations to demonstrate flexibility when it came to practicalities. British officials in the Northern Territories took pleasure from the fact that the boundary had reunified the Dagomba, but expressed an interest in shifting the line eastwards so as to gather in all of the Konkomba. The French were, however, no less intent on securing the Konkomba for themselves. Although their case was stated in terms of the need to secure an important arterial road, one British official believed that a more cynical motivation was operative: 'Personally I think that the French wish to have all the Konkombas because they are good fighting men, and may prove good recruits for their black army'.[101] Such was their interest in gaining the Konkomba that the French were prepared to trade the Adele, Agbaba and Akebu in return. However, Major Jackson expressed his opposition to any such deal because it would involve the loss of a thickly populated zone that was also reputedly rich in cattle. Further south, the Gold Coast authorities had taken possession of most of Adjuati territory, but not the town of Kjirina. They therefore bargained in the hope of moving the frontier eastwards at this point as well as in Adele, which had been cut in half. For their part, the French were interested in acquiring the western section of Akposso, or Litimé. In the event, the most ambitious plans for an exchange of territory came to nought because of an obsession about achieving equivalencies in the numbers of people and square miles exchanged. The only deal that actually went ahead was the exchange of French Adjuati (325 km^2) for British Akposso (500 km^2), which was provisionally agreed to in 1920.[102] Elsewhere, and most notably in respect of Eweland, the Milner–Simon line was preserved.

The next step was to set up a Boundary Commission to carry out the practical work of demarcating the frontier on the ground. In 1926, the parties agreed to a division of labour in which the French would measure and cut the boundary, and fix the longitude and latitude of various points along it, while the British would produce a topographical map covering an area of 4 kilometres on either side of the line. The work of actually erecting the beacons was divided between them. Over the course of three seasons between 1927 and 1929, the commission engaged in the laborious work of demarcating the frontier under the leadership of M. Bauché and Captain Lilley, respectively. This painstaking exercise was accomplished in spite of a considerable amount of mutual suspicion. Lilley, for example, complained of French attempts to push the British off the 'height of land', a strategy which was interpreted by a senior official as 'a general prejudice for good gun positions'.[103] Amouzouvi Akakpo has already published a fairly detailed account of the Commission, which considers its composition and some of the logistical problems that it faced.[104] Rather than repeating this in detail here, I will concentrate more particularly on the extent to which the Commission made a significant contribution towards shaping the boundary.

The work of the commission can be divided into three components. First of all, it was entrusted with interpreting the Milner–Simon agreement and implementing its

[101] A.W. Norris to Record Officer (3 April 1921), GNAA ADM 39/1/199.
[102] Akakpo, *Les frontières Togolaises*, p. 24.
[103] Acting Colonial Secretary to CEP (2 August 1927), GNAA ADM 39/1/199.
[104] Akakpo, *Les frontières Togolaises*.

36

provisions on the ground. This was not as straightforward as it might appear because the Sprigade map turned out to be misleading in many instances. This proved to be the case in respect of the one attempt to tidy up the southern boundary. The Milner–Simon agreement had stipulated that where the old Lomé–Akepe road crossed the frontier, the new line would run one kilometre south-west of the road so as to place all of it in French Togoland.[105] When it turned out that that the road did not actually cross the frontier and that this provision would have meant a cession of Gold Coast territory, the commissioners simply reverted to the 1890 convention. In some instances, a natural feature, which was identified on the map by an indigenous name, turned out to be unknown to the local population and could not be identified in the field.[106] In such cases, an alternative line had to be cut. Secondly, the commission was responsible for giving practical effect to the two modifications that had been agreed in respect of the Milner–Simon line. This involved mapping the Litimé and Adjuati regions and fixing a suitable boundary line in each case.

The third, and potentially more significant, task was to make modifications to the Milner–Simon line where this was considered desirable. The original agreement stated that the line could be deflected to prevent villagers from being separated from their lands. Prior to commencing work, the Boundary Commissioners indicated that they might be prepared to stretch this provision. In 1926, Captain Lilley proposed once again that an adherence to crude geographical outlines should give way to more meaningful ethnic criteria:

> I understand the mandate for our small portion of Togoland was given to us in order that we might reunite tribes which had been separated by the Anglo-German boundary and if we follow the tribal separation we shall act upon the spirit of our mandate. The tribal boundary will, I am aware, take longer to cut than one following natural features but though at the time it will involve land disputes, in the end will prevent them and avoid disputes in the future.[107]

In the final event, however, the Boundary Commission made relatively few modifications. When it was discovered that the specified watershed split the village of Kuma-Bala in two, Lilley did agree to the insertion of a straight line to keep it French.[108] Again, the original agreement specified 'a line generally running southwards following the watershed to the Fiamekito hills which it leaves to reach the River Damitsi. Thence the River Damitsi to its confluence with the Todschie (or Wuto).'[109] The village of Mayondi, which was marked on the Sprigade map as being on the left bank of the Damitsi, had since moved to the right bank. In principle, that made the village British, while depositing most of its farmlands in French territory. After French representations, it was decided to abandon the Damitsi and to draw a straight line

---

[105] Article 1, paragraph 41, reproduced at Brownlie, *African Boundaries*, p. 256.

[106] This was the case in northern Buem where a massif, a river and a waterfall could not be located. See 'Final report of the Commissioners appointed to delimit the boundary between the British and French Mandated Territories of Togoland', reproduced at Brownlie, *African Boundaries*, p. 262.

[107] 'Suggestions as to the boundary (southern section)' by Captain Lilley (25 January 1926), GNAA ADM 39/1/199.

[108] On this case, see Akakpo, *Les Frontières Togolaises*, pp. 22–3; see also section 5(c) of the final protocol, reproduced at Brownlie, *African Boundaries*, p. 267.

[109] Milner-Simon description of frontier, Article 1, paragraphs 35 and 36, reproduced at Brownlie, *African Boundaries*, p. 256.

further to the west, thereby placing Mayondi and its lands (on both sides of the Damitsi) in French Togoland.[110]

Elsewhere, however, the Boundary Commission was mostly content to follow the Milner–Simon line. Hence the modified frontier still followed natural features: out of a total of 997 km of frontier, 654 km consisted of rivers, 158 km of watersheds and 185 km of straight lines.[111] As the Kuma-Bala and Mayondi cases demonstrate, recourse to straight lines is not proof in itself of the arbitrariness of the demarcation exercise. They could also be used to avoid the undesirable consequences of following watersheds and rivers. It is tempting nonetheless to conclude from the partition of the Adele, the Konkomba, and more especially the Ewe, that the final product did not respect ethnic realities. This is, however, a more problematic issue than might at first appear. With the exception of the Lomé–Anlo borderlands, where the reshaping of identities was proceeding more quickly than elsewhere, there was not much sense of a common Ewe identity in the 1920s. The preference for remaining under the British flag reflected concerns about direct taxation and freedom of trade much more than a deeply felt sense of ethnic solidarity. When Ewe ethnicity did become a reality, it was because of and not in spite of the boundary. Hence Captain Lilley was probably correct when he argued that the focus of Ewe solidarity remained that of the division or *dukɔ*.[112]

In his capacity as Boundary Commissioner, Lilley worked hard to ensure that the line did not cut across divisions where this could be avoided, on the basis that this would only complicate management of the border zone. One place where this could not be achieved was in Agotime where, as we have seen, cession of the railway meant either that the entire division would have to pass to France or that it would be cut in two. The Milner–Simon agreement had placed three of the villages on the British side and the remaining nine in French territory. The headchief at Kpetoe campaigned for reunification under the British flag, but eventually opted to remain divided rather than reunite within the borders of French Togoland. North of Ho, where the boundary cut through the Togoland hills, the line weaved between the Ewe divisions and the Central Togo minorities. Hence the villages of Likpe and Buem were deposited on one side of the line, and those of Danyi, Ahlo and Akposso on the other. Although the Milner–Simon agreement was a fairly blunt instrument, the demarcated frontier did try to take some account of local political realities. As we shall see in the next chapter, this did not necessarily mean the border was free of contestation. At this point, however, I wish to consider the impact of the border upon trade.

Trade and the flag

Long before work on demarcation began, British policies imparted a practical significance to the Togoland boundary. In June 1920, Major Jackson proposed that

---

[110] On the Mayondi case, see Akakpo, *Les Frontières Togolaises*, pp. 18–20; see also section 4(g) of the final protocol, at Brownlie, *African Boundaries*, p. 266.

[111] 'Final report of the Commissioners appointed to delimit the boundary between the British and French Mandated Territories of Togoland', at Brownlie, *African Boundaries*, p. 261.

[112] 'Suggestions as to the boundary (southern section)' (25 January 1926), GNAA ADM 39/1/199.

rather than treat British Togoland as a separate unit, the various districts should be administered as part of the neighbouring territories of the Gold Coast: that is, the Northern Territories, Ashanti and the Colony, respectively.[113] The proposal was accepted and later given legitimacy by the Mandate agreement, which stated that:

> The Mandatory shall be authorised to constitute the territory into a customs, fiscal and administrative union or federation with the adjacent territories under his own sovereignty or control; provided always that the measures adopted to that end do not infringe the provisions of the mandate.[114]

The Gold Coast authorities wasted no time in putting administrative integration into effect. On 11 October 1920, following hard on the heels of the handover, Governor Guggisberg issued a proclamation to the effect that Gold Coast duties would henceforth be levied on the boundary between the two Togolands: comprising a 20 per cent *ad valorem* import duty and an export tax.[115] Viewed with historical hindsight, this might be construed as the first substantive attack on the idea of a united Togoland.

With immediate effect, the Customs Preventive Service (CPS) shifted its operations to the new border. This meant reverting to the old German–British line in the south, but also pushing eastward from the Volta River into areas that had once been under German rule. In the first instance, customs posts were hurriedly established on the main roads leading into Kpalimé – that is, at Leklebi-Dafo, Kpedze and Lokwe.[116] Shortly thereafter, Customs officials acknowledged that this coverage was inadequate because of the sheer volume of goods headloaded along bush paths. One Customs officer who conducted an on-the-spot inspection of the area between Wli and Buem ascertained that considerable trade crossed the Togoland hills into French territory. In respect of Wli itself, he reported that:

> The chief exports from this district are Kernels, Palm Oil and Raw Cotton. A small quantity of Cocoa is also exported but cocoa farming seems to be in its infancy as far as the Evhli [Wli] district is concerned. The produce is taken to Palime along a route which follows the main road as far as Acho, then along the Bush Path which runs from Uati [Woate] in the Liati district to the Kuma district in French territory. The people who take the produce into Palime return by this same route usually bringing with them Tobacco and European Goods.[117]

This was the same route to Kpalimé that the neighbouring Likpe people had become accustomed to using since at least German times and probably before.

As Customs officials woke up to the pull of the Kpalimé market on the whole of the Ho/Kpandu District, they found it necessary to establish temporary customs posts at Wli-Afegame, Likpe-Mate and Buem-Baglo. This arrangement had, in turn, to be modified when it was discovered that there was also a substantial trade

---

[113] Memorandum in Jackson to Colonial Secretary (12 June 1920), GNAA ADM 39/1/199. In the final event, the north was administered as part of the Northern Territories and the south as part of the Gold Coast Colony.

[114] 'Declaration relating to the Mandate for the part of Togoland assigned to Great Britain', PRO CO 724/1.

[115] As a matter of course, the same duties applied to the boundary between the Gold Coast and French Togoland. The cocoa duty was 12/- per load of cocoa. The French did not have such duties. A copy of Proclamation No. 22 of 1920 may be found at GNAA ADM 39/5/81.

[116] H.E. Davis to Acting COC (16 October 1920), GNAA ADM 39/5/81.

[117] Davis to Acting COC (31 October 1920), GNAA ADM 39/5/81.

north of Baglo, which drained into the other railway town of Atakpamé. By 1923, the Togoland frontier had been divided into three sections. The southern section consisted of two stations, at Kpetoe and Sokpe, manned by 17 Customs officials. The important central section, now comprising Wli-Afegame, Woate, Leklebi-Dafo, Ashanti-Kpoeta, Honuta, Shia and British Nyive, had a complement of 67 officers. Finally, the northern section consisted of stations at Kjirina, Dadiase, Pampawie, Kadjebi, Borada and Baglo, with a total strength of 53 officers.[118] As we will see more fully in Chapter 3, the function of these Customs officials was to collect duties and to mount regular anti-smuggling patrols.

The sudden imposition of a customs frontier where none had existed before was a source of considerable annoyance to the firms – most of them British – which had hitherto identified the French as the greatest potential threat to free trade. In mid-October, the principal firms – including John Holt, G.B. Ollivant and F. & A. Swanzy – protested that reasonable notice should have been given before the imposition of a customs regime.[119] Later that month, the French authorities forwarded complaints from lower down the commercial chain, that is, from African traders who had been intercepted while carrying produce across the frontier.[120] French representations posed a ticklish problem because, as British officials well knew, many French Togolanders had farm land in British territory and would continue to do so pending demarcation of the frontier. Indeed, in recognition of this reality, it had been suggested by representatives of the two administrations that 'the farmers who are cut off by the Boundary from their cocoa plantations should be permitted to have free access to the plantations on both sides'.[121] In fact, along stretches of the paper boundary, such as in the Batome area, nobody was entirely sure of the status of some villages.

Conscious of the possibility that the prosperity of Kpalimé could be undercut by British trade restrictions, the French insisted that it was quite unreasonable to impose a customs frontier before the final demarcation had been carried out, not least because there were farmers who were separated from their lands. The British riposte was that, unlike the French (and the Germans before them), they did not levy direct taxes, which meant that the costs of administration had to defrayed through a combination of import and export duties. To waive these duties would mean Gold Coasters subsidizing the entire Togoland administration, which was deemed unacceptable. Moreover, such a course of action would require the maintenance of a customs frontier between British Togoland and the rest of the Gold Coast, including the Keta district, which would engender hardships of its own. The British contention was that while strenuous efforts ought to be made to reduce unnecessary inconveniences, the creation of a customs frontier itself was an unavoidable evil.

It would appear that the British administration had not thought through the full implications of its policy because it appeared genuinely surprised by what transpired next. Rather than pay the new import and export duties, the European firms closed

[118] PRO CO 724/3, 'Annual Report for 1923'. These three sections were collapsed into two the following year. GNAA ADM 39/5/73.

[119] Letter from European firms to OCBF (15 October 1920), GNAA ADM 39/5/81.

[120] L'Administrateur en Chef to OCBF (26 October 1920), GNAA ADM 39/5/81.

[121] Recalled in Mansfield to CEP (8 June 1922), GNAA ADM 39/5/81.

their stores and retreated into French territory. They did so in the knowledge that British Togolanders would probably cross the frontier anyway in search of markets for their produce and consumer goods. This meant that they would be forced to pay the duties themselves or undertake the risks associated with smuggling. Even as early as October 1920, before the consequences of the new policy became apparent, a Customs officer was told by the headchief of Likpe that he had attempted to persuade his people to take their crops to Hohoe, but that they preferred to travel the greater distance to Kpalimé where prices were better.[122] Now they were left with very little option. At the end of 1921, Major Jackson visited the territory and painted a gloomy picture. He recorded that trade was virtually at a standstill and warned of the real possibility that people would relocate to French territory where they could live more cheaply.[123] Given that the French authorities levied an import duty of 10 per cent at the port of entry, the imposition of an additional British duty of 20 per cent at the border translated into substantially higher prices for consumer goods. To this has to be added the impact of export duties on crops such as cocoa. The fundamental problem, as a subsequent report acknowledged, was that 'the outstanding feature of the country east of the Volta is that from the standpoint of trade it faces eastwards'.[124] As we have already seen, this owed much to the spread of the German rail and road network. Although the railways would patently be a wasted asset if they were deprived of the trade of the Ho/Kpandu district, it was equally true that the latter depended utterly on the railways for access to the outside world.[125] Moreover, in 1920, there was not even a direct road link between British Togoland and the southern Gold Coast. Indeed, British administrators had to traverse French territory to get from one part of their district to the other. For example, anyone wanting to travel by car between Ho and Kpandu was forced to take a diversion through the former administrative headquarters of Misahöhe because there was no direct route across the hills.[126]

The British found themselves caught in a classic colonial bind. By agreeing to take over a portion of Togoland, they had committed themselves to meeting the costs of administration. And once the decision had been taken to attach the territory to the Gold Coast for administrative purposes, this meant that these costs would have to be charged to the finances of the colony. Furthermore, because of an aversion to direct taxation, the only means of defraying the expense was through the imposition of customs duties. But an ability to raise this category of revenue depended on there being a reasonable volume of trade to start with, which was precisely what was in question. Ever mindful of the need to balance the books, the Gold Coast authorities were reluctant to sink large sums of money into a territory that seemed to have limited economic prospects. For example, a report on the economic future of Togoland, carried out in 1921, offered the following bleak assessment:

[122] Davis to Acting COC (31 October 1920), GNAA ADM 39/5/81.
[123] Jackson to Acting CSA (20 December 1921), GNAA ADM 39/1/214.
[124] 'Report on condition of trade in Togoland' (January 1923), GNAA ADM 39/1/214.
[125] According to one estimate, 75 per cent of the volume of trade conducted along the railway came from British Togoland. 'The economic position of British Togoland' (May 1921), report enclosed in Captain Trotter to CEP (17 September 1921), GNAA ADM 39/1/214.
[126] First annual report for Togoland, enclosed in Guggisberg to Churchill (11 April 1922), PRO CO 724/2.

The construction of the Togoland border

Beyond this pocket of cocoa [in Buem] which ... is situated 100 miles, by a road not yet possible [passable?] in its entirety to motor traffic, from either suggested port on the Volta River, there are at present no resources either mineral or agricultural in the British Zone of Togoland which offer any immediate prospect, or in fact in the near future, of any lucrative basis for trade.[127]

Even in respect of cocoa, Lilley drew a comparison with Akuapem and professed himself 'not at all impressed by the amount grown by the Buems'.[128] Major Jackson, for his part, indicated that Togoland would have to take its place in the queue along with everybody else, and that meant somewhere near the back:

From the financial point [of view], the Mandated Area of Togoland is costing the Gold Coast a very large amount annually, whereas the revenue is very small; therefore until such time as we introduce means of increasing Trade generally, it is not advisable to expend large amounts in Togoland which could with advantage be expended in other parts of the Colony.[129]

The problem, which had its parallel in the Northern Territories, was that there was unlikely to be much trade in the absence of a new network of roads to match the new political topography.

The simplest solution to the dilemma was to request the French to grant a 'bond in transit' for imported goods destined for British territory.[130] When the matter was first broached in November 1920, the French Governor expressed a willingness to consider the matter, but implied that the *quid pro quo* would be the removal of the cocoa export tax.[131] The British administration opted instead to reduce the import duty to 10 per cent the following month. But any hope of reaching an accord faded as French suspicions about British intentions escalated. In the early months of 1921, French officials were incensed about the alleged dissemination of hostile propaganda by senior British officials and by the employees of British firms in Kpalimé, 'raising the possibility of our eventual departure from Togo'.[132] From this somewhat conspiratorial perspective, British frontier policy looked very much like an attempt to strangle the economy of French Togoland and thereby accelerate its retrocession. Jackson, for example, was quoted as bragging that he would ruin the Kpalimé railway. It was not surprising, therefore, that Governor Wöelffel indicated that there was no basis for a compromise:

This measure, against which I set myself, which brought the confines of the Gold Coast on to a frontier which has not yet been definitely fixed, cannot but operate in the most prejudicial manner possible against the Lome-Palime railway line in that it ruins the Palime market. In the circumstances, it does not seem to me possible to accord free transit of merchandise over which the British Authorities levy heavy duties of entry and export and the benefits of which are reserved for their zone alone.[133]

---

[127] 'The economic position of British Togoland', GNAA ADM 39/1/214.
[128] Lilley to Record Officer (22 September 1921), GNAA ADM 39/1/214.
[129] Jackson to Mansfield (13 October 1922), GNAA ADM 39/1/229.
[130] This would have meant that the French waived the import duties provided the goods were sent directly to British Togoland.
[131] Mansfield to CSA (8 November 1920), GNAA ADM 39/5/81.
[132] Cortot to Governor (19 May 1921), TNAL Klouto 2/APA 2.
[133] Wöelffel to Record Officer (26 May 1921), GNAA ADM 39/5/81.

When the French refused to countenance the precious 'bond in transit', the British authorities reintroduced the higher rate of duty on 6 July 1921.

While the impasse persisted, the hardships encountered by British Togolanders accumulated, leading to official concern about long-term damage to British prestige. In June 1922, by which time the firm of John Walkden was the only one still trading in the territory, Major Jackson reported that the situation had become desperate:

> The state of affairs is now truly lamentable, the natives have no means of selling their produce (other than in Palime) nor of buying essential European goods, which goods if bought in Palime, cost them at least 40% more than the imported cost as they pay 20% on the Palime cost when crossing the Frontier. Consequently it will be seen that the French get all the trade which legitimately ought to be ours.[134]

Jackson's reports from the field stimulated a vigorous debate, involving a number of government departments and the European firms, about how the crisis could best be resolved.[135] Whereas the firms saw very little point in trying to compete with the Kpalimé railway, officials were mostly in favour of taking decisive action to break the French stranglehold. Plans were immediately set in motion to construct a road between Ho and Adidome, which was in turn linked to Ada by river transport. At the same time, the authorities hoped to resuscitate the nineteenth-century river route from the more northerly reaches of the Volta River down to Ada. There was even brief speculation about the construction of a light railway to connect Togoland with the Gold Coast.

As an experiment, Jackson advocated abolition of the duty on cocoa exports passing through the Gold Coast. His reasoning was that this would draw Buem cocoa towards the river port nearest to Kwamikrom, while the remainder of the crop would be channelled along the Ho–Adidome route. Because the launches and lorries would be unlikely to return empty, Jackson reasoned, this would help to activate a return trade in consumer goods.[136] However, the Comptroller of Customs resisted this proposal on the grounds that the Kpalimé railway would still be the cheapest route – and if this option was imposed from above, the farmer would lose out to the tune of more than £4 per ton of cocoa, while the government would be £5,000 poorer in cocoa duties.[137] An alternative was to tinker with import duties, either by lowering (or abolishing) duties for goods crossing the border with French Togoland, or by granting a preferential tariff for Gold Coast imports destined for British Togoland. Although there were precedents for a differential tariff, dating back to the Anglo-German accord of 1894, the Comptroller expressed his opposition to any measure that would reinvent separate regulations for the Gold Coast and British Togoland. Whereas such compromises had once been forced upon an earlier generation of administrators, the maturation of the colonial state meant that a premium was now placed upon administrative uniformity. Summing up the debate, Governor Guggisberg indicated

---

[134] Jackson to Acting CSA (9 June 1922), GNAA ADM 39/5/81.

[135] For a synopsis of this debate, see Guggisberg to Colonial Secretary Duke of Devonshire (14 November 1922), PRO CO 724/2.

[136] Jackson to Acting CSA (9 June 1922), GNAA ADM 39/5/81.

[137] According to one estimate, it would cost £1.3.8 more per ton to export goods from Ho through Ada rather than Kpalimé. Guggisberg to the Duke of Devonshire (14 November 1922), PRO CO 724/2.

that the best solution still lay in securing a 'bond in transit', which would guarantee railway rates to the French, mollify the Gold Coast Treasury and reduce the cost of living for the inhabitants of British Togoland. But then this was really no solution at all because the French were not willing to play ball.

Increasingly, doubts were voiced about the practicality of beating the French at their own game. Under pressure from cocoa farmers in Buem, Lilley explored the possibility of building a 24-mile road from Jasikan to the Volta, but its navigability throughout the year turned out to problematic.[138] Moreover, the French threatened to slash their railway rates in order to secure the traffic for themselves, indicating to Lilley that 'the French have made up their minds to have all cocoa' whatever the cost.[139] Faced with the prospect of building roads that might never be used, British officials began to question the need to compete at all. Jackson was the leading convert to a policy of pragmatism, stating that:

> The present Policy appears (I regret to say) to be one of Dog in the Manger, that is to say we are endeavouring to prevent the French getting our produce, whereas we ourselves have not the means of exporting it. Until such time as we can say to the Native here is the way your produce must go and you will get a better price for it, I consider that in the interests of the Natives that we should make it possible for them to export via Palime.[140]

Indeed, the British administration even started to look upon the Kpalimé trade as a means to finance incremental infrastructural improvements by means of the duties that continued to be levied at the boundary.

Whereas the Public Works Department bore responsibility for maintaining roads in the Gold Coast proper, it was left to district officials in Togoland to carry out the work as best they could within a strictly limited budget. Captain Lilley devoted much of his considerable energy to the construction of bridges, culverts and roads, normally in close co-operation with the chiefs. Within strict budgetary constraints, there was some attempt to bind the constituent parts of British Togoland more tightly to the Gold Coast. For example, the natural barrier presented by the Togoland hills was breached by a new road across the mountain to Kpeve, which at last permitted freedom of movement between Ho and the rest of the district. At the same time, communications with the Gold Coast were considerably improved by means of a new road link between Ho and Senchi, although work on the route to Adidome was eventually abandoned. For the first time, it became possible to travel by road from the coast to Kete-Krachi, via Ho and Kpandu, without the need for a detour through French territory. Nevertheless, much of the investment was channelled into the construction of roads that actually fed the Kpalimé railway. This was true, for example, of the road that was built from Hohoe to Golokwati, which connected up with the Kpandu–Kpalimé route. Equally, the extension of the road beyond Hohoe, which was designed to liberate the cocoa economy of Buem, was

---

[138] Jackson noted that the water level became a problem in the dry season, while there were also the Senchi rapids to contend with. Jackson to Record Officer (13 October 1921), GNAA ADM 39/1/214.

[139] Lilley pointed out that while the French were being 'unbusinesslike', they were gambling that increased exports from France would help to stabilize the franc. Lilley to Mansfield (2 December 1922), enclosed in Mansfield to Jackson (26 December 1922), GNAA ADM 39/1/229.

[140] Jackson to Mansfield (13 October 1922), GNAA ADM 39/1/229.

actually destined to assist buying firms operating out of French Togoland.

Naturally, the French authorities were only too happy to continue tapping the trade of the British zone. There was a momentary scare when they imposed a duty on cocoa originating from British territory in January 1925.[141] This followed a metropolitan decision to grant preferential access to the French market for cocoa originating from its sphere of Togoland. It caused particular alarm among the cocoa farmers of the British zone, who formed a British Togoland Farmers' Association in order to campaign against the French duty. For a time, the bizarre prospect presented itself of British Togoland farmers holding back their stocks of cocoa from British firms in protest against a duty imposed by a French administration.[142] The threatened hold-up did not come to pass, but the farmers did start selling their crops to firms operating out of the Gold Coast. By July, the French authorities had woken up to the fact that the change of policy was harming the railway and was actually unnecessary. Because the farmers of French Togoland could not fill their imperial quota, it made sense to accept the crop from the British zone as well. Under a new card system, therefore, cocoa from the British zone was issued with a certificate of origin to enable it to be imported free of duty, although cocoa from the Gold Coast was excluded from the scheme.

By 1926, economic conditions in British Togoland had altered dramatically. A number of firms from the Gold Coast were reported to be opening stores in the leading towns, such as Kpandu, Ho and Hohoe.[143] Their stores were stocked with consumer goods brought in from Akuse and Keta, while their agents shipped stocks of cocoa southwards. Competition often required firms from French Togoland to reopen their own stores and buying centres, although in many cases these were the same firms anyway. An indication of the scale of the commercial recovery is that 19 of the leading firms were trading in Hohoe by 1929, whereas none had been present seven years earlier.[144] The larger firms, operating on both sides of the border, became adept at playing the two administrations off against each other. That is, they channelled trade along the route that held out the most favourable transport costs, customs duties and port/wharfage rates. As the two governments modified their rates accordingly, annual fluctuations in the flow of trade became a recurrent feature, as is indicated in Table 1.1. The survival of the Kpalimé–Lomé axis helped to foster an illusion that the partition had not significantly affected the economic integrity of former German Togoland. This illusion lies behind Claude Welch's suggestion that the boundary really only became an economic reality with the outbreak of the Second World War.[145] Impressions were, however, somewhat deceptive. Over time, a greater

---

[141] Lilley to CEP (19 January 1925), GNAA ADM 39/1/284.

[142] Mansfield met the farmers and dissuaded them from engaging in a hold-up. Mansfield to CEP (19 January 1925), GNAA ADM 39/1/214.

[143] Mansfield to CEP (10 May 1926), GNAA ADM 39/1/214.

[144] The firms that were notified of a road closure were F. & A. Swanzy, Millers; African and Eastern Trading Corporation; Russell & Co., Crombie Steedman, Batholomew; Commonwealth Trust Ltd; Anglo-Guinea Produce Co.; CFAO; J.J. Fischer; Pickering and Berthoud; G.B. Ollivant; Frames Agency; Union Trading Company, J. Schaad; John Walkden; Henry Werner, SCOA; and the Basel Mission Factory. GNAA ADM 39/1/205.

[145] Claude Welch, *Dream of Unity: Pan-Africanism and Political Unification in West Africa* (Ithaca: Cornell University Press, 1966), pp. 63–4.

proportion of the official trade was passing southwards to the Gold Coast, via the Senchi ferry, than was travelling along the Kpalimé–Lomé railway. This was true in respect of cocoa, but it was also true in respect of many other agricultural commodities, such as beans, maize, groundnuts and yams (see Table 1.1).

Whereas the total volume of this produce (including cocoa) in 1929 stood at only 1,346 tons, it had risen to 6,633 tons by 1934 and hit 12,258 tons in 1938. Contrary to the monocrop dependency thesis advanced by Ken Kwaku, British Togoland was actually becoming a significant exporter of foodstuffs.[146] Hence when food shortages became acute in parts of the Gold Coast during the War, one official noted that 'Demands in coastal markets are so large that large quantities of foodstuffs from this district are exported almost every day to Keta, Accra and Koforidua'.[147] Equally, the value of official imports from French Togoland peaked at the end of the 1920s, fell off rapidly during the Depression and never really recovered thereafter (see Table 1.2). As we shall see in Chapter 3, however, these figures tell only part of the story because there was also a considerable contraband trade that needs to be factored in. The bottom line is that infrastructural improvements in British Southern Togoland led the territory to face two ways at once: that is, towards Kpalimé and the Gold Coast market. This conferred a genuine advantage upon the local population who could acquire their wants from either source depending on the prevailing prices. It also created an opening for professional smugglers who could play the markets. However, this is just to jump ahead of the story.

Conclusion

In this chapter, I have advanced three propositions. The first is that the trans-Volta region had operated as a classic frontier zone for at least a century before the colonial partition. As the Kopytoff model would predict, the influx of successive waves of migrants and refugees forged hybridized societies that were composed of multiple layers. Beneath the apparent fixity of 'tribal' tradition lurked the reality of many divergent, and often discordant, versions of history that have continued to inflect local politics in the twentieth century. In addition to offering a sanctuary, this frontier zone also became a theatre of opportunity in the later nineteenth century as Hausa traders sought to evade Asante customs controls on the Volta. This, in turn, shaped the contours of the partition itself as the British and the Germans sought to monopolize the trade. Hence, if the partition was principally a European initiative, it was not strictly speaking arbitrary: on the contrary, it followed a geopolitical logic that had its roots in deeper historical processes.

Secondly, the early period of European rule was characterized by a broad measure of continuity. Although both the Germans and the British sought to manipulate trade to their own benefit, it proved extremely difficult to curb smuggling, which resulted from differentials in the rate of duty and availability of goods. A recognition

---

[146] Ken Kwaku, 'The political economy of peripheral development: a case-study of the Volta Region (Ghana) since 1920', Ph.D thesis, University of Toronto, 1975.

[147] John Duncan to CEP (9 August 1945), GNAA ADM 39/1/312.

Table 1.1 Exports From British Togoland (in tons).

Year	Cocoa via Gold Coast	Cocoa via French Togoland	Produce via Senchi Ferry
1922	n.a.	2,916	n.a.
1923	n.a.	3,473	n.a.
1924	n.a.	4,603	n.a.
1925	n.a.	4,941	n.a.
1926	n.a.	4,891	n.a.
1927	n.a.	4,842	n.a.
1928	n.a.	5,255	n.a.
1929	594	5,578	1,346
1930	710	3,808	2,307
1931	1,160	6,563	2,058
1932	3,193	5,456	5,187
1933	1,729	5,227	4,626
1934	5,914	4,575	6,883
1935	5,764	7,958	6,633
1936	6,731	9,003	8,064
1937	8,648	3,668	9,970
1938	10,701	5,750	12,258

Source: Colonial Office. *Togoland Annual Reports*, various.
Notes: n.a = not available. There is no estimate for the cocoa passing through the Gold Coast before 1929. In the early 1920s, it would have been negligible.

Table 1.2 Value of official imports from French Togoland (in £ sterling).

Year	Value of imports
1924	22,149
1925	21,211
1926	26,275
1927	50,832
1928	63,106
1929	55,511
1930	41,046
1931	19,391
1932	18,482
1933	18,463
1934	14,480
1935	10,785
1936	10,123
1937	16,208
1938	16,065

Source: Colonial Office. *Togoland Annual Reports*, various

of these realities led the two sets of authorities to tinker with, and eventually to co-ordinate, their customs duties. An element of rupture only really became evident in the early years of the twentieth century when the Germans embarked on a major infrastructural development programme. The arrival of railway lines and roads changed both the character and the composition of trade in Togoland. Moreover, communities that found themselves on the geographical margins of the colony were drawn towards the railheads where they increasingly marketed their agricultural produce and purchased their wants.

Thirdly, I have sought to demonstrate that the repartition of German Togo after the First World War severed Kpalimé from its economic hinterland, to the potential detriment of each. The British determination to impose the full schedule of Gold Coast customs duties at the new border had the immediate consequence of killing off trade. Whereas the inclination of some officials was to actively compete with the Kpalimé railway, the Customs Department argued against any such quixotic adventure. What transpired instead was a compromise solution. While the Kpalimé railway continued to carry much of the cocoa to the outside world, and consumer goods in the opposite direction, the British authorities taxed this trade at the border and used some of the money to improve their own road network. By the end of the 1920s, British Southern Togoland still faced towards Kpalimé, but now also conducted much of its trade with the Gold Coast. As we shall see, the Janus-faced character of the territory had much to do with the subsequent political history of these borderlands.

2

Cocoa Culture

Social Interaction & Land Litigation
along the Togoland Frontier

Introduction

Over the past three decades, a substantial corpus of historical and sociological literature has explored the impact of cocoa cultivation on the rich panoply of life in the
Gold Coast Colony and Ashanti from the time of its introduction at the end of the
nineteenth century down to the late twentieth century. As a consequence, we now
know a good deal about the ways in which cocoa transformed the utilization of land
and labour in the forest zone, and worked upon the very fabric of communities,
reshaping concepts of local citizenship, gender roles and household consumption
patterns.[1] The impact of cocoa upon southern British Togoland has not been
explored in anything like the same depth.[2] The reason is partly that Togoland was
always the poor relation, accounting for only a comparatively small fraction of the

---

[1] The pioneering account of cocoa cultivation in the former Eastern Province, in which issues of land and labour
are addressed, is Polly Hill, *Migrant Cocoa-Farmers of Southern Ghana* (Cambridge: Cambridge University
Press, 1963). More recently, Gareth Austin has taken up the mantle in respect of Ashanti. See especially 'The
emergence of capitalist relations in south Asante cocoa farming', *Journal of African History*, 28, 1987; 'Human
pawning in Asante 1800–1950: markets and coercion, gender and cocoa', in T. Falola and P. Lovejoy (eds),
Pawnship in Africa (Boulder: Westview, 1994); and 'Mode of production or mode of cultivation: explaining the
failure of European cocoa planters in competition with African farmers in colonial Ghana', in William Gervase
Clarence-Smith (ed.), *Cocoa Pioneer Fronts Since 1800: The Role of Smallholders, Planters and Merchants*
(Houndmills & London: Macmillan, 1996). Other treatments, which deal with gender and other dimensions,
are Christine Okali, *Cocoa and Kinship in Ghana: The Matrilineal Akan of Ghana* (London: Kegan Paul, 1983);
and Gwendolyn Mikell, *Cocoa and Chaos in Ghana* (New York: Paragon House, 1989). On the issue of citizenship and 'customary' rights, see Kathryn Firmin-Sellers, *The Transformation of Property Rights in the Gold
Coast: An Empirical Analysis Applying Rational Choice Theory* (Cambridge: Cambridge University Press,
1996), ch. 4, and Richard Rathbone, 'Defining Akyemfo: the construction of citizenship in Akyem Abuakwa,
Ghana, 1700–1939', *Africa*, 66, 4, 1996.

[2] The only published work is C. McGlade, *An Economic Survey of Cocoa Farmers in the Jasikan Area of Trans-
Volta/Togoland*, Economics Research Division, University of Ghana, Cocoa Research Series, 1957; C. Dorm-
Adzobu, 'The impact of migrant cocoa farmers in Buem, the Volta Region of Ghana', *Bulletin of the Ghana
Geographical Association*, 16, 1974; and R.A. Kotey, *Competition Between Cocoa and Coffee: A Case Study*, Legon:
Institute of Statistical, Social and Economic Research, University of Ghana, 1972. There also two relevant

total cocoa exports from the Gold Coast. And in part, this silence may also reflect the entrenched marginality of the region within Ghanaian studies. Nevertheless, many of the same observations about the socio-economic impact of cocoa production would hold equally true for British Togoland.

It is beyond the remit of this chapter to offer the kind of finely textured account that would be needed to adequately fill the historiographical gap. Yet so much of the story about the recomposition of space in Togoland – both economic and mental – revolves around cocoa that it deserves to be accorded a central place in the analysis that follows. My primary objective is to demonstrate how the wider processes associated with the expansion of cocoa production brought British Togolanders into closer imaginative proximity with their neighbours in the Gold Coast, while simultaneously helping to harden the newly created boundary with French Togoland.[3] This is a story that embodies doses of empathy and contestation in almost equal measure, and it is this duality of experience that constitutes the organizing principle in what follows. Whereas the previous chapter was largely concerned with European agency, the emphasis here falls squarely upon the role of Togolanders in the remaking of their own spatial universe.

Cocoa and new forms of social intercourse

Cocoa, roads and things

On the face of things, the early experience of cocoa production in Togoland was not a particularly auspicious one. For most of the German period, the crop hovered on the margins of the colonial export economy. The cash crops that found official favour in western Togoland, and which dominated the German export statistics, were palm products, rubber, cotton and maize. Some cocoa was grown under plantation conditions, but, according to Knoll, the authorities were worried that peasant producers would threaten the proposed forest reserves if given entirely free rein.[4] Once farmers in the Misahöhe area had demonstrated that the crop could successfully be grown, and the appropriate safeguards were in place, the government did lend some encouragement to their efforts. But officials were sufficiently deterred by the record of disease and adverse climatic conditions to actively discourage merchants from promoting the crop after 1908.[5] But, as in the Gold Coast itself, a lukewarm attitude on the part of government did not prevent Togolanders from exploring the options for themselves. Male migrants converged on the expanding cocoa frontiers of the

---

[2] (cont.) undergraduate dissertations by G.M. Austin, 'Colonialism and economic development in southern British Togoland, 1921–1945', B.A. dissertation, University of Cambridge, 1978; and Paul Coby, 'The development of the cocoa industry in Southern British Togoland', B.A. dissertation, University of Cambridge, 1978.

[3] 'Imaginative' in the sense that national communities are 'imagined'. See Benedict Anderson, *Imagined Communities: Reflections on the Origin and Spread of Nationalism* (London & New York: Verso, 1983).

[4] One of these plantations, at Kpeve, was taken over by the British after 1914. Although it was not a paying proposition, it was kept on as an agricultural station. Austin, 'Mode of production', deals with the failure of European cocoa planters in competition with African farmers, pp. 159, 163.

[5] Arthur J. Knoll, *Togo Under Imperial Germany, 1884–1914: A Case Study in Colonial Rule* (Stanford: Hoover Institution Press, 1978), p. 152.

Gold Coast, partly in order to raise enough money to pay their taxes and partly with a view to evading them altogether. Some of these farm labourers eventually returned bearing cocoa pods, the seeds from which they planted at home – remaining faithful to the spirit of enterprise first exhibited by Tetteh Quashie in the 1870s.[6] Others simply transported pods and seedlings across the border from Peki, which had itself become entranced by the crop in the first decade of the twentieth century.[7]

After 1900, when cocoa first entered the Togoland export statistics, there was a steady expansion of output, which was primarily attributable to the efforts of peasant producers rather than the German plantations.[8] Between 1906 and 1913 cocoa exports from Togoland increased tenfold to 335 tons, although some of the crop probably originated from Peki.[9] Under British occupation, exports increased a further eightfold to 2,851 tons which, on account of the delay between planting and bearing, would have reflected planting activity carried out during the last years of German rule. Nevertheless, it was after western Togoland was brought under the British flag that the economic transformation became most apparent in the export statistics as well as visible on the ground. During the war itself, many Togoland migrants chose to return from the Gold Coast, having encountered difficulties in securing remuneration for their labour. In 1917, one Customs official reported that:

> I understand that owing to the prohibition on the importation of Cocoa into England the Merchants have stopped buying the produce. The result is that thousands of natives who have been working on cocoa farms in the Gold Coast for practically the whole season are returning to Togoland without the major part of their pay. They state that owners of farms have not been able to pay them but have given them credit Notes against the time when they are in a position to dispose of their cocoa.[10]

This experience may have inclined many Togolanders to deploy their newly acquired skills at home rather than re-entering the cycle of migration to the Gold Coast. Certainly, this was the very moment when cocoa began to engage the attention of significant numbers of farmers within the territory. In Buem-Kute, Kotey identifies 1918 as the year when land sales began in earnest.[11] Equally, in the village of Likpe-Abrani, one elderly informant recalled planting his first cocoa farm in the year of a great epidemic, which can be identified with confidence as the influenza pandemic of 1918–19.[12]

[6] Austin, 'Mode of production', p. 162.

[7] Knoll, *Togo Under Imperial Germany*, p. 152. Birgit Meyer, *Translating the Devil: Religion and Modernity Among the Ewe in Ghana* (Edinburgh & London: Edinburgh University Press/International Africa Institute, 1999), pp. 6–7.

[8] Knoll, *Togo Under Imperial Germany*, p. 153. Knoll estimates that in 1904 Africans were responsible for 86 per cent of Togoland cocoa exports.

[9] These figures are extracted from a table contained in GNAA ADM 39/1/214.

[10] Extract from trade report for Quarter ending March 1917, by A.M. Archer, GNAA ADM 39/5/79. According to one informant, people from Likpe learned their craft from cocoa farmers in Worawora as well as in the Gold Coast. Interview with Mensah Ambor, Likpe-Abrani 14 March 1986.

[11] Kotey, *Competition*, p. 6.

[12] Interview with Mensah Ambor, Likpe-Abrani, 14 March 1986. Although Abrani did not exist as a village at that time, the farms would have been located in that area. M.B.K. Darkoh, 'An historical geography of the Ho-Kpandu-Buem area of the Volta Region of Ghana: 1884–1956', unpublished M.A. thesis, University of Ghana, 1966, notes in his introduction that it is often easiest to date events by concurrent events rather than relying on recollections of dates. One of his own benchmarks was the influenza pandemic.

Another informant from Likpe-Mate recalled planting his first cocoa farm a few years earlier, in 1914, and recalled that his trees started bearing in 1920.[13] This oral testimony corresponds with the documentary record. When a Customs officer embarked on a tour of the Kpandu district in 1920, he noted that the hills between Likpe-Mate and Buem-Baglo were covered with young cocoa farms. He also recorded the existence of some cocoa farming, albeit in its infancy, in Wli and Baglo proper.[14]

As we have seen, the partition of Togoland in 1920 was closely followed by the imposition of a customs frontier, which momentarily threatened the viability of the cocoa economy. The withdrawal of the European buying firms meant that farmers in more remote areas such as Buem were suddenly unable to find a ready market for their crops. However, the re-entry of the buying firms in the latter half of the decade gradually removed these impediments. As in the Gold Coast, the farmers were normally several steps ahead of the administration. In case of the Colony, G.B. Kay has argued that the colonial state, which was sensitive to the demands of the mining industry, was positively obstructive when it came to providing the infrastructure needed to service the cocoa industry.[15] Polly Hill has, however, pointed out that communities took the initiative in building their own roads when government support was not forthcoming.[16] In the case of British Togoland, the authorities sought to confine the construction of new roads, and even the upkeep of existing ones, to what they could felt they could afford. Within the Gold Coast pecking order, the Mandated Territory was not considered a great priority. Frustrated at the lack of government assistance, communities frequently built their own roads in the hope that the government could subsequently be persuaded to take them over. For example, when Captain Lilley met members of the 'Buem Literal Club' [sic] in 1928 and reported that there were no funds available for an extension of the road from Jasikan to Worawora, the chiefs expressed their desire to push ahead anyway.[17] Lilley was sufficiently impressed by their determination that he agreed to assist in the cutting of a line between these towns, leaving them to carry out the actual work as best they could. Similarly, the peoples of Likpe and Lolobi constructed their own road to Hohoe in 1935/36 because, in the words of one informant, 'we were tired of carrying cocoa on our heads' to Kpalimé.[18]

Where passable roads emerged, the European merchants tended to follow in close order. While they established themselves in the larger towns, their buying agents fanned out through the outlying villages, extending lines of credit in an attempt to secure a share of the next season's crop. Increasingly, therefore, the farmers were able to sell their cocoa without any real need to cross the border. At the same time, the firms brought with them a wide range of consumer goods that were exchanged in increasing quantities for the earnings derived from cocoa. A history of

[13] Interview with Emmanuel Osibo, Likpe-Mate, 9 March 1986.
[14] Report by H.E. Davis to Acting COC (31 October 1920), GNAA ADM 39/5/81.
[15] G.B. Kay, *The Political Economy of Colonialism in Ghana: A Collection of Documents and Statistics, 1900–1960* (Cambridge: Cambridge University Press, 1972), pp. 20–5.
[16] Hill, *Migrant Cocoa-Farmers*, pp. 234–47.
[17] Notes on Buem roads by Captain Lilley despatched to CEP (10 December 1928), GNAA ADM 39/1/205.
[18] Interview with Mensah Ambor, Likpe-Abrani, 14 March 1986.

commodification, along the lines of Timothy Burke's impressive study of Zimbabwe, has still to be written for Ghana.[19] But there can be little doubt that the spread of cocoa farming and the adoption of new patterns of consumption were mutually reinforcing processes. In the minds of oral informants, they are typically treated as part of a single package. For example, the late Nana Soglo Allo III of Likpe directly associated the emergence of local cocoa buying with the arrival of consumer goods:

> [People started to sell their cocoa locally] as the firms started to come here. When I used to go to Kpalimé, you also had the choice of going to Hohoe. The prices differed in the two places. If you went to Kpalimé, you could maybe buy a bag of salt or a cloth, but not in Hohoe, which was a small town. [But] later the UAC and GBO set up stores in town …[20]

The rise of Hohoe as the commercial hub serving the cocoa-growing areas was reflected in a near tripling of its population from 1,283 residents in 1921 to 3,785 10 years later. By this time, Hohoe had outstripped both Kpandu and Ho in size, which was no mean feat considering the fact that the former had hitherto been the pre-eminent commercial town and both served as the district headquarters at different times.[21] Furthermore, the Buem town of Jasikan emerged as a secondary commercial centre of considerable importance, boasting a population of its own of 2,150 by the time of the 1931 census.[22] Roads, towns and cocoa tended to finesse each other. The immediate effect of a road, however rudimentary, was not just to stimulate production in the immediate vicinity, but also to increase the demand for yet more roads just beyond it. At the roadhead itself, where concentrations of people accrued, a constituency typically emerged that was only too eager to push for further expansion. During the rainy season, when the cocoa trade was at its heaviest, the traffic invariably exacted a heavy toll on the fragile infrastructure. Faced with complaints from a loose coalition of European merchants, African traders, farmers and chiefs, the administration was repeatedly requested to step in to assist with the upkeep of roads and bridges, as well as the building of some new ones. Although Captain Lilley endeavoured to hold the line, the administration repeatedly found itself being dragged along as a half-hearted accomplice.

During the 1920s and the 1930s, two features of the burgeoning cocoa economy stood out. The first was quite simply the success of Togoland producers in steadily further increasing their output, despite the slide in prices after 1928. Hence exports from the territory almost doubled from 8,649 tons to 16,451 tons between 1932 and 1938, confounding conventional expectations about responsiveness to price signals (see Table 2.1). In the process, cocoa eclipsed more traditional exports from the territory. The export of rubber and palm-products had always depended heavily upon tapping wild trees, which had a finite potential for expansion. By contrast, the development of the cocoa industry represented, as Polly Hill has famously argued, a forward-looking investment in production that was limited only by the availability of

---

[19] Timothy Burke, *Lifebuoy Men, Lux Women: Commodification, Consumption and Cleanliness in Modern Zimbabwe* (London: Leicester University Press, 1996).

[20] Interview with Nana Soglo Allo III, Likpe-Mate, 20 August 1986.

[21] From 1921 to 1924, these towns shared the honour. Ho then served as the headquarters until 1928, when the administration moved to Kpandu, before finally returning in 1945.

[22] Colonial Office, *Togoland Annual Reports*, 1931, p. 30.

land and labour.[23] The planting and maintenance of cocoa farms also constituted less back-breaking work, and embodied a lower risk of crop failure than cotton production, which the authorities periodically sought to promote. Another attraction of cocoa was that it was compatible with food crop production under the local system of intercropping. If cocoa became king, the reason was that Togolanders considered that it represented the most lucrative and reliable option available to them, and not necessarily because the British wanted them to grow more of it.

Table 2.1 Producer prices and cocoa production in British Togoland (tons).

Crop year (October–September)	Mean producer price at Ho, £ per ton	Togoland production (in tons)
1922–23	no record	1,363*
1923–24	no record	2,916*
1924–25	no record	3,473*
1925–26	no record	4,603*
1926–27	no record	4,941*
1927–28	51	4,849
1928–29	31	5,442
1929–30	30	5,855
1930–31	13	6,172
1931–32	15	4,696
1932–33	14	7,763
1933–34	11	8,522
1934–35	13	10,860
1935–36	15	13,698
1936–37	17	15,734
1937–38	no record	12,316
1938–39	no record	16,451
1939–40	14	16,539

Source: Colonial Office, *Togoland Annual Reports*, 1948.
Note: * these figures are for calendar years.

The second noteworthy development was a shift in the centre of gravity away from the southern reaches of the territory around Peki towards the forest lands of Buem. During the 1930s, the authorities mapped the places of origin of the crop under the cocoa card scheme and thereby acquired a clearer picture of the spatial pattern of expansion. They distinguished between seven cocoa-growing areas (see Table 2.2). The first and second, comprising Sokode/Abutia and an area to the north of Ho, were judged to be of marginal significance and ceased even to be enumerated. The fourth area, which included Kpedze and Honuta, was of far greater importance, but production levels here remained virtually static. The third area, consisting of a

[23] Hill, *Migrant Cocoa-Farmers*; also Polly Hill, *The Gold Coast Cocoa Farmer: A Preliminary Survey* (Oxford: Oxford University Press, 1956); and *Studies in Rural Capitalism in West Africa* (Cambridge: Cambridge University Press, 1970).

Cocoa Culture

strip of territory along the Togoland hills, stretching from Likpe through Leklebi to Kpeve, was of less overall importance. However, it continued to register increases in production during the 1930s, an achievement that was mainly attributable to the efforts of farmers in Likpe and Lolobi. The curve was steeper for the sixth area, that is, Nkonya. But by far the heaviest increases were recorded in Buem (the fifth), which dwarfed the achievements of all the other areas combined. The forested hills to the north of Jasikan were ideally suited to cocoa cultivation. Moreover, as we have already seen, the expulsion of the Kwahu Dukoman after the defeat of Asante in 1874 had left much of this area denuded of population. In Buem, therefore, there was an open frontier with considerable scope for exploitation by indigenes and migrant farmers alike.

Table 2.2 Cocoa exports by area (tons)

Year	Area III	Area IV	Area V	Area VI	Total
1930/31	1,836	850	3,250	361	6,297
1931/32	1,605	965	3,222	384	6,176
1932/33	2,040	656	5,284	531	8,511
1933/34	1,828	893	5,929	576	9,226
1934/35	2,464	1,034	8,624	920	12,682
1935/36	1,977	636	9,646	916	13,175
1936/37	2,211	758	10,225	1,021	14,215

Source: GNAA ADM 39/1/284, 'Cocoa Card Scheme'.
Note: the lack of correlation with the total figures in Table 2.1 reflects a number of different factors: the use of different statistical bases (with their own shortcomings), the fact that Table 2.1 includes cocoa exports through the Gold Coast and the likelihood that some Gold Coast cocoa beans found their way into the cocoa card scheme.

Cocoa, land and community

None of this expansion would have been possible without the emergence of something approximating to a market in land. It was an article of faith among British officials across West Africa that there had been no such thing during pre-colonial times.[24] This was a preconception that was carried over to Mandated Togoland as well. Captain Lilley, for example, wrote that:

I think you will agree with me that 'in more or less ancient times' the Native Custom was not to sell land. It was sometimes pledged or pawned being redeemable but never sold. Land is often rented the usual conditions being a part of the produce to the landowner but beyond this no payment is made. This I consider satisfactory.[25]

The apparently sharp dividing line between pledging and sale might in practice be more difficult to define, particularly when the land in question was never actually reclaimed. In one case that came before the courts in 1930, the ownership of a piece of land in the village of Hoe was disputed between the plaintiff who claimed it had been pledged by his grandfather and the defendant who insisted that the land had

[24] On British attitudes towards the land question, see Anne Phillips, *The Enigma of Colonialism: British Policy in West Africa* (London: James Currey, 1989), chs 4, 6.
[25] Lilley to Record Officer (26 February 1923), GNAA ADM 39/1/574.

been sold outright. Neither party could be precise about the date of the transaction, but recalled that it had occurred some time around 1878 and that money had changed hands in the form of cowries.[26] In another case, which reached the courts in 1938, the defendant claimed that the land in question had been purchased by his grandfather from the plaintiff's grandfather for 12 baskets of cowries and that the latter had also pawned his son at the same time.[27] Admittedly, the evidence in these cases was being heard long after the respective events, when attitudes towards land had possibly changed. But the assertion that rights in land did change hands prior to the colonial period occurs so frequently in the legal record that one should be prepared to countenance the possibility.

One can feel rather more confident in asserting that such transactions became more frequent during the German period, when cash crops found a readier market. In many cases, usufruct rights were sold – for example, in favour of rubber tappers who paid landowners for the right to use the wild trees. But in other cases, a transfer of rights to the land itself occurred. The German authorities recognized this reality and merely sought to supervise the transactions, rather than seeking to enforce an absolute prohibition. Lilley recalled that his German counterpart, Dr Grüner, had consented to land purchases by people from the Peki area.[28] On assuming control of western Togoland, the British authorities were guided by German precedents as well as by the Mandate agreement itself, which stipulated that 'no native land may be transferred, except between natives, without the previous consent of the public authorities, and no real rights over native land in favour of non-natives may be created without the same consent'.[29] In 1923, Captain Mansfield observed that while the Germans had enacted legislation to regulate land transactions, the controls had been allowed to slip more recently, permitting a *de facto* market to emerge. The Acting Commissioner of the Eastern Province agreed that immediate action was needed to deal with a situation which threatened to get out of hand:

> I consider that steps should be taken to protect the natives of the Ho District against the result of the happy-go-lucky system in force in the Gold Coast and which was formerly prevented by the German Ordinance above-mentioned. What I would suggest is that a Proclamation on the lines of the German Ordinance should be issued and that giving or withholding approval to agreements affecting land should rest with the District Political Officer with a right of appeal to the Senior Political Officer.[30]

The British Sphere of Togoland Ordinance of 1924 followed the wording of the Mandate agreement closely, but stipulated that the consent of the DC was necessary before land could be alienated to a stranger. The definition of 'non-native' was taken to encompass both Gold Coasters and French Togolanders. In 1940 the prerogative of assent was passed upwards to the Governor.

---

[26] *Dabla Doe* v. *Anku Hogba*, 4 October 1930, GNAA ADM 29/4/28.

[27] *Frederick Agbezuge of Agotime* v. *Kposu Botoza of Takuve*, GNAA ADM 39/4/8 and ADM 39/4/9.

[28] Lilley to Komla Deh (4 June 1938), GNAA ADM 39/1/190. Oral informants often conflate the persons of Lilley and Grüner as the two officials who left the greatest mark on the district.

[29] 'Declaration Relating to the Mandate for the Part of Togoland Assigned to Great Britain', Article 8, PRO CO 724/1.

[30] Newlands, Acting CEP to Acting CSA (22 May 1923), GNAA ADM 39/1/574.

These measures proved entirely inadequate as the cocoa boom took hold. Much land changed hands under the so-called *dibi* system, which was an institution peculiar to Togoland. Under this arrangement, a stranger was given land on which to plant a cocoa farm, which was divided equally with the landowner once it started to bear.[31] Increasingly, strangers purchased land outright, either individually or as part of a 'company', normally comprising migrants from a single place of origin.[32] The actual acreage that changed hands for a given sum of money might differ considerably, both because of a somewhat imprecise system of measurement – the 'rope' – and the recognition that land was not of uniform quality.[33] But however imprecise the reckoning, there was never any doubt in the minds of the parties themselves that ownership of the land itself was changing hands. Hence one of the first acts of a purchaser was typically to plant special trees along the boundaries of his farm to signal to his neighbours where his land started and ended. Outright purchase and the *dibi* system were interlocking systems in that a stranger might acquire his first cocoa farms by means of the *dibi* method and then use the proceeds to purchase additional land in the same area. Equally, members of a company might purchase a block of land together and then acquire additional farms under a *dibi* arrangement.[34]

By 1932, there had been only six recorded transfers of lands to 'non-natives' in spite of what everyone recognized to be a thriving market in land. Three years later, Lilley acknowledged the scale of what had occurred under the nose of the administration, but expressed the view that it was too late to take remedial action:

> With regard to the sale of land generally, I do not see that Government can do anything useful now. In the Ahamansu, Kpedze and Honuta areas most of the land has already been sold.[35]

In addition, it was noted that much of the land in Bowiri had been alienated to outsiders. In some areas to the south of Buem, most notably Likpe and Lolobi, most of the cocoa was planted by indigenes on what had once been family land. Here the strangers found themselves in a numerical minority and their marginality was reflected in their residence on the farms rather than in the villages. By contrast, strangers came to constitute the majority in many Buem communities. The

---

[31] McGlade, *Economic Survey*, p. 15, refers to this as the 'abunu ownership' system, but it is more commonly known by the name of *dibi* in the Volta Region.

[32] On cocoa companies see Hill, *Migrant Cocoa-Farmers*, ch. 2; McGlade, *Economic Survey.*, p. 16, notes that in her survey areas in Togoland most of the land bought from chiefs was through these companies.

[33] In the Gold Coast, Hill notes that the 'rope' varied in size between the Shai rope of 12 or 14 hand-stretches and the Akuapem rope of 24 hand-stretches – that is, around 24 or 48 yards. Hill, *Migrant Cocoa-Farmers*, p. 44. According to Kotey, *Competition*, p. 29, a rope in Buem was reckoned to measure 24 yards. Evidence from the colonial court records does, however, suggest a considerable degree of variation. In one case, involving some land disputed between Likpe-Kukurantumi and Buem-Baika, a witness defined a rope as being 26 yards: GNAA ADM 39/4/7, *George Manokpor v. Kofi Bensu and David*, heard on 19 May 1936. In another case, where the disputed land was at Shia, the court ascertained that a rope was held to be around 100 feet, or 33 yards: GNAA ADM 39/4/5, *Ador Kwamla v. Atsiwoto Avutsu*, 5 January 1933. The more fundamental problem with the square rope as a unit of measurement is that a plot of land is typically measured accurately only along the base-line. A square rope may not, therefore, be square at all, and two pieces of land that are notionally of the same dimensions may differ in size.

[34] McGlade's chronology of land acquisition, *Economic Survey*, p. 17, does suggest that *dibi* became common in the latter half of the 1930s by which time land sales were already far advanced.

[35] Lilley to CEP (2 December 1935), GNAA ADM 39/1/574.

population of Ahamansu and the surrounding area was estimated at a mere 300 to 350 people in 1921, but ten years later the figure had jumped to 2,635 of whom no fewer than 2,304 were strangers. Similarly, the population of Bowiri was estimated at 2,588 of whom 1,084 were strangers.[36] These strangers would have included a mixture of farmers and labourers, including some who were in transition between the two. As in the Gold Coast, the pioneer cocoa farmers probably depended heavily upon family labour to start with. Once their first farms were bearing, however, they relied increasingly upon labourers drawn from the poorer parts of French Togoland – most especially Kotokolis and Kabrés from the north. Many farmers left their farms in the hands of their labourers and confined themselves to seasonal visits to Buem.

For our purposes, what is of paramount significance is the impact of these developments upon the evolving relationship between the Gold Coast and the Mandated Territory. Among the migrants flooding into Buem could be counted many natives of the Colony who came in search of good forest land. At various times, the authorities identified migrants drawn from Akuapem, Krobo, Peki, Ada and Anlo.[37] Even the occasional Ashanti farmer enters the official record. However, most of the migrants were actually drawn from other parts of British Togoland, where land was either scarce or not suitable for the cultivation of cocoa. For example, farmers from Anfoega spread out across the cocoa belt, and the money they accumulated is still visible in the houses that stand proudly in their home villages. Again, Dorm-Adzobu has identified farmers from Gbefi, located in the grasslands near to Kpandu, as being among the leading cocoa migrants in the vicinity of Guaman and Kadjebi during the 1920s. He also notes that farmers from Ve, whose lands were equally ill-suited to cocoa production, began to converge on Ahamansu and Papase in the 1930s.[38] The British authorities estimated that as many as 60 per cent of land sales involved migrants drawn from other parts of British Togoland who would not have required consent to purchase land.[39] A further 20 per cent were reckoned to involve migrants from Peki, which was experiencing an acute shortage of land suitable for cocoa cultivation.[40] The remainder was accounted for by natives of French Togoland, albeit mainly on land claimed by the Akpossos, and by coastal people drawn from Anlo and Ada. The latter were depicted as comparatively insignificant in numerical terms, but the pattern of chain-migration meant that they were concentrated in particular areas.

In numerous villages strung out along the cocoa frontier, Gold Coasters represented a visible, and often extremely vocal, element. They never regarded these adopted villages as home, and they channelled their earnings to their communities of origin, but their local presence was very obvious. Gold Coast Ewes were even more prominently placed among the ranks of the storekeepers, clerks and buying agents who represented the extended arm of the European firms. Furthermore, with the growth of commercial centres such as Hohoe and Jasikan, Anlo traders settled and

---

[36] Lilley to Reserve Settlement Commissioner, Hohoe (10 May 1931), GNAA ADM 39/1/190.

[37] CEP to CSA (14 March 1929), GNAA ADM 39/1/574.

[38] Dorm-Adzobu, 'Impact', p. 48.

[39] H.C. Ellershaw to CEP (6 January 1938), GNAA ADM 39/1/190.

[40] Meyer, *Translating the Devil*, p. 16.

secured a stranglehold over the produce trade.[41] During the inter-war years, the crucial link between the farmers of British Togoland and the external market was provided by these strangers from the Colony, while the Kpalimé nexus became somewhat weaker. Moreover, when British Togolanders attended church, there was a very good chance that their priest or pastor would be an Ewe from the Colony. And when Togolanders sought to defend themselves against the charge of smuggling or resorted to land litigation, they turned to Gold Coast lawyers to fight their corner. Hence one of the most influential Gold Coast intellectuals of the inter-war years, Dr J.B. Danquah, turns up repeatedly in the official records that concern Buem, which had more than its fair share of litigation. The attention was not entirely one-sided, in that the Gold Coast press also exhibited a growing interest in the affairs of the Mandated Territory.

While there is something highly seductive about the concept of 'imagined communities', it is devilishly difficult to be precise about the processes through which particular constructions come into being. One can point to associations between sets of actors, and draw reasonable inferences from them, but one establishes causal relations at one's peril. Such is the case of the creeping integration of British Togoland into the imaginative orbit of the Gold Coast, a process that was palpable but so subtle as to render it difficult to capture in non-reductionist terms. Nevertheless, there can be little doubt that by the second decade of British rule Togolanders were sharing in many of the wider concerns of the Colony. This can be illustrated with reference to the cocoa hold-ups of the 1930s, when farmers withheld their crops from the European buying firms in protest at successive pooling agreements designed to restrict competition.[42] In 1930/31, British Togolanders held back part of the crop, but because cocoa attracted a higher price in Kpalimé, many took advantage of this alternative.[43] The effects of the pooling agreement of 1937/38 seem to have been much more dramatic and, as everywhere, threatened to affect the brokers as much as the farmers.[44] Rhoda Howard understates the case when she observes

[41] On the spread of the Anlo-Ewe trading network, see Sandra Greene, *Gender, Ethnicity and Social Change on the Upper Slave Coast: A History of the Anlo-Ewe* (London: James Currey, 1996), pp. 171-80.

[42] There is a substantial literature on the cocoa hold-ups, although the Togoland dimension has not been considered in any depth. See Sam Rhodie, 'The Gold Coast cocoa hold-up of 1930–31', *Transactions of the Historical Society of Ghana* 9, 1968; John Miles, 'Rural protest in the Gold Coast: the cocoa hold-ups, 1908–1938', in Clive Dewey and A.G. Hopkins (eds), *The Imperial Impact: Studies in the Economic History of Africa and India* (London: Athlone Press, 1978); Rhoda Howard, 'Differential class participation in an African protest movement: the Ghana cocoa boycott of 1937–38', *Canadian Journal of African Studies* 10, 3, 1976; and Gareth Austin, 'Capitalists and chiefs in the cocoa hold-ups in south Asante, 1927–1938', *International Journal of African Historical Studies*, 21, 1, 1988.

[43] Although the average producer prices per ton fell from £31 in 1929 to £27 in 1930, the price was fully £14 per ton higher in French territory. Colonial Office, *Togoland Annual Reports*, 1930, p. 18. In 1931, prices fell still further. There was evidently some interest in the hold-up because John Amanie, a cocoa buyer and letter-writer based at Honuta (and a native of Buem), did recall that he 'was sent to Accra to represent by the farmers in the Cocoa Federation palaver'. See his evidence in GNAA ADM 39/4/4, 18 January 1932, *Martin D. Kwashie v. John Amanie*, 18 January 1932.

[44] It was one of the objects of the pool to break the power of the brokers. The Hohoe agent for Holt observed that there were few large brokers in Togoland, although there were many of them and they were engaged in playing the market. Document entitled 'Cocoa boycott', in Rhodes House Library, JHP, Mss. Afr. S.825, file 536 (ii), enclosed in a letter from Hohoe agent to District Agent, Accra, dated 24 March 1938.

that there was 'some minimal participation in the cocoa boycott in the cocoa growing areas of the British Mandated Territory'.[45] The active participation of Togolanders, and their gestures of defiance, were sufficient to elicit expressions of official concern.

As against the preceding season, the producer price in British Togoland fell precipitously from 25/- to 7/6 per load at the start of the 1937/38 buying season. The fact that this fall coincided with the inception of the latest Cocoa Pool suggested to farmers that producer prices were being artificially depressed, although the firms insisted that it was an accurate reflection of global market trends. The vehemence of the reaction in the Mandated Territory, where cocoa was burnt and employees of the firms were assaulted, caught the European merchants by surprise.[46] Given their assessment of Togolanders as essentially passive creatures, an explanation was sought in the guise of corrupting influences from outside. The Hohoe agent for John Holt, for example, pinned the blame on individuals who had picked up bad habits from the Gold Coast:

> We must remember that the BMT native is, in himself, much less subversive than the Accra native, for example, although in many cases his opinions are easily swayed by the numerous strangers who find their way into BMT. When an opinion does take hold of him, he is more dangerous than the ordinary African.[47]

A number of chiefs, especially in Buem, intervened directly in the dispute by preventing the movement of cocoa lorries and fining individuals who sold any of their crop. According to the same report, it was in Buem that the nefarious influences were most clearly manifested:

> Of course, the majority of the BMT chiefs are not intelligent, but there is always a power behind the Stool – either a Stool father who has been educated in Accra or a stranger occupying the post of Registrar to the Chief. These Registrars are clever and anti-white, belonging to the type of 'bush lawyer'... Such is the case with the State of Buem – the Paramount State in BMT. The Paramount Chief Nana Akpanja is malleable in the hands of the State Registrar. It is chiefly through the State Registrar of Buem, that the subtle change in the opinions advanced by the Chiefs as to the reason for the boycott, has taken place.

The European buyers also made much of the influence that the Gold Coast chiefs exercised over the minds of their supposedly more impressionable Togoland counterparts. The same agent, for example, claimed that when cocoa began to leak on to the market in Hohoe and Kpandu in February 1938, their chiefs were summoned to a chiefs' conference in Accra and instructed to close their roads.

This reading of events is clearly highly tendentious. There is no reason to believe that the farmers or chiefs of British Togoland farmers were especially gullible. If anything, their proximity to the border probably made them even more alert to price

---

[45] Rhoda Howard, *Colonialism and Underdevelopment in Ghana* (London: Croom Helm, 1978), p. 207.

[46] A police report on 'Riots and Disturbances' noted that 'while the people of Togoland are generally peacable', there had been two significant incidents connected to the hold-up at Kpedze and Hohoe. Senior Assistant Superintendant of Police, Koforidua, to Commissioner of Police, Accra (13 January 1939), GNAA ADM 39/1/570.

[47] 'Cocoa boycott'.

manipulation by the European firms. The Cocoa Pool would have been interpreted, not unreasonably, as an attempt to cheat the farmers. And given that the chiefs of the Colony had no sanction over their Togoland counterparts, one has to be sceptical of the notion that compliance was procured by means of 'dire threats' alone. The loaded reports of the European agents remain of some interest, however, because they do identify a growing interaction between farmers' representatives, chiefs and opinion leaders in the Gold Coast and British Mandated Togoland, respectively. On the other hand, the hold-up movement appears to have had a limited impact in French Togoland, where the issue of direct taxation provided the real focus of popular protest. These issues will be revisited in Chapter 5. At this point, I will I turn to consider some of the other side-effects of the cocoa boom.

Cocoa and discord

Land litigation

Although the cultivation of cocoa, and the expansion of related forms of commerce, brought peoples together in hitherto unimagined permutations, it also served up a recipe for social discord. In the days before cash crops figured prominently, rights to land among the northern Ewe and their neighbours were normally vested in patri-lineages and mediated by their respective lineage heads. According to the theory at least, initial rights were established by more or less distant ancestors having been the first to plant crops on a given piece of land. Any member of the lineage group might in principle cultivate the land at a later date, although, as Manoukian noted, 'in general, each member farms the land previously farmed by his immediate forbears'.[48] In practice, when land was relatively abundant and when food crops were the primary focus, land that was cultivated for a couple of years might have been allowed to revert to bush and could well have acquired the status of 'virgin' land once again. This goes some way towards explaining why, when competition for land began in earnest, so many rival claims could be staked. A second category, that of individual land, is linked by Manoukian to first cultivation, purchase, mortgage, donation and inheritance. A third category, that of stool land, was a feature of the southern Gold Coast, but did not exist in most of British Togoland. The notable exception is Buem, where stool rights were asserted over much of the forest lands that had been vacated by the Kwahu Dukoman.

Attitudes towards land use began to shift from the moment when agricultural commodities such as palm oil and rubber acquired a market value. But more than anything, it was cocoa that transformed the relationship between people and land. Because cocoa was a semi-permanent tree crop, it changed the meaning attached to usufruct. Whenever a lineage member created a cocoa farm, he effectively reduced the land available to other members of the group. Even worse, when lineage heads sold off land, as they did on a massive scale in Buem, they effectively extinguished the rights of their kinsmen in perpetuity. Not surprisingly, therefore, commodifica-

---

[48] Madeline Manoukian, *The Ewe-Speaking People of Togoland and the Gold Coast* (London: International Africa Institute, 1952), p. 40.

tion placed severe stresses on lineage solidarity. It is difficult to know quite when the shift began, and no doubt the timing varied from one place to the next, but it is noteworthy that in Likpe corporate rights had largely given way to individual land claims by the inter-war period. Hence the many family land disputes that came before the colonial courts tended to be fought on the basis of individual claims, with litigants referring back to the exploits of fathers and grandfathers. In one such case, a lineage head, who claimed knowledge of the land situation dating back to before the Asante wars, was keen to articulate the case for corporate ownership, while also acknowledging that cocoa had altered local practice:

> I am the senior member of the Ekudi family of which the Plaintiff and Defendants are members. From very ancient times nobody from this family could prevent another member from going to the land to fell palm trees. We have been farming for a long time on this land. With the advent of cocoa the land became apportioned... It is not customary for one man to lay claim to the land. Neither Plaintiff nor defendant can say the land is individual property.[49]

However, the fact that he was giving evidence at all was a consequence of the fact that both plaintiff and defendant were making precisely such individual claims. His observation about the effects of cocoa on local practice was echoed in an another case, when a witness observed that 'In olden days a man could farm on his neighbour's land. But this is not the case since the advent of cocoa'.[50]

At the same time, the expansion of the cocoa frontier led to a proliferation of disputes between communities. When land was abundant, the boundaries between pre-colonial *dukɔwo* had never needed to be very precisely delineated. But as land became associated with accumulation, farmers began to move into the buffer zones separating one community from the next. The dynamic was explained with some perspicuity by the Apesokubi chief in 1969, in the context of a land dispute with Asato that dated all the way back to the turn of the century:

> That by Akan customs and traditions when people settle like that and one is not under the other one, there is [*sic*] usually no established boundaries between them. Consequently the farmers and hunters from time to time meet at various places which in due course turn to establish a boundary between the two parties who remain independent people. Such an imaginary line which traditionally become their boundaries are not established by any straight line so that the so-called traditional boundaries are only determined by farms and hunting villages of people of the adjacent towns. Such has been the situation between Asato and Apesokubi people. Such condition has remained for the past 60 years. The trouble came as a result of cultivation of cocoa farms by the people of these two towns in which case some of the Asato people made farms in the far-reaching lands from their base and vice-versa by the Apesokubi people. In due course, as the cocoa farms increased, litigations started as to the ownership of the lands concerned at various points where [there were] lots of criss-cross cocoa farms belonging to both Apesokubi people and the Asato people.[51]

---

[49] Evidence of Emmanuel Ekudese in case of *Karl Akorli of Likpe-Mate* v. *Francis Kwabena and Amega Kwasi Ekudi*, 26 July 1938, GNAA ADM 43/4/16.

[50] Evidence of George Mensa in case of *William K. Asamoah* v. *Paul Kplente*, 26 July 1938, GNAA ADM 43/4/16.

[51] 'Apesokubi–Asato Land Case Petition For an Independent Enquiry and Arbitration Under the Auspices of the Ministry of Lands', dated October 1969', Stool Lands Boundaries Settlement Commission, Accra, File 6/76.

The Germans had responded to the first round of land cases by fixing boundaries as and when disputes arose. The exercise was often extremely arbitrary, reflecting a desire to establish a visible marker rather than to ascertain which claims were actually the stronger. For example, when the peoples of Vakpo and Anfoega became embroiled in a land dispute a few years before the First World War, Dr Grüner decided to fix a boundary between them. He detained the Vakpo chief and members of his entourage while he went to investigate. A witness recalls the blunt message that Grüner conveyed to the Vakpo side on his return:

> On the next day Dr. Grüner stood on the steps of the District Commissioner's bungalow. We were fetched from the cells. With his pencil he tapped his chest and said 'We are the landowners'. He said that as we were troubling the Anfoes and refusing to let them work on the land he was taking us to Misahöhe. We were given loads to carry.[52]

Grüner's idea of settling the dispute was simply to inform the two parties as to where their boundary would henceforth run and to graphically warn them of the consequences of failing to respect it. Another witness recalled that:

> He asked the elders of Anfoe and Vakpo to meet at Akefe. He fixed a machine gun in place and asked the chief of Vakpo to call his subjects out of the bush lest they should be injured. He aimed the gun at a Tsa tree. The tree fell down. He asked both chiefs if they saw this. 'That' he said 'would happen to them in if they again made palaver on the land'. He took £25 from each chief.[53]

This exercise in intimidation did not resolve matters in the longer term, however, because neither party felt that their claims had been seriously entertained. As the Provincial Commissioner's court later remarked:

> It is abundantly clear that Dr. Gruner did not take any evidence and did not apparently make any enquiry as to its previous history and ownership of the land.[54]

Predictably, these disputes resurfaced under British rule. In other land cases, it was not even possible to refer back to German precedents because in the absence of a dispute, the authorities had been happy to live without fixed boundaries. With the scramble to find land on which to plant cocoa in the 1920s, the British were deprived of this luxury. Captain Lilley's report referred to no fewer than 11 major land cases in Buem alone.

Cases involving land set well back from the border frequently had a frontier dimension in that local contestants were in the habit of selling land to strangers – often twice over. Among the migrants caught in the middle were farmers from the French sphere and from the Gold Coast. For example, Kpele farmers from French Togoland who bought land from the Papase chief later discovered that it was also claimed by the Dapa chief who was engaged in selling land to other strangers. As Captain Lilley remarked of this dispute, which threatened to escalate dangerously at one point:

---

[52] Evidence of Edward Kwasi in case of *Divisional Chief Gbogbolulu of Vakpo* v. *Chief Hodo of Anfoe*, 12 August 1938, GNAA ADM 43/4/16.

[53] Evidence of Chiami Kpong in case of *Divisional Chief Gbogbolulu of Vakpo* v. *Chief Hodo of Anfoe*, 19 August 1938, GNAA ADM 43/4/16.

[54] Judgment of Provincial Commissioner's Court, 13 June 1941, GNAA ADM 29/4/27.

The construction of the Togoland border

> The whole matter in the neighbourhood of Dapa and Papase is a stranger palaver and not really between the natives of Dapa and Papase. Each side, I am convinced, sells land to strangers. Often the same land is sold by both sides to different parties.[55]

From the standpoint of the vendor, this was the perfect ruse because, while he received payment from the purchaser, the latter was likely to bear the brunt of any conflict that might break out on the land itself. In the forests of British Togoland, the dictum of *caveat emptor* carried a particular resonance.

Land litigation and the frontier

The cases I wish to consider in detail concern claimants to land living on either side of the Togoland boundary. Despite the best efforts of the Boundary Commissioners, as outlined in the previous chapter, the final outcome was not without its shortcomings. Although they tried not to separate communities from their farm lands, this was sometimes unavoidable, while in other cases there was simply no consensus as to who owned the land. Indeed, the international boundary complicated the land question for reasons that the two sets of authorities had not fully anticipated. Despite an agreement that land rights would not be affected by the international boundary, and that farmers would be allowed unhindered access to their farms, local actors read a different meaning into the border. During the early 1920s, communities who claimed land on the other side began to complain that their neighbours were seeking to transpose the international borderline on to traditional communal boundaries. By making life difficult for the real owners, it was said, they were seeking to drive the latter off the land.

In 1936, the chief of Buem-Dzolu complained that whereas there had hitherto been a mutually accepted border with the Ahlo people, the international boundary had been drawn much further to the west, placing some of his land in French Togoland. The reason, he claimed, was that officials had not bothered to inspect conditions on the ground: if they had done so they would have seen the boundary trees marking out his farms. In this respect, the chief had perhaps misunderstood the demarcation exercise which, for logistical reasons, was never expected to follow the contours of individual farms. Be that as it may, he went on to report that when his son had tried to build a hut on the land, he had been harassed by a neighbouring (presumably Ahlo) farmer.[56] Later that year, he complained to the DC that armed Ahlo men had entered his farms and plucked cocoa.[57] Two years later armed conflict broke out, which continued sporadically until 1941.[58] Further to the south, the peoples of Wli and Danyi disputed the ownership of land on both sides of the boundary. Even the chosen site for the British Preventive Station at Wli-Afegame became a bone of contention between the peoples of Yikpa and Wli.[59] The sub-chief of Wli-

---

[55] Lilley to Spooner, DC Krachi (3 April 1936), GNAA ADM 39/1/212.

[56] Letter of complaint from Odikro Kasate, Dzolu (9 July 1936), TNAL Klouto 2 APA/2.

[57] Odikro Kasate to H.C. Ellershaw (22 December 1936), GNAA ADM 39/1/212.

[58] Ben K. Fred-Mensah, 'Bases of traditional conflict management among the Buems of the Ghana–Togo border', in I. William Zartman (ed.), *Traditional Cures for Modern Conflicts: African Conflict 'Medicine'* (Boulder & London: Lynne Rienner, 2000) p. 41.

[59] John Gutch to Commandant de Cercle de Klouto (13 June 1932), TNAL Klouto 2 APA/2.

Todzi echoed the complaint of the Dzolu petitioner when he noted that communal boundaries that had been accepted since German times were now bisected by the international border. He recalled that he had pointedly asked Lilley whether he still enjoyed undiminished rights to his land across the border and had been reassured that he did. Once again, he stated that his dilemma lay in the fact that Danyi people were starting to claim the land as their own and summoning the French authorities to their aid.[60] What emerges from the large body of court records and administrative documentation is evidence that border communities did indeed manipulate the contours of the international boundary to prosecute land claims. However, it bears reiteration that claims to the land were often confused, and the more hotly disputed for that reason.

The cases that proliferated during the inter-war years usually ended up being heard in the courts of that half of Togoland where the disputed land lay. The latter confronted a problem of reconciling fundamentally incompatible oral testimony and making sense of a highly fragmented documentary record. Even where German maps could be consulted, these were not always consistent and their accuracy was frequently what was at issue. Consequently, court decisions typically fell somewhere between a judgment and an exercise in arbitration in which the primary objective was to effect a reconciliation of the parties involved. The efficacy of the final settlement depended upon the willingness of the claimants to respect the outcome and on a determination on the part of the respective administrations to uphold it. The former proved problematic and, as we shall see in subsequent chapters, the same cases continued to recur with some regularity. As a result, the international border created the context in which a sense of mutual suspicion festered. In modern academic parlance, many British and French Togolanders living on either side of the boundary came to look upon their neighbours as a nefarious 'Other'. Although some felt that the border had complicated access to their farm lands, there were just as many who evidently benefited from the arrangements. Somewhere in the struggle between claimants and counter-claimants – in the production of winners and losers – lies the answer to the question of why the Togoland boundary stabilized so quickly and in the form it did.

For their part, the British and the French authorities felt the need to intervene in order to prevent the struggles over land from escalating into serious breaches of the peace. But they generally found themselves reacting to cross-border disputes whose dynamic was largely beyond their understanding and capacity to control. Whereas they were forced to sublimate their own mutual distrust and to pool their information, it was the border communities themselves who repeatedly sought to turn up the heat. This reading of the historical record cuts against a common interpretation of boundaries as bizarre European constructs imposed upon long-suffering Africans. Reality is a good deal more complicated than that. In order to develop this point, I will now turn to consider two specific land disputes that are particularly well-documented. The first derives from Eweland, while the other concerns the cocoa frontier between Buem and Akposso.

---

[60] Agbonotoh to DC (9 November 1927), TNAL Klouto 2 APA/2.

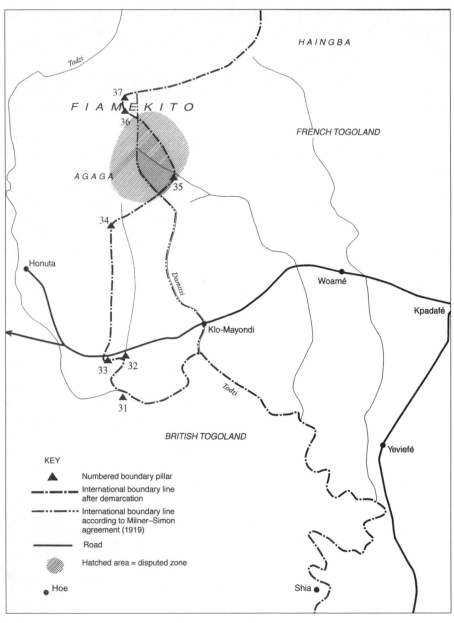

Map 2.1 The Woamé–Honuta dispute

Cocoa Culture

The Woamé–Honuta dispute

The dispute that engulfed the communities of Woamé and Honuta during the inter-war years could stand for so many others, in that it was a by-product of the cocoa revolution. The German authorities had previously fixed a physical boundary between the Haingbas and their neighbours, but because there had been no trouble between the Woamés and the Honutas, their boundary had remained undefined. However, a line was variously depicted on German maps, for reasons of cartographical tidiness. In this case, the supposed tyranny of the map led to some rather anarchic consequences.

With the expansion of cocoa cultivation, the two sides began to encroach on the same areas of land on the Agaga and Fiamekito hills that lay between them (see Map 2.1). The matter was complicated by virtue of uncertainty over where the international boundary ought to run. Although this was distinct from the issue of land ownership, the two became closely intertwined in the eyes of the litigants and the authorities themselves. Scanning from north to south, the Milner–Simon agreement of 1919 had specified 'a line generally running southwards following the [previously mentioned] watershed to the Fiamekito hills which it leaves to reach the River Damitsi. Thence the River Damitsi to its confluence with the Todschie (or Wuto)'.[61] This description was typical of the agreement as a whole, in that it followed natural features as identified on the 1905 map. But as has been noted in the previous chapter, it was quickly acknowledged that this arrangement was unsatisfactory because the effect would have been to separate the village of Mayondi from its farm lands. In the face of many complaints, Captain Mansfield and M. Coez visited the area and decided that it would be preferable to follow 'tribal' criteria rather than natural ones when drawing the international boundary.[62] This apparently straightforward solution achieved its principal objective when it came to fixing a line between Mayondi and Honuta. But when it came to defining the boundary between Honuta and Woamé, these officials ran up against conflicting evidence. According to a German map of 1902 (1: 100,000), their boundary lay at the summit of the Agaga hill, whereas the 1905 map (1: 200,000) placed it one kilometre to the east of the hill.[63] If the former was adhered to, a part of the hill would have belonged to either side, but if the 1905 map was followed the land would belong to Honuta in its entirety. The conclusion Mansfield and Coez came to was that a decision about where the 'tribal' boundary ran, and hence where the international frontier should follow, ought to be left to the Boundary Commissioners who could gather evidence on the spot.

This decision to temporize could not easily be sustained once the land became a serious bone of contention. The British and French authorities were unaware of any serious controversy until 1923 when Headchief Kwakutse of Honuta complained that Woamé people had jumped their traditional boundary and were starting to plant

---

[61] Milner–Simon description of frontier, Article 1, paragraphs 35 and 36, reproduced at Ian Brownlie, *African Boundaries: A Legal and Diplomatic Encyclopaedia* (London: Christopher Hurst/Royal Institute of International Affairs, 1979), p. 256.

[62] In this case, the 'tribes' in question were the *dukɔwo*, given that all the communities concerned were Ewe-speaking.

[63] Armand to Commissaire (5 June 1924), GNAA ADM 39/1/57.

cocoa on Agaga hill.[64] His understanding of what was traditional possibly accorded with the details shown on the 1905 map. Lilley and Coez responded by issuing a declaration that neither party should make new farms pending a final settlement. In 1924, Mansfield and Armand visited the land. They found only two cocoa farms on Agaga hill, both of which had been planted by farmers from Woamé. Despite talking to both sides, and calling on the services of the Mayondi chief as an arbiter, they found themselves incapable of deciding who were the rightful owners of the land. To add a touch of farce to proceedings, the Mayondi chief proceeded to claim the disputed land as his own.[65] Armand summed up the experience as follows:

> In the face of much bad faith on the part of the natives and in view of the numerous difficulties which confronted us in tracing a provisional Boundary at the heights of the above-mentioned hills, completely wooded and over-run by forests, we decided by mutual agreement, Captain Mansfield and I, that all the territory of the Agaga, Fiamekito and Kolokoto Hills, to the west of the River Damitsi, should remain temporarily a neutral zone, within which the inhabitants of Honuta and Woamé should not have the right to cultivate, and especially not to hunt.[66]

This amounted to the further postponement of a decision, although both governments were well aware that something would have to be done sooner or later.

By now, the two sets of officials had thoroughly conflated the definition of international and communal boundaries, and treated them in their correspondence as if they were interchangeable. The confusion was intimately bound up with the fact that the Milner–Simon line followed the contentious 1905 Sprigade map which depicted *dukɔ* boundaries. To follow this map in respect of the international boundary potentially meant that the Woamés would be separated from the land which the 1902 map suggested was theirs. Armand's preference was for abiding by the latter details, that would have meant dividing the disputed area in half, and redrawing the international boundary accordingly. Mansfield, on the other hand, cautioned against accepting this reading because it would entail the loss of valuable cocoa land. He therefore recommended sticking to the original Milner–Simon line along the Damitsi River.[67] However, as Lilley subsequently pointed out, the Mansfield solution would merely have had the effect of depriving Mayondi of its own farm lands, which was precisely what the initial accords had set out to avoid. In effect, these officials were starting to engage in the spirit of competition themselves.

While the administrations dithered, people on either side of the border started to take matters into their own hands. In contravention of the declaration of a neutral zone, farmers from both communities began to move into the Fiamekito and Agaga hills to plant cocoa, making a clash almost inevitable. In June 1925, one Bauman Alomevo reported a violent incident, in which he was allegedly the victim.[68] Being a native of Agotime, he claimed to have bought land on the Agaga hill from the Honuta chief in 1908. He had apparently just started to plant cocoa on this land, which he claimed lay outside the neutral zone. The incident in question allegedly

[64] Kwakutse to District Political Officer (17 July 1923), GNAA ADM 39/1/57.
[65] See the Honuta entry in GNAA ADM 39/5/73.
[66] Armand to Commissaire (5 June 1924), GNAA ADM 39/1/57.
[67] Mansfield to CEP (2 July 1924), GNAA ADM 39/1/57.
[68] Lilley to Commandant de Cercle de Klouto (13 June 1925), TNAL Klouto 2 APA/2.

occurred when one Motetse Bleku of Woamé and three other men confronted him on his farm and asked why he was still there when the French Commandant had allocated the land to the Woamés. A struggle ensued, during which a gun was discharged and Alomevo was struck with a cutlass. Lilley reported the incident to his French counterpart and Alomevo was invited to Misahöhe to lay charges. Motetse insisted that Alomevo had actually been the aggressor, and claimed that the Woamés had in fact been allocated the land on the right bank of the Damitsi River, which meant that this part of the hill belonged to them.[69] The initial incident was closely followed by another in which some women working on Alomevo's land were allegedly flogged and forcibly taken away to Misahöhe by Motetse.[70] The latter apparently believed that the French authorities were on his side, despite their evident embarrassment at this turn of events. Meanwhile, fresh points of friction were proliferating across the disputed area. In March 1925, for example, a group of migrant farmers, who claimed to have bought some land from the Honuta chief in 1914, complained that Woamé people were trying to drive them off. In this case, they asserted that their land had been placed in French territory and that the Woamés, backed up by the French authorities, were trying to dislodge them.[71] Given that a final decision on this stretch of frontier was not taken until 1927, it is unlikely that this area had been finally declared a part of French Togoland. And even if such a decision had been taken in principle, that would not have affected their pre-existing rights. But because of a singular failure to clarify matters, conspiracy theories abounded and farmers were inclined to fight for what they perceived as their entitlements before they were extinguished altogether.

In the final event, the Boundary Commissioners were forced to revert to practical expedients. The Damitsi River was abandoned and a straight line was drawn further to the west, thus reuniting Mayondi with its lands. But while the demarcation between Mayondi and Honuta did not become the cause for any subsequent concern, the problem of Agaga hill to the north was not really resolved. The final description defined the boundary (in this case scanning from south to north) as running in a straight line for 2,600 metres to pillar 34 located on Agaga hill (in the vicinity of Alomevo's dwelling), then following a series of straight lines along the edge of a cliff, to the confluence of the Adetugbe and Wumaklu Rivers at pillar 35, and finally upstream to the source of the former River at pillar 36.[72] The net effect was to deposit most of the disputed area in British Togoland, which approximated more to the 1905 than the 1902 map. The reality was that the Boundary Commissioners had effectively reneged on their promise to fix boundaries according to 'tribal' limits rather than natural features. Knowing full well that they had not been able to decide on communal limits, they fell back on the assurance that the international boundary did not affect prior rights of land ownership. This effort to disaggregate two issues which had been consistently elided did not satisfy local actors who felt that they were still intrinsically connected. For example, in the wake of the 1927 demarcation, the linguist for the Woamé chief complained that his land had been placed 'in English

---

[69] Motetse to Commandant de Cercle de Klouto (13 June 1925), TNAL Klouto 2 APA/2.
[70] Lilley to CEP (9 July 1925), GNAA ADM 39/1/57.
[71] Lawrence Atease and Philip Tedeku to DC (26 March 1925), GNAA ADM 39/1/57.
[72] Brownlie, *African Boundaries*, p. 266.

line' and that, as a consequence, he had been told by the DC that he could no longer use the land.[73] Although this is most unlikely, it does not alter the fact that this was how the matter was perceived by the Woamés. On the other hand, the Honutas felt that the demarcation had vindicated their claims. In fact, governmental reassurances begged the all-important question – which had been left in abeyance – of who did own the land.

In 1929, the dispute entered a fresh phase when the Woamé side decided to raise the stakes by petitioning the League of Nations. This embarrassed the administering authorities whose failure to act decisively was exposed to public view. Their response, after consulting among themselves, was to suggest that the case could only be resolved if it was brought to court.[74] Since most of the land lay in British Togoland, this meant that the case would have to be heard there. The Woamé chief seemed uninterested in this course of action until April 1932 when he finally took out a summons against the Honuta chief for trespass – although this did not prevent him from despatching a further petition to the League of Nations in 1933.[75] The Honuta chief responded with a counter-claim for damages, and in July 1933 the case finally came before the court, which was presided over by the Acting DC, John Gutch. The latter heard evidence from the two sides, and from their witnesses, and came to the conclusion that it was impossible to reconcile or decide between them. For example, both sides referred to the visible remains of an earlier settlement, but each claimed that it was their forebears who had lived there. Again, while it was agreed that Dr Grüner had laid down certain boundary markers after an earlier dispute with Hayingba, each side claimed that the intention had been to fix a boundary with themselves. The Honuta side performed rather better, in that they managed to produce a witness – a native of Avatime – who recalled seeking permission from their chief to hunt on the disputed land some 55 years earlier. On the basis of the tangled evidence, Gutch came to the conclusion that neither side was really aware of any clear pre-colonial boundaries, and that the dispute could be put down quite simply to the effects of cocoa mania:

> Since this time, the clearing of the forest and the planting of young cocoa trees in this area seems to have continued by both the Woames and the Honutas with frequent disputes and with resul-
> tant violence. I have actually been shown young cocoa trees which both a Woame and a Honuta
> man claim to have planted. I am convinced that the origin of the dispute lies in the fact that
> neither the Woames nor the Honutas have any idea where their boundaries really are, since they
> have never been fixed or agreed upon. As soon as cocoa was introduced and it was seen that the
> land was suitable for its cultivation on these hills, there issued a scramble for land, each party
> trying to stake as large a claim as possible.[76]

Unable to decide whose claim was the stronger, Gutch opted for an equitable division of the land based on present occupation. As a corollary, the claims for damages on either side were dismissed.

For the first time, Gutch entered on to the disputed land in order to establish a boundary between the two sides, but the result was to the liking of neither. The

---

[73] Adolph Tsogbe to DC (23 September 1927), GNAA ADM 39/1/57.
[74] T.S.W. Thomas to Cunliffe-Lister (7 December 1933), PRO CO 96/711/9.
[75] See petition dated 4 April 1933, PRO CO 96/711/9.
[76] *Chief Akoto* v. *Chief Ayisa*, in the Supreme Court, Ho, 19 May 1933, GNAA ADM 39/4/5.

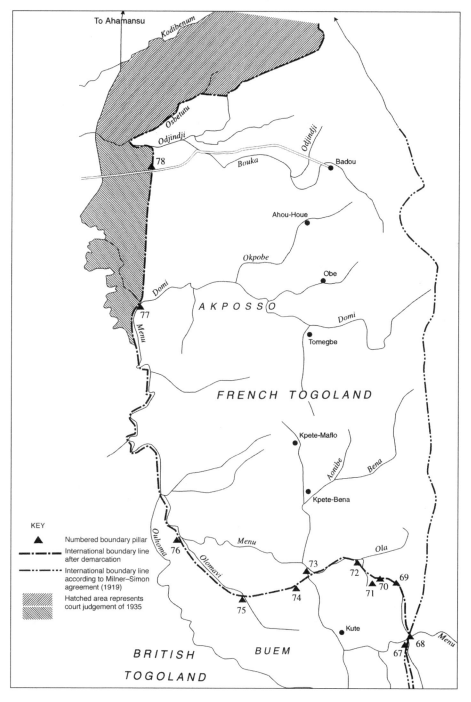

Map 2.2 The Buem–Akposso dispute

Honutas felt that they had lost much of their prime cocoa land, while the Woamé chief was so disgruntled that he refused to participate in the physical demarcation. After this final act, the dispute temporarily vanishes from the documentary record, although there is a reference to an ongoing dispute in 1940.[77] However, in the eyes of the participants, this was more of a ceasefire than a conclusive end to hostilities. In later decades, as we shall see, the Woamé–Honuta case resurfaced to tax the patience of a subsequent generation of administrators. In this dispute, it would be difficult to regard the British and French authorities as implementing a clearly defined frontier policy. While they had set the parameters in 1919, and muddled through in a highly confused fashion thereafter, it was members of the two communities who themselves imbued the boundary with most of its practical meaning. In that sense, the boundary was made by them as much as it was by the respective administrations.

The Buem–Akposso dispute

As was detailed in the previous chapter, the Milner–Simon agreement had placed the western portion of Akposso, or Litimé, in British Togoland. On hearing this decision, the chief of Kitchibo had walked all the way to Atakpamé to request that his people not be divided from the rest of Akposso.[78] This plea met with a broadly sympathetic response, and the swap of French Adjuati for British Akposso was agreed in principle at an early stage. The rationale was that a modification of the Milner–Simon line would permit the international border to follow 'tribal boundaries' as far as possible. But when it came to actually cutting a line between Buem and Akposso, the Boundary Commissioners experienced the same problem of interpreting inadequate maps and conflicting oral evidence. To the east of Kadjebi where the land question became acutely contentious, they adopted the simple expedient of a straight line, linking the point of confluence between the Menu and Domi Rivers and the Odjindji River, covering a total distance of some 7,000 metres (see Map 2.2).[79]

With the rapid expansion of cocoa production in this border zone, the peoples of Buem and Akposso, as well as the migrant farmers they both sold land to, began to contest ownership of forest land. There were, in fact, two separate disputes in the same general vicinity. The first, which involved the chiefs of Ahamansu and Kitchibo, concerned an area of land in the vicinity of pillar 78. This case came to court in 1935, where it was decided that the land belonged to the Ahamansus, subject to the provision that Kitchibo cocoa farmers were to remain in possession of any farms they had already made. There was at least one further court case in 1936, involving an area of land called Abotabe, after which this particular dispute fades from view.[80] The second was a rather more protracted affair. It concerned some 15 square miles of prime farm land that was located mostly to the west of the international frontier: bounded by the Kodibenum river in the north, the Kadjebi–Ahamansu road in the west and Kadjebi farmland along the Menu River in the south.

[77] See the final letter, dated 7 March 1940, in GNAA ADM 39/1/57.

[78] Amouzouvi Akakpo, *Les frontières Togolaises: les modifications de 1927–1929* (Lomé: Université du Benin, 1979), p. 24.

[79] Brownlie, *African Boundaries*, p. 268.

[80] *Chief Kwasi Kako v. Nipayena*, in the Magistrate's Court before V.H.K. Littlewood, 5 August 1936, GNAA ADM 39/4/7.

As in the case of the Woamé–Honuta dispute, a failure to swiftly resolve the issue encouraged both sides to continue extending their farms, culminating in physical clashes on the land.

Eventually, Fiaga Egblomese of Akposso-Badou was prevailed upon to sue Nana Akpandja, the Omanhene of Buem, before the DC's Court in May 1935.[81] Thomas Agbo, representing the Akposso chief, claimed that the Omanhene had wrongfully arrested some of his people who were working on land that actually belonged to them. The Akposso contention was that the international boundary had wrongly placed part of their land in British Togoland and that the Buems were using this oversight as an excuse to stake an illegitimate claim. In court, much of the evidence turned on conflicting versions of the turbulent history of these borderlands in the later nineteenth century. The Akpossos claimed that the land had always been theirs, but that they had allowed the Kwahu Dukoman to settle on a portion of it. As a consequence of Kwahu oppression, they recalled, the Buems and Akpossos had joined forces, and on the second attempt had succeeded in driving the strangers away. As a result of this victory, the land was supposedly divided between the Buems and Akpossos. However, the latter claimed that the Buem chief subsequently deemed the land to be too distant to be of much use and surrendered his portion in return for 36 people (presumably slaves), 30 sheep and 16 cloths, in addition to other people paid in compensation for the lives that had been lost in the wars. The Akposso side further asserted that there had been a dispute in German times, which had been decided in their favour. On the land itself, they drew attention to a heap of stones at a point on the Menu River, and a tree with extensive gunshot marks – Grüner's calling card – which supposedly represented the German boundary line. The Buems, for their part, insisted that the land had belonged to them since their initial migration into the area. They went on to repeat the story about the arrival of the Kwahu Dukoman, but with the significant difference that it was they who had given the strangers land.[82] The Buems also recited the history of warfare against the Kwahus and their Asante allies, but insisted that the Akpossos had taken no part in the campaigns. As a consequence of the final victory, they claimed, the land vacated by the Kwahus was attached once more to the Omanhene's stool. When confronted with the physical evidence of the heap of stones and the tree, the Buem side professed, rather weakly, to have never seen them before.

Confronted with silences and conflicting interpretations, the court declared itself unimpressed by the quality of the evidence which it regarded as heavily biased. Like its counterpart in the Woamé–Honuta case, the court came to the conclusion that there had probably been no clearly defined boundary in pre-colonial times:

> It is almost impossible to determine now with any certainty to whom the land originally belonged and I in fact incline to the view that it has long been a kind of 'No mans land' on which both parties have in course of time encroached.[83]

---

[81] See evidence and judgment in GNAA ADM 39/1/267. The judgment may also be found at GNAA ADM 39/1/228.

[82] This version of history was encountered by Lilley in another context. See his notes entitled 'Meeting with Head Chief of Buem' (undated) at GNAA ADM 39/1/212.

[83] Judgment at GNAA ADM 39/1/267.

The judge, R.E. Walker, inspected the land and found, both to his surprise – and no doubt his relief – that the Odjindji River separated the Buem and Akposso farms. South of the river, most of the cocoa farms belonged to Akpossos. His reading of the evidence on the spot was that this land had probably been farmed by them for some time and that the Omanhene of Buem was only now staking a claim because of the allure of cocoa. On the other hand, he felt that the reverse was true in the area to the north of the Odjindji River. His judgment was, therefore, a pragmatic one in which the land was partitioned along the line of that river. Damages were not awarded, the disputed lands on the French side of the border were not affected and a rider was inserted to the effect that farmers with cocoa on the wrong side of the river would remain the owners thereof.

This judgment was not to the liking of the Omanhene, who promptly appealed to the Provincial Commissioner's Court in May 1936. No new evidence was led and the judge, T.R.O. Mangin, confined himself to sifting through what had already been established in the lower court. He was persuaded that the Akpossos had once been subordinate to Buem, through whom they had paid tribute to the Kwahus – and by extension the Asante. He could find no reliable evidence that the Buems had sold land to the Akpossos after the final campaign against the Kwahus. Furthermore, he was impressed by the fact that one of the Akposso witnesses denied any knowledge of an earlier German decision in their favour. The court therefore upheld the appeal with costs.[84] Bitterly disappointed, the Akpossos then took the case to the West African Court of Appeal, where the initial judgment was restored in April 1937. Not willing to abandon the case at this point, Nana Akpandja decided to appeal to the Privy Council.

The fact that the case remained *sub judice* for so long aggravated tensions on the land. In October 1936, eight farm labourers – three Buem, one Kwahu and four French Togolanders – went to work on a cocoa farm belonging to a Buem linguist. They were ambushed by a party of some 40 Akpossos, captured and sent to Atakpamé as prisoners. When the Kwahu labourer escaped and reported the incident, around 300 Buems mobilized for war.[85] The immediate crisis was defused when it was reported that the captives had been released unharmed, but a number of attacks against Akposso farmers ensued. In the most serious incident, three Akposso men were murdered and their corpses secretly buried. To further fan the flames, the accused in the trial that followed were acquitted because of doubts about the impartiality of the evidence. The month after these violent incidents, District Commissioner Ellershaw warned his superiors that, with the onset of the main cocoa season, the situation could easily spiral out of control.[86] In particular, he regretted the fact that a writ of possession had been denied to the Omanhene in respect of the land north of the Odjindji River that had not been the subject of the appeal. Even on the neighbouring lands disputed between Ahamansu and Kitchibo, where a court ruling had already been made, the situation was still very tense. Here, the British authorities

---

[84] Judgment in Provincial Commissioner's Court, 22 May 1936, at GNAA ADM 39/1/228.

[85] These details are taken from a letter from Governor Arnold Hodson to Ormsby-Gore, which became the basis for 'Observations of His Majesty's Government in the United Kingdom' (April 1938) in response to the Togo Bund petition, PRO CO 96/751/8.

[86] H.C. Ellershaw to CEP(15 November 1936), GNAA ADM 39/1/267.

were forced to intervene to prevent the Ahamansus, who complained of Kitchibo harassment, from resorting to arms.[87] While the Buem and Akposso sides engaged in a low-intensity conflict on the land, the case was also starting to acquire greater publicity outside. Hence in August 1937, the Bund der Deutsche Togolander – consisting of Germanophiles from French Togoland resident in the Gold Coast – despatched a petition to the League of Nations.[88] In it, they argued that the contours of the international boundary had emboldened the Buem to seek a permanent alteration of traditional communal boundaries. They further expressed their opinion that the acquittal of the accused in the murder trial had tempted Nana Akpandja to pursue his claims in an even more reckless fashion.

While the British and French authorities understood the seriousness of the situation, they also recognized that they had limited room for manoeuvre. As long as the case was before the courts, they had little option other than to wait for the wheels of justice to grind to a halt. In the meantime, all they could do was to monitor the situation on the ground and to warn the contestants of the consequences of engaging in acts of violence. Eventually, in February 1939, the Privy Council delivered its judgment.[89] The court considered whether a German map, which appeared to locate the Buem–Akposso boundary further to the east, was admissible as new evidence. It ruled not, on the grounds that the map was unreliable. The court therefore upheld the DC's judgment and rejected the Buem appeal. This meant that the land was effectively divided along the line of the Odjindji River once more, so that Akposso farmers would continue to enjoy rights to their cocoa farms in British Togoland.

The British administration endeavoured to uphold the judgment of the courts and to persuade the Omanhene of Buem to accept the result with good grace. On the face of things, this put an end to the affair, but there were some further complications. On the one hand, the presence of Akposso farmers in British Togoland raised the delicate issue of how they would relate to the Buem Native Authority whose powers were in the process of being augmented. On the other hand, there remained certain areas of controversy in relation to the land. Both sides had spent large sums of money on litigation. In the case of the Akposso, a questionable figure of £14,000 was mentioned in the Togo Bund petition of 1937.[90] As for the Omanhene, he estimated his legal fees at more than £3,000.[91] His attempt to force stranger farmers to contribute £10 a head towards paying off the stool debt provoked a storm of protest. For their part, the Akpossos sought a court ruling that would dislodge Buem farmers from the area to the south of the Odjindji River, despite the guarantees specified within the court judgment.[92] Although the revised international boundary was supposed to coincide with communal boundaries between Buem and Akposso, this case-study confirms not just that the struggle for prime cocoa land could lead to disputes between communities, but that it could also assist in fixing the international boundary in the minds of the litigants.

[87] DC to CEP (1 February 1938), GNAA ADM 39/1/212.
[88] Petition dated 9 August 1937, PRO CO 96/751/8.
[89] The Privy Council judgment of 14 February 1939 may be found at GNAA ADM 29/1/52.
[90] Petition dated 9 August 1937, PRO CO 96/751/8.
[91] Nana Akpandja II to DC (27 May 1939), GNAA ADM 39/1/190.
[92] T.A. Mead to CEP (30 October 1946), GNAA ADM 39/1/267.

Conclusion

In this chapter, I have addressed the manner in which cocoa transformed not just the physical landscape, but also popular perceptions of social and political space. On the one hand, the cultivation of cocoa and the trade surrounding it brought Togolanders into new relationships of proximity with the peoples of the Gold Coast. While Togolanders continued to migrate westwards, Gold Coasters also became highly visible throughout the territory as stranger farmers, cocoa brokers, drivers, storekeepers, teachers and ministers. The growing mutual awareness, which was exhibited during the cocoa hold-ups of the 1930s, was eventually to impart a particular shape to the politics of unification. On the other hand, the rapidity with which land was turned over to cocoa production, and was sold with that object in mind, brought members of families, lineage groups and neighbouring communities into conflict with one another. As the surviving court records clearly demonstrate, land litigation was a growth industry in its own right. The pursuit of land claims before the courts was normally couched in terms of a defence of 'tradition', but colonial officialdom was probably correct to infer that the land requirements of cocoa had generated a need for clearly defined communal boundaries for the first time.

Some of the most bitterly contested cases involved claimants from either side of the international boundary. The Milner–Simon agreement had caused anxiety among communities who felt that they had been cut off from their lands. British and French officials suggested that these practical problems could be resolved by relying on 'tribal' boundaries when carrying out the final delimitation. However, by introducing the notion of a concurrence between two sets of boundaries – international and communal – they stirred up a veritable hornet's nest. Where these boundaries were perceived to be at variance, communities waged costly legal, and sometimes physical, battles to rectify perceived injustices. The authorities then temporized as they struggled to extricate themselves from the impasse they had helped to create. This merely had the effect of encouraging the litigants to take effective occupation. In the two cases examined here in detail, the Boundary Commissioners were forced to demarcate the international frontier before the courts had been able to decide on ownership of the land. Although land rights were not supposed to be affected by the former exercise, border communities continued to believe that the net result was to reallocate land. Hence they continued competing for what they regarded as their legitimate entitlements. When the courts did eventually step in, they resorted to a pragmatic partition of the disputed land, which tended to satisfy neither party.

By the outbreak of war in 1939, the relationship between communities across the line had been profoundly affected by these events. The ethnic categories of 'Buem' and 'Akposso', which are problematic in historical perspective, were largely forged in the heat of the struggle over land. In the case of the Woamé–Honuta dispute, both sides were 'Ewe', but emerged with a sense of difference which was no less profound. None of this had been anticipated, far less desired, by the two administrations who were deeply troubled by the events that unfolded. To view Africans as the passive recipients of European interventions is to entirely miss the point. It is true that the British and the French agreed to a partition in the first place, but the practical implications thereof were determined by border peoples themselves.

3

Display & Dissimulation

The Customs Preventive Service & Smugglers along the Togoland Frontier 1920–39

One purpose of delving into the intricacies of the land question in the last chapter was to sketch in levels of complexity that all too rarely intrude into more generalized images of Africa's colonial boundaries. By contrast, this chapter deals with subject matter that is seldom considered marginal, namely, the phenomenon of cross-border smuggling. The latter poses a greater challenge for the revisionist agenda because it may seem to bear out conventional wisdom rather well. On the one hand, since what constitutes contraband is defined by a given political authority, a campaign against smuggling could be construed as an attempt by the colonial authorities to impose their own sense of order and propriety on reluctant Africans – in that sense, representing the colonial project in microcosm. On the other hand, the fact that there was a smuggling problem at all might appear to testify to dogged resistance on the part of African peoples who had borders driven through their midst. Even if smuggling is not interpreted as an act of overt opposition, it might still be viewed as an instance of James C. Scott's 'everyday forms of peasant resistance', comprising part of the hidden transcript of power relations.[1] In Scott's terms, a consideration of resistance cannot be divorced from a discussion of power since the two stand in a dialectical relationship. This would hold true whether one was discussing New World slavery, the convict system in Australia or colonialism in Africa. There is, however, an alternative conception of power relations, which is associated with some of the writings of Michel Foucault even if it is not unique to them.[2] Here one is not talking about a 'thing', or even a resource, which one set of people wields over another, but of something arising out of the relationship between sets of actors yet which is external to all of them: what Foucault himself calls 'force relations'. This comes closer to what I am seeking to depict in this chapter.

---

[1] James C. Scott, *Weapons of the Weak: Everyday Forms of Peasant Resistance* (New Haven & London: Yale University Press, 1985); *Domination and the Arts of Resistance: Hidden Transcripts* (New Haven & London: Yale University Press, 1990).

[2] Most notably, the explicit discussion in Michel Foucault, *The History of Sexuality: An Introduction* (London: Penguin, 1978), pp. 92–102. It is striking, however, that Foucault's discussion mirrors the treatment of power in the literature on pluralism within political science.

In the first part, I suggest that while the coercive potential of the colonial state was limited, there was also restricted scope for the exercise of hegemony in the commonly understood sense. What transpires is a picture of a regime that was both pragmatic and skilled in the arts of dissimulation. One might say that the British authorities behaved more like the Great Oz than the custodians of some colonial panopticon: that is, power was exercised from behind the curtain rather than through the penetration of some all-encompassing colonial gaze.[3] The second part of the chapter, which takes in the south-eastern Gold Coast as well, deals more particularly with the theme of smuggling. There was undoubtedly much about the policing of the Togoland frontier, especially in the early years, that caused annoyance to the local population. This culminated in numerous incidents involving employees of the Customs Preventive Service and border communities. But an altogether more taxing contest arose out of the determination of significant numbers of border people to evade the payment of customs duties and the prohibitions against specific imports. The temptation is to interpret this behaviour as a subtle subversion of the colonial agenda. But I shall argue that the resistance paradigm risks becoming something of an intellectual strait-jacket in this context. Contrary to the view that Africans were the victims of a peculiarly European obsession with fixed boundaries, the reality was that there were distinct advantages to living in a border zone. Togolanders did not stubbornly ignore the new border, but actively exploited the opportunities thrown up by it. In that sense, I wish to argue, Togolanders were active participants in the remaking of colonial space. If smuggling was resistance at all, it was surely resistance of a very special kind. Finally, I will wrap things up by examining a specific court case that reinforces many of the points central to this chapter, while adding the kind of texture that I sought to provide in Chapter 2.

Peeping behind the colonial curtain: the Customs Preventive Service and border surveillance

The international boundary that was inserted between the two halves of Togoland came in a number of different disguises. At some distance from the scene of the action, it revealed itself in an abstracted form – that is, as a line on a map. On the spot, the border consisted of little more than a series of rough concrete pillars and cairns located at some distance from each other and joined by an imaginary line. Yet this construct, bizarre at it must have seemed to anyone who thought about it, did signify a line at which one set of rules and conventions formally ended and another came into effect. On the British side of that line, a range of different institutions – including the administrative, judicial and medical services – took over. In practice, however, most of these services would only have been encountered if one actively sought them out in the larger towns such as Ho, Kpandu and Hohoe. Whereas the decade of the 1920s,

---

[3] Jeremy Bentham's panopticon, which was designed to perfect the surveillance over the prisoner because he never knew when he was being observed, is a motif that stands out from Foucault's *Discipline and Punish: The Birth of the Prison* (Harmondsworth: Penguin, 1979).

especially during the tenure of Governor Guggisberg, was one in which the state apparatus was elaborated, retrenchment set in with a vengeance at the end of that decade and was not reversed until after 1945.[4] During the inter-war years, therefore, the clearest indication that a traveller might have had that he/she was moving from one sector to another was provided by the border officials themselves. On the British side of the line, officers of the Gold Coast Customs Preventive Service (CPS) functioned as the very embodiment of the colonial state. Their presence and their deportment made it clear to anyone passing through an official crossing point that they were entering a different realm. In that sense, they flew the flag for the British administration in both a figurative and a literal sense.

As the nomenclature would suggest, the CPS was responsible both for the collection of duties and for the co-ordination of anti-smuggling activity. These responsibilities pulled the service in different directions. Whereas the revenue aspect of its work required it to man the customs posts located at strategic points along the border, effective preventive measures required that officers patrol the more remote stretches of the frontier. The service always struggled to reconcile these duties and inevitably, because of governmental obsession with balancing the books, it tended to prioritize revenue collection over surveillance. The scale of the task confronting the service is apparent when one takes cognizance of the fact that in the mid-1930s a full complement of 191 African customs officials was expected to cover the entire eastern frontier, which stretched for a length of some 1,000 kilometres between Lomé in the south and the Upper Volta boundary in the north.[5] This amounted to roughly one customs official per 5.2 kilometres. In practice, the actual complement would normally have been smaller on account of sickness and leave entitlements, while a good many of the remaining officers would have been confined to duties at the fixed customs posts.[6] There was, in fact, a considerable variation in the local presence of the CPS. The latter does not seem to have maintained any substantive posts in Northern British Togoland, although there must have been some outposts. On the other hand, there were 78 officers responsible for the stretch of boundary between the Mpeyo customs post (in northern Buem) and Honuta, as compared with 113 for the shorter stretch down to the coast.[7] In other words, the CPS maintained a more visible presence the further south one travelled, which broadly reflected the economic centre of gravity. The isolated posts and outposts were linked up by European Collectors, who were responsible for the northern and southern sectors respectively. Their job consisted largely of travelling between these fixed points and ensuring that the regulations were properly enforced. The CPS was always acutely aware of the logistical constraints under which it operated. The extensive records that have survived suggest that the European officers who ran the service were of a pragmatic bent, and revelled in a collective image of themselves as

---

[4] A.H.M. Kirk-Greene, 'The thin white line: the size of the British colonial service in Africa', *African Affairs*, 79, 1980, p. 27.

[5] H.M. Customs, *Preventive Service Instructions* (Accra: Government Printer, 1935), p. 73.

[6] The leave entitlements for superintendents was one month every two years plus travelling time, while the other ranks received 14 days per annum. *Ibid.*, p. 18.

[7] *Ibid.*, p. 73.

the voice of sober reason within the colonial administration.[8] Their periodic interventions did a great deal to shape the tenor of government policy and to scotch some of the more ambitious plans that occasionally surfaced from within the political service.

Since the publication of Michel Foucault's pioneering work on crime and insanity, historians of colonialism have become inclined to look for possible relationships between the expansion of European fields of knowledge and the exercise of colonial power. As Megan Vaughan has frankly admitted, though, Foucault does not translate easily to a colonial African context.[9] The reason is that while Foucault was writing about the elaboration of systems of knowledge that helped to constitute power complexes, he also posited that everyone was complicit in elaboration of these discourses.[10] In his terms, power was not a commodity that was monopolized by any particular group of actors and wielded over another. To attach medical discourse to the exercise of colonial power in a straightforward instrumental sense is, therefore, to effectively jettison what is distinctive about Foucault's thinking. On the other hand, to remain loyal to Foucault's schema amounts to making a very large claim for the ability of the colonizer to get inside the minds of the colonized and to manufacture a common set of cultural assumptions. Here I wish to modify the Foucauldian problematic, suggesting that colonial officialdom operated on the explicit assumption that it was unable to call the shots, while border peoples themselves helped to forge the power relations that emerged at the border.

Being intensely concerned with surveillance of border populations, the CPS depended as much on the elaboration of systems of knowledge as any other branch of the colonial service. The very maps that purported to depict African realities were premised on a common code, which had evolved in Europe over centuries, according to which topographical features on the ground could be read as a series of contours and symbols.[11] Needless to say, maps represented reality in a highly selective manner. Much detail was necessarily omitted and much of what was featured turned out to have a loose correlation with what existed on the ground. More importantly, the cartographer's conventions fitted localities into a fixed spatial connection that did not always correspond with indigenous perceptions of space. Putting it very simply, while the standard map suggested a simple relationship between two given localities, which could be simply expressed in terms of a straight line, the actual relationship between them depended upon how the local populations perceived, and engaged with, their own landscape.

This consideration was of fundamental importance to the CPS in its efforts to monitor transactions across the frontier. Hence in the wake of the partition of Togoland, Customs officials set about seeking to understand the precise relationships between people living on either side of the boundary. They then drew their own

---

[8] At the risk of essentializing, one is tempted to suggest that it is perhaps no coincidence that Scots were so heavily over-represented within the Customs service!

[9] Megan Vaughan, *Curing Their Ills: Colonial Power and African Illness* (Cambridge: Polity Press, 1991), pp. 8–12.

[10] Foucault, *A History of Sexuality*, pp. 92–102.

[11] Jeremy Black, *Maps and History: Constructing Images of the Past* (New Haven & London: Yale University Press, 1997).

maps that purported to represent, in a way that the standard maps did not, the network of paths and trails that criss-crossed the border. This information was used in the location of customs posts. Subsequently, each station was provided with a map covering a radius of 12 miles, which, on a scale of one inch to one mile, was supposed to detail 'all roads, trails, villages and other important natural and topographical features'.[12] However, on the basis of past experience, Customs officials were also aware that they were not dealing with fixed essences, which could be captured and frozen on a map for all time. Because routes were capable of changing, not least in response to border surveillance, officials perceived the importance of constructing an intelligence-gathering system that would permit the service to update its snapshot of conditions on the ground. This, in turn, implied an ability to get inside border communities and discover what made them tick.

Megan Vaughan has observed that colonial medical discourse tended to deal not in terms of individual subjectivities, as a reading of Foucault might lead one to expect, but rather in terms of collectivities.[13] Much of the most instructive literature on colonial Africa has dealt with the manner in which colonial discourse slotted Africans into tribal categories, to which particular attributes were attached. In each case, historians have shown how the structures associated with European rule – including the political administration, the judiciary, the medical service, employers and missionaries – spawned their own systems of observation and classification. Comparative experience might lead one to regard the border as the ideal site for the construction of 'criminal tribes'. But one searches in vain through the legal and administrative record for such an optic. One is struck by the realization that Customs officers did not treat border peoples as 'the Other' who acted according to very different predilections. On the contrary, they construed their actions in terms of what could best be described as a rational actor model. They appreciated that the erection of a colonial boundary would create incentives to smuggle, which Togolanders, like any other human collectivity, would be tempted to exploit. Although particular communities were sometimes described as 'incorrigible smugglers', there was never any doubt in the minds of Customs officers that their behaviour was entirely rational – and even, up to a point, understandable. Precisely because they viewed smuggling as a rational response to the existence of an international border, senior Customs officials sought to dissuade government from enacting legislation that would have the effect of enhancing the incentive to break the law. In their view, border policing was not about reforming the innate criminality of Africans, but engaging in a delicate and pragmatic balancing act that actually avoided criminalizing border peoples without good cause. Although Customs officials conceded that the service existed to enforce the law, they were conscious of the reality that legislation was only as good as the ability to enforce it. By over-reaching itself, it was argued, the government risked bringing the entire colonial system into disrepute. This frank admission of the limits of state power was an important insight that was to be forgotten, at some cost, around the time of independence.

---

[12] *Preventive Service Instructions*, p. 22.
[13] Vaughan, *Curing Their Ills*, p. 11.

The construction of the Togoland border

The liquor question revisited

These points can best be substantiated through a reconsideration of the great debate surrounding imported alcohol at the end of the 1920s. From the very beginnings of colonial rule in Africa, regulation of the liquor trade had figured prominently in European definitions of the imperial burden. A rather vague injunction that Africans ought to be protected from the liquor traffic had been agreed at the Berlin Conference of 1884–85, and five years later the Brussels Convention had sought to prohibit alcohol from entering areas of Africa where it had not hitherto been consumed.[14] This was taken further by the Convention of Saint Germain-en-Laye in 1919, which required the signatories to prohibit the importation of 'trade spirits' into Africa.[15] The resolution of the British government, which inclined towards a strict definition of what constituted 'trade spirits', was reinforced by the responsibilities that came with control over western Togoland. Under the Mandate agreement, the British administration undertook 'to exercise a strict control over the traffic in arms and ammunition and the sale of spiritous liquors'.[16] However, as Emmanuel Akyeampong has demonstrated, the concerns of the Gold Coast authorities over the loss of revenue led to a watering down of the earlier commitments. In the Spiritous Liquors Ordinance of 1920, 'trade spirits' were defined by the government as 'spirits imported, for sale to natives, and not generally consumed by Europeans'. Although geneva (Dutch gin) was initially covered by the ban, it was readmitted three years later, alongside brandy, gin, rum and whisky, subject to verification as to ingredients and strength.[17]

The compromise solution briefly appeared to resolve the matter, but towards the end of the decade there was renewed pressure for the prohibition of all imported spirits. Akyeampong demonstrates that this did not emanate from within the ranks of the administration, but from an indigenous temperance lobby consisting of members of the intelligentsia and the chiefs, who enjoyed the backing of the Protestant mission organizations and temperance societies in Britain.[18] Prominent Gold Coast chiefs, such as Nana Ofori Atta I of Akyem Abuakwa, warned of the threat of social disorder unless action was taken to combat the importation of foreign liquor, particularly geneva.[19] Although the authorities were prepared to countenance stricter controls,

---

[14] Chapter VI of the Brussels Act of 1890 created a prohibition zone between 20° North and 22 South°.

[15] On the international liquor conventions, see Lynn Pan, *Alcohol in Colonial Africa* (Helsinki & Uppsala: Finnish Foundation for Alcohol Studies & Scandinavian Institute of African Studies, 1975), chs 6–8; R.O. Lasisi, 'Liquor traffic in Africa under the League of Nations 1919–1945: French Togo as an example', *Nordic Journal of African Studies*, 5, 1, 1996; and Emmanuel Akyeampong, *Drink, Power and Cultural Change: A Social History of Alcohol in Ghana c. 1800 to Recent Times* (Oxford: James Currey, 1996), pp. 82–5.

[16] Article 7 of 'Declaration Relating to the Mandate for the Part of Togoland Assigned to Great Britain', PRO CO 724/1.

[17] Ordinance No. 35 of 1923, amending the Second Spiritous Liquors Ordinance of 1920, at PRO CO 724/3; also Akyeampong, *Drink, Power and Cultural Change*, p. 84.

[18] The Wesleyans were the most fervently opposed to alcohol imports. By contrast, in a neat confirmation of popular stereotypes, the Catholic church in the Gold Coast was unenthusiastic about prohibition, preferring to fight against the evils of alcohol by inculcating 'Christian moral principles'. PRO CO 96/685/2.

[19] Akyeampong, *Drink, Power and Cultural Change*, ch. 3, has highlighted the increased social mobility associated with new sources of income, which threatened the primacy of older elites. The rise of drinking clubs was later paralleled by the founding of temperance societies.

including higher rates of duty and reduced licensing hours, they were reluctant to embrace outright prohibition. As early as 1926, J.M. Reid, the Comptroller of Customs, submitted a detailed memorandum that predicted that prohibition would simply lead to increased smuggling and would encourage Gold Coasters to learn the art of distillation.[20] Furthermore, he reasoned that if the effect of prohibition in the United States had been to undermine the respect of citizens for the statutory law, this effect was likely to be compounded in the colonial context.[21] Whereas the missionary lobby engaged in a classic discourse of alterity, in which strong drink was construed as an inherent hazard to the constitution of the African, Reid was intent on discussing the liquor question in a global context. Significantly, he chose to compare per capita alcohol consumption in the United Kingdom with the importation per head of spirits in the Gold Coast, and drew the conclusion that there was no great cause for concern. Throughout the debates that ensued, officials frequently made allusions to the experiences of prohibition and/or regulation in such disparate theatres as the United States, Ireland, Borneo and Malaya.

Following repeated demands for action within the Legislative Council, Governor A.R. Slater finally agreed to appoint a commission of enquiry, under the chairmanship of H.S. Newlands, which reported in 1930.[22] The conflicting evidence that was heard by, or submitted to, the Newlands Commission confirms the impression that the perceptions of Gold Coast opinion leaders and those of British officialdom were at significant odds. The chiefs and the missionaries mostly spoke in favour of tighter restrictions on imported spirits.[23] For example, Agyeman Prempeh (then still the Kumasihene), defended the merits of palm-wine, but supported a ban on imported spirits on the grounds that they undermined health; bred poverty and criminality; led to sterility; and were the cause of countless motor accidents. In addition his statement let the cat out of the bag when it observed that 'When a person is drunk he loses his sense of respect for his superiors'.[24] By contrast, Captain V.J. Lynch, a DC in Kumasi, asserted that 'Generally speaking, there is no big "drink problem" in any of the districts of Ashanti in which I have served'.[25] This was a view shared by Captain

---

[20] British officials insisted that there was no tradition of distillation in the Gold Coast. But Akyeampong, *ibid.*, pp. 106–7 posits that the Dutch (and later the Basel missionaries) brought their knowledge of distillation with them and that this had become implanted, but not widely disseminated, in the nineteenth century.

[21] 'Memorandum respecting the prohibition of imported spiritous liquors in West Africa' by J.M. Reid, COC (17 March 1926), PRO CO 96/681/8.

[22] Newlands, the SNA, had headed an earlier committee on the liquor question in 1928, which had led to tighter restrictions on the sale of liquor. The *Report of Committee Appointed to Consider the Spirit Licence Ordinance and its Amending Ordinance*, Sessional Paper XI, 1928-29, may be found at PRO CO 96/681/8.

[23] 'Of the fifteen Colony Paramount Chiefs who gave evidence six wanted prohibition of geneva only, five wanted prohibition of all spirits and the remaining four asked that there should be no change. Of the eight Ashanti Head Chiefs six desired prohibition of all spirits and two were in favour of introducing a system of permits to buy spirits. Of the three Head Chiefs from British Togoland two advocated no change and one wished to have geneva and rum excluded', *Report of the Commission of Inquiry Regarding the Consumption of Spirits in the Gold Coast*, No. XXIII of 1929–30, PRO CO 96/692/6.

[24] Evidence of Nana Agyeman Prempeh and statement presented to commission, contained in Enclosure No. 1: 'Notes of Evidence Taken by the Commission of Inquiry Regarding the Consumption of Spirits in the Gold-Coast' in Governor Slater to Lord Passfield (12 April 1930), PRO CO 96/692/6.

[25] Evidence of Captain V.J. Lynch, DC, Kumasi, in Slater to Passfield, PRO CO 96/692/6.

J.R. Dickinson, the DC for Obuasi, who opined that what drunkenness there was could be attributed to the effects of palm-wine rather than imported spirits.[26] Even the representative of Ashanti Goldfields, who might have been expected to take a dim view of excessive alcohol consumption, regarded the existing situation with apparent equanimity.[27]

But it was the officials who would be vested with responsibility for law enforcement who spoke with the greatest conviction against any rash attempt to introduce prohibition. The Inspector-General of Police, Lt-Col. H. Bamford, warned against any drastic alteration of the existing law that could lead to the emergence of illicit distillation and new forms of smuggling that the police might not be able to contain. His colleagues in the CPS were even more forthright. In a lengthy submission, A.J. Beckley, a Senior Collector of Customs with extensive experience of the eastern frontier, drew attention to the experience of the early 1920s when the implementation of a ban on 'trade spirits' had led to heightened smuggling activity. Like many other witnesses, Beckley acknowledged that alcohol played an important part in indigenous cultural practice. On this basis, he reasoned that there was bound to be a genuine demand for imported spirits regardless of what government might think on the matter.[28] A ban merely risked turning smuggling into a profitable business for those who were prepared to service that demand. In the words of Beckley:

> There are several types of smugglers running liquor; firstly there are those who live in areas adjacent to the Frontier and French Trading Centres but remote from our own licensed trading stores. Secondly, there are organised smugglers running liquor for specific festive occasions such as funeral customs obviously to obtain more for the amount of cash available and apparently encouraged to do so by the recent legislation limiting the expenditure. Thirdly, smuggling by organised gangs for profit. These are the most difficult to cope with and so long as there is a market for contraband in the interior nothing will stop them entirely. With the inducement offering to-day of only 3/- to 4/- per bottle natives jeopardize their liberty and even lives; they will certainly continue to do so if prohibition becomes operative.[29]

Beckley identified a particular problem along the south-eastern seaboard where contraband was transported by canoe from as far east as Anecho towards landing points beyond the Volta, conveniently guided by the lighthouse at Cape St Paul. By contrast, he claimed that the south-western frontier posed less of a problem because it was more sparsely populated. Finally, Beckley expressed the view that a further increase in the duty might be enforceable, especially if the French raised their own tariffs, but reckoned that prohibition would require a doubling in the strength of the Preventive Service along the eastern frontier.

The latter point was elaborated upon by Captain Dann, a Collector on the Togoland border, who reported that there was already a substantial contraband trade

---

[26] Evidence of Captain J.R. Dickinson, DC, Obuasi, in Slater to Passfield, PRO CO 96/692/6.

[27] Evidence of D.N. Richards, representative of Ashanti Goldfields, in Slater to Passfield, PRO CO 96/692/6.

[28] Beckley noted that the refusal of a spirits licence in Leklebi, on the grounds that it was too close to the border, had simply forced people to cross to Nkame on the French side when they needed drink. This was confirmed by Sam Aboku, the Headchief of Leklebi.

[29] Evidence of A.J. Beckley, Senior Collector of Customs, in Slater to Passfield, PRO CO 96/692/6.

in spirits on account of lower French tariffs.[30] He pointed out that the inevitable effect of prohibition would be to greatly increase the incentive to smuggle, which would in turn necessitate a substantial beefing up of the CPS:

> If geneva and schnapps were prohibited by law from entering the country in ten years time the smuggling menace would be enormously increased and the Preventive Service would have to be very much increased to cope with the traffic. Three Collectors could still manage unless we extended the line further north. If we embrace the northern portion, and were required to adequately protect the Eastern Frontier, five Europeans and 1,000 Africans would be necessary. Our present strength is three Collectors and 192 Africans. This would cost approximately £92,500 per annum or roughly five times [more] than at present. I am certain that it would become necessary to institute a system of constant patrols as the number of bush paths crossing the frontier is enormous and the country between Denu and Ziope is open. Even if such a scheme were to be adopted it would not, in my opinion, render smuggling completely impossible, but would control it considerably.

Both Beckley and Dann were drawing attention to the delicate balance that they felt the government needed to strike. If alcohol genuinely posed a social problem, which they sincerely doubted, then the measures that were taken to deal with it needed to be measured and realistic. If official policy increased the incentive to smuggle substantially, the net effect would be to raise the cost of border policing, possibly to prohibitive levels. Moreover, there was a high risk of failure that might create complications of its own. In the words of Captain Dickinson: 'It is a well known principle that it is a bad thing to have a law which cannot be enforced as it tends to bring all laws into contempt.'[31]

The warnings issued by these officials made some impression on the Newlands Commission. The fact that Captain Angus Durham Mackenzie, the Deputy Comptroller of Customs, was one of the four members of the commission no doubt helped. The commission accepted the force of the argument that outright prohibition was undesirable both because there appeared to be no liquor problem in the Gold Coast and because alcohol performed an important role in indigenous cultural practice.[32] For our purposes, what is more important is the finding that prohibition was impracticable in view of the comparative ease of smuggling from neighbouring French territory. In the case of French Togoland, the peculiar geography of the partition was clearly a factor in the equation:

> Considerable facilities exist for the smuggling of spirits across the land frontiers. Both in the Ivory Coast and in French Togoland railways run northwards from ports situated near the Gold Coast frontiers. Indeed, the railway in French Togoland is situated mainly within a few miles of the frontier and, along with excellent roads met with on both sides of the frontier, the conditions are almost ideal for successful smuggling operations. It is clear therefore that it is possible for

---

[30] Evidence of Captain Dann, in Slater to Passfield, PRO CO 96/692/6. The private papers of Captain Dann, some of which deal precisely with this period, are housed at Rhodes House Library at Mss. Afr. S.141.

[31] Evidence of Captain Dickinson.

[32] The statistics for liquor imports revealed a steady rise throughout the 1920s. Whereas 50,849 gallons of gin (including geneva) had been imported in 1920, this had risen to 859,169 gallons in 1925 and to 1,002,430 gallons in 1928. However, Governor Slater noted that the total spirit imports were still lower than in the pre-war period when imports of rum had dominated the scene. Slater to L.S. Amery (23 January 1929), PRO CO 96/685/2.

intending smugglers lawfully to obtain ample supplies of spirits close to the frontier. Another advantage in favour of smugglers is the fact that the tribes on both sides of the two land frontiers are closely related to each other and they also speak the same languages.[33]

Although the commission was sceptical about the alleged hazards attached to geneva, however, it did not feel that it could ignore the weight of African opinion against it. It therefore recommended the phasing out of geneva imports over a 10-year period. In addition, it proposed raising the rates of duty and tightening up the licensing laws.[34]

Slater, whose temperance leanings have been noted by Akyeampong, was prepared to accept most of the findings of the Newlands Commission.[35] However, in significant respects he urged that tighter restrictions be imposed. An immediate problem was likely to arise from a specific ban on geneva, which might appear discriminatory towards the Dutch product. In the view of Slater, if British gin had to be banned as well, in the interests of even-handedness, that course of action ought not to be avoided. He also recommended a prohibition against the importation of rum in casks.[36] Within the Colonial Office, there was grudging acceptance of the findings of the Newlands Commission and Slater's proposed modifications. It was agreed that outright prohibition would be impossible because the French authorities in Togoland would be unlikely to co-operate. It was also felt that even the desire to substantially raise import duties would have to be tempered in the light of French tariff policy.[37] Furthermore, it was pointed out that there was no significant difference in the quality of pot- and patent-still gin and that the phasing out of geneva would therefore have to include the British product as well.[38]

New legislation was passed in 1930 with the objective of phasing out all imports of gin over a 10-year period, restricting the imports of other cheap spirits, raising duties and tightening up the licensing laws. But even Slater recognized that the new policy was 'frankly experimental' and that its viability hinged on whether evasion, in the form of illicit distillation and smuggling, became a significant problem. In his words: 'If it is a failure it will have to be abandoned and whether it fails or not will depend largely on the extent to which smuggling and other evasions of the spirit law become prevalent'.[39] As Akyeampong has demonstrated, illicit distillation did indeed become

---

[33] *Report of the Commission of Inquiry Regarding the Consumption of Spirits in the Gold Coast*, No. XXIII, 1929–30, enclosure to PRO CO 96/692/6, paragraph 42.

[34] This included the licensing of palm-wine sellers for the first time.

[35] Akyeampong, *Drink, Power and Cultural Change*, p. 94.

[36] This actually came on the recommendation of Captain Durham Mackenzie, who was worried about gin consumption being replaced by rum sold by the tot.

[37] It was pointed out that the French duty of 2,000 francs per hectolitre of absolute alcohol was well above the 800 francs laid down in the Convention of St Germain-en-Laye. Minute by E.G. Compton, 4/3/1931, PRO CO 96/697/6. The PMC sought to persuade the Mandatory powers to harmonize their duties, but the French were reluctant to shift their ground.

[38] While the exclusion of all forms of gin was likely to lead to complaints from British distillers, Ormsby-Gore anticipated 'corresponding joy in the land of Dewar and Buchanan', Minute of 27/2/1929, PRO CO 96/685/2.

[39] Quoted in *Memorandum By the Governor on the Liquor Policy* (Accra: Government Printer, 1934), pp. 2–3, enclosure to PRO CO 96/715/10.

an immediate headache for the colonial authorities.[40] While this absorbed the attention of the Gold Coast Police, the running of gin across the eastern frontier presented the CPS with problems of its own. By 1934, the incoming Governor, Shenton Thomas, was asking the Colonial Office to consider a policy reversal, which (among other things) would have included a repeal of the decision to phase out gin imports.[41] At the time this was considered premature, but the government did quietly back down later on, substituting a quota system for outright abolition.[42]

It can safely be said that a policy of outright prohibition would have failed even more spectacularly. It was largely owing to the representations of Customs officials that the Gold Coast government steered clear of such a radical course of action. At every point in the liquor debate, senior Customs personnel had predicted that certain consequences would inevitably follow from government actions. This was premised not on greater knowledge of the 'African mind', but on the principle that it was human nature to respond to financial temptation. Relating these findings to the wider debate about colonial power, Vaughan's qualification of Foucault would seem unnecessary. To echo Foucault on the history of sexuality, African chiefs and intellectuals were only too keen to speak about alcohol and its effects on the body – not least on the virility of the Gold Coast male.[43] Equally, Customs officials debated policy implications in terms of the abstract rational actor rather than of tribal collectivities. To be sure, they alluded to the fact that members of the same 'tribe' lived on either side of the border, but the point they were seeking to make was that this facilitated the interaction between groups of would-be smugglers. Both the temperance lobby and the Customs service agreed that Africans had a hankering after imported spirits, but they differed on whether this constituted a peril and on whether government could do anything about it. Ever the realists, the Customs men believed that there was not much that could be done to reform human nature and only a limited amount that could be done to police its various outlets. With this in mind, I will now turn to consider how the CPS set out to accomplish the tasks that had been set for it.

Display and deception: the Customs Preventive Service at work

With hindsight, the CPS presents itself as a rather shambling beast, occupying a world where nothing quite worked as it was supposed to. The obvious disjuncture between the tasks that the service was expected to perform and the resources placed

---

[40] Predictably, there was a rapid expansion in the number of convictions for liquor offences. See Akyeampong, *Drink, Power and Cultural Change*, ch. 5.

[41] The Governor once again solicited local opinion on whether a change in the law was necessary. The substantial correspondence is contained in *Correspondence and Statistics Relating to the Consumption of Spirits in the Gold Coast* (Government Printer, 1934) PRO CO 96/715/10. Any change of policy was bound to have implications for the other West African colonies. Governor Arnold Hodson of Sierra Leone wrote: 'I am no bigot but strong drink (spirits) and the raw native are better kept apart. They don't mix well. However I must not start off now!', handwritten note dated 2/9/1934.

[42] The reason why gin imports ceased to be such a major concern was that they were dropping off anyway in the context of the Depression. The greater menace was felt to be the locally produced gin or *akpeteshie*.

[43] The contention that drink was affecting rates of sexual reproduction was made by a number of witnesses before the Newlands Commission.

at its disposal meant that the reality could not be otherwise. However, as we have seen, senior Customs officers were only too well aware of the constraints under which they operated and adapted their behaviour accordingly. At closer quarters, many of the apparent inconsistencies look more like a studied response to realities. Somewhere in the interplay between the overt and the covert exercise of power, the Customs service found a reasonably full deck of cards.

One half of the repertoire consisted of a self-conscious display of authority. The *Preventive Service Instructions* are revealing because they were issued for internal consumption and therefore give us an insight into official thinking. Significantly, they devoted almost as much space to the minutiae of daily life at the customs post as to advice on book-keeping, revenue collection and anti-smuggling measures.[44] Considerable detail was devoted to uniforms and how they were to be worn. African Customs officials were to be issued with three different sets of dress: one for inspections and official occasions; another for normal duty and travel; and a third for fatigue and night patrols. Whereas the normal working dress of a superintendent consisted of a tunic, belt and trousers, non-commissioned officers were kitted out with a blue jersey, 'knickers', belt and puttees. In addition, African Customs officials were provided with tasselled fezzes, cummerbunds and badges of rank that were to be appended to the tunic or jersey.[45] These uniforms were to be worn at all times, including on anti-smuggling patrols. One reason was that it prevented unscrupulous individuals from posing as undercover Customs men. But the reasoning was also that border peoples should be always be made aware of the presence of the Customs men who were the local embodiment of colonial power. If the intention was to impress the local population, it was also to stamp the symbol of state ownership – literally as well as figuratively – upon the heads of the Customs men. Out of uniform, the latter were Africans like any other. But in uniform they became the working property of the Crown. A conscious effort had always to be made to preserve the mystique surrounding the service. One of the means of achieving this was to minimize the points of social contact with the local population when the Customs men might be seen out of uniform. Hence barracks were constructed at the main customs posts and unauthorised entry by members of the public was expressly prohibited.

The Customs service also engaged in a series of rituals that were performed to a strict timetable. The flag was raised at 6.00 o'clock in the morning, when the border posts were opened, and lowered again at 6.00 o'clock in the evening when they were shut. The *Instructions* also insisted on regular drills and musketry practice, and even went so far as to detail the size of the targets and the prizes that were to be awarded in competition. The European Collectors, who travelled between the stations and outposts, checked that the rituals were carried out faithfully. Their task was not just to examine the books, but also to carry out snap inspections of guns and kit. The secret was to maintain the element of surprise. Without any hint of irony, the *Instructions* stated:

---

[44] The copy that is in my possession, which I found in a second-hand bookshop, was formerly the personal copy of Captain Durham Mackenzie. These minutiae are quite heavily annotated, which suggests they were taken seriously.

[45] *Preventive Service Instructions*, pp. 35–6.

The Customs Preventive Service & smugglers

The dates of monthly inspections should be varied as much as possible, as also should be the time of arrival at Stations. The element of surprise has obvious advantages. The dissemination of news, unless false, as to proposed itineraries, should be guarded against, and SURPRISE VISITS to Stations, by doubling one's tracks and taking other unexpected measures should be resorted to. [emphasis in original][46]

The object of the exercise was to impress on border peoples that the Preventive men always had an eye on them, but at the same time to convey to the latter that they were under observation as well.

The working through of the legal process was a further means by which power was displayed. When smugglers were arrested, they were normally taken back to the nearest customs station and detained pending a detailed investigation. The latter typically involved the Preventive men returning to search the houses and farms of suspects for contraband, sometimes in conjunction with the police. This would often involve the arrest of further suspects, some of whom may have been named by those who were already in custody. Although senior Customs and police officers were wary about being seen to harass border populations, these investigations provided a further opportunity for them to demonstrate that the state writ ran even in the most remote communities. African officers even took it upon themselves to represent the Empire to the villagers.[47]

A debate that ensued between the Keta District administration and the Customs service in 1927 reveals something of the latter's attitude in its dealings with border populations. The affair began when the Preventive Service learned of a smuggling ring operating out of the Anlo town of Tegbi. On searching the compound of one Moses Tormedogo, the Preventive men discovered 20 cases of contraband gin. When the suspect succeeded in escaping, the Preventive men mounted a concerted campaign to run him to ground. As the net closed, Tormedogo voluntarily turned himself in. However, he quickly followed up with a petition asking for remission of part of the financial penalty on the grounds that he had not known that the importation of spirits constituted an offence, and that he had surrendered willingly to the authorities. The DC was inclined to recommend leniency on the grounds that he had given himself up.[48] This produced a vigorous riposte from the Comptroller who insisted that the suspect, who had allegedly accumulated some personal wealth on the back of smuggling, had only surrendered because he had 'thoroughly tired of the chase'.[49] Furthermore, the Comptroller contended that the only means of dealing a decisive blow against smuggling was to make life difficult for the perpetrators. If that meant causing some local inconvenience, that was part of the price to be paid for an effective anti-smuggling policy:

I think that it is possible that this view of the matter has not been accorded by some Political Officers the weight I personally attach to it; but at the same time I fail to see any sound reason for

[46] *Ibid.*, p. 12
[47] For example, at one point during the Second World War, police patrols took it upon themselves to reassure border peoples that the loss of Singapore did not mean that Britain was about to lose the war and even resorted to exacting money for the Spitfire fund. See the reports in GNAA ADM 43/5/1.
[48] DC, Keta, to CEP (25 October 1927), GNAH KE/C27.
[49] Minute by Richard Sharpe, COC, dated 14/11/1927, GNAH KE/C27.

their suggestion that I should treat smugglers lightly because of the 'unrest' which our preventive campaign may have caused. The very intent of the campaign is to cause unrest.

On this occasion, the Governor took the point and sided with the Comptroller.

If contraband goods were found in the course of a search, they were seized. What happened next depended upon the scale of the offence. If the sum of treble the duty-paid value of the contraband did not exceed £10, this was construed as petty smuggling and the Collector was empowered to impose a penalty on the spot. If the culprit refused to pay, the Collector was expected to sue for a specified sum in the courts. In cases of serious smuggling offences, the Customs service was expected to initiate legal proceedings. Under the Customs Ordinance of 1923, the Comptroller was empowered to embark on either a criminal or a civil action.[50] In most cases, the service took out a civil action for recovery of a sum of money amounting to three times the duty-paid value of the goods or £100 – normally whichever was the greater.[51] If the action was successful, the goods were forfeited to the state and either sold or destroyed. Although the Governor was empowered to return any such goods once the duty had been paid, this was not common practice and did not apply to liquor, firearms and ammunition whose importation into the Mandated territory across the land frontier was specifically prohibited.

The hope of the Customs service was that the experience of going to court would have a salutary effect on even the most hardened smuggler. Under the Customs Ordinance, smuggling cases took precedence over all other civil proceedings, which sent a clear message that anybody who smuggled would be swiftly brought to justice.[52] Although some of the accused recruited lawyers to defend them, most could not afford to do so and so were left to negotiate an alien judicial procedure alone. In court, the standard procedure was that the Collector made a statement of claim against the defendants, which they responded to. If they pleaded liable, the court proceeded to impose the penalty that had been sued for. If they denied culpability, the case followed the procedure for civil suits. As the representative of the plaintiff, the Collector stated the facts of the case and then called witnesses, who included the Preventive men who had made the initial arrest. To underline the solemnity of the occasion, the *Preventive Service Instructions* stipulated that the latter were to appear in their dress uniforms. If a defendant wished to cross-examine the witnesses, he/she was free to do so. This was followed by the defendants stating their own case and summoning witnesses. Typically, the Collector then subjected the defendants and their witnesses to vigorous cross-examination.

At every point in the procedure, the accused faced an uphill struggle. Whereas the CPS could make sure that its witnesses appeared, it was not always easy for a defendant to ensure that his/her witnesses made it to court – especially if it was sitting at

---

[50] The Customs Ordinance of 1923 (No. 8), section 143 (1) stated that 'All duties, and all pecuniary penalties not specifically designated fines, and all forfeitures incurred or imposed by the Customs laws ... may be sued for, determined, enforced or recovered by suit, or other appropriate civil proceeding in the Court of the Police Magistrate or in the District Commissioner's Court...' The following sub-section stated that 'In all cases where any provision of the Customs laws is enforceable by fine or by imprisonment without the option of a fine, such provision shall be enforceable by the ordinary criminal procedure of the Colony applicable thereto.'

[51] *Ibid.*, section 126.

[52] *Ibid.*, section 150.

some distance from home. Moreover, while the courts did make use of interpreters, the medium of business was still English, which placed the defendant at an inherent disadvantage. Finally, the Customs Ordinance stipulated that the burden of proof rested on the accused in a smuggling case.[53] Where innocence could not be established, which was usually the case, the defendants incurred a financial penalty or, in default, a prison sentence with hard labour. The aesthetic attraction of a hefty financial penalty, at least to the Customs service, was that it paid the smuggler back in kind. What transpired in the courts was only partly an exercise in eliciting the truth. At a more profound level, it was expected to drive home the point that the state was capable of apprehending and punishing anyone who insisted on flouting the law.

There was, however, a strong element of bluff in the way that the Customs service went about its business, which brings us to a consideration of the more covert uses of power. There was a strict limit to the area that could be physically covered by the anti-smuggling patrols. For that reason, the vast majority of smugglers were actually intercepted within a few miles of the Customs stations. Along much of the border, especially in the northern sector, the presence of the Preventive men was so episodic that a smuggler must have counted himself very unlucky indeed to be caught. Even in relative proximity to the Customs stations, there were inherent limits to the intelligence-gathering capacities of the state. Most of the recruits to the CPS did not hail from southern Togoland, but from the Northern Territories or French West Africa.[54] In consequence, few of them spoke local languages at all fluently. Moreover, senior officials discouraged fraternization with the local population, which might otherwise have been expected to yield valuable information about smuggling networks.

Whatever intelligence came the way of the Customs service was provided by informers who were paid for the details they furnished about the identity of smugglers and the routes they used. Ever mindful of the need to achieve value for money, there was initially a reluctance to pay informers unless a successful action was brought. But as an internal memorandum of 1928 noted:

> An informer runs grave risks, his very life is endangered, and he will not come forward with really good information unless he knows that he is going to be paid for his information and to receive a certain amount of protection from the Preventive Service.[55]

Five years later, the Comptroller assured the Governor that informers were in fact being paid regardless of whether penalties were recovered.[56] The *Preventive Service Instructions* equally stressed the importance of protecting the anonymity of informers who had gone out on a limb.[57]

The attitude displayed towards informers was akin to the perception of what motivated the smugglers themselves: since border peoples were driven by anticipation of a financial reward, it was argued, there was a need to offer healthy and prompt

---

[53] *Ibid.*, section 155.

[54] This was a feature of the police service as well. See David Killingray, 'Guarding the extending frontier: policing the Gold Coast, 1865–1913', in David Anderson and David Killingray (eds), *Policing the Empire: Government, Authority and Control, 1830–1940* (Manchester: Manchester University Press, 1991).

[55] Quoted in Durham Mackenzie to Colonial Secretary (4 October 1933), GNAA CSO 6/5/14.

[56] Durham Mackenzie insisted that existing practice should not be altered. Letter to Colonial Secretary (4 October 1933), GNAA CSO 6/5/14.

[57] *Preventive Service Instructions*, section 64.

remuneration for services rendered. Yet Customs officers were forced to concede that there was more to becoming an informer than mere greed. In face-to-face communities, there were many points of friction between families and individuals waiting for an outlet. Some informers acted out of pure jealousy towards their neighbours who were not just accumulating wealth through smuggling, but also flaunting it. In a case that is probably connected to the one above, Joe Apetie and Thomas Kweidor of Anyako wrote a letter to the District Commissioner of Keta in which they identified one Degborlu Michael of Tegbi Apedome as the head of a smuggling ring operating between Lomé and the Keta area, and offered information on his movements. One can detect a hint of jealousy in part of the letter which stated that: 'The man commenced the work a very long time ago, and made plenty of money by it, [and] built a house roofed with iron sheets at Tegbe Apedome'.[58] The recriminations spawned by perennial chieftaincy disputes provided another reason for volunteering information. As Captain Dann admitted in one instance, 'I appreciate that Political bad feeling may, in some cases, be behind some of the information given'.[59] As we have already discussed in the previous chapter, and will see again in the next section, land disputes were a fertile source of intra-communal strife. Finally, commercial and marital disputes provided further incentives for would-be informers to blow the whistle on their neighbours.

Aside from the initial information, once the first wave of arrests had been made, even the most highly organized gang could quickly dissolve into warring factions who were prepared to volunteer incriminating evidence against their associates in the hope of securing more lenient treatment for themselves. Customs officials hammered away at every weak link and were not above practising a little chicanery along the way. For example, Alfred Acolatse, an employee of John Holt in Lomé, stood accused of supplying goods to smugglers in 1926. This would normally have attracted a fine of £100, but the Collector of Customs offered a deal in return for more detailed information about individuals who had received goods from the store.[60] According to Acolatse, the terms of the arrangement were that he would pay a £25 fine in return for protecting his anonymity. When he was subsequently cited as a witness in three court cases, Acolatse complained that the Collector had reneged on the deal and petitioned for a full remission of penalties. The DC conceded that the latter would be the only ethical course of action, both because the case against Acolatse was weak in law and because the firm of John Holt was equally complicit.[61] However, Acolatse was later informed that the Governor had rejected the plea and, moreover, considered that he was 'fortunate to have escaped so lightly'.[62]

Although the intelligence was often tainted, the CPS had little option other than to use whatever snippets of gossip came its way. Not surprisingly, Customs officials found themselves being dragged into local intrigue and score-settling. In one case, for example, an informer ('A') at Fenyi-Akanu was notified by a woman, whom he was

---

[58] Joe Apetie and Thomas Kweidor to DC, Keta (1 February 1927), GNAH KE/C27.

[59] The case involved one Bawa of Wute in Anlo. Captain Dann to Acting COC (28 February 1930), GNAH KE/C146.

[60] A.M. Archer to Alfred Acolatse (21 January 1928), GNAH KE/C27.

[61] DC, Keta, to CEP (16 February 1928), GNAH KE/C27.

[62] DC to Acolatse (15 June 1928), GNAH KE/C27.

having an affair with, that another man ('B'), whom she had previously been living with, had smuggled some tobacco. The Preventive men were tipped off and they investigated the allegations. Because the suspect could not account for the tobacco, he was duly arrested, but it later transpired that he had been framed. The Collector divulged that:

> After considerable trouble to this service and loss of time the woman confessed that she had bought the tobacco with the knowledge of 'A' and put in 'B''s house unknown to him, with a view to the latter being put away for a time as a smuggler, so that she might have the desired uninterrupted association with 'A' for some time! [63]

The Collector went on to solemnly record that the informer had been told that 'woman palavers were no concern of this Department'. The reality was, however, that the department depended heavily on personal grudges and petty jealousies in order to secure a peephole into societies that were otherwise a closed book to European and African officers alike.

The striking uniforms and mannered procedures of the CPS conjured up the image of a modern state institution carrying out surveillance according to universal norms of bureaucratic rationality. This was certainly the image that officialdom wished to project. But, as senior Customs officials freely admitted among themselves, the reality was starkly different. The service was incapable of maintaining much more than a skeletal presence along the frontier as a whole. If it caught a suspected smuggler, the judicial procedures were loaded in such a way that there was a very strong likelihood of bringing a successful action and exacting a heavy penalty. The real difficulty lay in effecting the arrest of smugglers in the first place. The frontier was stretched out along some very difficult terrain, and the Customs service simply did not have the personnel to patrol its entire length. It resorted, therefore, to the expedient of concentrating on selected areas where smuggling was perceived to pose a particular problem: chiefly the stretches of frontier lying adjacent to the commercial centres of Lomé and Kpalimé. In these target zones, the Preventive men carried out regular patrols and intercepted a good many smugglers. But the service was always heavily dependent upon the leads furnished by paid informants. In feeding off local gossip, the service risked taking some of the gloss off its finely honed image, but this was the price of making some progress towards the proclaimed objectives.

Resistance and opportunism: the secret world of the frontier

In his excellent account of the origins of Ewe nationalism, Claude Welch indicated that the boundary between the two halves of Togoland had not posed a significant barrier, either to trade or to the movement of people, before the outbreak of the Second World War.[64] My primary objective in what follows is to go a step further and to build a case to the effect that the frontier actually functioned more as a zone of opportunity. Before embarking on this line of argument, however, it is necessary to

---

[63] Collector, SEFPS, to DC, Keta (19 March 1936), GNAH KE/C146.
[64] Claude Welch, *Dream of Unity: Pan-Africanism and Political Unification in West Africa* (Ithaca: Cornell University Press, 1966), p. 63.

take account of the fact that the boundary affected communities differentially, as well as differently over time. In the early days, there were undoubtedly grievances associated with border policing that periodically spilled over into the 'smuggling affrays' that are strewn across the administrative record in the early 1920s.

The boundary as an impediment

As I have argued in the first chapter, the partition of Togoland had the effect of driving a line through the middle of a territorial entity that had developed a degree of integrity by 1914. By separating Kpalimé from its commercial hinterland, the partition was bound to create a measure of inconvenience. For many communities, the practical significance of the partition only really sank in when they travelled to Kpalimé to purchase consumer goods and were accosted by Customs men, demanding that they pay duties, on their return. Equally, French Togolanders with farms on the British side of the border were bemused by the levying of duties on loads of produce when they tried to carry them home. Numerous complaints about the new Customs regime reached the ears of both the French and the British authorities in the early 1920s, but once the latter had decided on a policy of administrative integration with the Gold Coast the issue of whether there should be a customs frontier was effectively closed. Over the next few years, a struggle ensued between the Preventive Service, struggling to make Togolanders accept the realities of partition, and border peoples endeavouring to maintain their former trading contacts.

It did not take long for the CPS to make itself highly unpopular. One reason was that, while the siting of a customs station might bring some revenue to the owners of the land on which it was located, the community was expected to furnish labour for the construction of offices and accommodation. Although the labour was remunerated, it was also onerous and competed with other demands. In 1921, the chief of Leklebi-Dafo complained to the DC about the labour demands of the Customs service, which had selected that town as its centre of operations. This provoked an acrimonious correspondence between the political administration and the Customs service. The Provincial Commissioner raised some hackles by suggesting that the structures being erected in Dafo were 'the most palatial residence ever built by the Preventive Service', a contention that was strenuously denied.[65] Furthermore, Captain Mansfield pointed to the problems caused when the Customs service made demands that competed with those of the District administration. He cited a case where he had asked a chief to repair a road and had been rebuffed on the grounds that the Collector had already requested labour to construct a customs station.[66] On the other hand, the Comptroller argued that the service had always relied on the practice of requesting chiefs to supply labour without having encountered any objection from the District authorities.[67]

The grievances surrounding the construction of customs stations were further exacerbated by the apparent arbitrariness of border policing. No sooner had the boundary come into effect than there were complaints that the French were levying

---

[65] Major Jackson to COC (14 January 1922), GNAA ADM 39/5/81.
[66] Mansfield to CEP (31 January 1922), GNAA ADM 39/5/81.
[67] J.L. Lauder, COC to CEP (7 January 1922), GNAA ADM 39/5/81.

taxes in British villages and that Preventive patrols were operating in French territory. On more than one occasion, the British authorities were forced to admit that the
Preventive men had indeed strayed across the line while giving chase. For example, in
March 1922, a Preventive patrol pursued some gin smugglers in the vicinity of British
Nkame and crossed the bridge to make their arrest in the French village with the same
name. The Collector put this incident down to 'partial excess of zeal and also vague-
ness of instruction regarding the two Nkamis'.[68] The confusion was understandable
because the British had previously laid claim to French Nkame. Moreover, while the
French Commandant insisted that the village was in fact French, it was mostly
populated by people from the British side who had moved there to profit from smuggling.[69] This episode was acutely embarrassing to the Gold Coast authorities, and
strict instructions were issued to the effect that the Preventive men should not
pursue suspects beyond the border. The problem was that it was not always immediately obvious where one zone ended and the other began.

A greater cause for concern was the recurrent complaint that the Preventive men
helped themselves to the possessions of the villages through which they passed. In
November 1920, for example, the French authorities complained that two Customs
officers from Kpetoe had crossed the border and stolen four sheep and two basket
loads of chickens from neighbouring French villages.[70] On this occasion, Major
Jackson agreed with the French Governor that 'the practice of looting must end at
once' and asked him to arrest anyone engaging in such practices.[71] But as French
complaints multiplied, the British authorities adopted a somewhat more sceptical
attitude. Senior Customs officials launched a staunch defence of their men, and the
Gold Coast authorities were inclined to dismiss many of the allegations as a deliberate attempt by border peoples to discredit the CPS. In the words of Major
Jackson:

> ... it is only natural that the Preventive Service is most unpopular, consequently are accused of
> many crimes, which doubtless some may be true, but in fairness to the Officers and Men of that
> Force, I would point out that they have arduous and unpleasant duties to perform with the result
> that many of their small indiscretions are multiplied to such an extent that on paper they appear
> to be most serious whereas in reality they are of a trivial nature.[72]

However, accusations about the abuse of power continued to be levelled on both sides
of the border. And while most of the blame was attached to African employees, European officials were not always free of blame themselves. At one point, the district
administration fielded complaints about the behaviour of the Collector at Jasikan
who had allegedly arrested a sub-chief for failing to supply palm-wine when

---

[68] Captain J.R. Braddick to Record Officer (16 April 1922), GNAA ADM 39/5/81. The Governor also put the
incident down to 'overzeal'. Guggisberg to Commissaire de la République (6 November 1922), TNAL Klouto
2 APA/2.
[69] Commandant de Cercle de Klouto to Governor (10 June 1925), reproduced in Amouzouvi Akakpo, *Les frontières Togolaises: les modifications de 1927–1929* (Lomé: Université du Benin, 1979), p. 40.
[70] Commissaire du Gouvernement Générale de l'A.O.F. to Major Jackson, OCBF (16 November 1920), GNAA
ADM 39/5/81.
[71] Jackson to Commissaire (23 November 1920), GNAA ADM 39/5/81.
[72] Jackson, CEP, to CSA (29 July 1922), GNAA ADM 39/5/81.

requested to do so, and who had allegedly insisted on purchasing sheep at reduced prices.[73]

On other occasions, the CPS carried out patrols in areas that they mistakenly believed to fall within the sphere of British administration. As we have already seen, there was initially a degree of confusion on where the border line ran in a number of places. The confusion was exemplified in November 1923 when a patrol arrested one Laklitza for smuggling firearms in the vicinity of Batome. This was an area where the precise location of the boundary was somewhat fuzzy. The Milner–Simon agreement had defined a line along the road from Kpetoe to Batome. The agreement placed the former town in British Togoland and the latter in French Togoland, but did not clarify where the exact boundary line between the two communities was located.[74] The Customs officers had already arrested Laklitza in 1922 and claimed that he was a recidivist who deserved to be punished. For their part, the French authorities asserted that the arrest had taken place 500 metres west of Batome, which meant that Laklitza was still in French territory at the time he was seized.[75] They disputed the contention that he was a hardened smuggler, and insisted that he had a perfect right to bear arms, given that he was on his own land and in French Togoland. In the testy correspondence that ensued between the two Governors, Bonnecarrère asserted that the Preventive service was pursuing a personal vendetta against Laklitza, while Guggisberg repeated the charge that he was an inveterate smuggler.[76] The fundamental issue of whether the arrest had taken place in British or French territory could not be resolved immediately and had to await demarcation by the Boundary Commission.

The manner in which the Customs service utilized informers was a further source of grievance. Peoples living east of the line resented the activities of informers from British Togoland and frequently alerted the French authorities to their presence. An arrest was typically followed by a formal complaint. For example, the villagers of Tomegbe arrested one Kodjo Adaquoua and handed him over to the French authorities in July 1922. When he was interrogated, he claimed that he had been employed by the Customs service at Dafo to lure some gin smugglers into a trap.[77] The CPS denied that he was their employee, but admitted that he had been promised a reward for information about routes being used for the smuggling of gunpowder and gin.[78] Although a formal apology was made on this occasion, and Customs officers were warned against sending informers into French territory, evidence led in court suggests that this practice was not altogether discontinued.[79]

[73] The DC reported that Mr A.D. Turner had been 'high-handed' in various dealings. Minute dated 11/8/1922, GNAA ADM 39/5/81.

[74] Milner-Simon agreement, reproduced in Ian Brownlie, *African Boundaries: A Legal and Diplomatic Encyclopaedia* (London: Christopher Hurst/Royal Institute of International Affairs, 1979), p. 256.

[75] Commandant de Cercle de Klouto to Commissaire de la République (19 November 1923), TNAL Klouto 2 APA/2.

[76] Guggisberg to Bonnecarrère (5 February 1924), and Bonnecarrère to Guggisberg (27 February 1924), TNAL Klouto 2 APA/2.

[77] 'Procès-verbal d'interrogatoire', 18 July 1922, TNAL Klouto 2 APA/2.

[78] Letter (author unknown) dated 21 July 1922, TNAL Klouto 2 APA/2.

[79] In one court case from 1933, a Preventive Service witness explained that when a suspect injured his leg in the course of being arrested and made good his escape to French Togoland, an informer had been despatched to

In British territory also, the use of informers was resented. A recurrent charge was that people were falsely accused, whether out of the expectation of financial gain or personal animus. In May 1927, the Awoamefia of Anlo, Togbe Sri II, sent a petition to the Governor in which he complained of 'the indiscriminate arrest and prosecution of persons alleged to have smuggled contraband goods'.[80] The crux of his argument was that the accused were treated unfairly because they did not have the opportunity of facing their accusers in open court and because the burden of proof was placed upon them. He went on to insist that this was causing a great deal of local resentment:

> His Excellency's petitioner further begs to show that people are being prosecuted on their names merely being given to the Collector of Customs Preventive Service, as smugglers by persons who cannot appear in Court to give evidence against the alleged smugglers. Because a person's name is given out as a smuggler, even though no smuggled goods are found in his possession, other goods legally purchased from the local firms in Keta and the Colony, are usually seized as contraband goods, thereby subjecting the person to several unnecessary questions. This procedure has created great consternation in the District, as it is possible to prosecute any innocent person at any time, and as result the people begin to evacuate the District, that it is feared before too long the District will become depopulated. It is also a menace to the progress of trade of the District.

The claim that the activities of the Preventive service were leading to a flight of population was reiterated by the chief of Wute in 1928.[81]

It is of interest to note that these chiefs were not objecting to the campaign against smuggling as such. Hence in June 1927, the Awoamefia circulated his chiefs, requesting them to report any cases of smuggling, which he claimed was causing 'great unrest', directly to him for action.[82] The DC also reported that a delegation of chiefs had been to see him to advocate more effective deterrents for prospective smugglers, which even he regarded as somewhat extreme. He recalled that '... the loose language used included such as "hanging offenders over the Keta Fort and the bodies to remain suspended there", "flogging" was another'.[83] The manner in which young smugglers flaunted their wealth, which had not been acquired by dint of what was deemed to be 'hard work', was one reason why some chiefs took a dim view of their activities. They were, however, insistent that any campaign to deal with the problem needed to be pursued through themselves rather than by an external agency operating through informers whose own credentials might be questionable. One chief protested to the Keta DC that the Preventive men did not report to him when they arrived in the village, but always went straight to a Lagosian trader who provided them

[79] (cont.) ascertain his identity. Evidence of Mama Kotokoli in case of *COC* v. *Kofi Dandoo* in Supreme Court, Ho, 26 October 1933, GNAA ADM 39/4/5. In another case, a Customs officer from Kpetoe was accused of having asked someone to bring him liquor from Assahun. His explanation was that the drink was supposed to have been left at Batome, on the French side of the border, to enable him to have a Christmas party with his informers. Evidence of Buckle in case of *COC* v. *Conrad Buckle* in Magistrate's Court, Ho, 15 February 1939, GNAA ADM 39/4/9.

[80] Awoamefia Sri II to Governor (28 May 1927), GNAH KE/C27.

[81] Reported in DC, Keta to Collector of Customs, Aflao (17 July 1928), GNAH KE/C27.

[82] Circular letter from Awoamefia to chiefs, dated 2 June 1927, GNAH KE/C27.

[83] DC to CEP (10 June 1927), GNAH KE/C27.

with lodgings.[84] Whereas the DC felt that it was desirable to work through the chiefs rather than 'Hausas' or 'Lagosians', the Collector argued that outsiders were often a more reliable source of information.[85]

Whereas ordinary people could limit much of the practical impact of the boundary by using secret trails, transport owners had little option other than to despatch their lorries through official crossing points. Apart from the customs duties that were levied on their cargoes, the Customs men imposed strict limitations on the movement of vehicles licensed on either side of the border. The regulations stipulated the towns which 'alien' vehicles were permitted to visit and the length of time they could stay. Hence vehicles registered in British territory were permitted to travel no further north than Kpalimé, while French vehicles could not go beyond Senchi without taking out a special licence. The ostensible purpose was to limit the smuggling of goods as well as the traffic in contraband vehicles.[86] Such was the level of commitment to enforcement that when a contingent of Boy Scouts or a party of mourners from British territory wished to spend some time in French Togoland, the DC thought it wise to appraise his French counterpart in advance.

These bureaucratic obstacles were a source of annoyance to many ordinary Togolanders. They also constituted a grievance to many lorry owners who fell foul of the law. In July 1932, one F.K. Gadabgui of Hohoe petitioned the DC to intercede with the French administration.[87] He claimed that although his lorries were properly licensed in British Togoland, the authorities at Kpalimé and Misahöhe had insisted that he pay for a French licence as well. He reasoned that since lorries licensed in French Togoland could travel as far as Worawora and Senchi, there ought to be no problem with his vehicles travelling to Kpalimé – especially in the view of the fact that the two territories were 'the same land'. In fact, the French regulations did permit British vehicles to travel as far as Kpalimé, for the simple reason that it was the destination of much of the cocoa trade. One assumes that the problem arose from over-zealous officials or the driver himself. British vehicles were, however, debarred from visiting Atakpamé. In 1929, a lorry owner from Nsawam petitioned the Governor of French Togoland about one of his vehicles that had been seized.[88] He claimed that he had been led to understand that he was entitled to travel beyond Kpalimé provided he paid the appropriate fee. After his lorry reached Atakpamé, it had been impounded for being in breach of the French Customs regulations. Whereas the French Consul in Accra was inclined to recommend leniency, the head of the Douanes in Lomé insisted that the owner of the vehicle should have been aware of the Customs regulations.[89]

[84] Fia Adzrakpanyato II, Apipwe, to DC, Keta (20 February 1936), GNAH KE/C146. The chief of Somé had made a similar complaint in 1935.

[85] The ethnic labels should not be taken too literally. Within the police and the Customs service, 'Hausa' was a term that covered a multitude of sins. Minute by DC to Collector of Customs, dated 22/2/1936 and response dated 26/2/1936, GNAH KE/C146.

[86] In 1928, the French authorities were petitioned by La Société des Usines Renault, which claimed that Togoland was a centre of the contraband vehicle trade, TNAL Douanes 7D/22.

[87] F.K. Gadabgui to DC (27 July 1932), TNAL Klouto 2 APA/2.

[88] F.J. Kumoji, Nsawam, to Governor of French Togoland (5 June 1929), TNAL Douanes 7D/68.

[89] L'Agent Consulaire de France, Accra to Commissaire de la République, Lomé (12 June 1929), and Chef du Service des Douanes, Lomé, to Commissaire de la République (2 October 1929) TNAL Douanes 7D/68.

The operations of the Customs frontier and the behaviour of the Preventive men created a great deal of resentment in the early years, which sometimes spilled over into direct confrontation. When a seizure had been made, it was not uncommon for members of a given community to band together to free the accused and to liberate the contraband. For example, in December 1933, Customs officers received information that a cow had been smuggled over the border to Atikpui.[90] The population of this town were evidently regarded as recalcitrants, and the Collector noted that they had previously thrown bricks at his men. On this occasion, the Preventive men seized the contraband cow with the intention of taking it to the Nyive customs station, but were surrounded by a hostile crowd. The chief apparently intervened to defuse the situation and promised to place the cow under the control of one of his own Native Authority policemen while the matter was discussed elsewhere. One of these policemen related that the chief subsequently sent a message ordering him to make himself scarce, at the risk of being beaten. When the Preventive officers returned, they found that the cow had been removed. The explanation was that it had been taken back across the border for grazing, but it later transpired that it had been killed. This triumph over the Customs officers was reinforced when the court ruled that they were at fault for having ceded control of the cow in the first place.

On another occasion, two Preventive men intercepted a couple of men near Have who they suspected of carrying smuggled goods.[91] One of the suspects managed to escape and alerted some people from the town who proceeded to assault the officers and to make off with the alleged contraband. The defendants claimed that the Preventive men were under the influence of alcohol, having gate-crashed a funeral ceremony, and that they had started the argument in their attempt to secure more palm-wine for themselves. On this occasion, the court was not persuaded, and four of the five defendants were found liable.

Such incidents are indicative of a collective hostility to the Customs men and a preparedness to take them on. It is tempting to locate such behaviour within a paradigm of resistance to artificial colonial boundaries. Although this would be a perfectly logical way of interpreting the evidence, the language of resistance does not fully capture the dynamic at the border. As we will now see, people also found ways of converting it into a resource that could be made to work to their distinct advantage.

The boundary as a resource

In the wake of the partition, British and French officials regarded each other with a certain amount of suspicion. But however inclined they might have been to monitor each other's actions from behind a defensive barrier, the practicalities of the situation required them to pool information and share experiences across a wide front. Their enforced co-operation had much to do with the way in which border peoples sought to exploit the new opportunities that presented themselves.

Not long after the partition was implemented, it dawned upon the two administrations that there would be abundant scope for people to play the system unless they did work closely together. In 1922, Captain Mansfield wrote to his opposite number

---

[90] *COC* v. *Felix Boso of Atikpui*, first heard in Supreme Court, Ho, 30 January 1934, GNAA ADM 39/4/5.
[91] *COC* v. *Yaw Ashiator and four others*, first heard in Supreme Court, Ho, 17 April 1934, GNAA ADM 39/4/5.

to draw attention to the ways in which judicial rulings were being frustrated in civil suits:

> I have the honour to inform you that it has become a practice for Defendants, who have had Judgements given against them in Civil actions before the courts of Ho and Kpando to make their escape either into the French Mandated Area or into the Gold Coast to avoid satisfying the judgement. I understand you experience the same difficulty.[92]

Much of the correspondence in the Ghanaian and Togolese archives concerns requests for assistance in tracking down individuals who had absconded without paying their debts. As if to illustrate the point he was making, Mansfield was forced to solicit French help in preventing one individual from emigrating to the Congo to evade the force of a judgment given against him in a suit brought by the firm of John Walkden.[93] Bad debts were a particular problem for the cocoa-buying firms operating out of Kpalimé, who offered cash advances at the start of a season in the hope of securing a greater share of the British Togoland crop. Brokers, who played the cocoa market, often gambled unwisely and found themselves unable to meet their obligations to the factors.[94] Those debtors who went to ground in British Togoland had first to be tracked down before they could be sued before the courts of either country. Tracing defaulters was not always an easy task when people commonly traded under more than one name.

Many of the cases involved Togolanders from either side of the boundary who had loaned each other money that had not been repaid, or had entered into contractual relationships which had not been fulfilled. For example, in 1936 the chief of Liati-Woate complained about two sawyers from Kpeme (in French territory) who had received a cash advance in respect of timber they were supposed to supply for construction of a bridge, but who 'had bolted away to the French Zone as soon as they got the money'.[95] One of the more colourful characters, whose brushes with the law are sprinkled across the administrative record, was Siegfried Delume. The latter was actually the headchief of Ve until 1923. He is described in the District Record Book as 'an ex-German dispenser who dealt with Hausa Magicians, crystal gazers and even went as far as to get in touch with a certain [name missing] in London who appears to have dealt in magic'.[96] The Record Book goes on to recall that he was forced to resign as headchief because of his unusual business interests. Thereafter, he migrated to French Togoland where he secured a job with the administration.[97] On contracting a venereal disease, he subsequently decided to return to British territory. He made a short-term loan of £3 from the chief of Yoh, promising to repay the money as soon as he reached the Gold Coast. He then disappeared until 1925 when the chief received information that he was trading in 'medicines' at a place called Abudi. After failing to secure a response to his various letters, the Yoh chief approached the Commandant

---

[92] Mansfield to Commandant de Cercle de Klouto (4 September 1922), TNAL Klouto 2 APA/2.

[93] Mansfield to Commandant de Cercle de Klouto (20 March 1922), TNAL Klouto 2 APA/2.

[94] The activities of the brokers were a constant source of annoyance to the Gold Coast firms as well, and the pooling agreement of 1937 was specifically designed to clip their wings.

[95] Chief of Liati Woate to Collector, Dafo (15 August 1936), TNAL Klouto 2 APA/2.

[96] Entry under Ve in GNAA ADM 39/5/73.

[97] Commandant de Cercle de Klouto to Commissaire (28 April 1927), TNAL Klouto 2 APA/2.

de Cercle for help. Following the intervention of the British authorities, Delume was sent back to Kpalimé where he was forced to meet with the Yoh chief and make good the debt.

When it came to extradition, legal technicalities tended to work in favour of the defaulter. For their part, the French were not inclined to allow red tape to impede the process of tracking down either bad debtors or criminals. In his final 'Handing Over Report', Captain Lilley noted that the French were prepared to deliver suspects at the border, without bothering with extradition proceedings, and expected the British to reciprocate.[98] However, British officials pointed out that their hands were tied by the laws of the Gold Coast. Although individuals engaged in criminal acts could be arrested and handed over, once the relevant extradition proceedings had been completed, they explained that they had no authority to intervene in respect of civil debts. The most they could do was to enquire whether an alleged debtor acknowledged the obligation. If he/she did not, the only recourse was for the creditor to bring an action in a British Togoland court, by which time the debtor might well have disappeared.[99]

Although there were occasional stories of lawlessness in border locations, fully-fledged banditry was rare. This owed as much to the determination of the chiefs to ensure safety of passage as to the activities of the Police and Customs services. Hence when a band of robbers briefly established itself along the border trail between Wli and Dayi Kakpa-Dzogbe, the chief of the latter village alerted the French authorities and they, in turn, sent word to their British counterparts.[100] By contrast, armed gangs of smugglers seem to have operated for long periods of time without being betrayed. Although brigandage was a rare occurrence, the enterprising thief could make use of the boundary. Neighbouring territory provided a refuge and a convenient market for stolen goods. When items of value went missing, the authorities assumed that they would quickly find their way across the border. Hence, in 1931 Lilley requested assistance in tracking down a goldsmith in Kpalimé who had allegedly purchased some gold articles that had originally been stolen in British territory.[101] On another occasion, the Gold Coast Police reported their suspicion that a blacksmith in Kpalimé, working in league with a Preventive serviceman from Dafo, had manufactured a duplicate key to the safe at the Customs station, from which £300 had been stolen.[102]

Another respect in which people were able to turn the boundary to their advantage was by exploiting the different tax regimes. The French relied heavily on poll taxes to meet their administrative costs. By contrast, the British administration did not levy direct taxes at all – although the Native Authorities were eventually empowered to raise levies – but relied instead on import and export duties. For border communities, the aim was to avoid paying direct taxes, while securing access to consumer goods at the lowest prices. At the time of the partition, it had been agreed that border populations should be allowed some time to relocate across the line if they so chose. There appears to have been some movement towards British territory, which was related to

---

[98] 'Handing over report by Captain C.C. Lilley', p. 9, GNAH DA/D78.

[99] Lindsell to Commandant de Cercle (15 April 1944), TNAL Klouto 2 APA/2.

[100] Commandant de Cercle de Klouto to DC, Kpandu (13 July 1939), TNAL Klouto 2 APA/2.

[101] Lilley to Commandant de Cercle de Klouto (16 November 1931), TNAL Klouto 2 APA/2.

[102] Assistant Commissioner of Police, Dafo, to Commandant, Kpalimé (29 November 1934), TNAL Klouto 2 APA/2.

a hearty distaste for the poll tax.[103] The haemorrhage of taxable populations was viewed with alarm by the French who sought to dissuade communities from decamping. But while the British felt comforted in the knowledge that the French taxation system was deeply unpopular, they were equally disturbed by the efforts of the same communities to avoid paying customs duties.

By shuttling between the two territories, border peoples could have their cake and eat it. The French authorities repeatedly requested the British to co-operate in handing over people they defined as tax defaulters. This presented British officials with an awkward dilemma because the individuals concerned often claimed to be formally resident in their territory. For example, in 1946 the Chef de Subdivision requested the DC to send one Abotchi back to his home village of Dzidrame, on the grounds that he owed a backlog of tax and labour obligations.[104] Lindsell replied that this individual had been living in Likpe-Mate for the past 28 years and had paid his taxes for all but the last two of them. Lindsell further noted that Abotchi was no longer willing to pay because he had never received a receipt, and because he had made his home in Mate where he now owned land and where his wife and family had since joined him. Whereas this was a fairly clear-cut case, it was often far from obvious where home really was. It was not uncommon for Togolanders to own farms on one side of the line, where they worked and constructed rudimentary shelters, only to return to their houses on the other side at the end of the day. It was also common to spend periods of time with kin on the other side. The burden of deciding who was eligible to pay tax fell largely upon the chiefs of French Togoland. Ambiguities abounded and were exploited by individuals who shuttled back and forth to escape the clutches of the tax man, often carrying contraband goods as they went. The French were intent on restricting such mobility and invoked medical risks in an attempt to persuade their British counterparts that it should be curtailed.[105] The latter were, however, reluctant to intervene, not least because they valued the labour of French Togolanders.

Communities living on the British side were determined to enjoy the benefits of the low tariff system that prevailed in French territory and were in the habit of crossing over to acquire their wants. However, the construction of a customs frontier also created opportunities for specialist smugglers who performed this service on behalf of others. The list of contraband included goods that were restricted in some way, as well as items which were simply cheaper in French Togoland. Guns and gunpowder fell into the first category. Access to these items was strictly regulated by the British

---

[103] In October 1920, H.E. Davis of the CPS reported that an Ahlo chief had asked him about the possibility of resettling in British Togoland. He further noted that 'The Kakpa Todji people are also coming across the Frontier into the English Zone'. Davis to Acting COC (31 October 1920), GNAA ADM 39/5/81.

[104] Chef de Subdivision, Klouto, to DC (3 January 1944), and handwritten response by Lindsell, TNAL Klouto 2 APA/2.

[105] The French claimed that unbridled migration would lead to a spread of sleeping sickness and claimed there had been a recent outbreak at Kpalimé. Bonnecarrère to Governor of Gold Coast (25 June 1929). The Acting SNA, Hugh Thomas, noted that communities had sprung up that had not existed at the time the boundary was drawn, and advised against co-operating with the French (minute of 20/7/1929). Slater agreed in a letter to Lord Passfield, and opined that 'immigrants into our territory are the reverse of being undesirable' (26 October 1929). PRO CO 96/691/10.

authorities, and it was specifically forbidden to import them across the Togoland frontier.[106] Into the second category fell items such as cigarettes, tobacco and cloth that could be acquired much more cheaply in French Togoland. European spirits fell somewhere in between these categories. They could not lawfully be brought over the eastern frontier and, as we have seen, they were subjected to tighter licensing regulations and import quotas from the end of the 1920s. But insofar as the consumption of imported spirits was still legal, what really counted was that gin, in particular, was much cheaper in French territory.

There is a temptation to interpret smuggling as something existing purely in the eyes of the beholder. According to a popular conception, a mysterious process of colonial accounting turned normal trading activity into something illicit. From this perspective, the historian merely has to place himself in the position of the 'smuggler' – to see things from his/her standpoint – and the very phenomenon of smuggling effectively evaporates. Going further, a stubborn attachment to trans-border trade might be construed as a form of resistance to the practical impact of European boundaries. The problem is that contraband cannot simply be viewed as pre-existing trade in different garb. The very creation of a boundary was bound to have an impact on the local economic geography, opening up avenues of profitable commerce where they had not previously existed. The fact that Kpalimé was the hub of smuggling operations might appear to support an image of continuity, but this is partly based on an optical illusion. There was no good reason, given the infrastructural changes that had been put in place by the end of the 1920s, why the same range of goods could not have been acquired from Ho or Keta. The reason why Kpalimé held its own was less because the railway conferred a natural advantage than because goods were cheaper there on account of French tariff policy. When economic conditions altered, as they did after 1939, the contours of smuggling mutated almost overnight. Apart from opening up new trade routes, the smuggling complex also summoned forth a new breed of entrepreneurs whose very livelihoods depended upon the perpetuation of the international boundary. It is important to emphasize that the most committed of smugglers, who were a familiar feature of every border town, were not resisting colonial borders so much as reinforcing them through their day-to-day activities. The strategies deployed by these actors are worthy of more detailed comment in their own right.

The artfulness and artistry of smuggling

Much as the effectiveness of the CPS rested upon the maintenance of a creative gap between theory and practice, border communities deployed different registers in their dealings with authority. By daylight, these communities often appeared to be populated by model subjects. On a routine basis, the chiefs functioned as the willing intermediaries of the administration, presiding over tribunal cases and overseeing communal work, while their subjects were apparently absorbed by the rigours of the farming calendar. By night, however, the very same communities took on a different aspect. Ostensibly loyal chiefs turned a blind eye as local men and women plied the

---

[106] This was stipulated in the Firearms and Ammunition Ordinance.

smuggling routes linking villages on either side of the border. In a number of cases, including one I will come to presently, chiefs were suspected of being directly implicated in illicit trade.

From a close reading of the court and administrative records, some general observations can safely be made. The success of a smuggling venture depended on playing the margins in at least two senses. On the one hand, the margin of profitability had to be sufficiently great to make the effort worthwhile. This margin was, in turn, affected by the purchase price of the goods that were being traded. It was important for the smuggler to acquire them at as close to the wholesale price as possible. For that reason, it was common practice for smugglers to strike up a personal relationship with employees of the European firms operating in the towns of French Togoland. The expectation was that, subject to a fee, the latter would provide consumer goods as well as a coasting pass that enabled them to be moved freely within French territory.[107] It was also considered wise for smugglers to strike a deal with clerks working for firms in British territory who could falsify coasting passes covering the same goods once they crossed the border. Although the unit size of the contraband was often a giveaway – such as the number of heads to a bundle of tobacco or the volume of a gin bottle – the possession of a coasting pass was often enough to satisfy an inattentive Customs officer. The CPS came to regard the merchant houses as the key to the smuggling complex and repeatedly blamed them for turning a blind eye to the activities of their African employees, especially in respect of gunpowder. Occasionally, European agents themselves acknowledged a level of complicity.[108]

At the other end of the process, the price at which the contraband was sold also had a bearing on the profit margin. Most obviously, the sale price had to be kept beneath the price of similar goods imported through the Gold Coast. Moreover, the proliferation of small traders competing for a sale tended to keep prices down. Hence the average smuggler depended on making a modest return over a succession of expeditions. In one case that came before the courts in 1928, a witness – who also happened to be an experienced smuggler – explained the logic behind fixing a sale price for contraband tobacco:

> I know from the way he [the accused] sold it [that] it did not come from Accra. He was selling it in a quantity of 6/- and if it had come from Accra it would be for 10/-... The whole thing is a smuggling goods [sic] and you must dispose of it quickly to go again. He will not sell it for 10/-.[109]

Under cross-examination, the witness explained that he would expect to make a profit of £2 on a case of smuggled tobacco bearing a duty-paid value of £12.

The latter might appear to be a very respectable rate of return, but there were expenses to be taken into account. These depended very much on the scale of the

---

[107] A coasting pass certified that a given quantity of goods had been purchased from a particular store. It was therefore *prima facie* proof of whether they constituted contraband or not.

[108] These issues presented themselves during correspondence concerning three Swanzy's storekeepers who were fined in 1927, GNAH KE/C.27. An admission of complicity on the part of some merchant houses is contained in an extract from a letter from agent of John Holt, Keta, to DC (24 April 1922), GNAA ADM 39/5/81.

[109] Evidence of Fia Manya, in *COC v. Lawrence Komla Noshi of Lume*, in Supreme Court, Ho, on 17 July 1928, GNAA ADM 39/4/3.

operation. At one end of the spectrum, petty smugglers dealt in relatively small quantities of goods in the hope of making some cash, often to meet a very specific need. In the court case just referred to, for example, one participant explained that he hoped to clear funeral debts by trading in contraband tobacco.[110] These petty smugglers would normally carry their own loads, perhaps calling on the labour of family members. At the other end of the spectrum were the larger operators whose investment could be very considerable. For example, in 1938, one storekeeper in the employ of G.B. Ollivant was unlucky enough to have his lorry intercepted at Koforidua, which was loaded with tobacco, cigarettes and gin to the tune of around £470. These goods had apparently been purchased from Kpalimé and did not represent company stock.[111] In an even more extraordinary case, the CPS intercepted a lorry at Attiteti (in Anlo) carrying 152 bottles of schnapps, 36 bottles of Cuban rum, 78 bottles of gin, 82 bottles of whisky, 9 bottles of tonic, 240,000 Capstan cigarettes and 399,000 Clipper cigarettes with a total market value of no less than £1,300. In this case, the Comptroller elected to sue for the hefty sum of £5,194.[112] In cases such as this, smuggling clearly represented a substantial business venture. The larger operators recruited teams of carriers and scouts to see to the loading of the contraband across the border. Hence a feature of many border towns was the presence of minority communities, often described as 'Hausas', who specialized in the provision of porterage services. Once the goods were safely landed in British territory, other workers might load them onto trucks and haul them deeper into the Gold Coast. All of these hired hands – the porters, scouts and drivers – needed to be paid out of the proceeds.

A smuggling venture was also about testing the margins of risk. Given the stiff penalties, it was a vital consideration that the risks of detection should be minimized. The acquisition of coasting passes was one means of improving the odds. Once the goods had been purchased, they were moved closer to the border and concealed until it was considered safe to move them over. This might necessitate an additional payment to the landowner on whose farms the goods were stashed. The act of smuggling was almost always carried out at night – the darker the better – in order to further reduce the likelihood of detection by Preventive patrols. It was also usual, even for petty smugglers, to travel in larger groups. Part of the reason for banding together was for companionship on a journey that might take several hours to complete. Another was that it afforded some protection in the event that robbers were lurking on the route. But perhaps the most important reason was that the members of a group could scatter in different directions if intercepted by a Preventive patrol, thereby minimizing the individual risks of being apprehended. Among wealthier smugglers, as we have seen, it was usual to leave the physical work to the porters and scouts. The latter were considered a very worthwhile precaution as well as a handy device for bamboozling the Preventive men. One report described their strategy as follows:

> It is to be regretted that most of the people smuggling large consignments escape but practically without exception they attempt to cross on the darkest of nights and also have scouts in the front

[110] Evidence of Ador Mensah.
[111] *COC* v. *Martin John Attipoe*, in Magistrate's Court, Ho, 1 December 1938, GNAA ADM 39/4/8 and 39/4/9.
[112] Details in case of *COC* v. *Mensah Amegashie and Frederick Kwashie Amegashie*, at GNAH KE/C146.

and in the rear. These scouts give the alarm as soon as a patrol is sighted and the carriers drop the goods and escape into the bush. The patrols dare not follow them too far for on their return they will find that the abandoned goods have disappeared.[113]

There was a potential risk attached to the recruitment of strangers, namely, that they were more likely to incriminate their employers if caught. But then it was the carriers themselves who would be arrested in the first instance, enabling the owners of the goods to make themselves scarce.

The smugglers of the Togoland frontier were extremely adept at making the terrain work for them. The open countryside south of Kpetoe and the Togoland hills to the north thereof each possessed their own distinct advantages. In the flat grass-land areas, it was easier to mount Preventive patrols, but equally the number of potential crossing points was almost limitless. In the hilly areas, the number of possible routes was significantly reduced and the labour involved in headloading was that much greater, but there were correspondingly more places of concealment. At night, the CPS faced an almost impossible task of monitoring movement along the myriad paths that criss-crossed the frontier. And if the Preventive men did become wise to a particular route, there was usually some scope for varying the point of entry in order to bypass them.

Nevertheless, not all smugglers were able to give the Preventive service men a wide enough berth. A Customs station might be located close by, thereby increasing the incidence of patrols. Equally, the smuggler might prefer to move the contraband by lorry, which became risky once the Customs service became wise to the practice of constructing concealed compartments.[114] In either event, it was possible to seek an additional insurance policy by cultivating a personal relationship with a Customs official. Senior staff were only too conscious of the possibility that their men might become seduced by local networks and, for that reason, endeavoured to restrict the points of social contact. But it was inevitable that if Customs men spent any length of time in a locality, drinking partnerships, friendships and sexual liaisons would be struck up. And it was no less inevitable that this would have a bearing on their capacity to function in the manner expected of them. Hence the image of endemic conflict between border peoples and the Preventive Service requires some qualification.

A couple of cases will serve to illustrate just how entangled local liaisons could become. In 1923, A.J. Beckley was notified by his superintendent at the Ahamansu station that he had received information to the effect that the chief was involved in gin smuggling from Atakpamé. A search duly revealed five bottles of spirits concealed in a corn bin. However, it transpired in court that the superintendent had actually paid a villager to smuggle the gin for his own purposes. He had subsequently quarrelled with the Ahamansu chief who had accused him of seducing his intended wife. Out of spite, the superintendent had then resolved to frame the chief by planting the bottles at his house.[115] In another case, the Collector-in-Charge of the

---

[113] Report on patrols, smuggling and seizures for the month of September 1941, by C. Duncan-Williams, Collector of Southern Section, GNAA CSO 6/5/21.

[114] A diagram of such a compartment may be found at GNAH KE/C146.

[115] The superintendent was found guilty of smuggling, but was cleared of the charge of seeking to injure the chief. The logic of this judgment is difficult to fathom. *COC* v. *Athanasius Cudjoe*, in Supreme Court, Dafo, 31 August 1923, GNAA ADM 43/4/18.

Southern Section received a petition from an aggrieved husband in Lomé. The latter claimed that his wife had been caught smuggling at Aflao and that, while she was in detention, she had struck up a sexual liaison, culminating in a pregnancy, with the superintendent. He further asserted that the Customs officer had since taken to assisting her in the smuggling of goods between Aflao and Lomé.[116]

The relationship between the Preventive service and border communities was, therefore, a roughly symmetrical one. While Customs officers depended on exploiting intra-communal rivalries and animosities, border peoples were no less adept at finding the weak links in the official chain. This made for a fascinating contest in which the balance of advantage shifted back and forth during the inter-war years. Whereas the Customs service believed that it had the smugglers on the run in 1927, this was shown to be a premature assessment of the situation, and the running of contraband continued right through to the war and beyond. With a view to drawing the threads of this chapter together, I will now examine a particular smuggling case in greater detail for the light it sheds on the behaviour of the Customs service and smugglers alike.

The Comptroller of Customs versus Togbe Sesinu Kuma IV

Along one of the routes passing north-east from Ho towards the Honuta border post is located the Ewe-speaking village of Hoe. Recording a mere 372 residents at the 1931 census, this was the kind of community where everyone knew everyone else.[117] This enforced intimacy accounts in large part for the bitterness with which village disputes were conducted, which, in turn, provide the key to understanding the dramatic events that unfolded in Hoe in 1928.

In June of that year the village chief, Togbe Sesinu Kuma IV, was arrested and sued by the Comptroller of Customs for 'having been knowingly concerned in a fraudulent evasion or attempt at evasion of Customs Duty on certain prohibited and uncustomed goods, to wit 26 gallons Trade Spirit value £65'.[118] This followed the discovery of a stash of alcohol on a farm. At the time of the search, the chief's linguist had apparently sought to deter the officers from digging there, claiming that it was a burial site.[119] Sesinu Kuma was defended by Ben Tamakloe, a young Cambridge-educated lawyer, who was later to be imprisoned for his part in orchestrating the ex-servicemen's march that culminated in the 1948 riots.[120] The principal contention of

[116] Frederic Ayih, l'Ecole Primaire Superieur, Lomé, to Collector, SEFPS (6 June 1943), GNAH KE/C146.
[117] Entry under Hoe in GNAA ADM 39/5/73.
[118] Statement of claim in *COC v. Sesinu Kuma*, in Supreme Court, Honuta, 5 June 1928, GNAA ADM 39/4/3. Curiously, the District Record Book lists the chief as Togbe Sesinu VII, whereas the present chief insists that he was Sesinu Kuma IV. I have followed the latter's guidance on the matter. Interview with Togbe Sesinu Kuma and S.L. Koffie, Hoe, 26 March 1997.
[119] Evidence of Sergeant Major Mama Bassari. This witness gave an insight into the mutual perceptions of the Preventive men and the local community when he explained how he knew the linguist was lying: 'I thought the linguist was telling lies. My reason was that he was a black man'.
[120] On the political activities of Tamakloe, see Marika Sherwood, *Kwame Nkrumah: The Years Abroad, 1935–1947* (Legon: Freedom Publications, 1996), p. 16 n. 11; and Dennis Austin, *Politics in Ghana, 1946–60* (Oxford: Oxford University Press, 1970), pp. 73–4, 139. Tamakloe defended a number of alleged smugglers around this time.

the Customs service was that the chief belonged to an active smuggling ring in Hoe. The most incriminating evidence was delivered by one Frederick Mereku who described himself as 'an old smuggler'.

Mereku told the court that in 1925 one Dente Kofi, who served as an aide to the chief, had pioneered a new smuggling route and had suggested forming a smuggling company to take advantage of it. Mereku recalled that they had persuaded 32 villagers – roughly a quarter of the adult male population of the village – to join the syndicate, which employed himself as secretary and Dente Kofi as 'headman'. Mereku further asserted that the members of the company had signed a formal agreement that specified their mutual obligations and entitlements. The membership dues allegedly took the form of one bottle of gin per case, the proceeds from which were paid over to the company and dutifully logged by Mereku in an account book. Mereku explained that one of the benefits of membership was assistance with arranging transportation of the loads. The preference was for carriers who were indigenes. In the event that an individual recruited his own 'Hausa' carriers, the company kept its distance because it was felt that they were more likely to crack under interrogation. In the words of Mereku: 'It is our rule that when Hausas carry we do not enter it in the book. If the Hausas are caught I will be mentioned and be [called] a smuggler'. The greatest benefit of all was that the company would club together and pay the penalty of anyone who was found guilty of smuggling. As Mereku described it, this was literally a form of insurance policy.

The substance of Mereku's testimony about the existence of an organized syndicate was confirmed by three other witnesses. One Age, who the court deemed to be a reliable witness, recalled that he had carried gin on behalf of the chief. Mattias Kwame, who was the younger brother of Mereku, also verified the existence of a written agreement, although he thought that there had been 29 rather than 32 members. He also recalled that one copy of the written constitution had been destroyed, but that a second had been lodged with Herman Tsogbe, a licensed spirit-seller based at Mayondi (in French Togoland). According to Mereku, the latter allowed them to store the contraband when it was brought from Kpalimé in return for a charge of 1/6- per case of gin. That there was a relationship between Tsogbe and the people of Hoe was confirmed by Dente Kofi himself who recalled that he had sent his son to serve an apprenticeship with him.[121] It may also be pertinent to note that Togbe Sesinu owned land at Mayondi, a community with which Hoe was reputedly closely connected. The chief also admitted that he knew Tsogbe intimately.[122]

Although there are references to smuggling networks in many other court cases, this is the best documented instance of a formal organization geared to taking advantage of the price differentials for items such as imported spirits, tobacco, cigarettes, lead pellets and bars.[123] The Hoe case is also instructive for what it reveals about the operations of the CPS. In this case, the Preventive men had been aware of smuggling

---

[121] Evidence of Dente Kofi, under cross-examination by A.J. Beckley.

[122] In 1928, Togbe Sesinu Kuma requested permission to be able to carry a gun into French territory because animals were spoiling his cocoa. Sesinu Kuma to DC (7 April 1928), TNAL Klouto 2 APA/2. In his evidence before the court, he stated: 'I used to go to Klo [Mayondi] to funerals with Herman Tsogbe. I used to drink gin if he gave it. They used to come to our customs. We are one town'.

[123] These were the contraband goods specifically mentioned by Mattias.

activity in the area for some time, but had failed to secure sufficiently detailed information on which to act. The breakthrough came when a bitter internal rift erupted within Hoe, which enabled the service to play different protagonists off against each other. The origins of this rift are remarkable in themselves, and, complicated as they are, are worth relating here. The story begins with shades of Martin Guerre. One day in 1923 a stranger going by the name of Avorgbedor arrived in Hoe and asserted that it was his natal home. Avorgbedor claimed that he had been enslaved during the Asante wars. He recalled that he had remained with his former masters at Srogbe until the last one died out, when he had performed the final funeral customs and headed for home.[124] In another court case, Mereku described what subsequently transpired:

> About six years ago the defendant [Avorgbedor] came from Awuna to Hoe and said he was a native of Hoe who was captured in the Ashanti war and taken to Awuna where has remained ever since. He had now returned to his village. The next day there was a meeting of the villagers. Defendant was asked the name of his father and he said Dzrosede. The elders in the town did not know his father's name but an old woman by the name Atsupunya said she had heard the name but had not met the person. She alleged the man came from the family of plaintiff appellant [Dable Doe]. The elders said this was plaintiff appellant's stranger so Dable Doe, plaintiff took him to his home.[125]

Avorgbedor was taken into the kin group of Dabla Doe and Mereku and given some land to farm on. Shortly afterwards, he began to dispute ownership of certain lands with Dabla Doe. When the dispute came before Togbe Sesinu's tribunal in 1926, the latter ruled that Avorgbedor was not only the rightful owner of the disputed land, but also that he was the proper head of the lineage. Not satisfied with the result, Dabla Doe succeeded in having the case referred to the DC's court in November 1928.[126] The substance of his appeal was that Avorgbedor had been accepted into the family in good faith, but was now seeking to claim what did not belong to him. Avorgbedor turned the argument on its head, asserting that his ancestors had always owned the land and that it was Dabla Doe's people who were originally strangers. He even claimed that he had been present when his paternal uncle had granted permission for Dabla Doe's parents to use the disputed land when they arrived as strangers from Haingba.[127] The struggle for ownership of the land exemplifies many of the

---

[124] Evidence of Avorgbedor in *Dabla Doe* v. *Avorgbedor*, in Supreme Court, Ho, 11 November 1929, GNAA ADM 29/4/28. This evidence would tend to support the contention of Raymond Dumett and Marion Johnson that slaves in the Gold Coast generally renegotiated their relationships with their former masters rather than deserting en masse. See 'Britain and the suppression of slavery in the Gold Coast Colony, Ashanti and the Northern Territories', in Suzanne Miers and Richard Roberts (eds), *The End of Slavery in Africa* (Madison: University of Wisconsin Press, 1988), pp. 71–118.

[125] Evidence of Frederick Mereku in *Dabla Doe* v. *Avorgbedor*, in Supreme Court, Ho, 11 November 1929, GNAA ADM 29/4/28.

[126] In his testimony in the case against Avorgbedor, Dabla Doe stated that he was not just unhappy with the land decision, but 'aggrieved because the chief of Hoe makes the defendant head of the family and not myself.' The case was decided in favour of Dabla Doe, but an appeal was made to the Provincial Commissioner's court. On the death of Dabla Doe in 1932, Kwasi Koko assumed the position of respondent. Submission granted in Supreme Court, Koforidua, 15 February 1932, GNAA ADM 29/4/28.

[127] According to local tradition, Mereku's grandmother was exceptionally beautiful and was taken away by an

tensions unleashed by the cocoa boom that were identified in the previous chapter. It also manifests the lack of commonly accepted rules of the game when it came to defining the grounds for communal membership. Various witnesses in the smuggling case implicitly accepted that the kinship system was flexible enough to accommodate outsiders. Hence Age, who hailed from Anlo, proclaimed: 'I live at Hoe. I am therefore a Hoe man.' In Dabla Doe's version of events, Avorgbedor was abusing the practice of incorporating outsiders as quasi-kin, whereas the latter was claiming the same in reverse.

The land and smuggling cases were directly linked because the hostilities unleashed by the former created schisms within the syndicate. The willingness of the chief to side with the 'stranger' in the land case was regarded by the immediate family of Dabla Doe as an affront. Significantly for what ensued, Mereku was a nephew to Dabla Doe and to Kwasi Koko, and it would seem that he shared their sense of grievance over the land case. At least, this was how Sesinu Kuma interpreted the allegations that had been levelled against him in court:

> I have had a land case with his uncles. It is now two years ago … I do not know whether it annoyed Mereku. I think that Mereku invented this owing to this land dispute. It has taken me 18 months to find that he is my enemy.[128]

Whereas the chief asserted that the charges arose out of sheer vindictiveness, Mereku claimed that members of the chief's entourage had previously sought to incriminate members of his family. What neither side fully appreciated, before they appeared in court, was that it was the Preventive Service that had germinated the existing seeds of mutual distrust.

The smuggling ring seems to have unravelled for reasons that were not fully appreciated by the local actors. A year earlier, a cocoa buyer from Yeviefe in French Togoland had been waylaid, robbed and almost killed near Hoe. One Agbadegbe Kwasi was apprehended by residents of the village and, after some rough treatment at the hands of Mereku and others, was handed over to the police. He claimed that he had previously been approached by both the chief and Mereku to carry contraband gin from French Togoland. Consequently, when the opportunity presented himself, he decided to exact his revenge by reporting the incidence of smuggling at Hoe. The police embarked on a thorough search, but were unable to discover any contraband at this time. However, official suspicions had been aroused and the Preventive Service began to take a particular interest in Hoe. It would seem that Mattias and Mereku were arrested around this time for gin smuggling, and the former was fined. At the time, Mereku had been forced to recruit his own 'Hausa' carriers because of a disagreement with other members of the company, which was presumably linked to the land dispute. Under the terms of the constitution, the company sought to keep a safe distance.

[127 (cont.)] Asante war-captain in return for sparing the people of Hoe. She was later married by Mereku's grandfather (presumably from Haingba), who took her back to live in Kpandu. At some point, people from Hoe rediscovered her as one of her own and, although she died at Kpandu, her family came to live at the village. Mereku was presumably born locally because his mother is described as coming from Hoe, but because of his paternity, he was still regarded by some as an outsider. As the uncle of Mereku, Dabla Doe would have been in the same position. Interview with Togbe Sesinu Kuma and S.L. Koffie, Hoe, 26 March 1997.

[128] Evidence of Sesinu Kuma, under cross-examination by A.J. Beckley.

It may be that Mereku felt sufficiently aggrieved that he then leaked some information about smuggling activity in the Hoe area. The CPS certainly received word that Dente Kofi and one Akakpo (who is described as a Lagosian) had permitted smugglers from Taviefe to pass through unhindered.[129] It is a reasonable presumption that Taviefe smugglers were using Hoe as a route to French Togoland, and were more than likely paying for the right of passage. Dente Kofi believed that he had been informed against and, as a close associate of the chief, naturally suspected Mereku. Both Dente Kofi and Akakpo recalled that they were then invited by A.M. Archer to become informers working for the Preventive Service. The former recalled the following exchange between them:

> I said I had seen people passing our town but I was not P.S. man to search them. They carried the things in their hunting gowns. They were passing towards Wiaso from Palime … [Archer] said that as I had said what I saw, from that day we would be friends & I should report to him anything I saw when I went home. I told him I am a black man & have no warrant. He told me I should not struggle with people or I should die for myself but should report to him.[130]

Piecing together the fragments of evidence, it would seem that Akakpo (and possibly Dente Kofi) sought to clear his name by reporting Mattias, the brother of Mereku, for having sold some unlicensed gin in town. This seems to have added fuel to Mereku's sense of grievance against his local enemies.

When Mereku was arrested for a second time in December 1927, the company again failed to come to his aid. Fearing that Mereku might blow the whistle, however, the chief sent him a sum of £20. But once Mereku was released, Sesinu Kuma made it clear that the money constituted a personal loan to cover the bail and did not come from the syndicate. Mereku explained that when he sought to persuade the members to honour their agreement, Dente Kofi refused to contribute because he now said 'his blood was akin to the Govt.' His stance provided the cue for everyone else to renege. This seems to have been the final straw for Mereku, who explained in court that he had only denounced the rest of the company because they had left him little option:

> I mentioned the members because they reported me as a smuggler & I was fined. I wouldn't have reported them if they hadn't reported me. There was an agreement among the members re. smuggling. Perhaps they disliked me & reported me. I [also] reported them because one of my brothers was reported.

In their testimony, the Preventive men recalled that they had indeed received a tip-off from an informer about goods that had been buried on a farm – on the very land, as it happened, that had been in dispute between Dabla Doe and Avorgbedor. When gin bottles were found there, the chief and Dente Kofi handed over Kwasi Koko – the brother to Dabla Doe and uncle to Mereku – alleging that the contraband belonged to him. It is presumably at this point that Mereku delivered the CPS a complete list of names, including that of Togbe Sesinu Kuma himself.

---

[129] Akakpo is manifestly an Ewe rather than a Yoruba name. It is possible that Akakpo was genuinely a Lagosian who had assumed a local name, but it is also possible that he was an Ewe whose parents had spent time in the Lagos area. In local terms, he was clearly still a stranger.

[130] Evidence of Dente Kofi, under cross-examination by A.J. Beckley.

The Hoe smuggling syndicate unravelled because of the deep level of mistrust between factions in the village who had crossed swords over the land issue. When someone was taking in for questioning, the inevitable suspicion was that they had been betrayed by their rivals. There was consequently little reason to hold back when the Preventive officers sought to strike a deal. Togbe Sesinu denied all along that he had been involved in smuggling, and his successor still insists that it was Mereku who was the real smuggler and that he sold the story of the gin to a gullible Preventive Service for reasons of personal vengeance.[131] This interpretation has the weight of historical hindsight behind it, because the chief and his co-accused were released on appeal to the Provincial Commissioner's court. However, the release was secured on the slimmest of technicalities. Ben Tamakloe repeated his argument that the evidence against Sesinu Kuma was contradictory, but what really carried the day was the fact that the writ of summons had been incorrectly worded.[132] Although the Comptroller was advised that he could bring a fresh action, he elected not to do so.

The final outcome was interpreted by a section of Hoe as a glorious victory over the CPS and the chief's local detractors, and the fact that Sesinu Kuma was carried home in a palanquin was meant to underscore the point.[133] The supporters of Mereku were less pleased and, such was the bitterness that ensued, that the town centre had to be relocated because it was situated on land that the losing side claimed as its own. The competing versions of events, which continue to resonate down to the present day, render it difficult to make a definitive conclusion about the truth of the original allegations.[134] But, on balance, the evidence for the existence of a smuggling ring is compelling. The fact that the case was eventually dropped is not conclusive proof of innocence. Arguably, it reflects both the organizational strengths and the limitations of the CPS. On the one hand, it was abundantly clear that the evidence against the accused was heavily coloured by personal animus and, to that extent, it might have proved problematic in the event of a retrial. Moreover, the CPS did not have much else to go on. On the other hand, the CPS had already made its point. It had demonstrated its capacity to uncover the most closely guarded secrets of the community. Togbe Sesinu and the people of Hoe had been served notice that they were under scrutiny. For senior Customs officials, that was probably enough.

Conclusion

The Hoe smuggling saga encapsulates the two principal theses that have been advanced in this chapter. The first is that because the CPS was incapable of implementing more sophisticated modes of border surveillance, it depended upon gossip and hearsay for its initial information and then sought to add detail to the picture by playing off local animosities. The public image of the service, and its actual modes of operation, were in reality two very different things. The second thesis is that the

[131] Interview with Togbe Sesinu Kuma and S.L. Koffie.
[132] Appeal to CEP's court on 15 March 1929, GNAA SCT 2/4/127.
[133] Interview with Togbe Sesinu Kuma and S.L. Koffie.
[134] Such was the continuing sensitivity over the case, that the present chief, Togbe Sesinu Kuma V, advised against seeking to interview members of Mereku's family, an injunction that I reluctantly agreed to.

boundary could offer untold advantages to communities living in close proximity to it. The fact that so many strangers – whether 'Hausas', 'Lagosians' or Anlos – actually chose to move into this border space is indicative of this fact. The Hoe smuggling syndicate is merely the best documented example of smuggling rings whose proliferation along the length of the Togoland frontier was frequently acknowledged by Customs officials.

There is much in the deportment of Togbe Sesinu and his supporters that could be read, in Scott's terms, as resistance. But this interpretation is problematic for two reasons. On the one hand, the people of Hoe clearly did not stand united against the structures of state power as one might have expected. On the other hand, it was the smugglers in places such as Hoe who imparted practical meaning to the boundary. Every act of smuggling affirmed the existence of the border and the advantages associated with it. Insofar as there was resistance, it lay in opposition to official attempts at restricting access to those opportunities. In their own very different ways, the CPS and the smugglers could therefore be described almost as partners in the creation of the Togoland boundary. Furthermore, it is this joint construction of a new complex of power relations at the border, arising out of the capillary actions of many different players, which approximates most closely to the Foucauldian model. Because power did not rest in one set of hands, as the Scott model would imply, it follows that there was also nothing as clear-cut as resistance in his terms either.

Part Two

Filling Spaces

The Politics of Identity along the Togoland Frontier

At this point, I wish to interrupt the narrative flow by introducing a rather different line of enquiry. Whereas I have so far been concerned with the socio-economic impact of the border, and its manifestations at the local level, I now turn to consider the politics of Ewe and Togoland unification. A history of the border that did not scrutinize the campaign to erase the line of territorial partition would clearly be less than complete, and it for this reason that I have chosen to revisit some fairly well-travelled terrain. It is in the nature of the subject matter that the spotlight pans across a wide field. Thus far, I have sought to recount the experiences of ordinary people who might not otherwise grace the pages of a history book. The characters who take centre-stage at this point in the production are far more recognizable, comprising politicians, chiefs and what might be called opinion-leaders. In writing this next part, I have been conscious of the possibility that the reader may find the sudden shift towards high politics at variance with the tone of what has gone before. The simple reality is, however, that the dream of unification was first hatched in the minds of a surprisingly small coterie of urban intellectuals who then endeavoured to sell it to a wider constituency. I wish to lay bare the ideological currents within unificationist thought, injecting a critical perspective that has largely been lacking up until now. But I also seek to consider the popular reception of these ideas, which inevitably involves a consideration of political dynamics at the grassroots. By the end of the exercise, therefore, I aim to have restored some continuity with the effort in Part One to understand the border as a local phenomenon. Moreover, in order to ease the transition from Part One to Part Two, I will begin by anatomizing the societal changes that conditioned the expression of identity politics, before turning to the trajectory of the unification movement in Chapters 5 and 6.

4

Us & Them

Christianity, Migrancy & Chieftaincy
in the Remaking of Identities

The Issue of Ewe Identity

The emergence of the unification movement after the Second World War, which sought the removal of the borders interposed between the Ewe people, is covered reasonably fully in the existing literature.[1] But while much of the published material has laid solid foundations for future research, it was generally executed well before the time that ethnicity became a problematized subject of enquiry within African studies.[2] Hence 'the Ewe' are typically treated as a straightforward ethnic category requiring little further interrogation. On this view, the Ewe came to an awareness of their hitherto latent identity in the midst of the hardships occasioned by the Second World War.[3] Of course, the writers concerned have not been unmindful of the existence of historic divisions among the Ewe-speakers – both as between the various *duk wo* and between the Anlo and the Krepi as a whole – but they have nevertheless tended to emphasize the manner in which European rule, and more specifically colonial boundaries, shaped a collective ethnic experience. This embodies a paradox in that what was distinctive about the Ewe was precisely the fact that they did not inhabit a single colonial space. But the underlying contention is that

---

[1] J.S. Coleman, 'Togoland', *International Conciliation*, no. 509, 1956; J.C. Pauvert, 'L'évolution politique des Ewe', *Cahiers d'Etudes Africaines*, 2, 1960; I.E. Aligwekwe, 'The Ewe and Togoland problem: a case-study in the paradoxes and problems of political transition in West Africa', unpublished Ph.D thesis, Ohio State University, 1960; Claude Welch, *Dream of Unity: Pan-Africanism and Political Unification in West Africa* (Ithaca: Cornell University Press, 1966), chs 2–3; B.W. Hodder, 'The Ewe problem: a reassessment', in C.A. Fisher (ed.), *Essays in Political Geography* (London: Methuen, 1968); D.E.K. Amenumey, *The Ewe Unification Movement: A Political History* (Accra: Ghana Universities Press, 1989).

[2] The obvious exception is Sandra E. Greene, *Gender, Ethnicity and Social Change on the Upper Slave Coast: A History of the Anlo-Ewe* (London: James Currey, 1996), ch. 5, although in this case the politics of unification forms a relatively minor part of the study.

[3] This, of course, mirrors the traditional interpretation of the war as a spur to African nationalism more generally.

they were made all the more conscious of their shared cultural and historical heritage by virtue of being artificially separated.

The most consistent exponent of this position has been D.E.K. Amenumey, who has also made the most substantial contribution to our understanding of post-war Ewe nationalism. In an early article on the subject, Amenumey went on the offensive, rejecting the 'platitude that the [Ewe] people so concerned had never been politically united in pre-colonial times' on the grounds that 'it is one thing to exist as a complex of disunited but sovereign chieftaincies free to co-operate when the occasion demanded, and quite another to have a colonial international boundary cutting across the country of a people who are one tribe'.[4] In this formulation, the 'tribe' exists anterior to the partition, and in that sense almost outside of history. Amenumey then set out to demonstrate that there was a linear thread linking post-war Ewe nationalism to the political expressions of earlier periods: in a nutshell, '1947 merely saw a continuation of what had been going on since the 1880s.' In his more recent monograph, Amenumey is less sanguine about the shared objectives of the constituent sections of the Ewe, but a residue of his earlier perspective is nevertheless evident in the text.[5]

Now there is an inherent difficulty involved in the study of all ethnic and nationalist movements, namely, that our evidence consists largely of the utterances of the actors themselves. Since the task of cultural brokers is to create neat symmetry out of baffling complexity, there is a danger of mistaking an ongoing political project for an accurate rendition of the past. The temptation to take ethnic discourse at face value is at its greatest where, as in the case of the Ewe, one can point to earlier expressions of dissent that can plausibly be linked up to form a continuous series. And yet the historian joins the historical dots at his peril. In the case of the unification movement, the perceptions of Amenumey and others have been shaped by the claims of post-war nationalists – notably those of Daniel Chapman and Ephraim Amu through the pages of the *Ewe News-letter* – that the Ewe were essentially one people who had always kicked against the boundaries that Europeans had erected between them. But, like many nationalists, Chapman and Amu were no slouches when it came to sweeping inconvenient historical facts under the carpet.

The Ewe case would seem to be over-ripe for what one might call the Vail/Ranger treatment. In line with recent research elsewhere, this would involve a close analysis of where the 'Ewe' ethnic category originated, how it came into popular usage and for whom it held the greatest appeal.[6] But in positing that the Ewe were 'invented', or

---

[4] D.E.K. Amenumey, 'The pre-1947 background to the Ewe unification question', *Transactions of the Historical Society of Ghana*, X, 1969, p. 65.

[5] Hence Amenumey opens his book with the admission that 'The idea of Ewe unification was espoused mainly by the coastal Ewe; those living inland either opposed it or at best remained lukewarm', *Ewe Unification Movement*, p. 1.

[6] I use this as a form of shorthand. Terence Ranger, 'The invention of tradition in colonial Africa', in E. Hobsbawm and T. Ranger (eds), *The Invention of Tradition* (Cambridge: Cambridge University Press, 1983) was of seminal importance in encouraging African historians to look again at the historicity of 'tribes'. The various contributions to Leroy Vail, *The Creation of Tribalism in Southern Africa* (London: James Currey, 1989), showed what could be done when ethnicity was taken as a historical problem rather than a given. Since the publication of this volume there has been a veritable explosion of research on ethnicity in different parts of

merely 'imagined', one may still be conceding too much.[7] Once the Ewe are deemed to exist, regardless of the route by which they reached that point, the way is left open to a teleology that is no less questionable. By seeking to map out the stages by which the 'Ewe' (or any other ethnic group) were created, one effectively privileges ethnicity over other modes of identity that may turn out to be every bit as salient.

I have therefore avoided the temptation to structure this chapter around the 'invention of the Ewe' and have opted instead for a more open-ended approach. The reasons for so doing deserve to be made explicit. To start with, southern Togoland consisted of a population that was far more diverse than a preoccupation with the Ewe would suggest. Secondly, there is really no evidence to suggest that Ewe nationalism commanded the support of the very people it was intended to attract, and this was true even at the height of the unification movement's powers. And finally, it is important to appreciate that Ewe ethnicity was not free-floating – a sort of higher plane of consciousness that was eventually attained – but was a refraction of identities at other levels.[8] An appropriate analogy might be that of a kaleidoscope, in which the net visual effect arises from the interaction of different layers that may themselves be constantly shifting. In the same way, Ewe ethnicity was a fractured phenomenon that derived its meaning from the interplay of other layers of identity. My aim is not to discount ethnicity altogether as a factor, but merely to observe it in proper relief.

During the inter-war period, there were three interconnected processes that had a dramatic impact on the internal ordering of communities in Togoland and the manner in which they came to view themselves: that is, the advance of Christianity, the proliferation of migration networks and the elaboration of British plans to ratio-nalize the structures of traditional rule. I will consider each of these in turn and conclude with three case-studies, which demonstrate how each of these processes interacted to produce novel expressions of identity within the communities concerned.

Socio-political changes and the roots of identity

The book and the word: Christianity and education

The long-term history of Christian conversion in Togoland is a subject that has been dealt with by a number of writers and so need not detain us unduly

---

[6 (cont.)] colonial Africa. Surprisingly little has been written in this vein in respect of Ghana, but see the contribu-tions to Carola Lentz and Paul Nugent (eds), *Ethnicity in Ghana: The Limits of Invention* (London & New York: Macmillan & St Martin's Press, 2000).

[7] Terence Ranger has more recently suggested that 'invention' is too strong a word and suggested that 'imagi-nation' might be a more accurate description. See 'The invention of tradition revisited: the case of colonial Africa', in Terence Ranger and Olufemi Vaughan (eds), *Legitimacy and the State in Twentieth-Century Africa* (London: Macmillan, 1993).

[8] Here I find myself in absolute sympathy with Sandra Greene's case, *Gender, Ethnicity and Social Change*, pp. 9–12, for treating the histories of ethnicity and gender as closely intertwined. I am merely going a bit further in deflating ethnicity as an independent variable.

here.[9] Following an early foray into the trans-Volta, the Asante invasion of 1868 momentarily disrupted the missionary advance, but defeat of the regional hegemon paved the way for a renewed assault on the region after 1874. Whereas the Bremen Mission concentrated on the Ewe-speaking areas, the Basel Mission became more active in Buem and to the north thereof. The Bremen missionaries were surprisingly ambivalent about the merits of the colonial project, but the entrenchment of European rule after the final division of Krepi in 1890, provided the kind of stability that ultimately assisted their operations.[10] In 1903, the Basel Mission ceded its own trans-Volta mission stations to its North German cousin, thereby leaving the Bremen Mission in control of the Protestant cause. By the outbreak of the First World War, the Bremen Mission was running stations both in German Togo (at Ho, Amedzofe, Lomé, Agu, Akpafu, Atakpamé and Kpalimé) and in the Gold Coast (Keta and Peki).[11] The Catholic Steyler Mission had begun its own advance from the coast in the 1890s and thereafter waged an uncompromising struggle for converts against the Bremen Mission. By the outbreak of war in 1914, the better-funded Catholic Mission could boast a larger membership (more than 20,000) than its cash-strapped Protestant counterpart.[12] In the years after the war, the expansion on both sides of the denominational divide was even more prolific. Over the next decade, membership of the Ewe Church (as the Bremen Mission was briefly renamed) jumped from 11,314 to 23,980.[13] In the case of the Catholic mission, there were some 31,085 Catholics in British Togoland by 1938, and 43,466 in the Lower Volta Vicariate, which included the south-eastern Gold Coast.[14] To these figures needs to be added the growing membership of alternative churches, such as the Methodists and the Jehovah's Witnesses, which began to sink their own roots in the 1930s.

The fundamental issue of why precisely people converted has recently been addressed in a excellent Peki case-study by Birgit Meyer.[15] It would appear that a crucial factor was that, as among the Tswana, Christianity came to be associated with a package called 'civilization', which 'insinuated new forms of individualism, new

---

[9] Eugene E. Grau, 'The Evangelical Presbyterian Church (Ghana and Togo), 1914–1946: a study of European mission relations affecting the beginning of an indigenous church', Ph.D. thesis, Hartford Seminary Foundation, 1964; Hans Debrunner, *A Church Between Colonial Powers: A Study of the Church in Togo* (London: Lutterworth Press, 1965); and Birgit Meyer, *Translating the Devil: Religion and Modernity Among the Ewe in Ghana* (Edinburgh & London: Edinburgh University Press/International Africa Institute, 1999).

[10] The Inspector of the mission, Franz Michael Zahn, was especially ambivalent. Grau, 'Evangelical Presbyterian Church', p. 105.

[11] Debrunner, *A Church Between Colonial Powers*, p. 109. According to Grau, 'Evangelical Presbyterian Church', p. 17, the mission also operated 164 outstations.

[12] Grau, 'Evangelical Presbyterian Church', p. 17; Debrunner, *A Church Between Colonial Powers*, pp. 110–12. Regrettably, there has been no detailed study of Catholic missionary enterprise in Togoland.

[13] During the First World War, the German missionaries were expelled from Togoland. In British Togoland and the Gold Coast, the Scottish Mission (of the Church of Scotland) assumed responsibility for the old Bremen Mission. However, most Church activities were turned over to the African membership. The choice of the name, the 'Ewe Church', was intended to convey the fact that this was a self-governing church. In 1927, it was renamed the Ewe Presbyterian Church. The thesis by Grau, 'Evangelical Presbyterian Church', deals with this aspect of church history. The figures for the Ewe Church are drawn from this thesis, pp. 17, 136.

[14] 'A brief account of the activities of the Catholic Mission in British Togoland', undated, enclosure to GNAA ADM 39/1/570.

[15] Meyer, *Translating the Devil, passim.*

regimes of value, new kinds of wealth, new means and relations of production, new religious practice'.[16] Bishop Herman himself attributed much of the pace of conversion to the flourishing links between the Togoland and the Gold Coast, which encouraged young people to look on the world with different eyes:

> It would be quite absurd and against the Christian mind to force a man to adopt a new religion. Nowadays the young people travel very much and they come back from other countries with open eyes (or so they say). Practically the young people do not [any] longer believe in the old Fetish Worship.[17]

As the new ideas and church structures caught hold, Christians, who had initially represented self-segregating minorities, increasingly represented the societal norm and came to exercise the dominant influence in their communities of origin. At the village level, this represented a veritable revolution.

Although conversion was construed as an individual voyage of discovery – and Meyer argues that part of the appeal lay precisely in insulating converts from the demands of kin[18] – the manner in which the churches rooted themselves had important social ramifications as regards relations between and within communities. As in others parts of colonial Africa, the missionary advance was associated with the expansion of educational access and stimulated the quest to find a satisfactory language of proselytization. Much of the attraction of the Bremen Mission in the early days lay in the practical skills that it endeavoured to teach to those who attended its schools. In subsequent years, it was literacy skills which exercised a far greater appeal. The siting of mission stations correlated closely with the provision of schools. While Protestant missionary enterprise privileged Ho, Avatime and Akpafu, the Catholic advance turned on Kpandu and Gbi-Hohoe.[19] The mission schools inevitably drew disproportionately from the host communities, giving them a head start in the education stakes, although they increasingly attracted pupils from across a wider catchment area.[20] Differential access to education provided an early source of discord, and prompted many communities to solicit church favours, often by playing the different denominations off against each other. Hence when the Bremen or Catholic mission elected to build a school in a particular town or village, its

---

[16] John L. Comaroff and Jean Comaroff, *Of Revelation and Revolution: The Dialectics of Modernity on a South African Frontier, Volume Two* (Chicago & London: University of Chicago Press, 1997), pp. 163–4. For another close comparison, see Thomas Spear, *Mountain Farmers: Moral Economies of Land and Agricultural Development in Arusha and Meru* (Oxford: James Currey, 1997), especially ch. 8.

[17] Notes by Bishop Herman enclosed in Captain D.N. Walker, DC, to CEP (23 February 1939), GNAA ADM 39/1/570.

[18] Meyer, *Translating the Devil*, p. 12.

[19] For a map of the field of Bremen Mission operations, see Debrunner, *A Church Between Colonial Powers*, map 11. On the Catholics, see p. 110. On the outbreak of the Second World War, the Catholic mission operated central stations, with a residential priest, at Ho, Kpandu, Liati, Hohoe, Likpe-Mate, Jasikan and Kete-Krachi, alongside 150 secondary stations. Notes by Bishop Herman enclosed in Captain D.N. Walker, DC, to CEP (23 February 1939), GNAA ADM 39/1/570.

[20] The Bremen Mission established a mission station at Amedzofe in 1890. Four years later, a teacher's training college and seminary were established there. Akpafu began as sub-station of Amedzofe, but was upgraded in 1905. Apart from Ho, these were two focal points of Bremen missionary activity, including education. Lynne Brydon, 'Status ambiguity in Amedzofe Avatime: women and men in a changing patrilineal society', unpublished Ph.D thesis, University of Cambridge, 1976, p. 9.

neighbour would frequently extend a parallel invitation to the rival church. This stood a chance of succeeding because the Catholics and Presbyterians were always seeking to drive a wedge into each other's field of operations. Hence the competition between mission organizations and between village communities tended to be mutually reinforcing. Indeed, it was not uncommon to encounter a situation where rival lineages within a single village gravitated towards different denominations. For example, in Likpe-Mate the Kalekato and Kalelenti clans turned to the Presbyterian and Catholic missions, respectively. Under the British Mandate, the administration exercised tighter regulation of schools, but also provided more generous funding. As a result, school enrolment in British Togoland increased substantially during the inter-war years.

As for language, Meyer observes that the German missionaries were convinced that they could only win genuine converts if they managed to express the Christian message in an indigenous medium.[21] The issue was not just that of rendering the Christian message formally intelligible, but also with 'cultivating' the language so as to make it a fitting receptacle for the word of God. In order to domesticate Ewe, the Protestant missionaries believed it was necessary to reduce it to a written form.[22] The final product, which was based on the Anlo dialect and transcribed through the international phonetic alphabet, represented a code that could be disseminated through the medium of the schools. The Bremen missionaries in Togo fought a dogged campaign to promote the use of Ewe in schools, thereby contradicting official policy which favoured the spread of German.[23] They even managed to delay the substitution of German for English, which was the foreign language of preference for Ewe converts by virtue of its currency in commerce.[24] During the inter-war period, an older generation of educated Togolanders took pride in the fact that its members were fully literate in both Ewe and German. The label of 'German scholars', which they attached to themselves, expressed this sense of pride in linguistic proficiency and educational attainment.[25] The partition of Togoland in 1919 had profound consequences because it drove a linguistic wedge between the two halves of the former German territory. Although some teaching in Ewe remained, the educational system in British Togoland now placed a greater degree of emphasis upon fluency in English. For those who hoped to migrate to the Colony, or even to acquire paid employment within the territory, a knowledge of English became even more highly prized than before. By contrast, the educational system on the other side of the border, where the state equally began to play a more interventionist role, revolved around the use of French. J.S. Coleman remarked of the cumulative effects of British

---

[21] The Catholics were less concerned to promote the Ewe language.

[22] Meyer, *Translating the Devil*, pp. 57–60.

[23] One of the criticisms that the Bremen missionaries later made of their Scottish counterparts, who took their place during the First World War, was they put too little emphasis upon an in-depth knowledge of the Ewe language.

[24] Debrunner, *A Church Between Colonial Powers*, p. 113, suggests that the Catholics were even more inclined to favour English ahead of German because that was where popular demand lay.

[25] In 1997, while in Ho, I was told that Gerald Awuma used to make a point of reading German newspapers up until his death. He wanted to be seen doing so, even if at times he appeared to be holding the newspaper upside down!

and French policy on either side of the border that: 'Westernization is a misnomer for the acculturation process; it would be far more accurate to refer to "Gallicization" and "Anglicization"'.[26] For a younger generation of educated British Togolanders, therefore, the imaginative world of the 'German scholars' became a thoroughly alien one – with political consequences we will come to in the next chapter.

On the face of things, the Presbyterian and Catholic churches still provided some mechanisms through which a common faith and a common ethnicity could straddle the border. At one level, the churches did appear to harden the ethnic boundary between the Ewes and their neighbours. The centre of gravity of both the main churches was located towards the south. The Basel Mission had made successful inroads into Buem in the last decades of the nineteenth century, using the medium of Twi. But the Bremen Mission, to which it handed over, was based in Ewe-speaking country. After the expulsion of the German missionaries and the indigenization of the church in British territory, its Ewe complexion was further accentuated. Indeed, the former Bremen Mission even adopted the new name of the Ewe Presbyterian Church (EPC). Although the Catholic mission was less explicitly anchored in its Ewe roots, its principal stations were similarly located in Eweland. All of this meant that, for some time, there was less church activity, and hence fewer schools, in the non-Ewe areas. To add insult to injury, the Bremen Mission and later the EPC concentrated on the promotion of Ewe as a liturgical language. This left little room for Twi and even less for the minority languages like Sekpele (Likpe) or Lelemi (Buem). From an early point, therefore, the language issue became emotively charged. In Buem, there was resistance in Worawora and some other towns to the replacement of Twi by Ewe when the Basel Mission withdrew. According to Hans Debrunner, the same issue provoked a serious schism within the church in Buem after the Second World War.[27] The underlying complaint was not merely that congregations were being forced to worship in an alien language. After all, the northern Ewe suffered many of the same problems in relation to written Ewe, which was based on the Anlo dialect. The more fundamental complaint was that the Akan and minority peoples suffered in educational terms because of their lack of fluency in Ewe.

Nevertheless, the suggestion that there was a clear fault line separating Ewe from non-Ewe communities cannot be sustained. The reality was that the EPC in particular came to be even more bitterly divided between southern Ewes – chiefly from Anlo and Peki – and British Togolanders of all ethnicities. Because the level of educational provision was far better in the Colony – it was not until the 1950s that the first secondary schools were established in British Togoland – it was Gold Coast Ewes who tended to predominate within the structures of the EPC. During the 1940s, the question of access to scholarships to study outside the territory became a highly emotive one. There was a deeply held perception that Togolanders as a whole did not receive a fair deal. Hence, at the end of 1947 the Paramount Chief of Avatime, Adja Tekpo V, proposed that the government impose a special tax on cocoa, which could be paid into a central fund to promote higher education upon which all Togolanders would be able to draw.[28] But in the longer term, the belief was that southerners would

[26] Coleman, 'Togoland', p. 15.
[27] Debrunner, *A Church Between Colonial Powers*, p. 135.
[28] Adja Tekpo V to CCC (22 December 1947), GNAA ADM 39/1/441.

continue to predominate until there were schools in Togoland to match those in the south. Within the teaching fraternity, there was an especially acute perception that the over-representation of Gold Coast Ewes in the EPC was perpetuating an unfair distribution of resources. In 1948, there was a campaign by Togolanders to oust Reverend Christian Baeta as the Synod Clerk and to replace him with Reverend F. Ametowobla (from Avatime). The case against Baeta, who was an Anlo, was that he consistently channelled scholarships towards fellow southerners.[29] Most Anlos and Pekis were also voted out of the EPC Teachers Union that year.[30]

Another site of conflict was the Ho/Kpandu District Education Committee, where G.O. Awuma was dismissed as secretary at the start of 1948. The ostensible reason was that the chiefs objected to his activities within the Asogli Youth League.[31] However, Awuma insisted that he had actually been the victim of calculated plot by Gold Coast Ewes, presumably to create a vacancy for one of their own number.[32] Awuma, an Ewe from Ho, proceeded to mount a vociferous campaign against alleged Anlo and Peki intrigues, which matched anything that Buem nativists could come up with:

> ... [A]ll the key positions in the Government, the Schools, Commerce and even the Native Administration, are filled with adventurers from Gold Coast Eweland, who, in nearly all cases, are so overbearing and intriguing. Should the inborn Togolander then be judged unreasonable when he rightly concludes that the Gold Coast Government, the Missionary Societies and the Merchant Houses seem to have conspired to support the Gold Coast Ewes in their intrigues and trickery to set up a Totalitarian Tyranny in Togoland and dominate, supplant and oppress the Togolander in his own home?[33]

As we shall see in the next chapter, much of the initial impetus for the Togoland unification movement came from northern Ewes like Awuma who insisted that Gold Coast Ewes were anything but close ethnic kinsmen.

Migrant mentalities

Although the rhetoric of Awuma and his associates seemed to point to a massive influx of Gold Coasters into British Togoland, the reality was that Togolanders were themselves exceptionally mobile and had been for some time. The pattern was established during the period of German rule, when Togolanders crossed in large numbers into the Gold Coast as farm workers. During the British period, Togolanders were more inclined to migrate towards urban centres, most notably Accra, in search of employment. And as we have already seen, there was a good deal of movement within the territory, as aspiring cocoa farmers from further south purchased land in the forest lands of Buem. In 1946, Barbara Ward conducted a survey in the Avatime town of Vane, which found that out of a population of 1,053 no fewer than 238 were absent from home.[34] Slightly less than half of that number (113 in total) had

[29] Welch, *Dream of Unity*, p. 86.

[30] *Ibid.*, p. 87.

[31] Amenumey, *Ewe Unification Movement*, p. 119. Also correspondence in GNAA ADM 39/1/665.

[32] His replacement was B.G. Kwami. It is not clear if he was a Gold Coast Ewe.

[33] Gerald O. Awuma to CSA, undated, GNAH DA/D113.

[34] Barbara Ward, 'Some notes on migration from Togoland', *African Affairs*, 49, 1950, pp. 129–35.

been away for two years or more, and a sizeable number (52) had been away for five years or more. Most of these migrants had travelled elsewhere in British Togoland (170 in total), followed by those who had gone to the Colony or overseas (46) and a comparatively small number who had migrated to French Togoland (22). Although schooling accounted for many of these absences (66 in all), many others had left to farm elsewhere (47), to engage in trade or ply a craft (33), or to find paid employment outside trade (26). The survey also suggested that women were just as likely to migrate as men, the only significant difference lying in the importance of marriage as a reason for the departure of women

This movement of population had a profound impact on the shaping of identities, both at the point of settlement and within the communities that represented home. In the first, changing demographic realities led to animated debates about the rights and responsibilities attached to host communities and migrant populations, respectively. Along the cocoa frontier of Buem, where the migrants were often in a majority, there was a growing reluctance to accept the financial demands of the Omanhene as well as a subordinate political status. On the other hand, the Buems complained that the migrants did not put their money into the community, but siphoned it out in order to build grand residential properties elsewhere. Buem nativists frequently pointed to the fact that it was their lands that produced the bulk of the wealth of British Togoland, and yet they were afflicted by the worst roads and inadequate schools. Within the communities of origin, the migrants also came to enjoy an enhanced profile. External observers were impressed by the spirit of self-help that was apparent in projects that were being initiated across the territory. One writer, for example, commented on a case in Ho where Presbyterians had been raising money to support a senior school and ended up by building it from scratch through communal labour.[35] Because migrants typically retained close links with home, and because they tended to have greater amounts of disposable income, their participation was critical to the fulfilment of most community projects. Of course, much of the wealth derived from cocoa, trade and employment was channelled into private consumption (including house building) and social activities such as the increasingly elaborate funeral ceremonies, but it is clear that much of it also went into collective projects. Following a familiar West African pattern, migrants formed associations in their places of settlement, which helped to maintain a sense of belonging as well as funnelling resources back to the community. By the 1940s, British officials became conscious of the proliferation of such migrant associations in the Gold Coast, noting that:

> The creation of such societies is usually quite spontaneous; the membership, as the names indicate, is often confined to Natives of a certain locality who would naturally seek each other's company in a strange town. The interests of the societies are mainly literary, political or merely social; very often their *raison d'être* is described as 'to advise our chiefs how to improve the town'. Their appeal is entirely to the literate.[36]

---

[35] Reinold Schober, 'Native co-operation in Togoland', *Africa*, 9, 1936, p. 491.

[36] 'Memorandum of the Governments of the United Kingdom and France on the Petition of the All-Ewe Conference to the United Nations', United Nations Trusteeship Council, *Official Records*, Second Session, First Part, 20 November 1947–16 December 1947, p. 28.

At Easter time, most of these migrants would endeavour to return home, where religious ceremonies were combined with hard-headed assessments of the progress that had been made in building schools, improving roads and so on. Within the world view of Christian converts, there was a integral relationship between piety, hard work and success in terms of communal upliftment. Whereas the literature on migration has often stressed its function in generating a sense of ethnic awareness, it is also important to emphasize its role in strengthening *dukɔ* identities – a point I shall return to shortly.

Chieftaincy and identity

One of the consequences of British parsimony in relation to the administration of British Togoland was that the authorities felt the need to devolve as much everyday responsibility as possible to the chiefs. The problem, as they saw it, was that they had inherited a highly fractured system of traditional rule from the Germans, which was ill-suited to the task. The reality, as we have already seen, was that the trans-Volta borderlands were characterized by a considerable measure of political pluralism and cultural diversity in the nineteenth century. German policies arguably amounted to a pragmatic recognition of that reality. Be that as it may, the British administration was less than happy at having to deal with 68 divisions in Southern Togoland, each of which claimed to be autonomous. Because each sub-divisional chief was permitted to operate his own tribunal, there were as many as 234 of these in the Ho District alone.[37] In the case of Buem, the British bemoaned an earlier German decision to disband a going concern by hiving off Tapa, Teteman, Akpafu, Santrokofi and Bowiri in 1907.[38] Here, the amalgamation policy simply involved putting Humpty-Dumpty back together again. Among the former Krepi divisions, however, it was difficult to base the case for amalgamation on historic ties of dependency. To be sure, the Peki headchief was ever willing to argue that the British should reconstitute his lost dominions, but his claims were hotly disputed by many of the northern Ewe divisions.[39] Instead of building upon Peki, therefore, the amalgamation policy came to rest on a supposedly voluntary grouping of the Southern Togoland divisions into larger Native Authorities (NAs).

As early as 1924, Captain E.T. Mansfield recorded that he was 'now making enquiries as to which chiefs are willing to come under the wing of their old Liege Lords once again'.[40] However, it was really under the vigorous direction of Captain Lilley that the amalgamation policy was given practical effect. Under the Native Administration Ordinance of 1933, the new NAs were to be empowered to raise local taxes, which would be paid into Native Treasuries and be used to finance local development activity. In addition, each of the divisional chiefs would sit on a joint State Council, which functioned as a kind of collective sounding board, but would retain their own separate tribunals. By contrast, the sub-divisional chiefs were to forfeit their tribunals. In theory, the British were prepared to sanction any amalgamation, provided the end

---

[37] 'Handing over report by Captain C.C. Lilley to D.N. Walker' (1938), in GNAH DA/D78.
[38] The 1907 order by Governor Zech is reproduced, in translation, in GNAA ADM 39/5/73.
[39] This comes across in Rattray's report at GNAA ADM 39/5/73.
[40] Mansfield to CEP (5 January 1924), GNAA ADM 39/1/545.

product was large enough (that is, covering a minimum of six divisions), geographically contiguous and commanded the support of all parts of the divisions concerned. The hope that he might be recognized as the leader of an amalgamated state encouraged many a headchief to solicit the backing of neighbouring chiefs, but because the latter typically entertained the very same ambitions the jockeying for position was acute. In practice, Lilley and his colleagues actively intervened in order to bring about certain amalgamations that were seen as 'natural', while frustrating other initiatives that were deemed to lack the essential ingredients. The overall consequence was to breathe life back into some historic animosities, and to give birth to some new ones.

By 1931, four states had been formally recognized: Buem, which was a marginally larger entity than the German rump; Awatime, which consisted of 10 divisions; Akpini, which embraced 19 divisions under the wing of the Kpandu chief; and Asogli, which united a further 13 divisions under the Ho chief. The first two states were led by headchiefs who belonged to the Central Togo minorities – namely, the Lefana and Avatime – while the second two were headed by the chiefs of prominent Ewe *dukɔwo*. That still left 47 divisions unaligned to any state, but Lilley was able to report that this figure had fallen to 14 by the time of his retirement in 1938.[41] Although British officials congratulated themselves on the success with which independent divisions had been persuaded to forgo their autonomy, the policy had begun to reach its upper limit by the outbreak of the Second World War. The reality was that many chiefs who had succumbed to official blandishments later regretted their decision to comply, while the record of the amalgamated states confirmed the recalcitrant divisions in their assessment that they had made the correct decision in staying out. The administrative reports for this period paint a consistently bleak picture of the four states that existed on paper, but did not really function as intended. The Kpandu District Quarterly Report for December 1938, for example, conceded that 'for the average Divisional Chief amalgamation can have produced no benefits'.[42] The unpromising record led some senior officials to question whether the policy had been properly conceived to start with. Hence in the immediate wake of Lilley's retirement, the CEP articulated what was effectively a damning indictment of government policy in the territory:

> I feel that the idea of amalgamating various divisions has somewhere and somehow gone wrong... I feel that to have made one chief paramount over all the others who have hitherto been independent is unsound and must lead to friction for a very long time.[43]

However, it was one thing to voice these doubts and quite another to set about jettisoning a policy that had been pursued as if the very fabric of British rule depended upon it. A detailed memorandum in 1944 conceded that many of the original safeguards, which had been used to reassure sceptical chiefs, had quietly been shelved. Most importantly, whereas the guidelines had portrayed the leaders of the amalgamated states as merely first among equals, the label of paramount chief had subsequently been adopted. And in reality, the incumbents had come to behave

[41] 'Handing over report', GNAH DA/D78.
[42] Quarterly Report, December 1938, by Captain D.N. Walker, GNAA ADM 39/1/305.
[43] CEP to DC, Kpandu (8 February 1939), GNAA ADM 39/1/305.

as if they did indeed occupy such an exalted position.[44] The context for this soul-searching was one in which the unamalgamated divisions, of which there were still 10 in 1944, were fighting a spirited rearguard action. With the outbreak of war in 1939, they made a veiled threat not to co-operate with the recruitment campaign because 'they had not been altogether fairly treated in the past'.[45] In 1941, seven of them – namely, the headchiefs of Gbi, Likpe, Ve, Santrokofi, Anfoega, Tsrukpe and Goviefe – submitted a petition to the Governor in which they pointed out that to join an existing state would mean subordinating themselves to an alien paramount chief. Their counter-proposal was that they should be allowed to forge a looser alliance in which the functions of the standard NA would be preserved, but without forcing the divisions to compromise their historic independence. The substance of the earlier petition was repeated in a further submission to the incoming Governor, Alan Burns, in 1945. The Governor, who quickly acquired a reputation as a reforming spirit, expressed his own fears that the administration was repeating the very mistakes that had led to serious trouble in southern-eastern Nigeria in 1929.[46] But in the end, the opinions of more experienced local officials carried the day. Their assessment of the situation was that to capitulate at this late stage risked unravelling the states that had been formed after so much painstaking effort. The petitioners were finally informed, therefore, that the government was not inclined to change its mind and that they ought simply to enlist with an existing state. Although some of the rebel divisions threw in the towel at this stage, the overall stalemate continued until the end of the decade when the administration finally agreed to recognize two federated Native Authorities, namely, Atando (covering Gbi, Ve and Likpe) and Ayonkodo (compromising Santrokofi and Nkonya), in which the hated oaths of allegiance were dispensed with. Anfoega, however, held out stubbornly until the bitter end.

The debate surrounding the amalgamation policy was of the utmost importance in bringing new actors to the fore and in sharpening the edges of identity. It has also left us with explicit statements about the ways in which these communities, or at least their appointed spokesmen, wished themselves to be regarded. The recalcitrant divisions can be divided into two categories. On the one side were those dukɔwo that were Ewe-speaking, but still insisted on their singularity. At the time of Lilley's retirement, this included Abutia, Adaklu, Agotime, Anfoega, Aveme, Gbi, Goviefe, Taviefe, Tsrukpe, Ve and Wusuta. Their resistance was premised on their independence in pre-colonial times. In some cases, the headchiefs went further and invoked traditions that purported to demonstrate that they were historically distinct from the rest of the northern Ewe, or even that they were not really Ewes at all. The Taviefe case, for example, rested on the claim that they were originally migrants from Anlo, which also helped explain their alignment with the latter during the

---

[44] 'Memorandum on amalgamation in British Togoland' (1944), GNAA ADM 39/1/545.

[45] Handing over notes from V.H.K. Littlewood to J.W. Chalmers, GNAA ADM 39/1/93.

[46] The observation is contained in a letter from Burns to G. Creasy, Colonial Office (dated 9 December 1944), in PRO CO 96/780, file 31458/6. On the warrant chief system and its contribution to the 'Aba riots', see E.A. Afigbo, *The Warrant Chiefs: Indirect Rule in South-Eastern Nigeria, 1891–1929* (London: Longman, 1972), and Judith Van Allen, '"Aba riots" or Igbo "women's war"? Ideology, stratification and the invisibility of women', in Nancy Hafkin and Edna Bay (eds), *Women in Africa: Studies in Social and Economic Change* (Stanford: Stanford University Press, 1976).

Asante wars.[47] Again, while most of the population of Agotime division spoke Ewe, they held out on the grounds that they were actually Adangmes.[48] The rebel divisions also cited the iniquity of being forced to suborn themselves to ancient rivals. For example, the Ve division initially sought to form an amalgamated state in its own right, and enjoyed some support from Lilley in this endeavour. But when the attempt failed, Ve resisted official pressure to join Akpini on the grounds that the Kpandu headchief was of equal standing.[49] Similarly, Taviefe, which was surrounded by the Asogli state, held out against incorporation for some years on the basis that Ho was an ancient enemy.

The second category of resisters consisted of those divisions that were not Ewe-speaking: namely, Likpe, Nkonya and Santrokofi. Since the attempt to resuscitate Peki's political ambitions after the First World War, they had become accustomed to asserting their rights to independence on the grounds that they were not just historically autonomous, but also ethnically distinct from their neighbours. The language of ethnicity was deployed with the greatest fluency in Nkonya. Located on the banks of the Volta River, Nkonya had enjoyed considerable commercial significance in the nineteenth century. This translated into a highly developed sense of its relative standing within the regional pecking order. In the face of British pressure to join either Buem or Akpini, the Nkonya headchief refused to co-operate on the grounds that his people were ethnically distinct from the Ewe, the Lefana and the Akan. In his opinion, it made all the difference that Nkonya were really Guans whose cultural ties lay with communities to the west of the Volta. It is a measure of his success in erecting this line of defence that Lilley and his colleagues accepted that the Nkonya case was somehow unique. The people of Likpe and Santrokofi were not so quick off the mark, but with time they too began to perceive the merits of adopting a public discourse of ethnic difference.

The expression of identity: three case-studies

Having examined the three principal factors that had a bearing on the morphology of identities, it remains to examine their interaction in three specific settings. For the benefit of contrast, I will examine one case where the effect was to accentuate *dukɔ* identity (Anfoega), another where ethnicity was activated (Buem), and a third where the outcome was extremely ambiguous (Likpe).

Heightened localism: the case of Anfoega

The division of Anfoega always presented something of a enigma for the district administration. On the one hand, Anfoega was generally viewed in positive terms as prosperous, by virtue of its involvement in the cocoa bonanza, as well as 'progressive' in outlook. But on the other hand, its perceived intransigence over the amalgamation

---

[47] For Taviefe traditions, see GNAA ADM 39/5/73.

[48] However, their traditions also recalled having lived at Notsie along with the Ewes. GNAA ADM 39/5/73.

[49] On the efforts of Ve, see David Brown, 'Politics in the Kpandu area of Ghana, 1925 to 1969: a study of the influence of central government and national politics upon local factional competition', unpublished Ph.D thesis, Birmingham University, 1977, pp. 33–5.

question was a source of considerable frustration. In fact, opinion in Anfoega was not hostile to the principle thereof, but merely to the suggestion that the division should be forced to degrade itself by acknowledging the primacy of a rival headchief. In 1931, when the amalgamation policy was at its zenith, the headchief, Togbe J.V. Hodo V, submitted a brief history of the Anfoega people to the authorities, in which he sought to establish the pre-eminence of his own division. He asserted that the Anfoegas had first learned the science of warfare from the Akwamus and had imparted that knowledge to the Peki.[50] The latter had, in turn, used it to good effect in instigating a revolt against their former overlords. In return, Togbe Hodo claimed, Kwadjo Dei had acknowledged the Anfoega chief as his effective deputy within the Krepi alliance. Later, when the Asante forces crossed the Volta, Togbe Hodo claimed, the neighbouring Ewe *dukɔwo*, including Kpandu, had sworn an oath of allegiance to the Anfoega chief as their military leader. In the light of these rather tendentious historical claims, Togbe Hodo insisted that it was only reasonable to expect that neighbouring *dukɔwo* would renew their bonds of allegiance to him rather than grouping themselves under the Kpandu headchief whose leadership pretensions had been vigorously contested since German times.

In later years, the feeling was that a state centred on Anfoega might well have come to fruition but for the meddling of Captain Lilley. In a petition of 1951, it was recalled that the divisions of Aveme and Tsrukpe had already indicated their willingness to swear an oath of allegiance to the Anfoega chief, but had been dissuaded from doing so by Lilley himself.[51] Once her own ambitions were thus frustrated, there was strong government pressure to join one of the existing states – preferably either Akpini or Awatime. Although the former was contiguous, there was hostility throughout Anfoega to anything that smacked of subjection to the Kpandu headchief. Such was the intensity of local feeling that when it was rumoured that the headchief had assented to joining Akpini in 1942, the sub-chiefs proceeded to destool him. Although the rumour turned out to be baseless, and the district administration sought to intercede on his behalf, the headchief was unable to recover his moral authority and the destoolment stood. A regent was then appointed until Togbe D.A.K. Hodo VI was enstooled as the new headchief two years later.[52]

After the war, the British may have expected a younger, more educated and more worldly-wise generation to exercise a moderating influence. However, increased migration tended to have the opposite effect. Anfoega provides a paradigmatic case of how hometown associations came to take command of domestic affairs. In February 1950, there were moves to destool Togbe Hodo VI on the grounds that he had used his stool title to raise loans to the tune of £595. The headchief explained that the loans were of a personal nature and had in fact been used to purchase a lorry.[53] The main conspirator was the ex-headchief, and the authorities doubted that

---

[50] 'Abstract of Anfoega traditional history', by J.V. Hodo V, Headchief of Anfoega, dated 6 January 1931, GNAA ADM 39/1/216.

[51] 'Petition from independent division of Anfoega to Honourable Minister of Local Government', dated 21 April 1951, GNAA ADM 39/1/95.

[52] These events are outlined in the Anfoega entry in GNAA ADM 39/5/73.

[53] Reported in letter from Acting Senior DC to CCC (9 May 1950), GNAA ADM 39/1/95.

he was constitutionally entitled to initiate the action in the first place. However, the divisional sub-chiefs appeared to subscribe to the opinion that Togbe Hodo VI had compromised the stool and should therefore be removed. In the midst of this political stalemate, the fate of the headchief came to hang on the attitude of emigrant Anfoega citizens. The latter were organized into an Anfoega Duonenyo Central Committee and a Working Committee that took an active interest in Anfoega affairs. In the context of the destoolment action, the DC noted that:

> Many natives of Anfoega live and work away from the Division and it is the custom that everyone who can returns home for the Easter holidays. A meeting of the prominent citizens is then held when the progress of the Division during the past year and future plans are discussed. No important decision affecting the future of the Division would be taken without first consulting this body.[54]

A meeting was duly convened in Anfoega, at which the evidence from both sides was listened to. Thereafter, the Central and Working Committees gave their seal of approval to the destoolment of the headchief, which sealed his fate.

While a regent was appointed to look after the affairs of the stool, pending a replacement, the Anfoega Duonenyo Organization played an enhanced role in the affairs of the community. Whereas its commitment to self-help was very much in harmony with government policy, the Duonenyo Organization also set out to protect the customary rights of Anfoega. Its underlying complaint was that Anfoega had not been fairly treated. In 1949, Togbe Hodo VI and his chiefs had despatched a petition requesting government assistance in order to complete a number of projects, notably a clinic, village wells and a social centre. In addition, the petition had requested an annual grant-in-aid to support two senior primary schools, one Catholic and the other Presbyterian, which had been built out of local resources.[55] The government response was that grants-in-aid needed to be dispensed through the NAs, and because Anfoega did not belong to one it could not be helped.[56] The official line was that Anfoega people could remedy the situation very simply by joining an amalgamated state. After the decision to recognize the Atando NA, the administration dug its heels in still deeper on the grounds that humiliating oaths of allegiance were no longer at issue. In 1950, Togbe Hodo VI had further raised the stakes by sending a petition to the Trusteeship Council, which was no doubt calculated to cause maximum embarrassment. However, by the time the petition came to be heard, the British representatives were able to stall on the basis that, in the wake of the Coussey Report, the whole structure of local government was going to have to change anyway.[57]

After the destoolment of Togbe Hodo VI, the regent and the Anfoega Duonenyo Organization kept up the pressure through a series of strongly worded petitions to the administration. By this time, a series of new political structures for British Togoland were being installed, which merely sharpened the sense of exclusion. The most important new body was the Southern Togoland Council. Although the council

---

[54] Acting Senior DC to CCC (9 May 1950), GNAA ADM 39/1/95.
[55] 'A petition from Togbe Hodo VI, Dufiaga and the Asafohenewo and the people of Anfoega Division to His Excellency the Governor', undated, GNAA ADM 39/1/95.
[56] J. Dixon to CCC (24 May 1949), GNAA ADM 39/1/95.
[57] Noted in J. Dixon to CCC (15 June 1951), GNAA ADM 39/1/95.

started with relatively few powers in 1949, its role in the distribution of finances was steadily augmented. Because its members were elected through the duly constituted NAs, Anfoega was cut out. The latter could not make its voice heard on the Rural Development Committee, which began to disburse significant development money, deriving from the Cocoa Marketing Board and central government. Although the committee was supposed to support projects with a proven self-help dimension, and this criterion was clearly met by Anfoega, the latter was considered ineligible for assistance.[58] Moreover, Anfoega was not represented on the Ho/Kpandu District Education Committee, which allocated assistance grants to schools. This meant that Anfoega schools continued to be denied financial support, although the division was permitted observer status at the close of 1950.[59] There was a further problem of raising funds independently of the administration. In the absence of a recognized tribunal, the stool revenues that might have accrued from court fees were not forthcoming. Moreover, the Anfoega chiefs could not even raise their own local levies for the support of community development work. With good reason, therefore, the Anfoega Duonenyo Organization complained that the vindictive attitude of British officialdom had led to the community being cut out of its rightful share of development funds.[60]

In Anfoega, therefore, an overarching Ewe ethnicity was far less salient than a heightened sense of divisional identity born out of a perception of unfair treatment. Leading the way were the eminent citizens, mostly living outside Anfoega proper, whose greater education and wealth empowered them to speak on behalf of their community. Their contention was that the peoples of Anfoega had demonstrated their 'progressive' nature through their achievements abroad and their self-help initiatives at home. In their opinion, the imperialist ambitions of the Akpini State represented a threat to progress, and this had to be opposed at every turn. As we shall see in Chapter 6, their deeply felt sense of grievance created a strategic opening for the Convention People's Party (CPP).

The emergence of ethnic politics: the case of Buem

If a sense of enhanced *dukɔ* solidarity was the upshot of British policy in Anfoega, the experience of Buem was very different. Characteristically for the trans-Volta borderlands, the nineteenth-century Buem state had been composed of diverse fragments. The Omanhene was drawn from the Lefana section, which was concentrated in the southern half of the state. Lefana oral traditions, which were collected by Rattray, claimed an initial place of origin in Asante.[61] However, the same traditions also alluded to a period of settlement alongside the Ewes at Notsie. The traditions of some Lefana villages, such as Dzolu, also amounted to claims to being autochthonous. The second major section consisted of the so-called Akans, located in the north of the state.

---

[58] It was explicitly stated that 'The Committee will be prepared to try to help those who are willing to help themselves'. J. Dixon to Assistant DC (20 June 1949), GNAA ADM 39/1/517.

[59] 'Minutes of the Ho/Kpandu District Education Committee meeting held at Ho on the 28th and 29th November, 1950', GNAA ADM 39/1/665.

[60] 'Petition from independent division of Anfoega to Honourable Minister of Local Government', dated 21 April 1951, GNAA ADM 39/1/95.

[61] Buem entry in GNAA ADM 39/5/73.

In fact, a 'Brief History of the Twi Peoples of the Buem State', which was commissioned from the Buem State Secretary by the DC in 1945, distinguished between no fewer than five historically distinct components: one that comprised migrants from the shores of Lake Bosomtwe in Asante who arrived via Aburi and Nkonya; another consisting of the remnants of the Kwahu Dukoman; two apparently autochthonous groups (the Dodis and the Adankafo) who had been assimilated; and a more obscure fifth group (the Oboguahsofo), which was apparently subdued by the first group of incomers.[62] Other traditions sub-divided the first category into the peoples of Worawora, who were described as speaking 'Akwapim', and the peoples of Asato, Kadjebi, Papase and Ahamansu who allegedly came on a more direct route from Asante.[63] No doubt, a more sustained effort at collecting traditions would have turned up still finer distinctions. What these fragments shared was their common usage of the Twi language rather than Lelemi. The third section consisted of neighbouring peoples who had apparently accepted the leadership of the Buem stool in the later nineteenth century. The traditions that were collected by the British listed Bowiri, Akpafu, Santrokofi, Likpe, Tapa, part of Ntribu and Litimé (or western Akposso).[64] The 'Brief History', which certainly did not represent a Lefana version of history, nevertheless claimed that the Akpafus, Lolobis, Bowiris and Likpes had all been brought together in a confederacy under the leadership of Nana Aburam at Borada.[65] Whatever the truth of the claim – and it was disputed in Likpe – the Germans had stripped these later additions, as well as Tapa, Teteman and Baika, from allegiance to the Buem stool.

During the inter-war period, the amalgamation policy and the forces of economic change pulled in different directions, stretching the Buem polity to crisis point. The administration set out to reconstitute the Buem state as it had supposedly existed before the German intervention. A first step was the decision to reunite Baika and Teteman with the rest of Buem during the First World War.[66] This was followed by the reintegration of Akpafu, Lolobi and Bowiri. At the same time, there was a reconfiguration of power within the state to the advantage of the Lefana chiefs. In the early years of British rule, it was by no means a forgone conclusion that battle lines would be drawn between the Lefana and Akan sections. For example, when the divisional chief of Kudje led a secessionist bid in 1926, he was supported by chiefs from both sides.[67] Moreover, when reconciliation was achieved in 1929, it was brokered by the Buem Melioration Club, which purported to represent the interests of Buem as a whole. In subsequent years, however, the Akan and Lefana sections of Buem were increasingly at loggerheads. The structural reasons lie in the demographic and economic shift towards the forested areas of the north as a result of the expansion of cocoa production. Whereas the population of the Akan towns numbered 4,782 at the

---

[62] 'A brief history of the Twi peoples of the Buem State', by S.D.O. Afari, undated, enclosure to GNAA ADM 39/1/567.

[63] T.A. Mead to CEP (26 February 1947), GNAA ADM 39/1/572.

[64] The last two were deposited in French Togoland after the repartition. Buem entry, GNAA ADM 39/5/73.

[65] 'A brief history of the Twi peoples of the Buem State'. This was in turn attached to the larger Brong confederation. D.J.E. Maier, *Priests and Power: The Case of the Dente Shrine in Nineteenth-Century Ghana* (Bloomington: Indiana University Press, 1983), p. 105.

[66] Buem entry in GNAA ADM 39/5/73.

[67] Lilley to CEP (1 October 1926), GNAA ADM 391/545.

time of the 1931 census, it was estimated at 10,671 by the mid-1940s.[68] The increase was attributable to the influx of strangers, who owed direct allegiance to Akan chiefs. As a result, the newer settlements came to outstrip the older Buem towns. By the mid-1940s, Ahamansu and Papase had overtaken Worawora and Kadjebi and were said to be considerably larger than their Lefana counterparts.[69] It was only a matter of time before the Akan section began to demand greater representation within the Buem State.

In 1944, the self-styled chiefs of the 'Twi section' submitted a detailed memorandum to the Buem State Council, which asserted that they had been treated as second-class citizens since the inception of the amalgamation policy.[70] It pointed out that while the Akan communities made up more than half of the population and contributed most of the revenue, none of their number was recognized as a divisional chief. Instead, they had been placed beneath the Lefana wing chiefs of Guaman (the Benkumhene) and Kudje (the Nifahene). The memorandum insisted that the structure of wing chiefs was actually a recent Akan imitation from west of the Volta, which had no basis in the pre-colonial dispensation when each of the chiefs had served the Omanhene directly. Indeed, the memorandum went on to assert that there had been no wing chiefs until as recently as 1931. The Akan demand was, therefore, that they be granted two or more divisional chiefs of their own, which was later scaled down to a demand for one wing chief.

Although the memorandum received short shrift from the State Council, British officials conceded that the Akan petitioners did have a point. That is, the Akan towns were indeed more populous and more prosperous than their Lefana counterparts, and had been treated contemptuously by the wing chiefs. However, since historical authenticity was the underlying tenet of the Indirect Rule canon, the authorities were reluctant to interfere with anything purporting to represent 'tradition'. Part of the problem was that the administration simply had no collective memory of what had pertained as recently as a quarter of a century before. In 1945, Lindsell appeared to concede the fundamental point of the memorandum, namely, that the wing structure had been imported in the early 1930s. His opinion was echoed by T.A. Mead in 1947 who stated that:

> The change brought about by Amalgamation was merely that instead of serving the Omanhene direct four of them were now made to serve him through the Nifa and Benkum Wing-Chiefs, to whom I do not think they have ever owed any allegiance, and their present restiveness can I think be traced to the arrangements made when the Buem State was re-established at that time.[71]

---

[68] P. Lindsell to CEP (25 June 1945), GNAA ADM 39/1/567; H.V. Wimshurst, Acting CEP, to Acting Senior DC (9 August 1947), GNAA ADM 39/1/572.

[69] However, the population estimates were questionable. Whereas the population of Papase had been estimated at 3,904 in 1945, the 1948 census figures produced a figure of 2,507, although it is possible that some of the population was counted as part of neighbouring hamlets. This compared with a census figure of 2,162 for Worawora, 2,460 for Kadjebi and 2,336 for Borada. *The Gold Coast Census of Population, 1948: Report and Tables* (Accra: Government Printer, 1950), pp. 172–4.

[70] 'Memorandum submitted to the President and members of the Buem State Council', GNAA ADM 39/1/567.

[71] T.A. Mead to CEP (26 February 1927), GNAA ADM 39/1/572.

This admission is somewhat surprising because at the time of the 1926 dispute, the Kudje chief was already referring to himself as Nifahene, and was seemingly accepted by the Worawora chief as such. Still, nobody appeared certain how much further back the title went.

The attempts to go back to the written record proved fruitless because the relevant German documentation could not be found. Furthermore, that trusty fall-back, the Rattray Report, had little to say on the matter – principally because the author had been more preoccupied with the historicity of Peki claims. The administration was left with a supposedly authoritative, but transparently speculative, assessment from Captain Lilley. Plucked from the District Record Book, this read as follows:

> The fact that the German policy was to disintegrate possibly meant that the constitution did not matter and was … forgotten … It is clear that at some time the Buems had some organization as the Akan expressions Nifahene are used… But even to the present day (1933) the various villages appear to serve the Omanhene rather than through their wing chiefs.'[72]

In reality, this only muddied the waters by signalling simultaneously that the wing structure was historically rooted but at the same time practically insignificant.

There seemed little doubt that the Akans had not constituted a separate division in the past. Inevitably, therefore, any reform of the chieftaincy structure to take account of their demands would involve some break with tradition. Although the district authorities were prepared to settle for a pragmatic course, the Provincial Commissioner declined to recognize a separate Akan division on the grounds that none had previously existed and that the definition of its boundaries was likely to lead to even greater altercation.[73] His preference was for amending the Native Administration Ordinance so as to permit sub-divisional chiefs to sit on the NA Council. Although the amendment was duly made, very much against the wishes of the senior Lefana chiefs, it failed to settle the matter. The Akan chiefs were granted three seats on the council in 1946, but the Lefana secretary ensured that they were not invited to its meetings.[74]

Although the Akan section had petitioned the Governor in 1945 to demand a separate division, the government procrastinated in the hope that tinkering would have the desired effect. Instead, this merely inflamed the dispute. The first of two 'reminder petitions' in August 1946 was indicative of the extent to which ethnicity was becoming a focus of mobilization. The document asserted that there was a sinister Lefana plot to extinguish the separate identity of the Akans:

> The present dismemberment and subjugation of the Twi Speakers brought about by the malicious intentions of the Lefana Chiefs whose language we do not understand, whose customs are in many cases the reciprocal of Akan customs, whose policy is to make us into hewers of wood and drawers of water, whose ambition is to suppress us, whose ultimate aim is to assimilate us as one Lefana Tribe thus compelling us under tragic circumstances to lose our identity as a Twi Tribe, is most incompatible with British Justice and Colonial policy.[75]

---

[72] John Duncan to T.A. Mead (13 January 1947), GNAA ADM 39/1/572.

[73] Acting CEP to CCC (18 March 1946), GNAA ADM 39/1/567.

[74] T.A. Mead to CEP (29 April 1947), GNAA ADM 39/1/572.

[75] 'Reminder petition of the Akan section of Buem State to His Excellency Sir Alan Burns', dated 1 August 1946, GNAA ADM 39/1/572.

In July 1946, the Akan chiefs convened a meeting at which they appeared to declare their secession from Buem under the leadership of the Woraworahene, although this was later denied.[76]

The situation was still further complicated by the emergence of other sets of players seeking to advance their own demands. One was made up of the chiefs of the eastern Lefana villages of Dzolu, New Ayoma and Baika who now insisted that they were the 'real aborigines' who had been wrongfully deprived of a divisional chief of their own.[77] What rankled was that the chief of Teteman had been recognized as the Kyidomhene in 1940, despite the fact that his forebears had collaborated with the Asante invaders seventy years earlier.[78] The administration regarded their demands, probably correctly, as a copycat response to the Akan campaign. An even more important challenge to the existing dispensation emanated from the migrant cocoa farmers. Although the population of the Akan settlements had increased rapidly in the past decade and a half, the majority in villages like Papase were in fact Ewes. In the midst of the constitutional crisis, the stranger farmers organized themselves into the Buem Strangers' Union and began to advance claims of their own, for which purpose they recruited the services of Dr J.B. Danquah.[79] Their case was that they were responsible for whatever wealth Buem enjoyed, and that they represented the largest single grouping, but were still treated as second-class citizens. It rankled that they were forced to pay sizeable NA taxes without experiencing the benefits thereof. As far as most of these migrants were concerned, they were already contributing the upkeep of their home communities and so resented having to make further contributions in Buem. Although the Buem State Treasury was established in 1940, three years later the stranger communities were still refusing to recognize it and were boycotting the markets in protest.[80]

Moreover, the strangers had been complaining for some years that the Omanhene, Nana Akpandja II, treated them as little more than a milch-cow. When the land dispute with Akposso allegedly culminated in a stool debt of over £3,000 in 1939, Nana Akpandja requested each stranger farmer to contribute £10 to pay it off.[81] When some refused to comply, they were allegedly forced off the land, which was then reallocated to individuals who were more compliant.[82] Insecurity of tenure had been a recurrent complaint throughout the 1930s. Migrants who purchased land outright often discovered later on that the Omanhene claimed it as stool land, for which they still needed to pay rent. In his defence, Nana Akpandja claimed that stool lands were alienated without his knowledge by Buem tenants, who paid only a sheep for the right to use the land and then proceeded to sell it on to strangers. His attempts to

---

[76] John Duncan to Acting President, Buem State Council (12 August 1946), and Nana Akuamoah IV, Acting President of Buem State Council, to Duncan (26 August 1946), GNAA ADM 39/1/572.

[77] Petition to Governor dated 21 December 1946, GNAA ADM 39/1/572.

[78] According to a tradition collected by Lilley, the Tetemans had betrayed the hiding place of the Omanhene of Buem to the Asante who proceeded to execute him. See handwritten notes in GNAA ADM 39/1/212.

[79] Danquah was involved in Buem politics on different sides at different times. Although he represented the Buem Strangers' Union, his services were also enlisted by the Buem State Council against the Akan chiefs.

[80] Quarterly reports for December 1943 and March 1944, GNAA ADM 39/1/305.

[81] Nana Akpandja II to DC (27 May 1939), GNAA ADM 39/1/190.

[82] Henrich Adai et al., Guaman, to DC (2 May 1939), GNAA ADM 39/1/190.

insist that all tenants register their claims was, however, treated with the greatest suspicion.[83] The underlying problem for those stranger farmers from Gold Coast Eweland and French Togoland who bought land outright, was that the law prohibited the alienation of land to non-natives of British Togoland.[84] In the perception of the stranger farmers, the Buem chiefs exploited their vulnerability by selling land and then claiming it back on the grounds that it was not supposed to have been alienated in the first place. Hence the Buem Strangers' Union demanded in October 1950:

> That the cruel ordinance No 15 of 1950 be repealed as we are all NATIVES OF WEST AFRICA. That the NON-NATIVE FARMERS in Buem feel themselves threatened since the Buems who form the minority in the Buem State have formulated plans to take back by intimidation and threats of violence those pieces of LAND acquired with COCOA now grown on them through many years of TOIL and EXPENSE. [emphasis in original][85]

In 1947, the Buem Strangers' Union did win representation on the NA Council, but this concession was regarded as inadequate. Hence in August 1948, their president, Amega Dogbe, sent a petition to Governor Gerald Creasy, which insisted that the strangers were still under-represented and taken for granted.[86] The demand of the union was for half of the seats on the NA Council and on the Buem State Council, and for representation on the Native Tribunals and the Finance Board. As in the case of the Akan complainants, the administration felt that the strangers had some cause for grievance. But they were reluctant to enforce substantial concessions on the grounds that the existing legislation did not allow for representation on the State Councils. There was also a perception that however much was conceded, Dogbe and Danquah were bound to ask for more.

At one level, the demands of the Strangers' Union undercut those of the Akan chiefs in that both were purporting to speak for the same constituency. But in practical terms, this did not seem to matter all that much. Together they complained that the Buem State was operated by a cabal of Lefana chiefs without due consultation and at the expense of the majority – however that might be defined. In each case, the protagonists increasingly found it convenient to mobilize around appeals to ethnicity. In this context, the labels of 'Akan' and 'Ewe' did not arise in opposition to each other, but in contradistinction to that of the 'Lefana'. As the 'Brief History of the Twi Peoples' implicitly conceded, an 'Akan' identity was of recent provenance. Equally, the 'Ewe' category that appeared unproblematic in Buem – encompassing as it did strangers from as far afield as Anlo, Peki and Anfoega – was precisely what was contested in other arenas. But in Buem, these ethnic packages came to comprise everything that was not 'Lefana', a term that was associated with arrogance, laziness, litigiousness and duplicity. British officials were inclined to agree, referring to the

---

[83] The *African Morning Post* reported on 20 July 1938 that Nana Akpandja had issued a public notice to this effect, giving all tenants (both Buem and strangers) just two weeks to register. Enclosure in GNAA ADM 39/1/574.

[84] Under Ordinance 15 of 1940, the consent of the Governor was required.

[85] 'A resolution by the non-natives of the Buem State formed into an association known as the "Buem Strangers Union"', dated 15 October 1950, GNAA ADM 39/1/123.

[86] Petition to Gerald Creasy, dated 8 August 1948, GNAA ADM 39/1/646.

Buem State Council as 'an oligarchy of an unpleasant nature' and attaching particular blame to 'unsavoury Borada "Bush Lawyers"'.[87] However, it was not until the emergence of new local government structures in the early 1950s, which created separate local councils for the Lefana and the Akan, that the grip of the Lefana chiefs was actually broken. By that time, the internal politics of Buem was feeding directly into the wider debate about the relative merits of Togoland unification and Gold Coast integration.

Contested identities: the case of Likpe

If there is a danger of reading backwards from successful efforts at ethnic engineering, there is also much to be learned from the projects that did not quite come off. A consideration of the rise of 'tribal' politics in Buem tends to confirm the general thesis that ethnicity did not act as a free-floating variable. As much theorizing would predict, it was both historically contingent and contextual. However, I would also underline that the symbolic values were a refraction of layers of identity that resided at lower levels than that of the *ethnie*. The discussion that follows amplifies these points, but also confirms the more or less conscious manner in which ethnic brokers set out to manipulate political discourse.

In the immediate post-war period, Likpe consisted of eight villages located along the Togoland frontier to the east of Hohoe. According to tradition, the core settlements were those of Mate (which provided the headchief), Todome, Bakwa, Bala and Avedzeme. As a result of disputes over chieftaincy, however, Kukurantumi seceded from Bala in 1927, and Koforidua and Agbozome broke away from Avedzeme in 1939/40. In Likpe (like Buem) the traditions that were collected by the British authorities painted a confused picture, albeit one that is perfectly comprehensible in terms of the nineteenth-century history. Rattray formed the impression that the Likpe people (or Bakpele) were originally immigrants from Ashanti.[88] This did not sit easily with the notion that, speaking their own unique tongue, the Bakpele were actually autochthonous. F.G. Crowther, the SNA, was one of those who believed that they had always been there. He reasoned that: 'Two groups, Santrokofi and Bogo (French) appear to comprise a mixture of aboriginal blood with the Ewe. It seems probable from the records that this original blood is associated with that of Buem and Likpe...'.[89] Lilley made enquiries of his own and concluded that the Likpe was actually composed of two different sets of people. He recalled the following incident, which took place in 1927 while he was cutting the revised international boundary:

> ... whilst at Mate I sat I one evening with the Likpes whilst they recounted their history. I was told that Mate meant the teacher and that they came from Attebubu [*sic*]. I asked the chief of Bakoa where he came from and he replied 'out of the ground'. Mr Koranteng nearly fell off his chair with merriment.[90]

[87] P. Lindsell to John Duncan (3 January 1946), GNAH DA/D309; John Duncan to T.A. Mead (13 January 1947), GNAA ADM 39/1/572.
[88] 'Togoland: a history of the tribal divisions of the district of Misahuhe and of the sub-districts of Ho and Kpandu', GNAH RAO/C2073.
[89] Comments by Crowther on Rattray's report at GNAA ADM 39/5/73.
[90] Minute by Lilley, dated 19 March 1931, GNAA ADM 39/1/216.

Quite what Mr Koranteng found so amusing we will never know. It was presumably not the image itself, given that certain Asante myths of origin make the same claim.[91] On the contrary, what probably tickled him was that these people were associating themselves with the great tradition of Asante. The suggestion that the Bakpele were composed of two distinct groups subsequently became firmly established through an official enquiry into the Likpe stool dispute in 1932.[92] The Assistant DC, John Gutch, had problems squaring the oral evidence, but nevertheless generated the first reasonably detailed history of Likpe. The fact that it was written down, and thereby codified, has made it a central reference point for litigants to this day. Gutch confirmed that there were indeed two distinct strands in Likpe, one claiming to be indigenous (Todome and Bakwa) and the other claiming to have migrated into the area from Atebubu via Notsie (the peoples of Mate, Avedzeme and Bala).[93] In all probability, the standard Ewe migration story had been grafted on to the Atebubu version, as was also the case with the Lefana traditions. Although it is tempting to dismiss the former on the grounds that Rattray had made no mention of it in 1915, one elderly local historian has claimed that it was actually the Atebubu story that was a recent invention that had originally been concocted to dissuade the Germans from uprooting the Bakpele from their present location.[94] For our purposes, it is important merely to note that two migration stories co-existed uneasily in the traditions collected by Gutch. His report provided the basis for an idealized version of events according to which the two sides supposedly came together as equal partners governed by a more or less formal constitution. Under the latter, certain families from Mate were supposedly entitled to provide a chief for all Likpe, while the enstoolment ceremony itself had to be performed under the supervision of the Todome chief as landowner.

As a result of the enquiry, Gutch confirmed the principle of rotation between the Kalekato and Kalelenti clans in Mate, and Togbui Boke Akototse III from the latter was duly enstooled as the headchief. To Akototse fell the task of negotiating the hazards of the amalgamation policy. The pressure from the administration was intense, and although Akototse insisted on the iniquity of being forced to join a state, he did at various points enter negotiations. At a point when the Gbi headchief was making the running, the chiefs of Todome and Bakwa were apparently in favour of amalgamating with the latter. This was not an attractive option to the rest of Likpe, which construed the Gbis as the historic enemy. When this amalgamation failed to come off, the two chiefs apparently favoured joining Akpini instead, but once more failed to convince the rest of Likpe that this would be advantageous. The latter move was finally blocked by Lilley himself, who raised the matter with the Kpandu headchief and 'earnestly entreated him not to allow the performance of customs as they are not related in any way, and the union, I am certain, would not have been satisfactory'.[95]

[91] Ivor Wilks, *Forests of Gold: Essays on the Akan and the Kingdom of Asante* (Athens: Ohio University Press, 1993), p. 65.

[92] The evidence and the conclusions of the enquiry may be found at GNAA ADM 39/1/216.

[93] 'Findings of Mr. John Gutch in the enquiry held at Likpe Mate on 17th–20th September, 1932', GNAA ADM 39/1/216.

[94] Emmanuel Osibo, 'A short history of the Bakpeles (Likpes)', typescript, undated.

[95] 'Handing over report', p. 116, GNAH DA/D78.

Lilley, curiously enough, insisted that the Bakpele were a 'Twi-speaking division' that really belonged with Buem.[96] However, the Buem option was, in turn, blocked by the chiefs of Bakwa and Todome, who argued – as the putative autochthons – that Likpe had always been quite separate from its more powerful neighbour to the north.

After the British rejection of a proposal for a confederacy in 1945, the pendulum swung back to a possible amalgamation with Gbi. In September 1947, the Assistant DC, John Green, held a meeting with the Likpe chiefs in order to ascertain where the balance of opinion lay. When asked, 'with whom do you wish to amalgamate and why?', the headchief and the chiefs of Todome, Bakwa and Koforidua expressed a preference for joining Gbi; the Bala and Kukurantumi chiefs signalled their lack of interest in any amalgamation; while the Avedzeme chief, with the support of the Agbozome chief, expressed his preference for amalgamation with Buem and his vehement opposition to any dealings with Gbi.[97] In a memorandum handed to Green at the meeting itself, the Avedzeme chief, Nana Agya Mensah II, went as far as to claim that the Buems (presumably the Lefana) and the Likpes were one people who had migrated together from the west under a common leader – although he also referred to an unhappy period of settlement at Notsie.[98] As it happened, these were to be the first shots in a long-running campaign by Agya Mensah to rewrite Likpe history and to remould a sense of Bakpele identity.

On the basis of the clear differences of opinion that were expressed, Green did not feel that he could recommend any amalgamation for the moment. However, the fact that Gbi, Likpe, Ve, Santrokofi, Anfoega and Nkonya remained unattached continued to cause concern, especially in the light of a pending visit from a United Nations Visiting Mission.[99] Whereas there was still a reluctance to endorse anything that fell short of outright amalgamation in 1948, the administration finally agreed to recognize a new-style Atando NA, covering Gbi, Likpe and Ve, the following year. This arrangement enabled Akototse to gain some of the advantages of integration into the native administration system, which (as we have seen) were denied to Anfoega. At the same time, the fact that a rotating chairmanship took the place of a paramount chief enabled Akototse to argue that he had not abandoned the principle of Bakpele independence. Indeed, this was precisely the more flexible arrangement that the independent divisions had been advocating for the best part of a decade. However, Agya Mensah and his associates did not see things in quite the same way, arguing that the arrangement amounted to a sell-out to the Gbis. In the three years that followed, Akototse and Agya Mensah became the principal combatants in a ding-dong battle for control of Likpe.

In background and outlook, the protagonists were as different as could be imagined. Indeed, the difference between them epitomized the social changes sweeping across southern Togoland. Akototse was very much a chief in the

---

[96] 'Handing over report'. This highly misleading depiction of Likpe was repeated in the 'Memorandum on amalgamation in British Togoland' of 1944, which stated that 'most of the Likpes are of Ashanti origin and speak Twi as well as Likpe, and it could be natural for the division to join Buem'. GNAA ADM 391/545.
[97] John Green to Senior DC (1 October 1947), GNAH D133.
[98] Agya Mensah to John Green (22 September 1947), GNAH D133.
[99] The concerns of T.A. Mead were alluded to in a letter from the DC to the CCC (6 July 1948), GNAA ADM 39/1/93.

traditional style. He had been selected for his age rather than for his education. In his final handing over report, Lilley described the headchief as 'an elderly man and not very bright'.[100] He was frequently depicted as an autocrat who expected more junior chiefs, or 'headmen', to fall into line once he had made up his own mind. This attitude was reflected in a rebuke he delivered to the District Commissioner in 1947:

> I shall be pleased if government through you will teach my people that they should respect authority by letting things follow their natural course; the engine must be responsible for the trailer but not the vice versa.[101]

By contrast, Agya Mensah was young, had acquired at least some formal education and was apparently well-travelled.[102] Moreover, he had evidently imbibed elements of a global post-war discourse on democracy. One DC was even sneakingly impressed by the figure he cut, writing that:

> This individual is an educated young man and frequent visitor to Accra, who quoted at length from the Coussey report and Abraham Lincoln.[103]

Although Agya Mensah had been enstooled as a chief, he nevertheless fits Dennis Austin's image of the new men who had acquired a measure of basic education but could not aspire to join the ranks of the intelligentsia. Austin writes that they were 'locally rooted in the village, yet beneficiaries also of an educational system which … endowed them with a common language – English – and an awareness of common interests which cut across tribal boundaries'.[104] Throughout the Gold Coast, these liminal men had exhibited a strong desire for self-improvement, which was manifested in their participation in debating societies and other voluntary associations.[105]

Agya Mensah was not highly educated, but he was evidently proud of whatever learning he had picked up along the way. His petitions were positively brimming with allusions to literature, history and international affairs. Much of his purple prose no doubt struck the authorities as bizarre – such as when he described his faction as the Likpe Liberal Party struggling against the malign Gbi socialists! – but it was calculated to impress his local audience. The following flourish was typical of the 'big English' he positively revelled in:

> That the inclusion of Likpe Division falls sharp below political data, very wanting in political principles, such as political grammer [sic], history, tradition, phylosophy [sic], metabolism very wanting also in constitution and democracy. For that inclusion of the membership of Likpe in this phase is rather very uncandid, irresponsible and unfounded as the formation of this Atando Native Authority is a direct illegal birth of a machinery propaganda, counterfeitedly coined and interpreted by a handful of self-interested persons or chiefs from Likpe Division who cannot at

---

[100] 'Handing over report'.

[101] Togbui B.K. Akototse to Senior DC (14 August 1947), GNAH D133.

[102] Agya Mensah noted that, despite the fact that he had been enstooled in 1943, he had to spend time away from Likpe owing to ill-health. Agya Mensah to CCC (28 March 1949), GNAH D133.

[103] Palmer to CCC (19 July 1950), GNAH D133.

[104] Dennis Austin, *Politics in Ghana, 1946–1960* (Oxford: Oxford University Press, 1964), p. 17.

[105] *Ibid.*, pp. 26–7; Yaw Twumasi, 'Prelude to the rise of mass nationalism in Ghana, 1920–49: nationalists and voluntary associations', *Ghana Social Science Journal*, 3, 1, 1976.

all stand any constitutional or democratic election or any form of public election of the people of Likpe.[106]

Agya Mensah was closely following events in the Gold Coast, and many of the nationalist slogans and catch-phrases also found their way into his own rhetoric. Whereas Akototse was very much tied in to the local milieu, Agya Mensah took it upon himself to translate the world beyond Likpe to his local audience. In that sense, he was very close to the 'progressive' element in Anfoega.

Shortly after the inauguration of the Atando NA, Agya Mensah set up a Likpe Grand Council in order to co-ordinate opposition to the new arrangements. The Grand Council conducted a vigorous campaign to break the NA, which was sustained despite intense official pressure. One means of so doing was to incite the Bakpele not to pay their local taxes. At the same time, the Grand Council despatched a steady barrage of petitions that set out the objections to the new arrangements. Now, Agya Mensah began to articulate a new vision of Bakpele history that was to create an important precedent for the future.[107] The crux of his thesis, which went far beyond the Atebubu migration story, was that the Bakpele were part of a greater Akan diaspora. In support thereof, he referred to the works of Bosman, Bowdich and Ellis, in which he suggested there were references to the Likpe people.[108] At the same time he argued that the Bakpele were historically quite distinct from the Ewes, with whom any past relationship had been conflictual. He placed a great deal of emphasis upon fundamental cultural differences between the Bakpele and the Ewes, deftly skirting over the even more obvious differences with the Akan (such as the patrilineal basis of Likpe society). At the same time, he poured scorn on the kind of claims that Nana Akototse was advancing:

> Among the people of Likpe [and] the Ewes the only Uniformity that exists is the accident of colour. The dissimilarity is as great as that which exists between a Greek and a Swede or a Bulgarian to a Dutchman or an Ashanti to a Hawsa [sic] or a Fanti to Ewe man.

By contrast, the headchief was inclined towards a version of the past in which the Likpe people, with the exception of the peoples of Bakwa and Todome, had supposedly lived alongside the Ewes at Notsie and participated in the great migration from that place. Indeed, the name of 'Atando' was supposedly drawn from a quarter of that town where they had resided together. Like the Akan origins posited by Agya Mensah, this recourse to the Notsie tradition might be construed as an attempt to

---

[106] Agya Mensah and others to the Governor at Hohoe (15 October 1949), GNAA ADM 39/1/93.

[107] On subsequent reworkings of history, see Paul Nugent, *Myths of Origin and the Origin of Myth: Local Politics and the Uses of History in Ghana's Volta Region*, Working Papers on African Societies, No. 22, 1997 (Berlin: Das Arabische Buch); and *The Flight-Lieutenant Rides (to Power) Again: National Delusions, Local Fixations and the 1996 Ghanaian Elections*, Occasional Paper, Centre of African Studies, University of Edinburgh, 1998, pp. 35–54.

[108] This was a figment of his imagination. Bosman was too early and dealt with the coastal strip. Bowdich was concerned with Asante proper. Even Ellis refers to the 'Krepi' in very general terms. The relevant texts are William Bosman, *A New and Accurate Description of the Coast of Guinea*, first published in 1704 (London: Frank Cass, 4th English edn, 1967); T.E. Bowdich, *Mission From Cape Coast Castle to Ashantee*, first published 1819 (London: Frank Cass, 3rd edn, 1966); and A.B. Ellis, *A History of the Gold Coast of West Africa*, first published 1893 (London & Dublin: Curzon Press, 1971).

associate with the great tradition of a culturally hegemonic group. A surviving school exercise book from 1931, which belonged to a later paramount chief, shows clearly that the Notsie story was being disseminated in the classroom and imbibed by people who might not previously have shared in it.[109] Going further, Akototse insisted that an association with Gbi was the most natural because of 'geographical unity and subsequent trade facilities and the freedom of expression in Ewe'.[110] He had a point in that the expansion of cocoa production in Likpe had indeed strengthened ties with Hohoe as the pre-eminent market town. Moreover, through the operations of trade and the church, the Ewe language had acquired considerable currency in Likpe. The official line that the Bakpele were 'Twi-speaking' was by this time clearly fallacious, if it had ever been true. For his part, Agya Mensah claimed that the Bakpele had reached the area long before the Gbis and other Ewe peoples arrived. His account laid emphasis upon the struggle by the Bakpele to hold on to what was rightfully theirs in the face of later Ewe arrivals. This version of the past enabled Agya Mensah to have his cake and eat it, in the sense that the Bakpele were described as Akan by origin, but also first-comers in their area of settlement. The Notsie dimension, which he had originally incorporated, was quietly erased from the record – in effect bringing the international boundary into convenient alignment with the pre-colonial traditions. Agya Mensah also made great play of the alleged duplicity of the Gbis who, he alleged, derived their commercial wealth from the sweat of the Likpe farmers, but contributed nothing to the common weal. In modern academic parlance, the Gbis were constructed by Agya Mensah as a concentrated form of the Ewe 'Other'. The clash of interpretations between Akototse and Agya Mensah over relations with the Ewe were played out in the correspondence that piled up on the desks of the district administration. They were even embodied in the chiefly titles that the protagonists adopted for themselves. Whereas the headchief always used the Ewe title of *Togbui*, Agya Mensah insisted upon the Akan designation of *Nana*.

Nana Agya Mensah was a sufficiently astute politician to realize that there were structural tensions within the chieftaincy set-up which could be exploited to his advantage. The chiefs of the newest settlements were treated by Togbui Akototse and the administration alike as mere 'headmen'. Agya Mensah nurtured their chiefly ambitions, although the fact that Agbozome and Koforidua had both split from Avedzeme also meant that he had to be careful about undercutting his own position within the hierarchy. Towards the end of 1949, a concerted effort was made to bring these 'headmen' on board or, failing that, to remove them from office. Nana Agyeman I of Kukurantumi became a particularly trusted ally, but in Agbozome Kofi Sekyere I actually sided with the headchief. The Grand Council therefore proceeded to mount a destoolment action against him, alleging that he was circumcised contrary to tradition and that he regularly failed to consult his elders. Two of the senior sub-chiefs, those of Todome and Bakwa, also backed the headchief and found themselves on the receiving end of destoolment actions. In each of these villages, the Grand Council purported to enstool new chiefs who, not surprisingly, were opposed to the Atando NA.

---

[109] The exercise book from the Presbyterian Senior School, Hohoe, belonged to the future Nana Soglo Allo III.
[110] Togbui B.K. Akototse III to Senior DC (14 August 1947), GNAH D133.

Although the district authorities felt that authoritarian tendencies of the head-chief were not helping matters, there was also concern that Agya Mensah was gaining the upper hand. If he were to succeed in undermining the Atando NA, that could also have serious implications for the administration in the rest of southern Togoland. At the end of 1949, therefore, Nana Agya Mensah was arraigned before the NA court on a charge of undermining its lawful authority and inciting people not to pay their taxes. Agya Mensah was found guilty, but proceeded to appeal. When the case came before the West African Court of Appeal early in 1950, he was acquitted. Far from being chastened by the experience, therefore, Agya Mensah acquired a heroic status and a heightened sense of his prowess. The Grand Council proceeded to impose a blockade on Mate town and to harass supporters of the headchief. Indeed the District Quarterly Report for April 1950 noted that the Grand Council had virtually seized power in Likpe:

> The present position is that five sub-chiefs support the head Chief, but two (Bakwa and Agbo-some) have been driven from their towns, and one other (Todome) is in a precarious position.

Going further, the supporters of the Grand Council announced that they were seeking to destool Togbui Akototse. The charges were released to the Gold Coast press, and were duly published in the pages of the *Gold Coast Express* at the end of March.[111] The following month, supporters of the Grand Council marched on Mate with the intention of effecting the destoolment, but were turned back by a detachment of police. At the same time, they sought to elevate their candidate for the Bakwa stool to the position of headchief.

Togbui Akototse was evidently in dire trouble and sought to bail himself out of his predicament by rekindling links with the non-Ewe divisions to the north. The context was one in which a modern local government system was being mooted to replace the discredited NA system. In 1950, the Atando NA expressed a preference for joining Buem, Krachi, Nkonya and Santrokofi in a proposed Northern District Council. This apparently enjoyed the support of Gbi division, if not of Ve. According to the District Quarterly Report for April, the proposal also appeared to have recaptured some sympathy for the beleaguered Likpe headchief at home.[112] However, self-styled 'scholars' from Buem, Nkonya and Santrokofi themselves petitioned against such an arrangement, which would include Gbi, on the grounds that they were quite distinct from the Ewe peoples. Their language was not dissimilar to that employed by Nana Agya Mensah:

> We have no grudge whatsoever against the Ewes as a race. We, however, feel correctly that our identity as an ethnic group should ever be preserved and not confused. We deplore that paragraph in the Joint Anglo-French Memorandum ... which described us as 'a few lesser peoples (the Buems, Likpes, Santrokofis, Akpafus, Bowiris and Nkonyas of British Togoland and Akpossos of French Togoland) who are not Ewes but whose interests are so confused with those of the latter that they cannot be excluded from consideration from the Ewe problem'. This statement clearly denies our identity as a race and this loss of identity has cost us dearly in matters of

---

[111] 'Charges preferred against Boke Akototse III', *Gold Coast Express*, 30 March 1950, and 'Unrest in Likpe Division', 6 April 1950, enclosed in GNAH D133.

[112] Kpandu Sub-District Quarterly Report, April–June 1950, enclosed in GNAH DA/240.

educational Scholarship, where because we are regarded as Ewes, whatever Scholarship is granted to Ewes is assumed to benefit us equally.[113]

The discourse of the Grand Council had, in effect, been transported to a higher plane. By this point, it should be noted, the language of ethnicity was being widely disseminated across the middle belt of southern Togoland. While macro-political events had a large part to play in this, as we shall see, it was British efforts to restructure chieftaincy that had actually set the ball in motion.

The Atando affair was ultimately resolved with the dissolution of the NA to make way for the new structures of local government. While Gbi received its own local council under the Kpandu District Council, a separate Likpe-Lolobi Local Council was created within the Buem-Krachi District. However, the destoolment actions rumbled on for some years more. Eventually, the Grand Council did drop the case against Togbui Akototse, but insisted that the other actions be recognized. In 1955, the authorities agreed to set up a commission of enquiry to resolve the matter once and for all. During the proceedings, Nana Amoah IV of Bakwa announced that he was not contesting the case against him. On the other hand, the Todome and Agbozome chiefs were cleared of the charges.[114] The underlying issue of whether the Bakpele were related to the Ewes or the Akans – the possibility that they were neither was not countenanced at this time – had not been decisively resolved. But it was to acquire added urgency as the Ewe/Togoland unification question began to demand an answer at the local level. This case has been dealt with in some detail because it demonstrates that discourses on ethnicity arose out of the interaction among layers of individual, village and divisional identities that themselves had unstable properties. It is also important to underline the fact that the historical claims were flatly contradictory.

Conclusion

In this chapter, I have demonstrated that whatever the importance of the Togoland boundary as a zone of continuing interaction, the processes that were playing themselves out behind the line were also extremely important. Those studies that start from the premise of a pre-existing greater Ewe identity arguably risk pre-judging the issue. They also make it very difficult to make sense of the patchy history of the Ewe unification movement, which comprises the subject matter of the next chapter. My own approach has been to begin with lower units of social organization, working both upwards and outwards towards an understanding of ethnic and territorial identities. I have mapped three deep-flowing social currents – namely, Christian conversion, migration and British chieftaincy policies – which combined and interacted in such a manner as to reconfigure the map of community relations. The proliferation of hometown, youth and improvement associations served as an important catalyst, but

---

[113] 'A resolution of the Buem State, Santrokofi and Nkonya Divisions Scholars Union to the Select Committee on Local Government', dated 10 June 1950, GNAH DA/240.

[114] Proceedings of committee of enquiry, quoted in Government Agent to Regional Officer (13 May 1955), GNAH DA/D314.

they did not contribute unequivocally to a heightened sense of ethnic identity. In some respects, as the Anfoega case demonstrates, they were rather more conducive towards a strengthening of *dukɔ* solidarities. Much the same could be said of the structures of traditional rule, which, under the amalgamation policy, tended to entrench sub-ethnic identities. When ethnicity did become an issue – as it did for the minorities like the Bakpele – it often became a matter of profound controversy because there was no latent pre-colonial *ethnie* waiting to be discovered. The complex history of the trans-Volta borderlands did not lend itself to such simplicities. As a result, the project of forging an ethnic consciousness was laborious, discontinuous and above all contested.

5

'*Imperialism is not Necessarily a Bad Thing*'

Togoland Reunification, Ewe Unification *& Gold Coast Imperialism* 1921–57

No one who knows anything about the Ewe people can pass from the British side to the French side of the frontier without being struck by the absurdity of the frontier arrangement. The frontier cuts indiscriminately through villages and farms. A man's house may be on the British side while his farm is on the French side, and vice versa. The real truth of the matter is that it is impossible to set up a satisfactory frontier anywhere between the lower Volta in the Gold Coast and the lower Mono on the western border of Dahomey.[1]

In the last chapter, I set out to avoid the fetishization of ethnicity and placed greater overall emphasis on the interplay between other levels of identification. In this chapter, which deals with what one might call 'meta-identities', I examine Ewe and minority ethnicity in tandem with two sets of competing territorial identities, centred on the concept of a reunified Togoland and a greater Gold Coast, respectively. By setting the discussion up in this fashion, I am conscious of swimming against a certain tide of opinion that is impressed by the depth of Ewe ethnic awareness cutting across international boundaries. I believe, however, that this approach is justified in the light of the manner in which the Ewe unification question played itself out.

It is true that in the immediate aftermath of the Second World War, the case for the reunification of the Ewe people was made more forcefully than ever before. But this project was always played out in tension with the reality that the Ewe were not just split between the Gold Coast, French Togoland and British Togoland, but also cohabited with other peoples in each of those territories. Hence any act of unification would inevitably have a bearing on existing relationships with other peoples, and would possibly create new boundaries to replace any that might end up being erased. Apart from the fact that non-Ewes were likely to have their own views, it was not immediately obvious to all 'Ewes' that this identification should override other relationships of affinity. My aim over the next two chapters is to explain why it was that the Ewe unificationist project failed so abjectly, and why the boundaries between partitioned Togoland and the Gold Coast ultimately remained in place.

---

[1] *Ewe News-Letter*, no. 2, June 1945, p. 4.

147

This chapter deals with the macro-politics of unification up to the end of 1956, whereas the one that follows traces the border question from the eve of independence down to the recent past.

The fact that there is already a substantial literature on the Ewe/Togoland unification question renders my task somewhat easier.[2] It is not necessary to provide a detailed narrative of events for the simple reason that this has been furnished by previous researchers in the field. Although I aim to offer some texture, the primary object is to map out a framework within which these events may be interpreted. Secondly, I will not dwell unduly on the protracted debates carried out within the fora of the United Nations, although these played an important part in determining the final outcome. Fortunately, D.E.K. Amenumey and John Kent have both provided fairly exhaustive accounts of the international dimension of the Ewe/Togoland question. Although I shall have cause to allude to the role of the Trusteeship Council, my principal concern is with the unfolding debate in Togoland itself. In order to gain a proper sense of perspective, I will situate the post-war debate in a somewhat longer historical time-frame, beginning with the moment of partition itself.

Interrogating boundaries: Francophobia, Germanophilia and the vision of a united Togoland

As we have already seen, D.E.K. Amenumey has made a case for tracing a conscious assertion of Ewe ethnic identity back to the initial partition of Eweland in the 1880s, and once more to the repartition of Togoland after the First World War. In the first case, however, it is surely anachronistic to refer to an overarching 'Ewe' identity. In fact, the discrete categories of 'Awuna' and 'Krepi' – which bore connotations not just of difference, but also of mutual antagonism – continued to be deployed until well into the second decade of the twentieth century. Admittedly, the Committee on Behalf of Togoland Natives voiced its 'opposition against a division of the Ewe-speaking tribe' in 1919, but the meaning here was ambiguous.[3] One of the proudest accomplishments of the German missionaries had been the standardization of a written form of the Ewe language, which could be deployed in church and school across the trans-Volta area. It would have been surprising, therefore, if this had not contributed to a heightened awareness of linguistic affinity. But the context suggests that when Octaviano Olympio and his colleagues referred to an 'Ewe-speaking tribe',

---

[2] L. Adam, *Het Eeenheidsstreven Der Ewe* (Leiden: Afrika-Instituut, 1952); J.S. Coleman, 'Togoland', *International Conciliation*, no. 509, 1956; J.C. Pauvert, 'L'évolution politique des Ewe', *Cahiers d'Etudes Africaines*, 2, 1960; I.E. Aligwekwe, 'The Ewe and Togoland problem: a case-study in the paradoxes and problems of political transition in West Africa', unpublished Ph.D thesis, Ohio State University, 1960; Claude Welch, *Dream of Unity: Pan-Africanism and Political Unification in West Africa* (Ithaca: Cornell University Press, 1966), chs 2–3; B.W. Hodder, 'The Ewe problem: a reassessment', in C.A. Fisher (ed.), *Essays in Political Geography* (London: Methuen, 1968); D.E.K. Amenumey, *The Ewe Unification Movement: A Political History* (Accra: Ghana Universities Press, 1989); John Kent, *The Internationalization of Colonialism* (Oxford: Clarendon Press, 1992), chs 9–10.

[3] Petition from President of Committee on Behalf of Togoland Natives via the Liverpool Chamber of Commerce, dated 12 December 1919, PRO CO 724/1.

they were really thinking of the peoples along the coastal stretch from Anlo proper to Lomé and its environs.[4] The northern Ewe, or 'Krepi', were still located at the margins of their cognitive map, and this remained the case until the 1940s when a more inclusive concept of 'Eweland' came into popular usage.

The early phases of political activity in partitioned Togoland are of interest primarily for the manner in which emergent ethnicities were subordinated to alternative political discourses. Although this book is primarily concerned with British Togoland, it is helpful to begin with a discussion of political developments in French territory for the simple reason that this is where the legitimacy of the boundary was first overtly questioned. As we have seen, the fact that the British administration relied upon customs duties rather than direct taxation shaped the character of its own interactions with border communities. Whereas official attempts to choke off the contraband trade constituted the dominant issue in British Togoland, an explicitly political battle was joined on the other side of the border.

From the start, popular misgivings about the partition were rooted in fears about the possible strictures that might accompany French rule. In 1919, petitioners recalled that German rule had been unpopular not just because of the arbitrary behaviour of its officials, but also on account of a plethora of taxes and licence fees that weighed heavily upon the population: these included head tax and road taxes, and licences covering general trading activity, the rubber trade, the sale of spirits, the possession of firearms and even the ownership of dogs. The petitioners also recalled that the British had won local favour by dispensing with these taxes in 1914. Their worst fears were realized in 1921 when the incoming French administration reintroduced many of the taxes. The most controversial were the poll tax, a tax on hawkers and market dues.[5] The latter was a source of particular grievance to the market women of Lomé who, on hearing of them, converged on the Court House to demand an audience with the Governor, Alfred Wöelffel.[6]

The Committee on Behalf of Togoland Natives sought to speak on behalf of the residents of the capital, but quickly found its position undercut by a new set of players who were typically younger and of a less elevated social background. The so-called 'band of irreconcilables' pointed to the failure of Olympio and his fellow patricians to sway the French, despite several meetings with the Governor.[7] They therefore advocated a tax boycott if the authorities insisted on introducing these measures against the will of the people. They also kept up a steady stream of petitions – which were forwarded to the British government and the League of Nations – that were designed to draw outside attention to their grievances.[8] Moreover, they did not

---

[4] Hence the fear '[T]hat the absorption of Togoland into France's Colonial Possessions will sever members of the Ewe-speaking tribe in Togoland from those in the south-eastern portion of the Gold Coast Colony and seriously interfere with their economic progress'. Petition to Viscount Milner via the Liverpool Chamber of Commerce, dated 16 September 1919, PRO CO 724/1.

[5] Other taxes that were the subject of complaints were those on strangers, cars, lorries and bicycles.

[6] J.T. Mensah to Pickering-Jones, Liverpool Chamber of Commerce (23 February 1921), PRO CO 724/2.

[7] This was how they were depicted by Captain Trotter in a letter to the Governor (24 August 1921), PRO CO 724/2.

[8] Among the recipients were David Lloyd George and W. Ormsby-Gore. The contents of one such petition were also relayed to, and published in, *West Africa*, 21 May 1921.

confine themselves to the taxation issue, but accused the French of recruiting forced labour for use within Togoland and theatres further afield.[9] Finally, a significant straw in the wind was their insistence that most Togolanders would prefer a reversion to German rule if the British could not be persuaded to take over the whole of Togoland themselves.[10]

The French authorities strongly suspected that not all British officials and merchants had reconciled themselves to the partition and that many at least tacitly supported the dissidents. This suspicion was backed up by a certain amount of circumstantial evidence. J.T. Mensah had previously been employed as the chief clerk to Major Jackson, while Martin Abibu worked as a storekeeper for the British trading firm of John Walkden in Lomé.[11] Abibu was also President of a Togo Union which had been formed in 1921, apparently with the active support of a Rev. Louis Ewart from Birmingham.[12] Moreover, some of the petitions were posted from across the border in Denu, whence they were routed through the Liverpool Chamber of Commerce. But whatever the sympathies of European merchants and individual officials, there is no evidence to suggest that the Gold Coast authorities were behind these protests. While they expressed some satisfaction at coming out top in the colonial popularity poll, they had no wish to complicate their relations with the French from whom they were presently trying to extract a customs agreement.

The French administration responded to the challenge to their authority with a judicious mixture of carrots and sticks. Mensah and Abibu were placed under police surveillance, and were allegedly threatened with deportation if they continued to incite opposition. At the same time, the government set out to build bridges with the 'respectable' sections of the population in Lomé and beyond. In 1922 the incoming Governor, Auguste Bonnecarrère, who quickly acquired a reputation as a liberal, withdrew some of the unpopular taxes and reduced others, most notably the hated poll tax.[13] Moreover, by contrast with the French West African colonies proper, women were exempted from payment of the latter tax.[14] A decision to allow sterling to continue circulating in Lomé also went some way towards alleviating the anxieties of the merchant community.[15] Finally, the Governor was astute enough to establish Councils of Notables in Lomé and the other main towns. Although these were purely advisory bodies, they performed a vitally important function as a two-way channel of communication between rulers and ruled. The Notables were initially nominated by

---

[9] The Gold Coast authorities found some evidence of the despatch of Kabré and Sokode military conscripts to other parts of French West Africa. Captain Trotter to the Governor (24 August 1921); and A.W.H. Wilkinson, Accra, to J.E.W. Flood, Colonial Office (7 September 1921), PRO CO 724/2.

[10] J.T. Mensah to Pickering-Jones (23 February 1921), PRO CO 724/2.

[11] Mensah and Abibu were apparently related as members of the Adjigo family in the Anecho area. C.D. Trotter to Governor (30 August 1921), PRO CO 724/2. Michael D. Callahan, *Mandates and Empire: The League of Nations and Africa, 1914–1931* (Brighton & Portland: Sussex Academic Press, 1999), p. 118.

[12] J.T. Beckley, Aflao, to Bettington, Gold Coast Police (27 August 1921), PRO CO 724/2.

[13] Bonnecarrère, who might be described as the Guggisberg of French Togoland, was Governor from 1922 to 1931. For a positive assessment of his tenure in office see Silivi K. D'Almeida and Seti Y. Gbedemah, *Le Gouverneur Bonnecarrère au Togo* (Lomé: Les Nouvelles Éditions Africaines, 1982).

[14] Silivi D'Almeida-Ékué, *La révolte des Loméennes 24–25 Janvier 1933* (Lomé: Les Nouvelles Éditions Africaines du Togo, 1992), p. 16.

[15] Welch, *Dream of Unity*, p. 58.

the Governor from among the ranks of the elite, but from 1925 the administration sought to widen the base of the councils, and thus enhance their legitimacy, by providing for election by ward and family heads.[16]

The Bonnecarrère reforms enjoyed some success in reconciling Togolanders to the fact of French rule, but this only lasted until the onset of the Great Depression in 1929. Faced with rapidly declining exports revenues, the new Governor, Robert de Guise, introduced a series of emergency measures. These included swingeing cuts in public spending, the reintroduction of some of the taxes that his predecessor had abolished – most notably the market tax – and the raising of others. Crucially, De Guise failed to consult the Councils of Notables before introducing these measures, perhaps anticipating the negative response that would greet them. This helped to weaken the public standing of the Notables, who were mocked as 'not able' in the street humour for which Lomé is famous.[17] Into the breach stepped an alternative leadership with closer links to the grassroots. The principal ringleaders were Kobina Garthey, a farmer-cum-clerk who originated from either Keta or Winneba, and Michel Johnson, an employee of John Holt in Lomé who hailed from Agoué in Dahomey.[18]

The malcontents rallied together under the label of the *Duawo* – roughly translated as 'the townspeople' – and convened a series of public meetings to debate the implications of the measures and the most appropriate means of combating them. The *Duawo* leaders claimed that they did not intend to replace the Notables, and indeed they professed a desire to work in tandem with them.[19] Ostensibly, their aim was simply to improve communications between the Notables and the people of Lomé. However, the unmistakable sub-text was that the Notables had hitherto failed to represent the populace effectively, and that there was a need to find alternative spokesmen who would be prepared to voice their opposition to French policy in a more forthright fashion. Indeed, their very choice of name implied a significant gap between Notables and 'people'. Significantly, when the arrest of Garthey and Johnson was followed by demonstrations in Lomé in January 1933, the home of Jonathan Savi de Tové was stoned and then torched. Savi de Tové, being one of the most prominent Notables, was perceived as being too closely aligned with the French administration. This action on the part of the crowd – supposedly 'composed of the lower class of natives, peasants from the outskirts of town, market women, young boys, with a collection of the usual thieves and bad characters' – speaks volumes

---

[16] D'Almeida-Ékué, *La révolte*, p. 17, n. 4. For more details on the Councils of Notables, see D'Almeida and Gbedemah, *Le Gouverneur Bonnecarrère*, pp. 44–65.

[17] The fact that this was a play on English is significant. See Comi Toulabor, 'Jeu de mots, jeu de vilains: lexique de la dérision politique au Togo', in J-F. Bayart, A. Mbembe and C. Toulabor (eds), *La politique par la bas en Afrique noire: contributions à une problématique de la démocratie* (Paris: Karthala, 1992); 'Political satire past and present in Togo', *Critique of Anthropology*, 14, 1, 1994; Also Yves Marguerat (ed.), *Dynamique urbaine: jeunesse et histoire au Togo* (Lomé: Les Presses de l'Université du Bénin, 1993).

[18] D'Almeida-Ékué, *La révolte*, p. 35. Garthey's Winneba connection is mentioned in 'Report on Disturbances in Lomé, 25th January 1933', PRO CO 96/710/6. He was possibly the same Garthey who had also been a signatory to one of the petitions of 1921, when he would have been 32 years old.

[19] Letter from Garthey to J.V. Cazeaux, Inspector of Colonies, Lomé (12 March 1933), reproduced in D'Almeida-Ékué, *La révolte.*, pp. 147–50.

about the gulf that had emerged between sections of the educated elite and the mass of the urban population.[20]

The continuities with the events of 1921 lie in the immediate issues at stake (principally taxation), the anti-French undertones, and the social composition of the leadership. The difference was that whereas Mensah and Abibu made no secret of their desire to reunify the two Togolands under the British flag, the *Duawo* were more inclined to frame the issues within the context of French Togoland. Given that the French were by now deeply entrenched, it made more sense to concentrate on reminding them of their responsibilities under the Mandate agreement. Hence the comparisons that were drawn were no longer so much with the Gold Coast as with Dahomey and other parts of the French empire, where taxation policies were allegedly more benign.[21] It is difficult to judge whether the *Duawo* had genuinely ceased to aspire towards reunification of the two Togolands under the British flag. It is more than likely that this was still their preferred option.

Overlapping chronologically with these challenges to French rule was the campaign mounted by the Bund der Deutsche Togolander. An organization by that name had been established with official patronage during the German era. Its corpse was then disinterred by French Togolanders resident in Accra in 1922. The Togo Bund came to prominence by virtue of a series of petitions that it despatched to the League of Nations between 1925 and 1933. The fact that it gathered strength at a time when the French had recaptured the political initiative in Lomé suggests that it was born out of something other than the immediate crisis over taxation.[22] The petitions rehearsed earlier complaints about French colonial rule, but they also struck a radically different tone in demanding reunification of the two Togolands under the German flag. A circular letter designed to rally the peoples of Togoland in 1925 stated the objectives as follows:

> We have the honour to inform you herewith that, two years ago, we constituted at Accra a League of German Togolanders, through which we claim, as native-born Togolanders, the right to watch over the welfare of the country and to rescue it from the misery to which it is exposed by the present French Administration. The Bund aims at establishing close liaison with Germany and has undertaken to represent Togoland at the League of Nations, and to defend her interests... Petitions have twice been addressed by us on behalf of the whole people of Togoland to the League of Nations at Geneva, demanding that Togoland be evacuated by the French and that the country be restored to the Germans.[23]

Surprisingly little is known about the Togo Bund, and this is reflected in its consignment to the margins of most historical writing.[24] At the time, the British and

---

[20] 'Report on Disturbances in Lomé', PRO CO 96/710/6.

[21] Letter from the *Duawo* of Lomé to Governor (18 December 1932), reproduced in D'Almeida-Ékué, *La révolte*, pp. 143–4.

[22] Andrew Crozier, *Appeasement and Germany's Last Bid For Colonies* (Houndmills: Macmillan, 1988), p. 71, creates a misleading impression that the Bund arose in response to the events of 1933.

[23] Circular letter signed by Agboka and Blicon, dated Accra, 19 December 1925, PRO CO 96/719/3.

[24] There is minimal documentation in the Ghanaian and Togolese archives, while most of the relevant Colonial Office records have been destroyed under statute. It is possible that the archives in Germany would shed further light on the Bund, but I have been unable to follow up this lead. The marginalization of the Bund is reflected in the fact that Amenumey, *Ewe Unification Movement*, devotes only half a page to its activities, while

French authorities were themselves unsure about the membership and activities of the organization. Admittedly, it was convenient for the authorities to frame the Bund in the most shadowy light because that made it possible to avoid engaging directly with its demands. Hence successive petitions to the League of Nations were disregarded on the grounds that the appended signatures were pseudonyms.[25] When the French representative to the Permanent Mandates Commission was asked to furnish more detailed information, he was only able to identify a handful of individuals in the leadership: namely, Johann Agboka, Akplamakpe Ousah (or Ansah), Johan Kany and Alfred Lawrence. The last two were apparently related to Garthey, and Kany had previously been employed by the German administration.[26] From another source, it would appear that Ousah/Ansah also went by the name of Johnson and came from the Anecho area.[27] In other material details, the statement of the French representative remained distinctly vague. The internal correspondence of both administrations suggests that they were genuinely unsure about what exactly they were dealing with. The French were, however, convinced that the Germans had propagated a network of spies across West Africa as part of a master plan to recapture their lost colonies.[28] The implication was that the Togo Bund was sustained with German money.

This possibility cannot be ruled out, but equally it should not be assumed that the Bund was merely an instrument of a rejuvenated German imperialism under the Nazis.[29] Apart from the named activists in Accra, there was also a genuine constituency on both sides of the Togoland border. According to Welch, the Bund had its most active network in the Kpalimé/Klouto area. To this should be added Akposso where Bund members were intimately involved in the land dispute with Buem. After their expulsion from French Togoland in 1939, many members apparently made their way back to Akposso and holed themselves up there for the duration of the war.[30] There is also some evidence of Bund activity in British Togoland. Although border peoples were content to exploit the chances to engage in smuggling, not everybody was in favour of the status quo. In 1935, one Zeman Aboh of Ve-Koloenu was reportedly reproducing a photograph of Hitler for general sale, which is indicative of a level of popular interest in things German.[31] Three years later, the same individual allegedly convened a meeting at Koloenu, at which delegates from Kpalimé were present. On this occasion an overtly political agenda was married to plans to

---

[24] (cont.) Welch, *Dream of Unity*, pp. 59–60, offers a single paragraph. The most recent study, by Callahan, *Mandates and Empire*, pp. 120, 150–2, is similarly thin. Its front cover does, however, carry a rare photograph of Bund members. For a parallel phenomenon in Cameroun, see Richard Joseph, 'The German question in French Cameroun, 1919-1939', *Comparative Studies in Society and History*, 17, 1, 1975.

[25] Two names which appeared on the petitions of 1926 were Alioys Gagée and Karl Dugamey which surnames were translated as 'in the balance' and 'in the big city'. These were rejected by the French representative as false signatures. Extract from minute of 25th session of PMC, 30 May–12 June 1934, PRO CO 96/719/3.

[26] Extract from minute of 25th session of PMC, 30 May–12 June 1934, PRO CO 96/719/3.

[27] An Akplamakpe Ansah surfaced in Accra in 1934 where he was recognized by the Ga Manche as a headman. GNAA ADM 39/1/295.

[28] On this aspect, see D'Almeida-Ékué, *La révolte*, pp. 127–33. The official record suggests that this was a real French concern. See correspondence in TNAL 8 APA/101.

[29] On the Nazis and the lost colonies, see Crozier, *Appeasement, passim*.

[30] Welch, *Dream of Unity*, p. 58.

[31] Lilley to M. Goujon, Misahöhe (21 April 1935), TNAL Klouto/70.

channel cocoa sales through the German representative of the Deutsche Togo Gesellschaft, rather than the established British and French firms.[32] Brown has also noted that support for the Bund was greater among the unamalgamated divisions where people looked to a German recall to effect a reversal of chieftaincy policy.[33] Significantly, the headchiefs of Anfoega and Gbi were both sympathizers, as was a future claimant to the Kpandu stool.[34] All of this is consistent with my own encounter with informants in Likpe in the mid-1980s who were able to recall the names of 'German scholars' who had been active members of the Bund. These appear to have been the literate products of mission schools and, as in the Klouto area, they may have been disproportionately Presbyterian.[35] These fragments of additional evidence are significant because they significantly qualify the image of the Togo Bund as purely an Accra affair.

Given the anti-German sentiments that abounded in 1914, it is perhaps surprising that anyone should look upon the prospect of their return with anything but foreboding – not least members of the older generation for whom heavy taxation, forced labour and arbitrary punishments were recent memories. The apparent amnesia can, however, be accounted for in the light of several factors. The first is that the 'scholars' were themselves casualties of the end of German rule, because the British and the French dispensed with the services of clerks who lacked the requisite fluency in the new languages of administration and replaced them with recruits from the Gold Coast and Dahomey, respectively. Hence in April 1922, a group calling itself the Ho Native Scholars petitioned the British authorities to draw attention to the plight of its members:

> From the beginning of the war up till now most of us who are educated are left without finding any more position. This is so because they did not mastered [sic] the English language. It is so that in this new Colony the people had been taught in German language, and by means of the language they found positions and worked for their livings... Now as they went away owing to the war and its consequences and the English came, most of the clerks they brought with them were those who knew the English language already so that even the lowest position is not to be found in their departments. Consequently those who know German language are left without finding any employment.[36]

The predictable riposte was that there was nothing that the government could do for them, but that if the German clerks worked hard to overcome their disability some work would probably come their way. It is likely that most never made the transition,

---

[32] The context was, of course, one in which cocoa farmers were engaged in a hold-up. Unsigned letter from Kpalimé to Commandant de Cercle du Centre, Atakpamé (17 January 1938), TNAL Klouto/70. A DTG employee, Robert Armattoe, was also reputed to be the leading pro-German activist in Kpalimé.

[33] David Brown, 'Politics in the Kpandu area of Ghana, 1925 to 1969: a study of the influence of central government and national politics upon local factional competition', unpublished Ph.D thesis, Birmingham University, 1977, p. 61.

[34] Togbui Gabusu IV was the Gbi headchief from 1934 to 1958. Togbui Jonuta Dumoga, the father of Kofi Dumoga, was the Anfoega headchief between 1915 and 1919 and again between 1931 and 1934. Dionysius Nyavor was apparently the leading Bund supporter in Kpandu. He fled to Akposso in 1940. *Ibid.*, n. 12, p. 411.

[35] Commandant de Cercle de Klouto to Commissaire de la République (27 August 1928), TNAL Klouto/70.

[36] Ho Native Scholars to Major Jackson (April 1922), GNAA ADM 39/1/216. As has already been said, English enjoyed some currency in German Togo. The issue was one of proficiency.

and many of those who did would have lost their jobs during the retrenchment that ensued on both sides of the border after 1929. As a result, there was a generation of older 'scholars' who firmly believed that the return of the Germans might facilitate a recovery of their employment and social status. Nor was this attitude necessarily confined to the ranks of the unemployed. Lilley was taken aback to discover that his own cook remained in secret correspondence with his German predecessor, Dr Grüner, as late as the 1930s.[37]

Secondly, in the context of the Depression, the German regnum began to be remembered as a period of comparative prosperity. Although older people still recalled the forced labour and taxation, there was a willingness to credit the Germans for having made an effort to promote economic activity in the territory, most notably through road and railway construction. The critique of French rule in the early 1930s was that it imposed many of the same burdens, but failed to deliver any of the benefits. The British were less interventionist in their own section of Togoland, but the 'German scholars' were equally inclined to chide them for their lack of ambition. And, thirdly, one should not underestimate the extent to which German rule had created a framework within which people had come to think of themselves as Togolanders. It is striking that the Togo Bund made almost no reference to ethnicity, and when it referred to 'rights of self-determination' these were understood to revolve around a putative Togoland nation. Those who had been sent to mission schools genuinely did discover Togoland as an imagined community in terms very close to those outlined by Benedict Anderson.[38]

As I have already pointed out, the Togo Bund came to prominence through successive petitions to the League of Nations. But there is also some evidence that it sought to disseminate its message through the pages of the Gold Coast press. In the opinion of one French official, *The Gold Coast Spectator* was nothing less than an organ of the Togo Bund.[39] *The Spectator* did indeed pursue a consistently critical line against the French administration. But while the newspaper shared the wider concerns of the Bund, it also asserted that the latter 'was being directed from Berlin' and insisted that British Togolanders had no desire to be attached to a reunified Togoland under German rule:

> What of British Togo? It is in the interest of the Bund not to make enemies for themselves. None of the members of the Bund would complain that he has been unnecessarily taxed or he has been put on forced labour for days since he took refuge in the Gold Coast. If such is the case, as the Bund itself would admit, do the members by their plea for the Germans want the British to evacuate their sphere of influence in Togoland? Do the inhabitants in the British zone want back

---

[37] Lilley claimed to have seen letters and postcards from Grüner. He observed that the Germans had tended to recruit servants from Ve, which might explain why it remained a centre of pro-German sympathies. Lilley to M. Goujon, Misahöhe (21 April 1935), TNAL Klouto/70.

[38] I refer here to Anderson's motif of functionaries embarking on a 'bureaucratic pilgrimage', which takes them along certain pathways, normally leading to the colonial capital, and in the course of which they became conscious of commonalities shared with their travelling companions. Interestingly, Anderson uses Accra as one of his examples. Benedict Anderson, *Imagined Communities: Reflections on the Origin and Spread of Nationalism* (London & New York: Verso, 1983), p. 105.

[39] R. Mary, Commandant de Cercle, Misahöhe, to Commissaire de la République, 25 June 1934, TNAL Klouto 2 APA/2.

the Germans? Would it not be ungratefulness on their part to the power that now affords them an asylum? I hold no brief for the British. They have their faults. But I know them. I know the Germans too. Watch Hitler. Watch Hitlerism.[40]

To complete the picture, the same article revived the claim of Peki to its lost territories – the significance lying in the fact that Peki was an integral part of the Gold Coast. The logical implication of *The Spectator*'s argument was that if the two Togolands were to be reunited, this would have to come about through fusion with the Gold Coast as it stood. None of this is surprising if one takes cognizance of the fact that the newspaper was owned by Alfred Ocansey, who was not a Togolander himself, but hailed from Ada. Interestingly, the one newspaper that did pursue a line that was somewhat closer to that of the Togo Bund was the *African Morning Post*. It kept up the anti-French invective, but also argued that if the Germans were to return to West Africa 'all the tribes who speak Ewe' should be placed under their control rather than being divided once more.[41] Whereas *The Spectator* was making the case for a greater Gold Coast, the *African Morning Post* appeared to be arguing for a possible enlargement of Togoland as it had originally been constituted.

These competing currents were regarded with concern by the French authorities who stood to be the principal losers in any territorial shake-up. Their response was to crack down hard on expressions of dissent. After making some concessions to the crowd in January 1933, the opposition was suppressed with considerable violence and loss of life. Many of the protagonists were subsequently put on trial and handed down stiff prison sentences.[42] The repression led to the flight of refugees into British territory, including many of the women traders who had been at the centre of much of the action. And yet the Togo Bund must have retained some local presence because there remained a rump of members and 'sympathizers' who needed to be physically ejected in 1939. Needless to say, the flight and expulsion of dissident elements merely displaced the problem to British territory, where they sought to keep up the campaign against French rule. This could not be avoided, but the French authorities hoped to at least isolate the exiles from public opinion in Togoland. Hence the most hostile Gold Coast newspapers, including the *African Morning Post*, were banned from circulation in French territory. There was also a conscious effort to cultivate a friendly press at home. The key to this strategy was Jonathan Savi de Tové, who was regarded as eminently pliable. During German times, he had hitched his wagon to the colonial power and at one point had even worked in the German embassy in Madrid.[43] Thereafter, he had switched his loyalties to the French, serving on the Council of Notables and pursuing a decidedly pro-French line in his newspaper *Le Guide de Togo*. The authorities particularly valued his forthright stance in opposition to the campaigns of the Gold Coast press and the Togo Bund. In their internal correspondence, French officials discussed ways of feeding government propaganda to Savi de Tové. In 1936, he was actually appointed to head the government informa-

---

[40] 'The French in Togoland, the German Propagandists', *Gold Coast Spectator*, 29 December 1934, a copy of which is in PRO CO 96/719/3.

[41] Article in *African Morning Post*, 11 July 1935, a copy of which is in TNAL 8 APA/171.

[42] D'Almeida-Ékué, *La révolte*, pp. 99–107.

[43] Samuel Decalo (ed.), *Historical Dictionary of Togo*, 2nd edn (Metuchen & London: Scarecrow Press, 1987), p. 185.

tion service. Although this undermined any pretensions towards impartiality, the French were by this time looking for open manifestations of support to keep the twin threats of German imperialism and Gold Coast irredentism at bay.

At the same time, the French administration set about rebuilding bridges with valued sections of the African population. In the wake of 1933 riots, the government abrogated the most controversial measures, most notably the market tax. It also proposed to balance the books by effectively fusing the administration with that of Dahomey. Ostensibly, this was about alleviating the tax burden, but the French authorities were also seeking to shore up their position by binding Togoland to the neighbouring colony. Not surprisingly, this was construed by the Togo Bund as a blatant attempt to obstruct the future reunification of the two Togolands.[44] As in Cameroun, the government also endeavoured to neutralize the pro-German lobby by sponsoring its own support groups. In 1936, a Cercle des Amitiés was founded as part of a conscious effort to bring Europeans and members of the African elite into closer contact. According to D'Almeida-Ékué, intellectuals like Sylvanus Olympio were drawn to the circle out of a sense of apprehension at the possible installation of a Nazi administration in Lomé.[45] This initiative was taken further in 1941 when the Comité de l'Unité Togolaise (CUT) was formed with government backing in an effort to spread these support networks to the rest of the territory. Predictably, Savi de Tové was installed as the secretary-general of this enlarged association.

These developments brought the first cycle of Togoland politics to a close. With an eye on the analysis to follow, it is worth underlining three features in particular. The first is that while the epicentre of political activity lay in French Togoland, and more particularly in Lomé, it spilled over into the Gold Coast and British Togoland. Secondly, these political movements were not simply directed by members of the elite, but involved the lower echelons of society who on several occasions took matters into their own hands. Finally, it is striking that organizations like the *Duawo* and the Togo Bund scarcely ever resorted to the language of ethnicity, concentrating instead upon the rights of 'Togolanders'. This casts further doubt on the notion that there was a linear progression from the protests of 1919–21 to the Ewe unification movement of the post-1945 period.

Challenging boundaries:
the rise of the Ewe unification movement

The outbreak of a fresh bout of global conflict in 1939 served to create a political hiatus on both sides of the border. Following the expulsion of Togo Bund members from French territory, the British authorities resorted to the internment of individuals who were thought to harbour pro-German sympathies.[46] By the time the debate

---

[44] D'Almeida-Ékué, *La révolte*, p. 120.

[45] *Ibid.*, p. 135.

[46] Many were deported back to French Togoland after the war. In a petition to the United Nations, Johann Agboka later demanded compensation. See Trusteeship Council, *Official Records*, Seventh Session, Annex Volume II, p. 57.

was rejoined at the end of the war, the case for a German return had effectively been discredited. Although the underlying plan for a reunification of the two halves of Togoland was later reactivated, the initiative now lay with the advocates of Ewe unification. I will begin this account by addressing the sources of Ewe ethnic expression before considering in greater detail the organizational forms it assumed.

The concept of Ewe unity

This shift in the balance of forces in favour of Ewe unificationism could be said to reflect two loosely connected developments. The first was the emergence of social networks arising out of the process of migration. The latter crossed borders in that the economic hardships of the 1930s, and the requisitioning and forced labour of the war years, resulted in a steady outflow of French Togolanders towards the Gold Coast. The mingling of these migrants in their new places of residence in turn spawned associations based on the concept of a common ethnicity or place of origin. It is important, however, not to oversimplify the processes at work. To imply that the migrants became aware of a latent Ewe identity in their new settings is arguably to put the cart before the horse. In fact, it was the experience of migration itself that helped to forge a sense of common identity where the preconditions had hitherto been absent. Because ethnic identities did not exist *out there*, their boundaries had to be negotiated and hence they were frequently contested. For example, Mina migrants in Accra strongly objected to being lumped with the Ewe, insisting that they were a distinct people who should be granted their own 'headman'. As it happened, their preferred candidate in 1934 was none other than Akplamakpe Ansah of the Togo Bund. Their petition queried the boundaries of Ewe ethnicity explicitly, stating that:

> We are Natives of that part of Togoland known as the French Togo and we are all called and styled 'Ganyi' by all the people who are described by the Gold Coast Government as the Ewe speaking people. We are entirely a race or tribe different and distinct from the rest of the Ewe speaking people. We have difference [sic] customs and ceremonies... Our names are distinct from the Ewe people and thus you see, we do not form part of either the Anlos and the Pekis [sic] who are known as the Ewe speaking peoples.[47]

The petitioners went on to argue that it made no more sense to group them with the Ewes than it would have done to lump the Fante and the Akyem on the basis that they both spoke Twi – a fair point, perhaps.

In 1947, the representatives of Britain and France at the United Nations Trusteeship Council tabled a joint memorandum, which posited that the stirrings of Ewe nationalism might be rooted in the voluntary associations that had begun to proliferate in the Gold Coast some years before. Among those they listed were some that were evidently organized around place of origin and that were strictly speaking subethnic – like the Anyako Union, the Togoville Union and the Agome Palime and District Union. Others were ethnic in character, but were ambiguous in respect of the Ewe category – most notably the Glidzi Union and the Anecho Union. Finally, there were associations that were constructed around a notional Ewe constituency – such

---

[47] Petition of French Togoland community, Accra, to Acting Governor G.A.S. Northcote, dated 16 October 1934, GNAA ADM 39/1/295.

as the Ewe Benevolent Association, the Ewe Speaking Catholic Union, the Ewe Speaking Society and the Ewe Charity Union.[48] The activities of most of these unions are obscure, but in one case it is possible to link up the local activities of an association with the pan-Ewe movement. As we have already seen, the Buem Strangers' Union mobilized its mostly Ewe following in the fractious environment of the cocoa frontier. The head of that union, Amega Dogbe, was a frequent petitioner in defence of the rights of the stranger population. In 1936, he wrote a letter to *West Africa* magazine that chastised the British and French representatives to the Permanent Mandates Commission for claiming that the Togoland border had imposed no hardship upon the inhabitants. In what was to become a familiar line of argument after the war, Dogbe asserted that the Ewe had suffered from being 'subjected to two different sovereignties with entirely different systems of administration and a Customs barrier'.[49] He elaborated on what made the Ewe unique, stressing their propensity to travel in pursuit of self-betterment:

> The inhabitants [of Togoland] have emigrated in large numbers, and particularly the Ewe people, one of the most sympathetic, industrious and intelligent tribes of the whole of West Africa, are to be found to-day in almost every place of importance from Dakar to the Congo, where they were compelled to emigrate in order to earn their living.

It comes as no surprise to discover that Amega Dogbe was a signatory to the Ewe Convention of 1946.

The ethnic claims advanced by Dogbe contrast in interesting ways with the statements of the Ewe chiefs in British Togoland a few years later. Although some did express an interest in unification during the war, they were apparently thinking more in terms of a reunification of partitioned Togoland.[50] Hence a petition from all the Paramount Chiefs to the Secretary of State in September 1943 expressed the desire that 'the whole country namely "Togoland" should be under one government'.[51] Similarly, a petition from the Asogli State to Governor Alan Burns in 1944 stated that 'we value the restoration of Ewe unity', but qualified this as 'unity with our families in French Togoland'.[52] Although unification of the two Togolands and of the Ewe people were compatible objectives, they were evidently not the same thing. To the extent that the former was prioritized, the latter was rendered more problematic.

The second development was the emergence of a lobby within the Gold Coast that

---

[48] 'Memorandum of the Governments of the United Kingdom and France on the Petition of the All-Ewe Conference to the United Nations', Trusteeship Council, *Official Records*, Second Session, First Part, 20 November 1947–16 December 1947, p. 28.

[49] This is a reasonable inference since a copy of the letter to *West Africa* on 10 April 1936, signed 'Amega', is to be found in the file GNAA ADM 39/1/570 relating to the Buem Strangers' Union. Amega Dogbe was active in the Ewe unification movement after the war.

[50] For that reason, it is questionable whether these petitions should be assimilated to a history of demands for Ewe unification, as Amenumey does, *Ewe Unification Movement*, pp. 37–8.

[51] Quoted in Trusteeship Council, *Official Records*. Verbatim Records, Annex Volume II, 1947, 2nd Series, Appendix A, p. 185. Amenumey, *Ewe Unification Movement*, p. 37 describes this as a petition of the Ewe Paramount Chiefs, but the Trusteeship Council records refer to a petition from the British Togoland Paramount Chiefs. The distinction is an important one.

[52] Trusteeship Council, *Official Records*, Annex Volume II, Appendix A, p. 186. Again Amenumey, *Ewe Unification Movement*, p. 38, puts a somewhat different gloss on the petition.

set out to articulate the case for Ewe unification. The leadership was distinctly elitist in terms of its background, organizational tactics and mode of political expression. It is perhaps fitting to note that the first initiatives were taken in January 1945 at a cocktail party hosted by Daniel Chapman, an Oxford graduate and at that point a teacher at Achimota College in Accra.[53] The meeting was attended by a number of prominent Anlo educationalists and businessmen, including his brother, C.H. Chapman, Philip Gbeho (who also taught at Achimota) and S.S. Newlands, who worked with the United Africa Company (UAC). It was decided at this point that Daniel Chapman should publish a broadsheet to draw attention to the Ewe predicament. The first edition of the *Ewe News-Letter* appeared in May of that year. It continued as a monthly publication and claimed a circulation of a thousand copies per issue by 1947.[54]

The format of the *Ewe News-Letter* reflected a shrewd calculation that unification of the Ewe people would only be achieved by winning over the British authorities – who always received their complimentary copy – as well as international opinion. The immediate obstacle was posed by France. Whereas the British government indicated early on that it was prepared to submit its Mandates to international trusteeship, the French intimated that their preference was for outright annexation. African opinion had been ignored in 1919, but Chapman and his colleagues were heartened by Article 76 of the new United Nations Charter, which stipulated that the goal of the trusteeship system was 'development towards self-government or independence as may be appropriate to the particular circumstances of each territory and its peoples *and the freely expressed wishes of the peoples concerned*' [my emphasis].[55] The immediate goal was to ensure that French Togoland was brought within the purview of the trusteeship system. Once that battle was won, the next step was to demonstrate that the Ewe people's freely expressed wish was, in fact, for unification under a single administration – preferably British.

While framing the Ewe case for an external audience, the *Ewe News-Letter* endeavoured to reach out to the Ewe-speaking population itself in order to persuade it of the need to rally in defence of its interests. The existence of a cross-cutting network of Ewe associations strengthened the belief that a constituency already existed in an incipient form. There was a palpable tension here in that the *Ewe News-Letter* was written in rather bookish English – what Welch calls 'a gentle, school masterly tone'[56] – which threatened to exclude the mass of the population. Daniel Chapman and Ephraim Amu, who took over the task of editing towards the end of 1946, sought to resolve this difficulty by publishing some of the editions in the Ewe language.[57] But this did not amount to much more than a token gesture. Significantly, the international boundary was negotiated not through the use of Ewe, but by

---

[53] Welch, *Dream of Unity*, pp. 65–6.

[54] Copies of this publication may be found at GNAA ADM 39/1/339. The circulation claims were made in the *Ewe News-Letter*, no. 25, May 1947.

[55] *Ewe News-Letter*, no. 8, December 1945. This would seem to have weighed more heavily than Article 73, which is highlighted in Welch, *Dreams of Unity*, p. 67.

[56] Welch, *Dream of Unity*, p. 66.

[57] Chapman left the Gold Coast in 1946 to take up a position with the United Nations, leaving Amu to edit the newsletter. The occasional Ewe edition was called *Nukexletivi*.

seeking a Francophone counterpart. Hence, Chapman and his colleagues set out to co-ordinate their campaign with *Le Guide du Togo*, the newspaper that was owned by Savi de Tové. In Partha Chatterjee's terms, therefore, the outward, political form of nationalism drowned out the inner voice of Ewe cultural nationalism.[58] The reason was perhaps that Ewe nationalism did not aim to throw off the external yoke entirely, but merely to reposition it.[59]

A close analysis of Ewe nationalist discourse is rewarding because it reveals all the inconsistencies that are characteristic of the genre. It is also essential for our purposes because so much subsequent historical interpretation has been coloured by the theses advanced in the pages of the *Ewe News-Letter*. One recurring theme was the underlying unity of the Ewe-speaking people despite their apparent fragmentation into many separate *dukɔwo*. The very first issue set out to trace the outlines of a common Ewe history not just to Ketu and Notsie, but even back to Old Oyo.[60] A subsequent issue proclaimed that 'in Notsie we were a Nation, the Ewe Nation, members of one State', but went on to explain that this unity had subsequently been broken as a result of the dispersal from that town and the divisive influences of the slave trade.[61] Within this discursive framework, the nineteenth-century antagonisms between the Anlo and the Krepi were conveniently displaced to the era of European contact – and hence could be depicted as aberrant. As I have already indicated, the Notsie myth had been disseminated throughout Eweland (and beyond) by the mission schools, and hence it provided a convenient resource for the *Ewe News-Letter*.[62] But it should still be regarded as an ethnic charter that, by its very nature, sought to blot out other histories – not least those that emphasized the long-standing antagonisms between the Anlos and the Krepis.

A second theme was that the partition of the region between Britain and Germany, and then between Britain and France, had imposed an intolerable burden on the Ewe people who were otherwise closely connected with one another:

> We have repeatedly stated in these news-letters that the people of Eweland are one and indivisible, and that the partition of Eweland between two different colonizing powers is a serious social crime which should be rectified without delay. It is most grievous to think of a people who are

---

[58] Partha Chatterjee, *The Nation and its Fragments: Colonial and Postcolonial Histories* (Princeton: Princeton University Press, 1993). Interestingly, Ephraim Amu was a staunch cultural nationalist in other contexts. He was forced to leave Akropong Presbyterian Training College in 1933 because of his insistence on wearing African cloth and his use of drumming and African languages in church. See Fred Agyemang, *Amu The African: A Study in Vision and Courage* (Accra: Asempa, 1988), pp. 87–91. Later on, he took the French to task for not promoting the use of Ewe in their schools.

[59] In the words of Sylvanus Olympio in 1947: 'We do not ask for self-government at the moment because we are incapable of governing ourselves just now'. Discussion of 8 December, Trusteeship Council, *Official Records*, Second Session, First Part, 20 November 1947– 16 December 1947, p. 336.

[60] *Ewe News-Letter*, no. 1, 21 May 1945.

[61] *Ewe News-Letter*, no. 14, June 1946. This bears more than a passing resemblance to Samuel Johnson's attempts to simultaneously assert the timelessness of Yoruba identity while accounting for a history of discord between its various kingdoms. See *The History of the Yorubas* (Lagos: C.M.S. Bookshop, 1921), and, for an analysis, Robin Law, 'Constructing "a real national history": a comparison of Edward Blyden and Samuel Johnson', in P.F. de Moraes Farias and Karin Barber (eds), *Self-Assertion and Brokerage: Early Cultural Nationalism in West Africa* (University of Birmingham: Centre of West African Studies 1990), pp. 88–99.

[62] Again, the parallel with the Yoruba myth of the sons of Oduduwa is instructive.

united by close ties of kinship, language and culture being divided between two totally different colonizing powers whose colonial policies are diametrically opposed.[63]

The reasoning here was in many respects self-contradictory. The complaint that the implementation of different educational and administrative policies on either side of the line had driven a wedge between sections of the Ewe people was difficult to reconcile with the assertion that they still thought and acted as one 'nation'. Hence Ewe nationalists sought to assert simultaneously that colonialism had hardly made any dent on the cultural landscape and, conversely, that it had been acutely divisive. As part of the same stock of arguments, the *Ewe News-Letter* also asserted that these boundaries had functioned as a barrier to normal social intercourse. The reality, as argued in an earlier chapter, was that people and goods had flowed relatively freely across both sets of borders.

This point was tacitly conceded in a third recurrent theme, which invoked the increased wartime hardships as a turning point in Ewe self-realization. Both Welch and Amenumey have followed Chapman in attributing crucial significance to wartime exigencies, but these claims deserve to be examined more critically.[64] On the French side of the border, the resort to forced labour and requisitioning were undoubtedly resented by a population that had actively resisted earlier impositions. But the assertion that the closure of the border by the Vichyite authorities between 1939 and 1943 effectively severed contacts between communities is questionable. It is reasonable to suppose that annoying obstacles were placed in the way of parties of people who wanted to cross over en masse, for example, to attend funeral ceremonies. But it is difficult to believe that the French authorities could have prevented population movement beyond the immediate environs of their customs posts. Indeed, the flight of population into British territory, which was alluded to in the *Ewe News-Letter* and is acknowledged by Welch, would seem to demonstrate that the French were powerless to regulate such flows.

Welch places further importance upon the interruption to normal commercial interaction, writing that:

> To reduce the possibilities of subversion, French authorities sealed the border with British Togoland and the Gold Coast; no persons or products were permitted to cross. The thriving commercial network of 'Eweland' was sundered. As a result, residents of French Togoland could not obtain many commodities, notably salt, which had been imported from Keta.[65]

However, the shortages of foodstuffs appear to have been the direct result of French requisitioning rather than the effects of border closure. Indeed, the introduction of the former seems to have ameliorated implementation of the latter. Hence the French Governor, Lucien Montagné, reportedly turned a blind eye to cross-border trade, knowing full well that his territory needed supplies from the other side.[66] In fact, British intelligence reports in 1941 indicated that the French authorities were actively encouraging the smuggling of foodstuffs from their territory.[67] The leakage

---

[63] *Ewe News-Letter*, no. 22, February 1947.
[64] Welch, *Dream of Unity*, p. 65; Amenumey, *Ewe Unification Movement*, p. 36.
[65] Welch, *Dream of Unity*, p. 65.
[66] Yves Marguerat, 'La seconde guerre mondiale au Togo' in Marguerat, *Dynamique urbaine*, p. 214.
[67] CSA to CEP (20 November 1941), GNAA ADM 39/1/312.

of agricultural produce into French Togoland and the Gold Coast alike seems to have led to a serious food shortage across British Togoland, which is recalled as having been even worse than in 1983.[68] Not for the last time in the history of this border, the public declaration of closure was belied by the reality of vigorous frontier exchange.

There is no reason to dispute that Chapman and his associates empathized with the plight of the Ewe population of French Togoland. The arrival of substantial numbers of refugees from French territory must surely have drawn attention to their hardships. Moreover, the fact that the Gold Coast press had cultivated an interest in French Togoland during the 1930s ensured that its affairs received some coverage. But as real as the empathy might have been, it needs to be distinguished from the self-conscious arguments that began to be advanced in the pages of the *Ewe News-Letter*. The latter traced some well-worn footsteps in singling out French misrule as an integral dimension of the problem. But when it deviated from this path in order to advance the case for Ewe unification, it needed to come up with arguments of an altogether different order. As seductive as the appeal to an ethnic essence might be, it is incumbent upon the historian to bear in mind that it constituted a project and not a description of the world as it actually existed.

The All-Ewe Conference and the mobilization of Ewe opinion

Our next task is to consider the means by which Ewe nationalist discourse left the cocktail party, as it were, and solicited a wider audience. Daniel Chapman and his colleagues never doubted that they had the moral authority to speak on behalf of the mass of the population.[69] Yet because they had to pass the credibility test at the bar of the United Nations, they also had to be seen to be speaking in tandem with the people. This imperative, in turn, required that they develop visible organizational structures. Not surprisingly, they turned to the network of voluntary associations that already existed on the ground.

The initial attempts at political outreach were decidedly limited in scope. Hence the first resolution in December 1945, was signed by a mere 26 concerned Ewe citizens. Most of the signatories were Anlos of relatively high social status, although J.W.K. Dumoga from Anfoega was to be found among their number.[70] The resolution, which was forwarded to the Secretary of State for the Colonies, set the tone for later despatches in calling for the whole of Eweland to be turned into a single Trust Territory under British administration. Shortly afterwards, an Ewe Unionist Association was formed in Accra, which set out about trying to unite the existing Ewe associations, and to spread the political networks into British Togoland and French territory. The Ewe Convention of 1946, which was its principal achievement,

---

[68] According to one informant, the source of the problem went back to the 1937/38 cocoa hold-ups when farmers had been forced to sell rice instead. When drought followed, farmers found themselves without adequate food supplies. Interview with Arnold Gidiga, Likpe-Abrani, 29 May 1986.

[69] In that sense, the Ewe unification movement was really no different from those elitist political organizations, such as the ARPS and the NCBWA, that held sway in the Gold Coast before the war. Significantly, the efforts of the NCBWA, and Casely Hayford in particular, on behalf of the Ewe cause were recalled with admiration in the *Ewe News-Letter*, no. 14, June 1946. The best account of the ARPS and the NCBWA remains David Kimble, *A Political History of Ghana, 1850–1928* (Oxford: Oxford University Press, 1963), chs 9–10.

[70] 'A resolution on Eweland', reproduced in the *Ewe News-Letter*, no. 9, January 1946.

reiterated the demand for 'unification of Eweland under a single Administering Power', on this occasion leaving open the question of who that might be.[71] Given that the signatures of Daniel Chapman, S.T. Agbeko and G.K. Amegbe appeared both on the 1945 resolution and on the subsequent Ewe Convention, it would seem reasonable to conclude that the second initiative was really an outgrowth of the first. What was different was that there was a larger pool of signatories to the second document, encompassing 22 chiefs and Notables from French Togoland, eight chiefs from British Togoland, and 15 chiefs and six members of the Ewe Unionist Association from the Gold Coast. These signatures nevertheless betrayed the limited social base of the Ewe movement – that is, as an alliance between the educated elites of Lomé and the south-eastern Gold Coast, and the chiefs of all three territories.

With respect to British Togoland, the organizers recognized the importance of securing the signatures of the Paramount Chiefs of the amalgamated states and as many of the unamalgamated divisions as possible. Hence the Paramount Chiefs of the three mostly Ewe-speaking states – namely, Akpini, Asogli and Awatime – were signatories, although the Omanhene of Buem was a noteworthy omission. Again, the convention also included the signatures of the headchiefs of Gbi, Ve, Nkonya and Anfoega who, by virtue of their protracted opposition to the amalgamation policy, were by now old hands at the art of petitioning. It is doubtful, though, whether all the chiefs fully appreciated what was at stake. The Nkonya and Avatime chiefs were not themselves Ewe-speaking, and the former had a history of asserting a separate Guan identity. As regards the intellectual elites, there were already close links across the southern section of the border. The leading pro-unificationist organization to emanate from within French Togoland was the CUT, which was reinvented in 1946. Its leading lights were members of the Afro-Brazilian elite, such as Augustino De Souza, Sylvanus Olympio and Jonathan Savi de Tové. The latter had a history of close dealings with the French, but many also had family and business connections across the border. A classic example is Sylvanus Olympio, who attended the London School of Economics in the 1920s, returned to work for the UAC, and subsequently made a point of sending his own children to school in the Gold Coast.[72] The striking feature of British Togoland, on the other hand, is that it did not have a true educated elite beyond a narrow cadre of school teachers. As we shall see in due course, this imbalance was to prove the undoing of the Ewe unification movement.

On the back of these initiatives, further steps were taken towards creating an umbrella organization for all three territories. A diverse collection of individuals and associations, including the CUT, gathered in Accra in June 1946 and established the All-Ewe Conference (AEC). The AEC, which was to serve as the principal vehicle over the next few years, boasted an organizational structure of a complexity much beloved by the coastal elites. It comprised an Ewe Central Committee, an Ewe Working Committee (an executive of three members) and an Ewe Central Fund. The latter lay at the heart of an ambitious plan for raising financial contributions across Eweland – initially set at 4s. per man and 2s. per woman – that were to be used to

---

[71] Amenumey, *Ewe Unification Movement*, pp. 54–6.

[72] Olympio also attended the University of Vienna. He later rose to become the UAC General Manager for French Togoland. Welch, *Dream of Unity*, pp. 46–7.

cover the costs of international travel and campaigning.[73] Whereas the first four sessions of the AEC were held in Accra, the next meeting was deliberately staged at Tsito in August 1947, as part of the outreach programme. On this occasion, the *Ewe News-Letter* boasted that 'as many as sixty Chiefs were able to attend the conference and in full state too'.[74] And the following year, the unificationist roadshow travelled to Kpalimé, in line with the desire to make inroads into French territory beyond the confines of Lomé. On this occasion, the meeting apparently attracted 8,000 participants.[75]

Having established a political presence in each of the three territories, the AEC concentrated most of its energies on securing a favourable audience at the United Nations. On the surface of things, the AEC charm offensive was extremely success-ful, but at a deeper level the internal contradictions always lay on the verge of being exposed. Whereas the Permanent Mandates Commission had functioned as a club for the mandatory powers, the Trusteeship Council included representatives from countries without an obvious vested interest, which enabled it to take its supervisory function more seriously. When the AEC sent a series of petitions to the Trusteeship Council in 1947, these were given a considered airing, and the British and French authorities were forced to respond to the demands contained within them. Placed on the defensive, they issued a Joint Memorandum, which appeared to make substantial concessions to the petitioners. To start with, this document acknowl-edged that:

> There can be no doubt of the existence of an Ewe tribe, which possesses marked characteristics clearly distinguishing it from neighbouring peoples and which is becoming increasingly aware of its own identity.[76]

This was a substantial concession, in view of the fact that Lilley had previously insisted that there was no such thing as an Ewe tribe.[77] Even more strikingly, the Memorandum did not seek to undermine the credibility of the AEC, remarking instead that:

> ... there is good reason to believe that the objects and views which the Conference have expressed, both in the telegram and the convention to which it refers, and in the last petition, are those of the mass of the people (whether educated or not) and the latter would almost certainly endorse the action taken by the Conference in setting up its Working Committee.

But the apparent tractability on the part of the administering authorities was a tac-tical gambit, and contained very great dangers for the AEC. The Joint Memorandum argued that there was little mileage in creating a separate state for the Ewe people. This was not really contentious given that the AEC itself believed that such a state

---

[73] *Ewe News-Letter*, no. 20, December 1946.

[74] *Ewe News-Letter*, no. 28, August 1947.

[75] This estimate was made by Governor Creasy in a letter to the Secretary of State for the Colonies (26 June 1948), PRO CO96/809/31614.

[76] 'Memorandum of the Government of the United Kingdom and France on the Petition of the All-Ewe Conference', p. 27.

[77] This was the essence of the statement by Lilley before the 35th session of the Permanent Mandates Commis-sion in 1938.

would not be viable. The logical implication was that the Ewe problem would have to be resolved as part of a wider settlement. The memorandum insisted that a reunification of the two Togolands was not a solution either because the former German colony was 'in no sense a national entity' and that such a course of action would mean dividing groups like the Dagomba who had actually been reunited by the Milner–Simon agreement. Furthermore, the memorandum reminded the Trusteeship Council that the Ewes of the Gold Coast could not be included in a reunified Togoland because they lay beyond the remit of the trusteeship system.

Having disposed of the arguments in favour of a fresh territorial carve-up, the memorandum then turned to the practical difficulties arising from the existence of the border. The administering authorities professed to take the AEC complaints seriously, and responded with practical measures aimed at 'co-ordinating their activities in the social, economic, political and cultural spheres'. One such complaint was that exchange controls and customs duties inhibited dealings between communities on either side of the line. The two governments therefore proposed to 'remove as far as possible obstacles which at present impede the movement of individuals and their transport of personal property, as well as commerce in local goods and the carriage of individual loads of locally produced foodstuffs'. They also promised to look into the idea of a conventional zone in which a single Customs regime might operate across the two Togolands – although this was not expected to interfere with the underlying principle of exchange control. They further promised to harmonize the tax burden on both sides of the line. In response to the AEC contention that different administrative practices were an impediment to social intercourse, the two governments also advocated the teaching of English and French in each other's schools. Finally, in order to bring people from across the border into closer proximity, and to give them an active role in decision-making, the governments announced their intention to set up a Standing Consultative Commission (SCC), in which representatives from both Togolands would meet to give practical effect to these ameliorative measures.

In December 1947, an important precedent was created when Sylvanus Olympio was allowed to speak before the Trusteeship Council on behalf of the AEC. The supremely urbane Olympio, who chose to speak in English rather than French, made an immediate impact upon his audience. In the words of one observer:

> We heard that there was a petitioner coming from Africa and didn't know quite what to expect. None of the delegates knew much about Africa, and I sincerely believe that many of them expected someone to come rushing into the Council in a leopard skin and accompanied by a rumble of drums. Instead of which in strolled Sylvanus Olympio in his natty business suit. The delegates may not have known it, but they were seeing, for the first time, the shape of things to come.[78]

Olympio did, however, have his work cut out because the joint memorandum had stolen much of his thunder. His reaction was to assert that the reforms did not solve the underlying problem, which was that the Ewe would always be disadvantaged unless they were brought beneath a single administration pursuing common educational, economic and political objectives. When subjected to sustained

[78] Quoted in Alex Quaison-Sackey, *Africa Unbound: Reflections of an African Statesman* (New York: Praeger, 1963), pp. 129–30.

questioning, Olympio came close to admitting that the border as a practical obstacle was not really an issue at all: what the AEC really wanted, it transpired, was a single political homeland for all the Ewe people.[79]

This is further confirmed by the experience of the Working Party, which was mandated to enquire into the creation of a conventional zone in April 1949. The members travelled extensively through the three territories, canvassing local opinion. Although the Working Party eventually rejected the scheme for other reasons, it was also struck by how little the border really mattered as a physical barrier.[80] In fact, the guidelines under which it was established already acknowledged that:

> ... the permeability of the frontier between the two Territories, together with the relaxations already introduced, is in fact greatly reducing the real inconveniences arising from the frontier, at least in so far as persons other than traders are concerned.[81]

Whereas large traders seeking to move their goods by road faced genuine inconveniences deriving from exchange controls, customs duties and restrictions on the circulation of commercial vehicles, ordinary people were much less affected. Hence, following a meeting with Anlo chiefs and citizens in Keta, one member penned the following note:

> They looked at the whole question from a political point of view instead of from a practical problem of customs frontiers. They are not really inconvenienced by the customs frontier?[82]

Indeed, the Working Party was informed that some Ewes preferred the customs frontier to remain precisely where it was because it guaranteed a livelihood through smuggling. The same member reported that:

> The Reverend Baeta mentioned that there was some Ewes who were interested in maintaining the present customs frontier because of the livelihood they made out of smuggling. One smuggler said to him 'He hoped the customs frontier would remain until he had made sufficient profit to finish the house he was building'.[83]

---

[79] Hence Olympio's reply to a question from the Iraqi representative that 'Our point really is that we want unification; it is not so much that there are inadequacies in certain parts of the area'. Discussion of 8 December, Trusteeship Council, *Official Records*, Second Session, First Part, 20 November 1947–16 December 1947, p. 336.

[80] The principal sticking point was that to have created a conventional zone for the two Togolands would have meant introducing new customs frontiers between French Togoland and Dahomey, on the one hand, and British Togoland and the Gold Coast on the other. Olympio and Amu specifically rejected such a solution on the grounds that it would still have meant that sections of the Ewe population would be divided by a customs frontier. The Bank of England also noted that if the principle of exchange control was to be upheld, sterling and the franc would not be able to circulate alongside each other. See copy of a letter from E. Cranshaw, Bank of England, to W.A.J. Marshall, the Treasury (dated 2 April 1949), Rhodes House, Mss. Afr. s.414. Finally, both the Gold Coast and the French Togoland governments worried about a possible fall in customs revenue that might result from a harmonization of their customs regimes. The French Governor, Cédile, in particular, argued that free trade might augment the trade of the Gold Coast, but would do little for French Togoland. Eventually, the plan for a conventional zone was dropped as impractical.

[81] 'Anglo-French Working Party: Principles of Operation', Rhodes House, Mss. Afr. s.414.

[82] Notes on a meeting with 17 Anlo chiefs and people, including C.H. Chapman, at Keta, 1 November 1949, Mss. Afr. s.414.

[83] Notes on a visit to Achimota to discuss Ewe affairs with E. Amu, Rev. Baeta and another, 25 October 1949, Mss. Afr. s.414.

The shortages that prevailed on the French side of the border from the end of the war through the early 1950s ensured that there was a steady profit to be made from illegally importing items that were in comparative abundance in British territory: such as cement, cloth, flour, petrol and tinware. When specific items, such as iron roofing sheets, bicycles and even gramophone records, were in short supply throughout the region, the scarcity factor held out the prospect of substantial economic rents. Hence in the early 1950s, a British official noted that

> There are, I think, long lists of people [in British territory] waiting for bicycles and, possibly, for iron sheets. I hear, however, that some hundreds of bicycles escape each year from the Gold Coast into French Territory.[84]

This evidence offers striking confirmation of an earlier argument that the border functioned as a resource rather than as an unnatural barrier for border communities. Insofar as the AEC was giving expression to genuine grievances about the boundary, these reflected the concerns of the wealthier Lomé and Anlo merchants, who were over-represented in the leadership of the unification movement. They did not necessarily represent the agenda of the mass of smugglers and petty traders.

To admit that the Ewe claim was based on something other than practical grievances arising from the border raised other difficulties for the AEC. On the one hand, it needed to define quite unambiguously who belonged to the 'Ewe nation' on which everything hinged. On the other hand, given that the AEC was not seeking a separate Ewe state, it had to wrestle with the implication that other peoples might be adversely affected by any subsequent territorial division. With regard to the first of these problems, the *Ewe News-Letter* initially treated 'the Ewe' as an unproblematic category, bounded by a common language and history. But a more nuanced picture subsequently emerged as the AEC endeavoured to expand the boundaries of 'Eweland'. The *Ewe News-Letter* stated, in a formula that has been echoed many times since then, that the 'The real truth of the matter is that it is impossible to set up a satisfactory frontier anywhere between the lower Volta in the Gold Coast and the lower Mono on the western border of Dahomey.'[85] The Mono was defined as the eastern boundary despite a French assertion that the Fon beyond it were also closely related to the Ewes. The AEC feared that introducing Dahomean peoples into the ethnic equation would only complicate matters and create an excuse for the French to drag their feet. Although the *Ewe News-Letter* conceded that there were 'ancient connections' between the Ewe and the Fon, Chapman insisted that they spoke distinct languages and did not consider themselves to be the same people.

Behind the Mono River, on the other hand, the AEC leaders were prepared to blur the differences. Hence the people of the Anecho area were defined as Ewe despite the fact that the Minas were historically a mixture of immigrants from the vicinity of Accra and Elmina.[86] As we have already seen, Mina migrants to Accra themselves

---

[84] Comment by George Sinclair, Gold Coast Government representative on Joint Council for Togoland Affairs, fourth sitting, 8 August 1952, GNAA ADM 39/1/171.

[85] *Ewe News-Letter*, no. 2, June 1945.

[86] On the history of the Mina people, see Nicoué Lodjou Gayibor, *Le Genyi: un royaume oublie de la côte de Guinee au tempe de la traite des noirs* (Lomé & Paris: Editions Haho & Karthala, 1990); and the new edition of the 1934 account by Fio Agbanon II, *Histoire de Petit-Popo et du royaume Guin* (Lomé & Paris: Editions

insisted that they were in fact distinct from the Ewe, both culturally and historically. Yet Sylvanus Olympio informed the Trusteeship Council in 1947 that:

> Further, the Minas and the Adangbes speak no language today other than Ewe, and practise the same general customs. They have become absorbed by the Ewes and do not owe allegiance to any Paramount Chief outside the Ewe country.[87]

The differential consideration extended to the Mina and the Fon was very obviously an instance of creative ethnic accounting. The French were only too aware of that fact and, as Amenumey has shown, they proceeded to define the Minas and Ouatchi as existing outside the Ewe category in order to deflate the significance of the AEC.[88] The numbers game, in other words, was one that could be played by more than one party.

On the northern fringes, the AEC contrived to expand the boundaries of Eweland so as to embrace the Central Togo minorities. Hence Olympio asserted that the Avatime, Woadze, Nyangbo and Agotimes could be considered as Ewes on the same linguistic principle as the Minas were. On a subsequent occasion, he made the even bolder claim that the Adeles and Akpossos could be considered as Ewes as well:

> Both the Akpossos and the Adeles had centuries ago migrated from the Watchi district. There was not in the whole Akposso district a single person who spoke any language other than Ewe. Those people had lost all trace of separate identity.[89]

If language was taken as the basis for ethnic ascription, which is assuming a great deal, these peoples were manifestly not Ewes. More to the point, the claim that most Adeles and Akpossos regarded themselves as 'Ewe' was highly tendentious. These subterfuges were necessary, however, because Olympio knew that the campaign for unification would only ever be taken seriously if the AEC could claim to speak on behalf of a large enough Ewe 'nation'.

In the debates of 1947, the Trusteeship Council was already beginning to comprehend that if there was an Ewe view to be listened to, there might well be alternative opinions – not least among the Dagomba population.[90] With considerable disingenuity, Olympio asserted that non-Ewes were a numerical minority in both Togolands, and that the Dagomba would probably agree with any proposal to bring the two Togolands together.[91] This sleight of hand may have just about satisfied his audience in 1947, but in the longer term it could not be sustained. Dissonant northern voices inevitably began to be heard and were deliberately amplified by the administering authorities as part of their own strategy for preserving the status quo.

---

[86] (cont.) Haho & Karthala, 1991).

[87] Formal statement by Olympio on 8 December 1947, Trusteeship Council, *Official Records*, Second Session, First Part, 20 November 1947–16 December 1947, p. 325.

[88] Amenumey, *Ewe Unification Movement*, p. 62.

[89] Oral evidence of Sylvanus Olympio, Trusteeship Council, *Official Records*, Sixth Session, 19 January–4 April 1950, p. 504.

[90] This point was made explicitly by Sir Carl Berendsen, the representative of New Zealand, in the discussion of 8 December 1957. Trusteeship Council, *Official Records*, Second Session, First Part, 20 November 1947–16 December 1947, p. 339.

[91] Discussion of 8 December 1957, *ibid.*, pp. 38–40.

At the same time, dissenting opinions began to emanate from the minority communities who had been verbally appropriated by Olympio. As we have seen in the previous chapter, this was around the time that sections of the Central Togo minorities were becoming sensitive to the insinuation that they were merely 'a few lesser peoples' whose interests were bound up with those of the Ewe.[92]

While the AEC was increasingly hoist on its own petard at the Trusteeship Council, its vulnerability was also being exposed on the ground. Because the AEC strategy revolved around the petitioning of the United Nations, it did not feel the need to go much beyond securing the signatures of influential chiefs. Amenumey has asserted that while the AEC initially commanded the support of the old and new elites, it 'quickly began to command a loyal following among the masses'.[93] At least as far as British Togoland is concerned, it is difficult to find much evidence to substantiate this view. There undoubtedly were regular channels of communication with the Gold Coast, along which news and rumour could travel with lightning speed. In the larger towns such as Ho and Kpandu, traders and transport operators maintained daily contacts with the Colony that kept them fully abreast of developments there. Equally, those who migrated in search of employment served as a vector for ideas emanating from the Gold Coast. However, a perusal of the official record leaves the distinct impression that involvement in AEC affairs was confined to a handful of chiefs and a few individuals who were closely connected to stool affairs.

An example would be F.Y. Medie, who served for a time as secretary to the Asogli State Council. Medie, who enters the record as a cocoa buyer in Anfoega at the end of the 1920s, seems to have settled down in Ho after the war.[94] In one administrative report, he was described as wielding 'a tremendous influence over the chiefs' and was credited with the successful enlargement of the Asogli State under the amalgamation policy.[95] In the early days of the AEC, it was his enthusiasm that apparently turned Ho into an AEC stronghold. Elsewhere, however, one searches in vain for evidence of significant AEC activity. Successive handing over reports for 1947 and 1948 are entirely devoid of references to the AEC. Given the attention that the Ewe unification cause was attracting at higher levels, it would have been most surprising if district officials had not kept their ears to the ground. Given that these reports represented the collective short-term memory of the administration, the AEC should have left a trace in these documents if anywhere. In this instance, silence can plausibly be read as evidence for an absence of significant Ewe unificationist activity. This also goes some way towards explaining how the AEC was rolled back with such comparative ease after 1947.

---

[92] For example, see 'A resolution of the Buem State, Santrokofi and Nkonya Divisions Scholars Union to the Select Committee on Local Government', dated 10 June 1950, GNAH DA/240.

[93] Amenumey, *Ewe Unification Movement*, p. 45.

[94] In April 1930, he was sued by the firm of F. & A. Swanzy for failure to deliver on a cash advance against cocoa purchases. *F. & A. Swanzy per Seddoh v. Felix Y. Medie*, in the Supreme Court, Ho, 28 April 1930, GNAA ADM 39/4/3.

[95] Handing over notes from C.M. Weatherburn to A.V. Cameron, 1950, GNAH DA/D78.

The parting of the Ewes:
the ascendancy of the Togoland Union

Had the AEC managed to carry its chosen constituency with it, it might have been able to sustain its pressure upon the administering authorities and secured more lasting support from the international community. As it happened, though, the AEC began to unravel almost as soon as it made its grand entrance on the global stage. Moreover, it came undone at its weakest point, that is, in British Togoland. The rapidity and the virulence of the backlash caught by surprise the AEC leadership and the British administration alike.

The revival of the vision of a reunified Togoland dates from 1947 when an association calling itself the Togoland Union (TU) announced itself. The leaders claimed that its origins lay in a body of the same name that had been formed in 1943, through an amalgamation of various improvement associations, with a view to lobbying the Resident Minister in West Africa about conditions in Togoland.[96] At this time, the TU had presented a memorandum requesting improved amenities, but had then sunk back into obscurity. The emergence of the TU as an active political organization can only be dated from the later period. It seems to have emerged as a direct response to the success of the AEC in drawing attention to the Ewe problem in 1947.[97] The importance attributed to the United Nations dimension was reflected in the fact that the TU also operated under the name of the Togoland United Nations Association (TUNA).[98] The fundamental difference between the TU and the AEC was that whereas the latter aspired towards unification of all the Ewe under a single administration, the TU campaigned exclusively for the reunification of the two halves of Togoland. Indeed, the TU leadership specifically sought to exclude the Gold Coast Ewes from the equation, for reasons I shall shortly come to. While the TU sought to emulate the AEC in making its demands directly to the Trusteeship Council, it was rather more astute at building a constituency at the local level.

To start with, British officials downplayed the significance of the TU, noting that it was restricted socially to the 'teacher class' and confined geographically to Buem.[99] As a thumbnail sketch, this was not entirely wide of the mark. Amenumey observes that there was a link between the leadership of the TU and rebels in the Ewe Presbyterian Education Unit who had railed against Anlo intrigues in 1937.[100] In 1948 itself, as we have seen, there was an outright struggle for power within the educational structures of the EPC between Togolanders and Gold Coast Ewes. Indeed, some of the leaders of the TU in 1948 were the same individuals who were embroiled in this conflict.[101] It is equally true that the TU gained much of its initial following from

---

[96] V.O. Anku, President of TU, to CSA (9 August 1948), GNAH DA/D113.

[97] In fact, Amenumey, *Ewe Unification Movement*, p. 119, claims that it arose out of the AEC.

[98] Originally, the organization was calling itself TU internally and TUNA internationally. 'The Togoland Union (What it is and how it functions)', undated, GNAH DA/D113.

[99] Undated memorandum by DC, GNAH DA/D113.

[100] Amenumey, *Ewe Unification Movement*, p. 119.

[101] V.O. Anku, the president of the TU in 1948, was based at the Ewe Presbyterian Teachers Training College. E.O. Kofi Dumoga and G.O. Awuma were both teachers in British Togoland, while S.G. Antor was teaching at Koforidua.

among the Central Togo minorities, who balked at being dragged along on the coat-tails of southern Ewe opinion. But however narrow the political foundations of the TU was to start with, it wasted little time in building a wider base of support, which straddled the Ewe and minority communities as well as different social strata.

Much of the success of the TU can be attributed to the way in which it tapped into the existing network of youth and hometown associations. In 1947, as we have seen, G.O. Awuma was dismissed from his position as secretary to the Ho–Kpandu District Education Committee after chiefs from Asogli complained about his conduct. Precisely what Awuma had done to antagonize the chiefs is somewhat unclear, but according to Amenumey it was his involvement in the Asogli Youth League that was deemed to be subversive of traditional authority.[102] Imagined Anlo conspiracies apart, Awuma complained to the Trusteeship Council that it was his participation in a Togoland Association for the United Associations that had led to his sacking.[103] Assuming the latter was simply another name for TUNA, this would imply that there was a direct connection between Awuma's involvement in the TU and in the Asogli Youth League, and it was this that was held to be so threatening by the chiefs. Although Awuma lost the early rounds of this contest, the position had been entirely reversed a couple of years later. Hence an administrative report in 1950 observed that:

> Asogli has been a stronghold of the All Ewe Conference, and the majority of the chiefs and elders gave their full backing to this party. The young men of Dome on the other hand began to give active support to the Togo Union two years ago and now the whole of Ho except Bankoe is nearly 100% Togo Union.[104]

In the process, the spell that had been cast by F.Y. Medie was broken. Indeed, even the Paramount Chief of Asogli, Togbe Howusu, had been drawn into the embrace of the TU by the time of this report. The latter also indicated that the TU had effectively spread itself beyond the confines of Ho town, primarily through the activities of the young men:

> In addition to this the young men from Dome have been very active in gaining support from amongst the Asafo in the outlying Divisions and as a result many of the young men in all of the Divisions are actively opposed to the political opinions of their Chiefs and elders.

The 1949 United Nations Visiting Mission was itself struck by the depth of popular feeling, reflecting on its reception over two days in Ho and Kpandu that:

> Rarely did the Mission enter a locality without being faced with cries for unification, petitions to that end and demonstrations clamouring for it. They were usually mass demonstrations, and the enthusiasm and spontaneous response were unmistakable.[105]

Evidently, therefore, unification politics had moved out of the confines of the chiefs' palaces and on to the streets.

---

[102] Amenumey, *Ewe Unification Movement*, p. 119.

[103] This version of events was echoed by the Philippines representative to the Trusteeship Council. See the exchange at Trusteeship Council, *Official Records*, Fourth Session, 24 January–25 March 1949, p. 316.

[104] Handing over notes from C.M. Weatherburn to A.V. Cameron, September 1950, GNAA ADM 39/1/456.

[105] The context of the earlier remarks would suggest that the cries were for Togoland unification. 'Report on Togoland under British administration', United Nations, *Reports of the United Nations Visiting Mission to Trust Territories in West Africa*, Supplement No. 2 (T/798), 1951, p. 99.

It would, however, be misleading to imply that there was a deep rift between chiefs and people. Indeed, the success of the TU also lay in the skill with which it also projected itself as the defender of the interests of traditional authority in British Togoland. As early as 1944, Governor Burns was advocating the incorporation of the British Togoland Ewes into a single district with their counterparts in the Colony.[106] These proposals had many implications, but for the Togoland chiefs they raised the immediate prospect of a revival of Peki claims to hegemony. While the Paramount Chiefs feared they might lose their enhanced status through closer union, there was nothing much to be gained by the independent chiefs either. In 1948, Chief Commissioner T.R.O. Mangin canvassed opinion on government proposals to harmonize NA legislation with that of the Gold Coast and to bring the Togoland chiefs on to the Joint Provincial Council of Chiefs (JPC).[107] Mangin, who depicted his audience as 'a backward people with only limited powers of mental absorption', had to admit to a less than enthusiastic response.[108] The chiefs were suspicious of anything that would dilute their powers, especially in respect of the native tribunals, but they were also reluctant to sit alongside the larger Gold Coast chiefs on the JPC. Although AEC spokesmen expressed their own concerns, Mangin noted that the most vigorous support for the chiefs came from TU delegates who demanded an entirely separate council of chiefs for southern and northern Togoland. Mangin concluded that it would be unwise to do anything that might foster an alliance between the chiefs and the TU, and therefore dropped the second proposal in favour of a separate Southern Togoland Council. In the aftermath of this debate, the TU became closely associated with a more or less formalized alliance of Togoland chiefs, styling themselves the Natural Rulers Association.[109] In 1949, the latter convened meetings to protest against the proposed alterations to the Native Administration Ordinance. This campaign drew much of its support from the Paramount Chiefs, but the Natural Rulers and the TU also took up the cause of the unamalgamated chiefs, insisting that they should be adequately represented on the Southern Togoland Council.

The TU was also the principal beneficiary of the wrangle surrounding the election of two members to the SCC by representatives of the Native Authorities in 1948. The election of Ephraim Amu and W.S. Honu, both leading members of the AEC, was followed by complaints that, as Gold Coast Ewes, they should be ineligible to stand.[110] Many chiefs felt that the interests of Togoland could only be adequately be represented by people from the territory. Leading the charge was the Acting President of the Buem Native Authority, Nana Akuamoa IV of Kudje, whose

---

[106] In 1944, Burns commissioned a report from the CCC and welcomed his proposals. See correspondence in PRO 96/780/31458.

[107] 'Address given in Togoland by His Honour T.R.O. Mangin, Chief Commissioner, October 1948', GNAA ADM 39/1/495.

[108] Memorandum on Togoland by T.R.O. Mangin, undated GNAA ADM 39/1/495.

[109] A Natural Rulers Society dates back to September 1932 when chiefs opposed to the amalgamation policy rallied together. Brown, 'Politics in the Kpandu area', p. 38.

[110] Amu was from Peki. Welch, *Dream of Unity*, p. 87, asserts that Honu was also a Gold Coaster, although the DC insisted he was a 'native of Gbi'. Letter to CCC (8 October 1948), GNAA ADM 39/1/676. In 1949, Amu had to give way to F.Y. Asare of Buem because he was not resident in Togoland. Amenumey, *Ewe Unification Movement*, p. 92.

representatives had cast all of their votes against Amu and Honu.[111] The petition that was submitted also contained the signatures of the headchiefs, or those of their representatives, from Anfoega, Gbi, Likpe, Nkonya, Santrokofi and Ve.[112] Some of the latter had been signatories to the Ewe Convention of 1946, but had since begun to distance themselves from their AEC associates. The concerns of the chiefs closely echoed the contention of TU leaders, such as Awuma, that Gold Coast Ewes had muscled themselves into most positions of importance within Togoland.

Whereas the AEC leadership sought to smooth over any differences within the united Ewe front, it was in the interests of the TU to play up the theme of Gold Coast Ewe dominance. Hence Awuma, who could assert at one moment that 'the Gold Coast Ewes are not our enemies' and indeed that 'they are our own brothers', repeatedly reverted to the crudest diatribes against the Anlo and Peki.[113] There were various attempts at mediation between the AEC and the TU in 1949, which were brokered by certain chiefs – although Amenumey notes that those of Anfoega, Akpini, Atando, Buem and Krachi had already declared for the TU at a meeting in Borada in July. The final attempt at bridging the gulf, at a meeting in Ho later that month, ended in chaos after TU supporters rejected the results of the arbitration.[114] Thereafter, the TU quickly consolidated its position, appealing both to the most senior chiefs and to those who had been alienated by the amalgamation policy. At the same time, the TU sought to firm up its support among the youth associations by sponsoring a Togoland Youth Movement.[115] The AEC, which had always depended rather narrowly upon chiefly support, increasingly found itself squeezed out of the picture. As one Buem chief put it, the AEC was now 'debunked, defunct, derelict and condemned'.[116] Hence the 1949 Visiting Mission remarked that while the AEC was still supported by the Gold Coast Ewe, it had forfeited its position in British Togoland to the TU, except in the extreme south of the territory.[117]

In order to make sense of the success of the TU in mobilizing a broader constituency, one must return to the process of creeping integration that was outlined in Chapter 1. Increased contact with the Gold Coast helped to created a common imaginative space, but at another level it contributed to a perception that British Togoland was the poor relation. That this was not a mere figment is clear from the reaction of Governor Burns to his first visit to the territory in 1942:

> I have just returned from a hurried trip through Togoland where I was struck by how little had been done to develop the Mandated Territory. In the Gold Coast itself the roads are, generally

[111] 'Resolution of the Natural Rulers of Southern Togoland including the Togoland Union on the Consultative Commission for Togoland Affairs', dated 10 September 1948, GNAA ADM 39/1/676.

[112] Signatures purporting to be those of the Paramount Chiefs of Akpini, Asogli and Awatime were also appended, but their veracity was in some doubt.

[113] In June 1949, a meeting was held at Hohoe to smooth out the differences, and it was here that a conciliatory letter from Awuma was made known. *Gold Coast Express*, 22 June 1949.

[114] Welch, *Dream of Unity*, p. 90, notes that Togbe Howusu was threatened with destoolment by TU supporters for accepting the resolution. See also Amenumey, *Ewe Unification Movement*, p. 121.

[115] The TYM did not have the most auspicious start: allegedly only one person turned up for the inauguration. J. Dixon to CCC (24 February 1950), GNAA ADM 39/1/652.

[116] Welch, *Dream of Unity*, p. 90, n.15.

[117] 'Report on Togoland under British administration', United Nations, *Reports of the United Nations Visiting Mission to Trust Territories in West Africa*, Supplement No. 2 (T/798), 1951, p. 103.

speaking, very good: in Togoland they are very bad. In the Gold Coast telegraph and telephone communication is provided at every important centre: in Togoland no such facilities exist. In some cases even the work done by the Germans has been allowed to deteriorate. Although nothing is in writing on the subject, I understand that Hodson, fearing (before the present war) the possibility that the mandated Territory would be given up deliberately discouraged any expenditure on development and refused to approve of some much-needed works.[118]

Apart from the ailing infrastructure, Togolanders were sensitive to the fact (as we have seen) that educational facilities were markedly inferior to those of the Gold Coast. Part of the reason why the AEC may initially have gained some support from the chiefs was that it drew attention to the lack of basic amenities, while laying the blame at the door of partition. In his first appearance before the Trusteeship Council in 1947, for example, Olympio made a point of highlighting the lack of proper roads and the absence of a single secondary school or a decent hospital in either British or French territory.[119] But whereas Olympio sought to blur the distinction between Togoland and 'Eweland', the TU stressed the comparative abundance of Gold Coast Eweland. In that sense, it was asserted, they did not share a common predicament at all.

A particular worry of the TU was that Gold Coast Ewes might benefit from measures intended to improve the lot of Togolanders. In 1950, the British authorities were forced to admit, in response to an individual petition, that scholarships earmarked for British Togolanders had in fact gone to Gold Coast Ewes.[120] This underlined the importance of protecting the separate status of British Togoland. Going further, the TU leadership asserted that the lessons of history were that closer integration with the Gold Coast would only lead to a widening of the gap. It followed that the surest means of achieving parity lay in gaining parallel structures for British Togoland. In 1950, S.G. Antor informed the Trusteeship Council that because the Gold Coast Cocoa Marketing Board (CMB) persistently underestimated the production of British Togoland, and hence its contributions to general revenues, the territory was losing out.[121] His demand was therefore for a separate marketing board for Togoland. The assumption was that a separate Togoland administration would have greater resources at its disposal if it was freed from the drain imposed by the neighbouring colony.

Once the TU had broken the monopoly of the AEC, it was able to state its own case directly before the United Nations. Hence, in 1950, F.Y. Asare and Antor shared the platform with Olympio at the Trusteeship Council.[122] No less important was the

---

[118] Governor Alan Burns to Dawe, Colonial Office (6 December 1942), PRO CO 96/776/31467. There was an acknowledgement in the Colonial Office (minute by U. Williams) that 'there does appear to have been some tendency to neglect the development of Togoland though not to an extent that attracted the attention of the Permanent Mandates Commission'. An anonymous minute simply remarked 'So much for mandates!'.

[119] Statement by Sylvanus Olympio on 8 December 1947, Trusteeship Council, *Official Records*, Second Session, First Part, 20 November 1947–16 December 1947, p. 326.

[120] The petition was from one G.K. Noamesi. See Trusteeship Council, *Official Records*, Seventh Session, 1950, Annex, Volume II, p. 24.

[121] Antor was representing the Mandated Togoland Farmers Association, in addition to the Natural Rulers of Western Togoland and the TU. Trusteeship Council, *Official Records*, Seventh Session, 10 July 1950, pp. 185–6.

[122] This followed a TU complaint that allowing the AEC to appear would misrepresent Togoland opinion. President of TU to Secretary General, United Nations Trusteeship Council (9 March 1950), GNAA ADM

impression created by the mass of petitions submitted by individuals and organizations from within the territory, ranging from the Liati Literate Union to the Akpini Youth Society and the Women Teachers of Togoland. Most of these petitions focused on the inadequate provision of infrastructure and social amenities, either in specific localities or in British Togoland more generally. Although some of the associations were possibly fronts for the TU, the petitions were too many and too varied for this to be a convincing explanation. It is more likely that the TU was itself tapping into a widely held perception that Togoland was simply not receiving its fair share of resources. The alacrity with which ordinary Togolanders engaged in the debate underscores the point that the political landscape, which had once been dominated by a handful of traditional rulers, had become much more undulating by 1948.

The language of 'development' was attractive to the TU for a variety of reasons. It resonated with the community improvement ethic that had been such a feature of the inter-war years, while underscoring the point that government had a responsibility to assist local initiatives. Crucially, it could be moulded to appeal simultaneously to the chiefs, youth movements and hometown associations. It also chimed in with the new post-war international discourse of 'development', which was in turn reinforced by the internal ideology of the trusteeship system. The British found themselves in the position, from which they had been spared under the Mandate system, of having to demonstrate that they were making steady and tangible improvements to the lives of their wards. Their well-chosen response was to work with the grain of the prevailing discourse and to manipulate it for their own ends. In due course, developmentalism became a keystone of the decolonization package in the Gold Coast. The irony was that 'developmental decolonization' was associated with the extinction of the separate status of British Togoland. In a sense, unificationists had helped to unleash a monster that ultimately devoured them.

British trusteeship and Gold Coast imperialism

At this juncture, I wish to the shift the focus towards policy at the state level, before returning to the local political dynamic once more. My particular concern is the shift in the British stance from being semi-conscious imperialists to outright annexationists in the post-war period. The relative success of the Ewe and Togoland unification movements in stating the case for a rectification of borders forced both the British and the French to come up with a response that would both satisfy international opinion and protect the status quo. This was a tall order because there was considerable sympathy within the United Nations for the unificationist case. The recent release of relevant British government papers makes it possible to identify core elements of an official strategy that turned on buying time at the United Nations, while nurturing a local constituency that would favour integration with the Gold Coast. Both dimensions are worthy of further comment.

[122 (cont.)] 39/1/675. Amenumey, *Ewe Unification Movement*, p. 124, observes that Asare and Antor presented a confused picture when they said they wanted the Gold Coast Ewe to be included in a united Togoland. It is true that this demand cut against the anti-southern rhetoric of the TU, but it was consistent with the position that the first priority was to keep the Gold Coast at bay. The Anlos and Pekis were at best an add-on.

Frustrating the United Nations

As observed above, the administering authorities responded to AEC demands for a wholesale revision of the map by offering reforms to mitigate the practical effect of existing borders. The creation of the SCC was intended to demonstrate to international opinion that the two governments took the issue of cross-border co-operation seriously. In response to SCC recommendations, some concrete measures were in fact implemented. Hence in response to the observation that many farmers worked lands on the other side of the border, the authorities agreed to permit the duty-free movement of foodstuffs (but not cocoa) from farm to homestead.[123] Moreover, individual headloads of foodstuffs, local manufactures and medicines were specifically exempted from duties. Greater restrictions remained on the circulation of imported goods because of ongoing concerns about consumer shortages, but non-commercial quantities were permitted to be transported across the border without duty. Moreover, in response to complaints about stringent exchange controls, the authorities agreed to increase the amount of foreign currency that could be taken across the border with a verbal declaration, to £10 or its franc equivalent.

But while the authorities sought to make a public display of their good faith, they were also worried that the SCC might become altogether too successful. The danger was that its interventions would merely strengthen the case for dissolving the border altogether. As originally constituted, three of the four African members – Olympio, Amu and Honu – were AEC spokesmen.[124] Although they were prepared to co-operate in suggesting ways and means of lessening the practical effect of the boundary, they insisted that there was no adequate substitute for its complete removal. To the intense discomfort of the government co-chairmen, Amu and Olympio repeatedly sought to place the Ewe unification issue squarely on the SCC agenda. When F.Y. Asare replaced Amu, the monopoly of the AEC was helpfully undercut. Because the TU purported to represent the interests of Togolanders, this reinforced the official position that the Ewes were not the only players in the game. On the other hand, the TU was no less of a thorn in the flesh because of its demand that the borderline between the two Togolands be erased.

In June 1950, the two governments executed a master stroke by announcing their intention to establish an Enlarged Consultative Commission (ECC) to replace the SCC. In another joint memorandum, they conceded that the remit of the SCC had been too narrowly confined to frontier issues, and declared that the ECC would be charged 'with the responsibility of submitting to the two Governments its views as to the practical means of satisfying, within the framework of French and British administration, the wishes of the inhabitants of all parts of the two Trust Territories'.[125] This went some way towards responding to the observation of the 1949 Visiting Mission that the unification problem 'had taken on a political aspect' and that the

---

[123] Notes by Muchmore (undated), Rhodes House, Mss. Afr. s.414. 'Special Report on the Ewe Problem', United Nations, *Reports of the United Nations Visiting Mission to Trust Territories in West Africa*, Supplement No. 2 (T/798), 1951, pp. 72–4. Cocoa was the exception because of the buying monopsony created under the auspices of the CMB.

[124] The fourth was Fare Djato from French Togoland.

[125] 'Anglo–French memorandum to the Trusteeship Council, June 1950', GNAA ADM 39/1/676.

SCC was 'a most valuable institution which might be further developed'. By increasing the membership to 45 elected representatives, it could also be made to seem as if the governments were taking the new body much more seriously. Moreover, by weighting representation on the ECC according to population – with 28 seats going to French and 17 to British Togoland – they could even be seen to be treating the two Togolands as a single entity. However, it is difficult to escape the conclusion that more cynical motives were afoot. As Amenumey has shown, the French set out to manipulate the system of indirect elections to ensure that candidates who were opposed to any form of unification were elected.[126] Their behaviour was partly rooted in a perception that the revamped CUT was anti-French. But they also feared that any weakening of their position in Togoland would create dangerous precedents for the rest of their African empire. And because French Togoland representatives were in the overall majority, this ensured that AEC and TU representatives from the British side of the border would be unable to dictate the agenda.

In view of the repression of the CUT in French Togoland, Ewe unificationists from both territories resolved to boycott the ECC.[127] While the TU, the TYA and the Anfoega Duonenyo Organization protested that the two Togolands ought to receive equal numbers of seats, they were initially just as concerned with ensuring that AEC members were excluded.[128] However, when the practical question of participation arose, the TU was forced to consider its own position more carefully. Most of the party went along with the assessment of S.G. Antor that electoral anomalies in French Togoland and unequal representation made it undesirable to lend legitimacy to the ECC. In October a joint meeting of chiefs, the TU, the TYA, the Togoland Farmers Association and the AEC was convened at Antor's home town of Logba-Alakpeti, at which it was decided to boycott the ECC. However, there was a section within the TU that was still inclined to give the ECC a chance. Those who had been most hostile to the AEC in the past were of the opinion that the travails of the CUT were of no great concern to themselves.[129] Awuma also judged that the ECC offered a valuable training in self-government, and stuck to this position in spite of the Logba resolution. He prevailed upon the Asogli Paramount Chief, Togbe Howusu, to endorse a stance in favour of participation, although this was opposed by other chiefs within that State.[130] Awuma was supported in his assessment of the situation by Kofi Dumoga, who wielded some influence over the chiefs in Anfoega. When the ECC held its first meeting in Lomé in November 1950, therefore, it was attended by Dumoga, a representative of the Asogli Native Authority (B.G. Kwami), a

---

[126] This led the CUT to boycott the elections. Amenumey, *Ewe Unification Movement*, pp. 64–73.

[127] E. Amu, General Secretary of AEC, to co-presidents of ECC (27 October 1950), GNAA ADM 39/1/676.

[128] 'Petition from the Togoland Union of the Enlarged Joint Anglo French Standing Consultative Commission for Togoland' (undated), GNAA ADM 39/1/676.

[129] After all, the TU had held a joint meeting in May 1950 with the PTP – one of the parties that was being sponsored against the CUT – on a platform of uniting against 'Ewe tribal conspiracies'. The PTP was fundamentally opposed to Ewe unificationism, and while it was not opposed to Togoland unification in principle, it took the view that the two territories should move independently towards self-government and then unify at the end of the process. The TU eventually declined to ratify their joint convention because of its own preference for immediate reunification. Note on a convention between PTP and the TU dated 21 May 1950, GNAH DA/D113.

[130] Notably by Togbe Noe Keteku II of Agotime.

representative of the independent divisions of Anfoega, Santrokofi and Nkonya (J.K. Kwami) and eight members from Northern British Togoland. It was, however, boycotted by the rest of the Southern Togoland delegates. Dumoga, who purported to represent the TU, was promptly expelled from the party. In January 1951, the CUT, the AEC and the TU met in Kpalimé to formalize their new-found alliance on a platform that sought to reconcile Ewe and Togoland unificationist objectives. The resolution prioritized the reunification of the two trust territories, but recognized that the interests of Gold Coast Ewes needed to be accommodated, and even acknowledged the possibility of a future federation with the colony.[131] In keeping with his earlier stance, Kofi Dumoga and his brother, J.W.K. Dumoga, bitterly attacked this entente in the Gold Coast press.[132]

The eventual outcome was actually to the liking of the two governments. By adhering to a boycott, the leadership of the CUT and the TU could be accused of an unwillingness to abide by the principles of democracy. Indeed, the British questioned whether Antor even represented the views of his own party. At the same time, the authorities could point to the ECC as a representative forum, in the knowledge that while it might recommend further cross-border co-operation, it was unlikely to question the existence of the boundary itself. In the event, the ECC only ever held two sessions. Having recommended a further alleviation of specific frontier controls, and expressed its opposition to Ewe unification, the ECC ceased to have a meaningful role to perform. The two governments would have been happy to leave it at that, but there remained strong support from within the Trusteeship Council for trying to build upon cross-border initiatives. Rather than risk alienating this opinion, the authorities sought to maintain the appearance of compliance while seeking to blunt the practical impact of what was being advocated.

In July 1951, the British and French proposed to substitute a Joint Council for Togoland Affairs for the ECC, but sought to limit its scope to the co-ordination of development policies across the border. To their dismay, however, the General Assembly recommended in January 1952 that such a council be empowered to consider all aspects of the Ewe and Togoland problem. Furthermore, the Visiting Mission of that year urged that the remit of the proposed council be expanded to cover the whole spectrum of cultural, economic, educational and political affairs. As Amenumey has observed, the two governments were by now loathe to establish the Joint Council at all, far less to enlarge its powers.[133] Nevertheless, by declining to grant parity of representation on the Joint Council, they were virtually assured of a renewed boycott by the unificationist parties. Following a walk-out by the unificationist parties in August 1952, the Joint Council quickly became moribund.

But even this did not lay cross-border initiatives to rest. In December 1953, the General Assembly recommended the re-establishment of the Joint Council 'with the power to consider and make recommendations on the question of unification, as well as on all political, economic and social and educational matters affecting the two Trust Territories'.[134] The French were in favour of simply declaring that the

---

[131] Amenumey, *Ewe Unification Movement*, pp. 124–5.

[132] J.W.K. Dumoga was Assistant Editor of the *Ashanti Pioneer*. Amenumey, *Ewe Unification Movement*, p. 126.

[133] Amenumey, *Ewe Unification Movement*, p. 103.

[134] Resolution adopted at 469th plenary meeting, 8 December 1953, at PRO CO 554/1032.

Joint Council would never be reactivated, but the British government feared that this might provoke open criticism and possibly lead to the passage of a resolution in favour of some form of unification. This was to be avoided, not least because it would 'render the task of the integration parties in the forthcoming general election in British Togoland more difficult'.[135] The British strategy was, therefore, to make excuses for failing to re-create the council immediately rather than repudiating it outright. The underlying calculation was that if the integrationist parties won a majority of the British Togoland seats in the 1954 elections, the Joint Council could safely be jettisoned and both administrations could then concentrate on integrating their respective sections of Togoland into their alternative spheres.[136] For that reason, everything came to hinge on the promotion of a local constituency that would support the case for integration with the Gold Coast – to which I now turn.

Benign imperialism?:
the Convention People's Party and integration

At the same time as the British authorities were engaged in neutralizing the threat of cross-border co-operation, they proceeded to tighten the bonds linking the trust territory and the Gold Coast. Because administrative union was permissible under the Trusteeship Agreement, closer union could be justified without much difficulty. Indeed, the British authorities pointed to an extension of political rights to Togolanders as an step towards fulfilling their responsibilities under Article 76 of the agreement. Most Togoland unificationists, however, opposed political and administrative reforms as the thin end of the wedge, designed to render future disengagement from the Gold Coast practically impossible.

The Coussey Commission, which was set up to frame a new constitution for the Gold Coast in the wake of the 1948 riots, came up with proposals that had important implications for British Togoland. First of all, it recommended a single region to unite the southern half of the trust territory with Gold Coast Eweland, as had already been mooted some years before. The commission further suggested that Togoland should be fully represented on the Gold Coast legislature. The new constitution, which was adopted in December 1950, duly provided for three Southern Togoland seats on the Legislative Assembly: that is, one territorial member elected by the Southern Togoland Council and two rural members chosen through a two-stage election. Some TU leaders – notably Asare, Awuma and Dumoga – welcomed this development on the grounds that Togoland would only receive its fair share of resources if it were directly represented in Gold Coast institutions. But most of the party followed Antor's reasoning that closer association threatened the distinct status of the territory and rendered the prospects for union with French Togoland even more problematic. In November 1950, Antor convened a meeting at Borada, which was attended by a number of chiefs (under the banner of the Natural Rulers), the TU and the Togoland National Farmers Union (TNFU). This meeting heralded the

[135] Note for United Kingdom representative for Franco-British meeting in Paris, 14–15 January 1954, PRO CO 554/1032.
[136] W.L. Gorell Barnes, Colonial Office, to Arden-Clarke, PRO CO 554/1033.

beginnings of a new unificationist party, which finally came to be known as the Togoland Congress (TC).[137] The resolutions that were passed at this meeting advocated a boycott not just of the ECC, but also of the Gold Coast elections.[138] The TC set out to discourage the population of the territory from registering, and when this strategy failed, it sought to persuade them to abstain from actually voting.[139] The TC's counter-proposal was that the Southern Togoland Council should be turned into a separate legislature in its own right.

As it happened, the decision to boycott the elections merely opened the way for the minority faction of the TU to steal a march on its opponents. Asare was duly elected as the territorial member, while Awuma and Joseph Kodzo were elected as the two rural members. Not surprisingly, their failure to respect the boycott further poisoned their relations with former colleagues. Dumoga later complained to Awuma that Anku Morny and M.C. Batse had embarked on a smear campaign, alleging that the government had paid him £2,000 and offered him a scholarship in return for attending the ECC meetings. He further alleged that the headmaster of the Anfoega school where he was teaching was being used by these 'Hohoe people' to heap humiliations upon him and thus drive him out of the teaching field:

> Apart from the salary one receives, prestige also counts and to some of us the latter even matters more. Since my coming here I have been made to work on the staff of my juniors and less efficient teachers and even now under my old school boys as headmasters. Is this not very insulting?[140]

Both Dumoga and Awuma went as far as to allege that an assassination squad had been formed to liquidate them for their disloyalty to the unification cause.[141] Finding themselves isolated, the dissidents turned to embrace the party that had triumphed in the Gold Coast as a whole – namely, the CPP. Asare was promptly given the position of Ministerial Secretary in the new Nkrumah government, as part of an effort to prove that Togolanders were adequately represented at the centre.

These developments heralded a wholesale reconfiguration of political alliances that worked to the ultimate disadvantage of the TC. The CPP was a late entrant to the political fray in British Togoland. The United Gold Coast Convention (UGCC), out of which it emerged, had made almost no attempt to rally support east of the Volta. Hence when Mangin embarked on his tour of the territory at the end of 1948, he encountered a lone member of that party.[142] The CPP, which seceded from the UGCC in June 1949, was equally slow to take an active interest in Togoland affairs. Although the 1949 Visiting Mission received one petition from the CPP, it did not

---

[137] In a lengthy memorandum, the Senior DC, John Dixon, denied that the Togoland Congress had ever been formally constituted. See his 'Commentary on Mr. Antor's statement to the Trusteeship Council on 16 March 1951'. When representatives at the Southern Togoland Council were asked if the Congress did exist, there was a division of opinion. See letter from the secretary to D. Barnard, Ministry of Defence and External Affairs (9 July 1951). Both at GNAA ADM 39/1/676.

[138] 'Resolution adopted by the Natural Rulers and the peoples of Western Togoland during their second meeting at Borada on November 3rd 1950', GNAH RAO/C705.

[139] The registration rate was 25.5 per cent in Southern Togoland.

[140] Kofi Dumoga, Presbyterian School, Anfoega-Akukome to G.O. Awuma (25 May 1951), GNAA ADM 39/1/676.

[141] G.O. Awuma, Ho, to S.G. Antor at United Nations (5 June 1951), GNAA ADM 39/1/676.

[142] Memorandum on Togoland by T.R.O. Mangin, undated, GNAA ADM 39/1/495.

find its contribution to the debate worthy of specific comment.[143] In October 1950, G.K. Amegbe launched a CPP branch in Ho, but this does not seem to have been a resounding success because the membership was estimated at a mere 14 people early the following year.[144] Equally, David Brown has noted that the pioneering efforts of the CPP in Kpandu fell on stony ground.[145] Some commentators interpreted the slow progress of the CPP as reflecting a conscious desire to remain aloof from the struggle between the AEC and the TU by virtue of its links to both.[146] But while AEC members, like Komla Gbedemah and Amegbe himself, were among the founders of the CPP, it is difficult to identify a TU element prior to the 1951 elections. It is much more likely that the CPP failed to make earlier inroads because the AEC, with which it was closely associated, had itself been squeezed out of most of British Togoland.

On the back of the 1951 elections, however, the CPP began to exhibit a more serious interest in the Togoland question. It may well be true that Nkrumah feared that a failure to settle the unification question quickly would provide an excuse to delay Gold Coast independence. Whatever the reasons, the CPP adopted the line of least resistance by enlisting disaffected TU leaders like Asare, Awuma and Dumoga, and then set about building party structures around their existing bases of support. The CPP purported to offer the definitive answer to the unification riddle, promising that if British Togoland marched alongside the rest of the Gold Coast towards independence, the French could be persuaded to hand over their own section of Togoland at the end of the process.[147] Within the framework of a greater Gold Coast, therefore, the competing demands of Ewe and Togoland unificationists might successfully be reconciled. The decision to carve out a separate Trans-Volta Togoland (TVT) Region in 1952 could be presented, in these terms, as a fulfilment of a long-standing Ewe unificationist objective. However, it exposed an immediate rift within the ranks of the AEC which had been latent since the Kpalimé accord of January 1951. Some members of the AEC felt that there was a serious danger that closer integration would provide an excuse for the French to annex their section of Togoland. Far from squaring the circle, they argued, over-eagerness on the part of the CPP risked jeopardizing Ewe and Togoland unification alike. This apprehension was strongest among the CUT leadership, but also shared by some Gold Coast Ewes like Amu. However, most of the Gold Coast Ewe leadership placed its faith in the ability of the CPP to deliver the goods. The upshot was that the AEC split and long-standing members like Daniel Chapman, C.H. Chapman and Philip Gbeho

---

[143] By contrast, detailed consideration was given to the stance of the major pro- and anti-unificationist parties. 'Special report on the Ewe problem', United Nations, *Reports of the United Nations Visiting Mission to Trust Territories in West Africa*, Supplement No. 2 (T/798), 1951, pp. 76–8.

[144] Amenumey, *Ewe Unification Movement*, p. 166; Welch, *Dream of Unity*, p. 92. Amegbe was a 'prison graduate'.

[145] The branch that was set up in 1951 collapsed almost immediately. Brown, 'Politics in the Kpandu area', p. 261.

[146] *West Africa* magazine quoted in Amenumey, *Ewe Unification Movement.*, p. 167.

[147] This was the one respect in which the British and Nkrumah held differing views. The Colonial Office in fact worried that Nkrumah might be tempted to forgo immediate integration in the hope of adding French Togoland, which was regarded as an unrealistic scenario. Gorell Barnes to Arden-Clarke (21 May 1954), PRO CO 554/1033.

decamped to the CPP.[148] The supreme irony was that they found themselves settling into the same party structures as their former tormentors from the TU.

There is an enduring image of the CPP as the black nationalist knight that slew the imperialist dragon. East of the Volta River, however, the CPP and the British administration were close collaborators in pursuit of what was quite evidently a shared imperialist agenda. This was summed up in typically candid fashion by none other than the last Governor, Sir Charles Arden-Clarke, in the wake of the 1956 plebiscite:

> It seemed to all of us that the natural destiny of Togoland under United Kingdom Trusteeship was to become an integral part of the Gold Coast: it had been administered as such since its capture from the Germans in 1914. I was interested to see how cordially all my Ministers agreed with this view. Indeed, I had occasion to twit them on the subject. After listening to a diatribe about British imperialism I suggested that in the case of Togoland there seemed to be quite a lot of Gold Coast imperialism and imperialism was not necessarily a bad thing! I am glad to say that Gold Coast imperialism has won the day and that British Togoland is now an integral part of independent Ghana.[149]

Indeed, one might also say that successful dyarchy between CPP and the British was built upon the mutual trust that arose out of their working alliance in Togoland.

This collaboration was underpinned by a political division of labour. While the British sought to buy time at the United Nations, the CPP assumed the task of building up a local constituency that would sign up to integration with the Gold Coast. British officials took a close, pastoral interest in the progress of the CPP, but were careful not to be seen to openly champion its cause. After all, the tenuous credibility of the nationalist movement rested on maintaining a certain distance from the colonial power. But the authorities in Accra were undoubtedly partisan towards the CPP. Whereas some officials with experience of Ashanti had sympathy for the NLM, officials in Togoland were universally hostile to Antor and his associates.[150] In 1954, as we have seen, the British looked to the CPP to win enough Parliamentary seats to make it possible to kill off the Joint Council for Togoland Affairs. In the opinion of Reginald Saloway, the CPP was actually rather vulnerable at this time:

> The C.P.P. organisation is improving slowly but only very slowly and at the moment it seems likely that in the general election two or even three seats in the Southern Section might be won by the Togoland Congress. I am not satisfied that even now the Prime Minister realises the

---

[148] Amenumey, *Ewe Unification Movement*, p. 137. C.H. Chapman became the Deputy Speaker of the Assembly before independence, and subsequently a Regional Commissioner. Daniel Chapman went to work for the United Nations in 1946, but while he had withdrawn from active politics by 1954 he intimated that his sympathies lay with the CPP. Telegram from British delegation, New York, to Secretary of State for the Colonies (11 January 1954), PRO CO 554/1032. In 1954, he returned as Secretary to the Cabinet and to Nkrumah, and then became the Ghanaian Ambassador to the United Nations in 1957. He subsequently returned to Achimota as headmaster in 1959. See the pen-portrait in *West Africa*, 5 September 1959, p. 679.

[149] Quoted in Welch, *Dream of Unity*, p. 117.

[150] The contrast between the attitudes of A.C. Russell in Ashanti and George Sinclair in Trans-Volta Togoland is striking. Russell indicated his own inclination to do something to help the 'Ashantis' in an interview on the 'End of Empire' television series. Sinclair has left his views on record at Rhodes House, Mss. Afr.s.1622.

seriousness of the implications of this. Nevertheless C.P.P. activity is likely to be stepped up between now and the date of the election and may turn the scales.[151]

This assessment was borne out at the polls when the CPP won three of the six southern Togoland seats. Fortunately for the British, the eight northern seats were won by pro-integration candidates of the CPP or the Northern People's Party (NPP).[152] On this basis, it was possible to despatch petitioners to the United Nations to put the case against Togoland unification and a revival of the Joint Council. British officials advised on the composition of the best team and tutored its members on what to say when they reached the United Nations. By contrast, while there remained a lingering respect for Olympio, TC petitioners were dismissed as mere 'riff-raff'.[153]

All of this begs the question of why there should have been such a close meeting of minds between the CPP and the British. Undoubtedly, the fact that the Gold Coast and British Togoland had grown together since 1920 contributed to an unspoken assumption that integration was in the natural order of things. But there may also have been a more hard-nosed reason why the two sides were determined to resolve the Togoland question in their favour. Ambitious plans for damming the Volta River had been mooted in the inter-war period, but it was only in the early 1950s that detailed plans were drawn up. The Volta River Project introduced geopolitical considerations that had not been present at the time of the Milner–Simon agreement. On the British side, the project embodied the new-found British enthusiasm for the 'big push' in developmental terms. As far as Nkrumah was concerned, hydro-electric power held the key to modernization. But the viability of the entire project rested on the presumption that the government enjoyed absolute rights over the Volta. While it is true that the secession of British Togoland should have left the entirety of the river within the Gold Coast, as had been the case prior to 1914, the left bank would have constituted foreign soil. Because the flooding was bound to affect communities on this side of the river, the status of British Togoland was of fundamental importance to the project as a whole. The TC thought it detected a direct link between the sudden display of interest in Togoland on the part of the CPP, and the advancement of plans for the project. Certainly, the manner in which the CPP government handled the issue was not calculated to allay their suspicions. When a National Committee was announced in July 1953, its membership did not include a single Togolander, which led even Kofi Dumoga to express concern at the lack of respect for the separate status of the territory.[154] Increasingly, the TC set itself in opposition to the Volta River Project, arguing that this was merely the latest example of the way in which Togoland was taken for granted. In September 1954, Antor proclaimed that 'as long as the leaders of the Togoland Congress live the Volta River Project can never be

---

[151] Undated note from Saloway, Accra to Gorell Barnes, PRO CO 554/1033.

[152] Although the NPP was opposed to the CPP, and allied itself with the NLM, it was also against Togoland unification on the grounds that this would mean dividing the peoples of the north once more. On the NPP, see Martin Staniland, *The Lions of Dagbon: Political Change in Northern Ghana* (Cambridge: Cambridge University Press, 1975), ch. 8; and Paul Ladouceur, *Chiefs and Politicians: The Politics of Regionalism in Northern Ghana* (London: Longman, 1979).

[153] Draft of a letter from Vile, Colonial Office, to Arden-Clarke (1 September 1954), PRO CO 554/1035.

[154] Amenumey, *Ewe Unification Movement*, pp. 144–5, notes that Dumoga's response was to return to the Togoland unificationist fold.

implemented', and pledged to take the case against it all the way to the International Court of Justice if necessary.[155]

The obdurate stance of the TC introduced a destabilizing element into the equation. Project planners wished to insulate the scheme from party politics as far as possible. Hence R.G.A. Jackson, who headed the Preparatory Commission, was of the view that planning should not proceed until the status of the territory was definitively settled, lest it become a political football. From the perspective of the CPP, this only underscored the necessity of producing a surgical solution to the Togoland question. In 1954, Komla Gbedemah sought to persuade the British of the need to push ahead with a Togoland plebiscite that would enable the Trusteeship Agreement to be terminated.[156] Once that was safely accomplished, the Volta scheme could be debated in Parliament and the scheme could be carried forward. Although the CPP had performed reasonably well in the 1954 elections, Gbedemah was worried that the machinery of the party would 'go rusty' if the plebiscite was delayed into 1956. This is as clear an indication as any that Togoland was perceived as a worrisome obstacle that needed to be negotiated if the future prosperity of an independent Ghana was to be secured. Whether the CPP would have devoted so much of its energy to the Togoland question in the absence of such an economic imperative is intriguing to ponder upon.

Finessing the electorate

After 1951, an increasingly bitter contest ensued between the TC, which insisted that the CPP, had no place dabbling in Togoland affairs, and the CPP, which was intent on absorbing Togoland with the utmost haste. Although the levels of political violence never matched those in Ashanti, there was a good deal of conflict in those communities that constituted the primary battlegrounds. And, as in Ashanti, Nkrumah was unable to travel freely in the territory without running the risk of demonstrations and attempts to block his passage.[157] Up until the moment of Ghanaian independence, the contest was also fairly evenly balanced, although the CPP progressively ate into the TC support base. In what follows, I will examine the political messages that were disseminated by both sides before turning to consider the patterns of support in greater detail.

With the benefit of hindsight, one can conclude that the TC leadership chose the wrong terrain on which to fight. The success of the TU in rolling back the AEC had resided in its capacity to appeal to different constituencies at once. After 1951, however, the TC chose to present itself as the spokesmen of more specific interests, thereby creating a political space into which the CPP could insert itself. The shift of emphasis can be dated to the moment the TC was conceived. At the time, Antor claimed that the new party was not the brainchild of the TU, but actually the creation of the Natural Rulers. As he explained to the Trusteeship Council in March 1951:

---

[155] Reported in extract of a letter from R.G.A. Jackson to J.A.R. Pimlott, Board of Trade (30 September 1954), PRO CO 554/1035.

[156] Telegram from Secretary of State of Colonies to Arden-Clarke (9 September 1954), PRO CO 554/1035.

[157] In June 1952, a party of TC supporters attempted to impose a blockade at Goviefe to prevent Nkrumah entering Togoland and, when that failed, his car was stoned at Logba. 'Incident in Togoland', *West Africa*, 28 June 1952, p. 587.

The Congress is not a new organization. It is an organization of all the Chiefs in Togoland, who meet in cases of emergency when an important decision is required. For a long time, that meeting of all the Chiefs has been known as the Congress of Chiefs. Because of the unification and other political developments in the Territory, the Chiefs decided at their last meeting to admit representatives from the Togoland Union, the Togoland Youth Association and the Togoland National Farmers' Union.[158]

A possible reason for deferring to the chiefs was that the TC wished to pre-empt British claims that it lacked legitimacy. Given the ideological investment the British had made in chieftaincy over the preceding decades, an appeal to chiefly authority was in many ways a clever one. But it did enable the CPP to set up its own stall as the party of the youngmen. Whereas the myriad youth and improvement associations had once provided a solid base of support for the TU, the CPP enjoyed some success in gathering them in on a platform of promoting 'progress' as against defending 'tradition' – although, as we shall see, the CPP also counted a good many chiefs among its ranks.

This narrowing of the social base of the TC was related to another set of tactical considerations. Whereas the Togo Bund had appealed to the integrity of former German Togoland as a desirable goal in its own right, the TC concentrated on the material disadvantages of association with the Gold Coast. Like the TU before it, the TC emphasized the legacy of uneven development and asserted that this was a necessary consequence of closer union. The TC leadership made a special pitch for the support of the cocoa farmers, claiming that they were being forced to subsidize developments in the Gold Coast. The decision to make cocoa pricing an issue arose out of an awareness that British Togoland farmers were unhappy about the conduct of the CMB. By virtue of their proximity to the border, they were well aware of what their counterparts were receiving in French Togoland.[159] Whereas Coleman asserts that the TNFU championed a free market in cocoa, it actually campaigned for a separate marketing board for Togoland.[160] This acceptance of statutory marketing was consistent with the fact that the TC leadership shared much of the post-war consensus. It was merely demanding that taxes derived from Togoland cocoa should be spent within the territory.

In the 1951 cocoa season, the TNFU threatened to hold up sales altogether, while looking into the possibility of establishing direct links with purchasers in New York.[161] The authorities also suspected the TNFU of imparting legitimacy to

---

[158] Extract from verbatim record of Eighth Session of the 343rd meeting of the Trusteeship Council, 15 March 1951, GNAH RAO/C705.

[159] In August 1950, Togbe S.W. Atsridom IV of Kpedze claimed that the mid-crop price per ton of cocoa was £83 in British Togoland, but £160 in French Togoland. Letter to General Manager, CMB (28 August 1950), GNAH DA/C31.

[160] Coleman, 'Togoland', p. 36. This is presumably based upon a summary of a petition in 'Special report on the Ewe problem', pp. 76–8.

[161] Interestingly, one of the old hands of the Gold Coast farmers' movement, Ashie Nikoi, was for a time the secretary to the Mandated Togoland Farmers' Association and a vocal critic of the CMB. See Antor's statement at Trusteeship Council, *Official Records*, Seventh Session, 10 July 1950, p. 188. He was also secretary to the Conference of Natural Rulers in 1949. See report in *Ashanti Pioneer*, 9 July 1949. On the plans to market cocoa independently, see J.A.R. Williams, Accra, to Gates (6 January 1952), Rhodes House, Mss. Afr.536 (v).

smuggling activity. Certainly, there is evidence that farmers' leaders were prepared to use the contraband option as a form of blackmail. In January 1953, for example, the Dzigbe Local Council informed the CMB that local people intended to defy the authorities by sending their cocoa to Kpalimé, as had been the practice before the war, rather than selling through official channels.[162] After the CPP government froze producer prices in 1954 – thereby providing the catalyst for the formation of the NLM in Ashanti – the TNFU was accused of actively encouraging the farmers to smuggle their crops into French Togoland.[163] In view of the sensitivity of border peoples to price differentials, it is doubtful that they needed very much encouragement.

In pressing home the price issue, the TC evidently felt that it was on to a winner. However, the reality was that the greater part of British Togoland grew little or no cocoa, and therefore had a minimal stake in the campaign. The CPP sold its own pricing policy to Togolanders on the basis that judicious taxes on cocoa would be used to finance development projects that benefited every community. In response to TC complaints that the territory was persistently neglected, the CPP put the blame on the British and promised an immediate injection of funding into the territory in excess of what was extracted in the form of taxes on cocoa. In practice, this commitment to new spending was not merely rhetorical. Apart from the initiation of a Ten-Year Development Plan for the Gold Coast, out of which the territory would receive its due share, Nkrumah and the British together decided on a special package for Togoland. The then Regional Officer, George Sinclair, claims that he actually came up with the plan for a financial inducement, but credits CPP politicians with being astute enough to appreciate the political dividends. In his words:

> I realized that if we were to persuade the [Ewes] in British Togoland to come and join a greater number of them who were in the Gold Coast Colony proper, in the Keta area, then we would have to show them that a closer association with the Gold Coast under a new form of representative government was something which could be seen to bring a stream of material benefits... So I then started a campaign to get a million pounds out of the Government which would be at the disposal of a regional council for T.V.T. to spend on development additional to that provided in the National Development Plan. This took a good deal of persuasion but we were fortunate in these days in having some political Ministers who could see the political argument....[164]

The upshot was that an additional £1 million was gifted to the Trans-Volta Togoland Council for expenditure on development projects in the territory. This enabled CPP politicians to target areas that were of the greatest concern to ordinary Togolanders. Most of the money went into road construction and the provision of rural water supplies.[165] At the same time, other government money was funnelled into larger infrastructural projects, the most symbolic of which was the suspension bridge over the Volta near Senchi, which established unfettered road communications between Accra and Togoland for the first time. The opening of the first secondary school in Ho in 1950, and the expansion of educational and medical facilities across the board, was equally calculated to leave an impression on the electorate.

---

[162] Acting clerk to Dzigbe Local Council, Matse, to CMB (30 January 1953), GNAH DA/C31.

[163] A.C. Russell, Secretary to Governor, to TNFU, Hohoe (26 October 1954), GNAH DA/C31.

[164] Rhodes House, Mss. Afr.s.1622.

[165] 'Address by the Honourable the Prime Minister Dr Kwame Nkrumah to the Trans-Volta/Togoland Council at Ho on the 24th August, 1954'.

In 1953, the TC announced the leak of a 'most secret' government document that detailed a covert strategy for bribing Togolanders through the offer of material benefits.[166] Although its authenticity was disputed, one Colonial Office functionary expressed the opinion that it was genuine, adding that 'with its advocacy of bribery and strong arm methods to deal with the opponents of integration, the C.P.P. document is not pretty reading'.[167] As Coleman suggests, the methods advocated within 'most secret' were entirely consistent with the policies that were in fact pursued jointly by the CPP and the British. The TC continued to assert that the territory would be better off if left to its own devices. But for many voters the CPP contention that separation from the Gold Coast would come at considerable material cost seemed a serious one. Furthermore, the comparative poverty of French Togoland raised the spectre of having to subsidize communities across the border. These considerations, taken together with the tactical alliance with the NLM, may partly explain the growing acceptance by the TC of the principle of some form of federation with the Gold Coast. On the whole, then, a willingness to fight on the terrain of material development tended to strengthen the hand of the CPP over time.

In May 1956, the electorate of British Togoland was asked to vote in a plebiscite, in which the choice was between union with an independent Gold Coast or separation from the latter pending the ultimate determination of the future of the territory. The youngmen who aligned themselves with the CPP interpreted it as a choice between material progress in harmony with the Gold Coast and stagnation in an unnatural union with French Togoland. TC followers, by contrast, saw the choice as lying between *Ablode* (or freedom) and subordination to a larger and overbearing neighbour. Each party had its concentrations of support and its grey areas, and I will now seek to account for the distribution of support in the light of the analysis that was offered in the previous chapter.

Unification versus integration: the patterns of local support

Among existing interpretations of voting patterns, it is possible to distinguish those which prioritize either local attachments or ethnic solidarities, or serve up some concoction of the two.[168] Apart from David Brown, whose detailed study of Kpandu tends to highlight the force of local factional alignments, the best example of the first genre is the interpretation of James Coleman. He writes that:

> The broader issue of integration vs separation was perceived by a large number of voters in terms of immediate local issues. This is seen in the efforts made by political leaders to equate 'integration' or 'separation' with different local tensions and conflicts which agitated the minds of the people concerned... The predominance of local issues is also suggested by the rather striking pattern of voting revealed by the plebiscite results. In 61 per cent of the 344 wards, which were the primary electoral units, voting tended to be overwhelmingly for or against integration.[169]

---

[166] See *'Most Secret' Politics in Togoland: The British Government's Attempt to Annex Togoland to the Gold Coast* (New York: Contemporary Press, 1953).

[167] Minute by M.G. Smith, dated 1 June 1954, PRO CO 554/1034.

[168] Amenumey, *Ewe Unification Movement*, pp. 265–8, combines the two.

[169] Coleman, 'Togoland', p. 74. He does, however, go on to suggest that this was nothing unusual and to argue that it cannot be assumed that the plebiscite did not represent the will of the people on the question of union with the Gold Coast.

The implication is that voting decisions were influenced by numerous factors that strictly speaking had nothing to do with the plebiscite. The second position is exemplified by Dennis Austin, who first asserts that the TC leaders 'wanted a "homeland" under Ewe leadership' and then goes on to suggest that its appeal was correspondingly limited among non-Ewe communities. Hence:

> In the south the non-Ewe states of the Krachi, Nkonya, Likpe and Santrokofi peoples (whose ties lay westwards with the Gold Coast) looked with suspicion on all Congress propaganda.[170]

Curiously, this statement is reproduced almost word for word by Amenumey.[171]

Neither interpretation is entirely satisfactory as it stands. On closer inspection, as Brown recognizes, phenomena which are deemed to be local often turn out to have their roots in processes that were far wider in scope. At the same time, essentialist ethnic categories are more of a hindrance than an aid to understanding. Although the Austin text has stood the test of time remarkably well, it is positively misleading in respect of its depiction of politics in Togoland. The TC never construed itself as an Ewe party and many of its key leaders, most notably Antor himself, do not fit comfortably into an Ewe bracket.[172] The point is not to resurrect the idea that there was an authentic Ewe category, which Antor happened to lie outside of, but to reiterate that what it was to be 'Ewe' was precisely what was hotly disputed.

The limits of ethnicity

The plebiscite results will serve as the basis for discussion here because they give us a clearer sense of the preferences of Togolanders than either the 1954 or the 1956 elections – in part because the issue was framed more precisely, but also because electoral constituencies straddled the invisible border with the Gold Coast.[173] A cursory glance at the plebiscite results reveals a clear north–south pattern of voting, which might appear to support a straightforward ethnic interpretation (see Table 5.1). Most obviously, the electorate of Northern British Togoland voted for union – particularly in the Dagomba and Mamprusi Districts – while that of Southern Togoland voted mostly for separation from the Gold Coast. Here I will confine myself to a detailed discussion of Southern Togoland. Within the southern half of the trust territory, there was equally a north-south distribution of voting. Whereas support for integration was concentrated in the Buem-Krachi District, the Ho and Kpandu Districts mostly opted for separation from the Gold Coast.

Relating this pattern back to the Austin thesis, it would be fair to say that the peoples of the Krachi area did indeed have close historical and cultural links with peoples west of the Volta. Equally, the Nkonya peoples had long insisted on a link with

---

[170] Dennis Austin, *Politics in Ghana 1946–1960* (Oxford: Oxford University Press, 1970), p. 234.

[171] Amenumey, *Ewe Unification Movement*, p. 146. Much the same is reported in a highly misleading article by Barbara Callaway, 'Local politics in Ho and Aba', *Canadian Journal of African Studies*, 4.1, 1970, p. 132.

[172] The Ewe label is attached to Antor by every commentator I have encountered, despite the fact that he actually hailed from Logba. See, for example, Welch, *Dream of Unity*, p. 88 and Richard Rathbone (ed.), *British Documents on the End of Empire, Series B Volume 1: Ghana, Part II 1952–1957* (London: HMSO, 1992), p. 90, n. 1. Among the other key leaders, Alex Odame was from Buem and Rev. F.R. Ametowobla was from Avatime. In fact, A.K. Senoo and Kodzo Ayeke, a former Customs officer from Taviefe, were the only Ewes in the first rank of leaders.

[173] Austin, *Politics in Ghana*, pp. 234–5.

Table 5.1 Pattern of voting in May 1956 plebiscite by District Council area

Council area	Integration	Separation
Mamprusi District	17,870	3,429
Dagomba District	28,083	6,549
Gonja District	3,166	2,729
Northern votes	*49,119*	*12,707*
Buem–Krachi	28,178	18,775
Kpandu	8,581	17,029
Ho	7,217	18,981
Southern votes	*43,976*	*54,785*
Grand total	*93,095 (58%)*	*67,492 (42%)*

Source: United Nations Trusteeship Council, *Report of the United Nations Plebiscite Commissioner.*

Table 5.2. Voting in 1956 plebiscite in Southern Togoland by District and Local Council area

District and local Council area	For integration	For separation
Buem Krachi District	*28,178*	*18,775*
Krachi	10,004	2,861
Akan	8,299	6,837
Buem	3,127	4,315
Biakoye	2,210	1,957
Likpe-Lolobi	1,027	2,114
Nkonya	3,511	691
Kpandu District	*8,581*	*17,029*
Gbi-Hohoe	547	3,667
Akpini	2,287	4,861
East Dain	2,001	5,564
Ablode	1,287	2,828
Anfoega	2,549	109
Ho District	*7,217*	*18,981*
Yingor	1,663	5,574
Asogli	1,586	4,049
Anyigbe	2,063	1,092
Adaklu	185	1,861
Dutaso	1,720	6,405
Grand Total	*43,976*	*54,785*

Source: United Nations Trusteeship Council, *Report of the United Nations Plebiscite Commissioner.*

the Guans of the Gold Coast. These realities may account for their preferences. In Buem, however, the picture was more confused. As we have seen, the Akan section of Buem had fought long and hard for recognition of its distinct identity. And yet the margin in favour of integration in this sector was actually fairly narrow (see Table 5.2), which would suggest that the Akan card worked better in some contexts than in others. In fact, because the Akan category had emerged less in opposition to an 'Ewe' than a 'Lefana' foil, it cannot be assumed that Akan voters were necessarily primed to reject political appeals emanating from 'Eweland'. Moreover, other factors almost certainly played an additional part in tilting the outcome in favour of integration. One was a perception that northern Buem was particularly deprived in terms of access to basic social amenities, despite producing most of the cocoa. Although the TC appealed to the interests of the cocoa farmers, it was out-trumped by CPP promises of immediate material rewards.[174] Furthermore, ongoing land disputes with Akposso probably helped to harden attitudes in favour of maintenance of the border – although some of the settlements closest to the highly disputed zone actually voted for separation.[175]

Ethnicity possesses even less explanatory value among the other Central Togo minorities, where identities were both more fluid and highly contested. Hence Bowiri and Santrokofi mostly voted for integration, while Akpafu, Likpe, Lolobi, and the Lefana section of Buem opted for separation. Contrary to what Austin asserts, Santrokofi did not have particularly strong affinities with the Gold Coast, while the voting statistics show that Likpe evidently did not spurn the TC.

An ethnic interpretation of voting is inherently problematic in respect of the Ewe-speaking communities of the Ho and Kpandu Districts for the simple reason that there was no straightforward choice on those lines: after all, there were Ewes to be found both in the Gold Coast and across the border in French Togoland. The chiefs of the Anyigbe Local Council area actually expressed a desire to opt out of the plebiscite altogether, and to be joined with the Gold Coast without further ado, on the grounds that they had nothing in common with the peoples of the Ho District, but were related to the Anlos.[176] In this theatre, the margin in favour of union was clear-cut. The preferences of voters in the Anyigbe area might be thought to reflect the force of sub-ethnic solidarities, in that the Agotime traditions claimed a distinct origin from the northern Ewe.[177] But even this is problematic in view of the fact that Agotime provided the one clear instance of a *dukɔ* that was split down the middle by the Milner-Simon line. A vote in favour of union therefore amounted – quite remarkably – to endorsement of the boundary that partitioned the Agotime people. The plebiscite results would suggest either that Agotime identity had become

---

[174] Interview with Henry Yao Gyambibby, Asato, 19 September 1992.

[175] In Dzindzi, the vote was 344 for separation and 100 for union, and in Menusu it was 479 for separation and 179 for union. One should probably not read too much into these figures, because it is likely that many of the voters were themselves from French Togoland.

[176] 'Petition by the Natural Rulers of the Anyigbe Local Council Area praying for exemption from the forthcoming plebiscite and for the direct integration with the Gold Coast', dated 8 November 1955, GNAH RAO/C749.

[177] Rattray was emphatically told in 1915 that 'We are not Ewes' although the traditions did refer to a migration from Notsie. GNAA ADM 39/5/73. Apart from the Agotimes, the Anyigbe area also included the Dakpas.

attenuated or that the inhabitants of towns like Kpetoe and Afegame did not find the border that irksome. The same was possibly true of other border villages like Shia, Atikpui and Nyive within the Dutaso Local Council area, all of which backed the integration option.[178] Although the greater part of Eweland nevertheless voted for separation, it also has to be emphasized that there were many CPP strongholds throughout Southern Togoland. Integrationist opinions dominated Anfoega, but the larger towns of Ho and Kpandu, and rural *dukɔwo* such as Abutia, Vakpo and Ve, also boasted a considerable CPP presence. All of this would tend to suggest that ethnicity is far too blunt an instrument with which to meaningfully dissect popular opinion in Southern Togoland, and raises the question of whether local dynamics were indeed more decisive.

Local factionalism and the Togoland debate

It makes obvious sense to pay close attention to the internal dynamics of particular communities because these were likely to act as a filter for the larger political questions. However, as I set out to demonstrate in the previous chapter, it is untenable to treat localities as if they were hermetically sealed from one another and from the wider political environment. As I will now seek to argue with reference to three specific communities, the micro- and macro-processes really need to be read in tandem.

(i) *Likpe*. Likpe divided right down the middle on the plebiscite question, and this happened to replicate the lines of fracture surrounding the Atando NA.[179] Although the issues were ostensibly unrelated, they raised the same matters of principle in the eyes of the protagonists. It is possible to identify a unificationist strand in Likpe politics from the beginnings of the TU. The headchief, Boke Akototse III, was one of the founders of the Natural Rulers Society that had kicked against the amalgamation policy during the 1930s and 1940s. When the TU established common cause with the Natural Rulers in 1948, Akototse was drawn into the fold. And when Antor announced the membership of the TC executive, it included Togbui Jacob Sekyere I of Likpe-Agbozome as vice-chairman and vice-president of the party.[180] Akototse chaired one of the party committees and was a regular signatory to its political communications.[181] Political preferences were also reinforced by less formal contacts. The Atando NA swiftly acquired a reputation as a hotbed of unificationist activity. This was signalled in the grudging – and distinctly inaccurate – words of John Dixon in 1951 when he opined that: 'Mr. Antor represents nothing but a handful of political adventurers in the town of Borada and the Atando Native Authority area'.[182] Many of

---

[178] In Shia, the vote was 237 for union and 180 for separation, and in Atikpui/Nyive it was 321 for separation and 253 for union. North of Klave, border settlements were more inclined to vote for separation.

[179] In Likpe, the vote was distributed as follows: in Mate 49 for integration and 532 for separation; in Bala 37 for integration and 280 for separation; in Kukurantumi 354 for integration and 14 for separation; in Todome/Bakwa 304 for integration and 188 for separation; and in Avedzeme/Agbozome/Koforidua 11 for integration and 192 for separation.

[180] Antor to Senior DC (5 February 1951), GNAH RAO/C705.

[181] 'Observations of the political committee of the Togoland Congress on the resolution adopted by the Congress at Logba-Alakpeti on 28 January 1951', GNAH RAO/C705.

[182] 'Commentary on Mr Antor's statement to the Trusteeship Council on 16 March 1951' by John Duncan, GNAA ADM 39/1/676.

the closest associates of Antor, like A.K. Senoo, originated from Hohoe and wielded some influence over the Gbi headchief, Togbui Gabusu IV. The latter had co-operated with Akototse in the Natural Rulers Society, and the two worked closely together as rotating presidents of the new Native Authority. As we have already seen, the Likpe Grand Council was formed with a mission to subvert the NA, and embarked on a campaign to destool those chiefs who backed the initiative. When Togbui Sekyere was forced to vacate his village, he settled in Hohoe and married the daughter of Togbui Gabusu. From his base in Hohoe, he was able to play an even more active role in unificationist politics. Significantly, these political-cum-personal alliances remained operative long after the Atando NA had been replaced by separate Gbi and Likpe-Lolobi Local Councils. The headchief's town of Mate served as the bastion of unificationist politics in Likpe, with additional pockets of support in Bala, Koforidua and Agbozome.

Predictably, the central figure behind the CPP was Nana Agya Mensah III of Likpe-Avedzeme. The latter claimed to have been a member of the UGCC in Accra, to have joined the CPP when it broke away in 1949 and to have been given an explicit mandate by the party to proselytize in the territory.[183] When the CPP began to seek a means of inserting itself into Togoland, the Likpe Grand Council served as a ready-made vehicle. Interestingly, Agya Mensah presented himself to his local audience almost as a local incarnation of Kwame Nkrumah. For example, he made much play of his victory over the combined efforts of the British and the NA to have him impris-oned, suggesting a link with Nkrumah's own triumphant emergence from jail. Although the creation of the Likpe-Lolobi Council in 1952 removed the rationale for the Grand Council, the insistence on seeing the destoolment actions through to their conclusion kept local politics on the boil. The Grand Council sought to remove the chiefs of Agbozome, Bakwa, Todome and the headchief himself and to replace them with pro-CPP candidates. Hence in January 1954, Agya Mensah led a delegation to F.Y. Asare, then the Ministerial Secretary for Local Government, to solicit his support for the destoolments and for the recognition of one Nicholas Soglo as Mate chief.[184] The latter, who worked as a contractor outside the area, was nominated precisely because he was known to be a keen member of the CPP. Given that Agya Mensah was campaigning for the re-election of Asare to Parliament, this plan was bound to meet with a positive reception. However, Asare lacked the wherewithal to carry through this local coup, and final resolution of the matter had to await a committee of enquiry the following year.[185] As with the TC, the spillover of political sympathies from one arena to the other is very apparent. In the plebiscite, the villages that had backed the Grand Council most strongly – especially Kukurantumi and Bakwa – voted overwhelmingly for the integration option.

However, this should not be taken to mean that local issues were autonomous or determinant. Akototse and Agya Mensah lined up on opposite sides of the Atando and unification debates precisely because they regarded the underlying issues as

---

[183] Interview with Nana Agya Mensah III, Avedzeme, 19 February 1986.

[184] Under this plan the Mate chief would have ceased to be the headchief, thereby overturning the 'Likpe Constitution'.

[185] Letter from F.Y. Asare to Minister of Justice (27 January 1954) and Government Agent, Jasikan, to Regional Officer (13 March 1954), GNAH DA/D31.

cognate. Akototse had defended the Atando arrangements on the grounds that the cocoa economy of Likpe and the commercial power of Hohoe were mutually complementary. He had also inclined towards a version of history that presented the Bakpele and the Ewes on both sides of the border as closely related peoples. For these reasons, it seemed logical that he should endorse the Togoland unification campaign. Local informants also suggest that the hand of the headchief was steadied by a concentration of 'German scholars' in Mate who had once been members of the Togo Bund and who had transferred their loyalties to the TC. As Victor Soglo, who later succeeded to the paramountcy, put it: 'The old German-educated people were *Ablode*. Mate had many of these people and so was strongly *Ablode* unlike Kukurantumi, Bakwa and Avedzeme'.[186] Exactly the same observation was made by one of the CPP stalwarts with reference to Hohoe itself.[187]

On the other side, Agya Mensah appealed to a generation that had no memory of a united Togoland. Those who had travelled to work in the Gold Coast were inclined to measure local developments against those of the Colony, whereas they typically regarded French Togoland as little more than a backwater. Agya Mensah had also opposed the Atando NA on the grounds that the Bakpele were quite unlike the Ewes and were traditional enemies of the Gbis. On the basis that the Bakpele were really an offshoot of a greater Akan diaspora, he contended that both Ewe and Togoland unificationism were of no concern to his people, and campaigned for outright integration with the Gold Coast. Although Agya Mensah was himself a chief, and a fairly senior one at that, he was adept at playing the populist card. Hence he appealed to the youngmen against the authoritarianism of the headchief, and to junior chiefs against the traditional hierarchy. Whereas the TC leadership tended to be advancing in years, CPP activists were typically younger, more highly educated and thoroughly seduced by the modernist vision articulated by Nkrumah. In certain instances, generational schisms manifested themselves within the same family. Hence Nicholas and Victor Soglo found themselves at serious odds with their father, a former Togo Bund member, and senior members of their family who were ardent unificationists.[188] For most CPP enthusiasts, 'progress' was a package that converted the local and the national into a common political currency.

(ii) *Buem*. The second area that warrants closer attention is the Lefana section of Buem which, like Likpe, divided over the 1956 plebiscite. In the early days of the TU, some of the most virulent opposition to the AEC had emanated from Buem. This had precedents in the inter-war period, when Buem nativists railed against a perceived Ewe cultural hegemony within the church. As already mentioned, the Kudje chief, Nana Akuamoa IV, petitioned against the election of Gold Coast Ewes to the SCC in 1948. The subsequent replacement of Amu by F.Y Asare (from Borada) brought a Buem politician to the forefront of unification politics for the first time. However, the subsequent disagreement over participation in Gold Coast institutions generated a rift in Buem itself. F.Y. Asare and Nana Akuamoa accepted

---

[186] Interview with Nana Soglo Allo III, Mate, 16 October 1986.

[187] Interview with Frank Tsaku, Hohoe, 14 October 1986.

[188] Their father was arrested at the start of the war for his pro-German sympathies, as was the father of Victor Soglo's wife. Interview with Nana Soglo Allo III, Mate, 10 February 1986.

the merits of inclusion and went over to the CPP in 1951. On the other hand, the regent in Borada, John Amanie, allied himself with the Antor faction.[189] Under his leadership, Borada acquired a reputation, second only to Hohoe itself, as a hotbed of *Ablode* militancy. At the founding meeting of the TC in Borada, Amanie accepted the position of chairman and president of the party, and remained one of the most influential members in subsequent years.[190] In the mid-1950s, Asare and Nana Akuamoa squared up against Amanie and Alex Odame in a struggle for the political loyalties of Buem.

The TC appealed to the cocoa farmers, and had an effective mouthpiece in Amanie who had played a key role in the hold-ups of the 1930s. On the other hand, the CPP highlighted the material gains that would follow from union with the Gold Coast. However, an examination of the plebiscite results suggests that local factors may also have had a part to play. Borada, Jasikan, Nsuta and Teteman contained substantial numbers of supporters from both sides, but the rest of Buem tended to line up on one side or the other. Whereas New Ayoma, Old Ayoma, Lekanti, Baika, Baglo and Kute were firmly rooted in the unificationist camp, Okadjakrom, Atonkor, Guaman and Kudje voted for integration. Although this reveals itself as a geographical division between a pro-CPP north and a pro-TC south, the key to understanding this pattern lies in a continuation of chieftaincy struggles. The most pro-CPP towns were those that were presided over by senior wing chiefs, while the TC drew its support from towns which felt most excluded from the hierarchy and were claiming an autochthonous status.[191] Chieftaincy conflicts reinforced the contours of the larger political debate because the wing chiefs were – ironically enough – inclined to defend the existing hierarchy on the basis of Akan precedents. Nana Akuamoa regarded John Amanie as such a threat precisely because he was seeking to elevate the regent to the position of a substantive Omanhene. As the senior wing chief, and Acting President of the Buem NA, Nana Akuamoa was intent on preserving the rules of precedence. What he defended as 'tradition' was rejected by the southern sub-chiefs as sheer historical fabrication. By allying themselves with John Amanie, they hoped to restore a structure in which all Buem settlements would be of equivalent status and all chiefs would serve the Omanhene directly. For that reason, they were inclined to distance Buem from Gold Coast models and practices.

(iii) *Anfoega*. Finally, it would be instructive to return to the case of Anfoega. As the plebiscite results reveal, this Ewe-speaking *dukɔ* was fully behind the integrationist platform. After the 1951 elections, Anfoega was reputed to be the safest CPP stronghold in the territory, with the possible exception of Nkonya. Kofi Dumoga had parted company with the CPP over the Volta River Project, but Togbe S.T. Fleku and the new headchief, Togbe Tepre Hodo III (enstooled in 1952), took up the mantle and performed sterling work on behalf of the governing party. The former served on the national committee for the Volta project, held the position of regional

---

[189] In 1946, Nana Akpandja II ceased to be capable of performing his duties as Omanhene. Amanie therefore assumed the position of Regent.

[190] Although Asare and Nana Akuamoa were apparently present at the Borada meeting, they later disassociated themselves from the TC.

[191] The chief of Kudje was the Nifahene, while the chief of Guaman was the Benkumhene.

secretary of the CPP and appeared before the Trusteeship Council to state the case for integration in 1954.[192] For his part, Tepre Hodo filled the strategic position of chairman of the TVT Council and campaigned actively on behalf of the CPP across Togoland.

The reason why Anfoega aligned itself so completely with the CPP has everything to do with local politics, but of a kind that was itself grounded in the larger issues of the day. As in Nkonya, there was a profound sense that the community had been penalized for its principled opposition to the amalgamation policy. In April 1951, yet another petition was despatched to the Ministry of Local Government, demanding that Anfoega be entitled to draw on the Rural Development Fund. When this met with the standard rebuff, the Anfoega Duonenyo Organization proceeded to write directly to the newly installed Leader of Government Business, Kwame Nkrumah. British civil servants complained about this failure to respect the proper lines of communication, but the petitioners defiantly proclaimed that they would henceforth continue to take the direct route.[193] By a happy coincidence, the CPP was seeking to secure a foothold in Togoland at the very moment when Anfoega spokesmen were seeking a fair hearing in government. The CPP leadership indicated that it was sympathetic and signalled a willingness to help redress the injury in exchange for political support. In this manner, an enduring alliance was forged.

However, the accord was not purely a matter of expedience on both sides. It was crucial that there was also a comfortable fit between the CPP vision of 'progress' and the world view of the educated youngmen who dominated community affairs through the Anfoega Duonenyo Organization. The fact that the newly enstooled headchief was youthful and distinctly 'modern' in outlook helped to fortify the position of the CPP in Anfoega. In fact, Tepre Hodo used every sanction at his disposal to banish the TC from the community. When Kodzo Ayeke addressed a public meeting in Anfoega in February 1954, he was arrested and charged before the Anfoega Native Court for having used insulting language against the chief.[194] Antor and his supporters subsequently attended an election rally at Anfoega-Tokome, and they too were arrested for abetting Ayeke. The Government Agent, David Heaton, took the view that Tepre Hodo had acted improperly in the matter and succeeded in having the charges withdrawn. Although he was inclined to blame the provocative stance of the TC politicians, he also identified an unwillingness to accept dissenting opinions. As he put it:

> The Anfoegas are extremely intolerant of activity by anyone not of their political persuasion and it has been necessary to draw their attention to regulation 62 of the Electoral Provisions (Assembly Elections) Regulations, 1954.[195]

In the plebiscite itself, the separation option received precious few votes in Anfoega. The evidence of coercion is compelling, but even on a level playing field it

---

[192] Amenumey, *Ewe Unification Movement*, p. 145.

[193] Hayibor, General Secretary of Anfoega Duonenyo Organization, to Senior DC (7 July 1951), GNAA ADM 39/1/95.

[194] The case was later transferred to the Magistrate's Court, which found Ayeke guilty and fined him £10 plus costs, while binding him over for £50.

[195] David Heaton to Regional Officer (17 May 1954), GNAH TA/31.

is doubtful whether the TC would have made very much headway. The truth of the matter was that a collective sense of Anfoega identity was far stronger than any groundswell of Ewe or Togoland solidarity. And while this was undoubtedly grounded in a local dynamic, it also synchronised remarkably well with the modernist myth around which Ghanaian independence was built.

Conclusion

In a review of Coleman's monograph, Thomas Hodgkin remarked that 'It is easy to lose one's way in the "Togoland question". There are so many actors in the drama, like a Dostoyevsky novel'.[196] To the lengthy list of characters needs to be added a plot that is sometimes difficult to follow and even occasionally implausible. In this chapter, I have sought to chart a course through the various sub-plots, while showing how the story might still be viewed as a whole.

It bears reiteration that the case for a reunified Togoland preceded arguments in favour of Ewe unification by some two decades. Hence, the suggestion that there was an unbroken thread linking the campaigns of the AEC with protests at the time of the nineteenth-century partition is misleading. Much of the agitation in the 1920s was inspired by a distaste for French rule, but the Togo Bund went further in articulating the merits of a unified Togoland in its own right. It was only after 1945 that the Ewe unification movement really became a significant political force. Although the AEC won substantial support in the Gold Coast and in French Togoland, opinion in British Togoland quickly turned against it. Whereas the *Ewe News-Letter* chose to emphasize the latent unity of the Ewe people, the TU contended that Ewe unificationism was no more than a cover for Anlo and Peki interests, thereby flatly contradicting the ethnic charter of Chapman and his colleagues.

Subsequently, most of the Gold Coast Ewe leadership defected to the CPP, in the hope that Nkrumah could deliver on the promise of ultimate unification. Here they were joined by a dissident section of the TU that believed that the territory would only receive its fair share of resources if Togolanders had some representation at the centre. After 1951, the British and the CPP worked closely together to bring about full integration with the Gold Coast. This was driven by an annexationist agenda that was rooted as much in Gold Coast mentalities as in the predilections of the colonial power. Some Togolanders remained distrustful of their larger neighbour to the west and reacted negatively to the efforts to entice them into a closer embrace. Others were prepared to agree with Arden-Clarke that imperialism was not necessarily a bad thing. When it came to the final choice in 1956, ethnicity played a role – albeit a smaller one than is often thought – but it still derived its practical salience from the local context. At the same time, I have sought to demonstrate that local politics was also informed by ideas and processes which were really territorial in scope. It is the elusive character of identity politics in Togoland which makes it so devilishly difficult to nail down.

The plebiscite results finally forced the United Nations to make up its mind on

---

[196] 'Sure guide in Togoland', *West Africa*, 1 December 1956.

whether the two Togolands were to share a common destiny or to go their separate ways.[197] Because north and south had voted for different options, interpreting the results was by no means a straightforward affair. Whereas unificationists argued that the two halves should be considered separately, the British government underlined the fact that an overall majority had endorsed union with the Gold Coast, while observing that Southern Togoland was too small to stand on its own. Furthermore, the British had pointed out as early as 1954 that they would be unable to fulfil their trusteeship obligations once the Gold Coast became independent. These points were made in the full knowledge that it would be difficult to unscramble Trans-Volta Togoland without causing considerable disruption. Manoeuvred into a corner, the United Nations felt it had little option than to consider the results for British Togoland as a whole, thereby setting its seal of approval on the final partition of Togoland.[198] On 6 March 1957, therefore, the territory forfeited its distinct status and became an integral part of an independent Ghana. Across the border, the CUT under Sylvanus Olympio succeeded in winning the national elections of 1958, and thereafter opted for a separate independence in April 1960.[199] The result was that the partition of Togoland became a permanent dispensation etched into the map of a newly independent Africa.

[197] For the final debates at the United Nations, see Amenumey, *Ewe Unification Movement*, pp. 266–75.

[198] The fact that the United Nations distinguished between north and south in the Cameroons plebiscite of 1961 shows that there was an alternative. Welch, *Dream of Unity*, pp. 224–43.

[199] On the 1958 elections in French Togoland, see D.E.K. Amenumey, 'The general elections in the "Autonomous Republic of Togo", April 1958: background and interpretation', *Transactions of the Historical Society of Ghana*, 15, 2, 1974.

Part Three

Inscribing Spaces
The Political Economy of the Ghana–Togo Border
since Independence

Towards the end of 1959, which was a critical point in the unfolding Togoland saga, *West Africa* magazine observed that 'No West African frontier has caused more trouble or is more resented than that between Ghana and the Togo Republic'.[1] Going further, the article predicted that 'so long as the frontier exists, at least in its present form, it may always cause trouble'. Such an assessment would not have sounded alarmist or out of place at the time of writing. Indeed, the Ghana–Togo borderlands have retained a reputation as one of the more contentious frontier zones of independent Africa. In many ways, this is a reputation that is undeserved. Four decades after independence, the boundary has ossified and now seems unlikely to alter its shape or import, except conceivably within the more inclusive framework of the Economic Community of West African States (ECOWAS). By contrast with other notorious trouble spots, such as Kashmir and the Ogaden, the Ghana–Togo border has not provided the occasion for a clash of arms, although there have been many verbal exchanges between the respective governments over the years. In a series of incisive articles, David Brown has argued that while this border has been a constant irritant in relations between governments, there has been little interest in secession from within 'western Togoland'.[2] Equally, little popular irredentism has emanated from the Togolese side. If the border was ever actively resented, therefore, it seems to have acquired a broad measure of acceptance with time. As far as former British Togoland is concerned, this outcome cannot be attributed in any simple sense to the material benefits of being associated with Ghana, given that the experience was one of accumulating hardships after independence. Although Togo fared comparatively better, at least in economic terms, it is significant that it has not functioned as a political magnet for its former sibling.

The next two chapters seek to account for this curious state of affairs, but come at

---

[1] 'Dr. Nkrumah and M. Olympio', *West Africa*, 7 November 1959, p. 929.

[2] David Brown, 'Borderline politics in Ghana: the National Liberation Movement of Western Togoland', *The Journal of Modern African Studies*, 18, 4, 1980; 'Who are the tribalists? Social pluralism and political ideology in Ghana', *African Affairs*, 81, 322, 1982; and 'Sieges and scapegoats: the politics of pluralism in Ghana and Togo', *The Journal of Modern African Studies*, 21, 34, 1983.

the question from rather different angles. Chapter 6 resumes the political discussion where the previous one left off, with a view to accounting for the collapse of the unification movement after 1957. Much of the analysis will centre on the First Republic, because it was at this time that the *Ablode* cause imploded while the concept of Ghana took greater hold. Chapter 7 seeks to demonstrate how ordinary people have contributed to the construction of border spaces since independence, with reference to the contraband trade and land disputes. In a reprise of Chapter 3, I also set out to examine the interactions between border communities and the Ghanaian state.

6

The Cessation of Secession

The Political Paradox
of the Ghana–Togo Border

The United Nations decision to assess the British Togoland plebiscite results as a whole, and thus to accept the majority verdict in favour of integration, was a heavy blow to campaigners for Ewe and Togoland unification. The latter worried that the outcome would free the hands of the French authorities to integrate their section of Togoland into the French Union, thereby foreclosing any chance of unification in the future. However, the electoral victory of the Comité de l'Unité Togolaise (CUT) in 1958 restored hopes that such an eventuality might still be forestalled. At some level, the Convention People's Party (CPP), the CUT and the Togoland Congress (TC) all agreed that the boundary question could be best resolved by a coming together of Ghana and French Togoland. In the final event, however, the opportunity was lost owing to mutual suspicions between the three sets of protagonists. The rift between Kwame Nkrumah and Sylvanus Olympio has received fairly detailed treatment elsewhere, and I will seek to do no more than sketch an outline of the dispute here.[1] The division between Nkrumah and Antor had deeper roots in the battle over political turf in British Togoland. In this case, the determination of the CPP to extinguish opposition in the Trans-Volta Togoland (TVT) Region ruled out any chance of co-operation. In the longer term, it also had the effect of dismantling the one constituency that had an abiding interest in unification. The legacy of Nkrumah, the self-professed prophet of pan-Africanism, was a profoundly contradictory one. He contributed more than any other politician to the entrenchment of the border, partly because of his limitations as an international statesman, but partly also because he was such a consummate politician on the domestic stage.[2] Both added up to the same thing in the long run: namely, the reinforcement of the

[1] E.O. Saffu, 'Nkrumah and the Togoland question', *Economic Bulletin of Ghana*, 12, 2/3, 1968; W. Scott Thompson, *Ghana's Foreign Policy, 1957–1966: Diplomacy, Ideology, and the New State* (Princeton: Princeton University Press, 1969), pp. 81–7; Saadia Touval, *The Boundary Politics of Independent Africa* (Cambridge, Mass.: Harvard University Press, 1972), pp. 155–8, 203–11; and D.E.K. Amenumey, *The Ewe Unification Movement: A Political History* (Accra: Ghana Universities Press, 1989), ch. 9.

[2] Ironically, it is a stock observation on the Nkrumah period that he concentrated on foreign affairs to the neglect of domestic ones.

territorial status quo. In what follows, I will examine the record of the Nkrumah government in relation to the border question in a certain amount of detail. I will then proceed to evaluate the renewed rumblings of secessionism during the decade of the 1970s.

Greater Ghana:
the Nkrumah regime and the pursuit of integration

Artificial barriers which have irritated and annoyed us and our kinsmen on the other side for all these years and which led to the initiation of the unification movement can be removed only by total integration of Togoland under French Trusteeship with Ghana into a single and indivisible nation.[3]

A union of master and boy?
Nkrumah, Olympio and the border equation

Throughout the first half of the 1950s, the Nkrumah government had subscribed to the view that the principal obstacle to unification was posed by the French. Although his British advisers urged him to abandon any ambition of joining up with French Togoland, on the grounds that the French had their own legitimate interests to protect, Nkrumah continued to hope that events might still turn in his favour.[4] The immediate problem was that the dominant parties in French Togoland, namely, the Parti Togolais du Progrès (PTP) and the Union des Chefs et Populations du Nord-Togo (UCPN), were supportive of French designs for the territory. The CUT was resolutely opposed to the latter, but found it difficult to advance its own agenda because of official manipulation of the electoral process. The poll of February 1958 did, however, present a fresh opportunity, in that voting on this occasion was to be observed by the United Nations. The CUT contested the elections in alliance with Juvento on a platform of outright independence.[5] The parties did not campaign very actively on the issue of reunification, but they did advocate the negotiation of a customs union agreement with Ghana.[6] There is some disagreement as to whether the Nkrumah government actually offered material assistance to the CUT/Juvento alliance, but it certainly offered its moral support.[7]

---

[3] Speech by Nkrumah at Ho, cited in telegram from J.H.A. Watson to Commonwealth Relations Office, 29 October 1959, PRO FO 371/138171.

[4] Nkrumah was allegedly being encouraged by Nehru and Krishna Menon, the Indian representative to the Trusteeship Council, to play for French Togoland as well. The British endeavoured to keep Nehru and Nkrumah as far apart as possible. H.T. Bourdillon, Colonial Office, to W.A.W. Clarke, Commonwealth Relations Office (20 May 1954), and W.L. Gorell Barnes to Sir Charles Arden-Clarke, Accra (21 May 1954), PRO CO 554/1033.

[5] Juvento stood for Mouvement de la Jeunesse Togolaise. For more about this party, see Amenumey, *Ewe Unification Movement*, pp. 133–4, 314–23.

[6] 'Togoland before the elections', *West Africa*, 3 May 1958, p. 413. Some pro-unification posters were, however, to be seen in southern villages, according to Amenumey, *Ewe Unification Movement*, p. 316.

[7] Saffu, 'Nkrumah', p. 38, cites Michael Dei-Anang in support of the view that material support was provided. Thompson, *Ghana's Foreign Policy*, p. 82 cites S.W. Kumah to the same effect, but insists that there is no evidence that this was actually the case.

The Cessation of Secession

The overwhelming victory of the CUT over Nicholas Grunitzky raised expectations that Nkrumah and Olympio might be able to come to a mutually satisfactory arrangement.[8] As far as the Ghanaian authorities were concerned, this was best hammered out sooner rather than later – and preferably before Togolese independence. What Nkrumah envisaged was a complete merger of sovereignty after the withdrawal of the French. On the back of his electoral triumph, Olympio signalled his willingness to contemplate joining a new political dispensation in the future, possibly as part of a greater West African Federation. However, he also indicated his lack of interest in an outright merger with Ghana. Instead, he stressed that the immediate priority ought to be the fostering of closer economic links, and in particular the creation of a customs union that would mitigate the practical consequences of the boundary. From the Ghanaian point of view, this amounted to the abandonment of a long-standing commitment to political union. They had a point, in that Olympio had himself responded to an earlier Franco-British pledge to ease frontier restrictions by asserting that the maintenance of any border between the Volta and the Mono Rivers was untenable. Nkrumah now repeated the claim that ordinary people felt affronted by this legacy of European imperialism, and pronounced that:

> ... by integration of Ghana and Togoland we mean the removal of the artificial frontiers between Ghana and French Togoland to enable the people of these two sister territories to be reunited as they were in former days before the division of their territory by colonial powers.[9]

Increasingly, Nkrumah appealed over the head of Olympio to ordinary Togolanders who, he believed, were hankering after an effective union.

As Olympio became increasingly suspicious of the territorial ambitions of his Ghanaian counterpart, he did not stop at asserting the right of Togo to defend its hard-won independence, but also began to question the equity of integrating British Togoland into Ghana. As Touval suggests, this perceived interference in Ghanaian internal affairs rendered a break between the two sides more or less inevitable.[10] If Olympio had abandoned much of his earlier commitment to unification, by effectively retreating behind the boundary line, Nkrumah was being thoroughly consistent in seeking to expand the borders of his country. He had never exhibited much concern for the sensitivities of political leaders in the former Trust territories. At the same time, he was strengthened in his resolve by certain southern Ewe politicians, notably Komla Gbedemah. In one of his more tactless speeches, Nkrumah even went so far as to declare that Togo belonged to Ghana 'by right' and that he would 'see to it that [Togo] became the seventh region of Ghana'.[11] Olympio responded in kind, asserting at one point that 'the former territory of British Togoland belongs without contestation to the Republic of Togo.'[12]

---

[8] CUT and Juvento won 29 seats to the 10 seats of the UCPN and the three seats of the PTP. There were also four successful independent candidates. Amenumey, *Ewe Unification Movement*, p. 320.

[9] 'Ghana–Togoland integration?', *West Africa*, 6 February 1960, p. 158.

[10] Touval, *Boundary Politics*, p. 205.

[11] A speech of October 1959, apparently at Keta, quoted in Thompson, *Ghana's Foreign Policy*, p. 84.

[12] Translation of release by Ministère de l'Interieur, de l'Information et de la Presse, quoting monthly Presidential broadcast of 7 July 1961, Padmore Library, Bureau of African Affairs, file No. 915.

Amid the clash of irredentist claim and counter-claim, the two governments also began to suspect each other of fomenting, or at least tolerating, subversive activity along the border. For his part, Olympio accused Ghana of harbouring Juvento dissidents who had split from the government in 1959 and were alleged to be plotting a coup. On the other side, the Nkrumah government complained that exiled dissidents from the TVT Region were preparing to carry out armed incursions across the border with the connivance of the Togolese authorities. The Togolese were also implicated in the Ahwaitey affair, during which it was alleged that military equipment had been stored across the border for use against the Nkrumah government.[13] The Ghanaian response was to step up security along the frontier, and, in the run-up to Togolese independence, to carry out military manoeuvres there. According to W. Scott Thompson, Nkrumah even instructed General Alexander to draw up an invasion plan.[14] The net effect was merely to drive Olympio into the unlikely embrace of the French, who now seemed the most likely guarantor of Togolese sovereignty. Within days of independence in April 1960, Olympio had signed a defence pact with the former administering power, which he delighted in brandishing in the face of his Ghanaian neighbours.

Even after Togolese independence became a *fait accompli*, Nkrumah believed that Olympio might still be brought to his senses if sufficient pressure were applied. In June 1960, the Ghanaian leader paid a visit to Lomé, where he proposed a formula according to which 'neither country would surrender sovereignty, but would co-operate closely in the matter of diplomatic relations, defence and currency'.[15] Interestingly, in the light of his earlier declarations before the Trusteeship Council, Olympio now cited basic differences of language and history as a barrier to political union. The meeting broke up with agreement only on a proposal that Olympio would submit plans for closer economic co-operation. The Togolese President subsequently entered into discussions with the Guineans and Nigerians with a view to widening the geographical scope thereof.[16] At this point, Olympio was apparently still willing to countenance the adoption of the Ghanaian (or some other) currency as well as membership of a common customs union.[17] However, the Ghana government interpreted the delay as deliberate stalling, and decided to raise the stakes. In October 1960, the Ghana government imposed tough frontier restrictions, which virtually prohibited the export of goods, instituted tighter currency controls and restricted access for Togolese vehicles. F.Y. Asare, then the Regional Commissioner, intimated that the intention was to send a reminder to Olympio that there was still some serious

---

[13] In December 1958, Captain Awhaitey alleged that he had been approached by opposition politicians, Reginald Amponsah and M.K. Apaloo, with a view to staging a coup. Amenumey, *Ewe Unification Movement*, p. 340. See also Dennis Austin, *Politics in Ghana 1946–1960* (Oxford: Oxford University Press, 1970), pp. 424–9 and Simon Baynham, *The Military and Politics in Nkrumah's Ghana* (Boulder & London: Westview, 1988), pp. 87–92.

[14] Thompson, *Ghana's Foreign Policy*, p. 85.

[15] *Ibid.*, p. 86.

[16] 'Togo report No. 2, 1 November 1960', by J.F.S. Corbett, Chargé d'Affaires, British Embassy, Lomé', PRO FO 371/147612.

[17] Olympio apparently regarded membership of the franc zone as something of a straitjacket. Telegram from J.H.A. Watson, British Embassy, Dakar, to Foreign Office (28 December 1960), PRO FO 371/147613.

business to transact. At a speech in Ho in December, Nkrumah was even more forth-right:

> This action has brought home as forcibly as no other action could the hardships and absurdity involved in maintaining an artificial border between us and in proving to M. Olympio that Togoland and Ghana are one and that no amount of lies and deception to the people can disprove this fact.[18]

This attempt to apply an economic stranglehold was based on a couple of critical calculations. The first was that Togo was dependent upon Ghana for her supplies of manufactured goods and foodstuffs. Although Togo did receive many of its consumer items from Ghana at this time, there was no reason why it needed to do so. Hence Olympio signalled his intention to simply import more commodities directly from Europe and the United States. As he put it:

> The Republic of Togo has practically no need of Ghana to achieve its need of imported goods. The pre-war statistical figures can prove this fact. In short, refusing to sell one's neighbour goods which can be found in all world markets where that neighbour would also go, does not constitute a safe means of [exerting] economic pressure. Even a first year student in economics knows that.[19]

British intelligence reports indicated that the port of Lomé was probably equal to the task and that the principal losers were likely to be Ghanaian exporters.[20] The second assumption was that the Ghanaian authorities were capable of imposing an effective blockade. The reality was that the border was altogether too porous for this to be a realistic proposition. Hence an early British assessment of the frontier controls stated that:

> The Ghanaian near-blockade of Togo merely caused irritation: legitimate trade was affected, but the traditional smuggling of Ghanaian cocoa and manufactured British goods into Togo continued as before.[21]

It was also reported that 'large quantities of francs have been regularly sold on the black market in Ghana at a discount of up to ten per cent in order to buy British goods and bring them back into Togo'.[22] The *Evening News* tacitly admitted the prevalence of smuggling when it claimed that Olympio wanted the border to remain in place because he himself was doing so well out of the contraband trade.[23] Although the Ghanaian press asserted that tightening of the frontier had led to famine conditions in Togo, food shortages in the north were really the consequence of a drought there.[24] Coupled with unrelenting *ad hominem* attacks on Olympio in the

---

[18] Reported in *West Africa*, 31 December 1960, p. 1468.
[19] Translation of release by Ministère de l'Interieur, de l'Information et de la Presse, quoting monthly presidential broadcast of 7 July 1961, Padmore Library, Bureau of African Affairs, file No. 915. On the trade flows, see Edouard Kwam Kouassi, 'Les échanges frontaliers entre Le Togo et le Ghana', mémoire pour le diplôme de l'Institut d'Etudes Politiques du Paris, 1969.
[20] 'Togo report No. 1, 17 October 1960', PRO FO 371/147612.
[21] J.H.A. Watson to E.B. Boothby (2 January 1961), PRO FO 371/147612.
[22] J.H.A. Watson to Earl of Home (2 January 1961), PRO FO 371/155656.
[23] 'Olympio: Africa's No. 2 Tshombe!', *Evening News*, 15 December 1961.
[24] 'Hunger strikes Togo: where is Olympio? Sensation', *Evening News*, 20 March 1962.

Accra newspapers – ranging from the shape of his 'Brazilian nose' to his maternal slave origins and capitalist inclinations – the crude attempts at using the border as a weapon merely confirmed the wisdom of keeping a safe political distance from Accra.[25] It is difficult, therefore, to disagree with W. Scott Thompson when he concludes that, while there was a real chance of finding a mutually satisfactory solution to the Togoland question in the late 1950s, 'Ghana was to fail no test more thoroughly than this one'.[26]

Throughout the stand-off, the government of Sylvanus Olympio was treading a perilously thin line. Although the threat of an invasion from Ghana was always a possibility, Olympio was reluctant to augment his own armed forces, on the grounds that they were a luxury that a small country could ill afford. This made Togo entirely reliant upon a French defence pact, to the evident discomfort of the latter. But while Olympio was willing to use France, he was also intent on diversifying his international links, both in order to retain a degree of autonomy and to cultivate powerful friends. Hence he went out of his way to court the Germans, British, Americans and Nigerians, and sought to involve United Nations bodies directly in the country. Before independence, one British official summed up the Togolese master-plan as follows:

> Some Ministers hinted rather optimistically that Togo would like to become a little Switzerland in West Africa, living quietly, without any strings from abroad, subsidised by the French and anyone else who cared to help, exporting a little cocoa and some phosphates, and indulging in modest contraband trade across its several frontiers.[27]

As it turned out, this was a very prescient observation. In the context of decolonization, when political ties were up for renegotiation, both the British and the Americans came to look upon Olympio as a leader of real stature who projected an influence out of all proportion to the size of his country. By comparison, Nkrumah appeared an increasingly unpredictable figure. One Foreign Office bureaucrat felt sufficiently enthused about the Togolese leader to resort to doggerel:

> In Olympio Olympeius
> Quis portabit Togam eius?[28]

Unfortunately, the answer to this question was to emerge rather quicker than anyone imagined. In line with the Swiss option, Olympio declined to use French aid to absorb demobilized colonial troops into an expanded Togolese army. On 13 January 1963, the veterans and some serving soldiers seized power in Lomé, killing the President as he tried to escape into the American Embassy compound.[29] Suspicion immediately fell upon the Ghana government. From the Nigerian corner, Jaja Wachuku warned darkly that '[f]or the purposes of security, Nigeria considers

---

[25] A selection of the anti-Olympio clippings may be found in the files of the Bureau of African Affairs in the Padmore Library, Accra.

[26] Thompson, *Ghana's Foreign Policy*, p. 81.

[27] A.T. Oldham, Consulate-General, Dakar to H.F.T. Smith, Foreign Office (24 April 1959), PRO FO 371/138270.

[28] An anonymous note penned on the cover of PRO FO 371/167653.

[29] Samuel Decalo, *Coups and Army Rule in Africa; Studies in Military Style* (New Haven & London: Yale University Press, 1976), pp. 98–9.

her boundary extends to the Ghana–Togo border'.[30] Nkrumah momentarily considered sending troops across the border, but after consultations with Dahomey, decided to let the crisis resolve itself internally.[31] To have done otherwise would have looked like a blatant attempt at annexation. Although Ghana did become the first country to recognize the new regime, and the CPP press was distinctly uneulogistic about the assassinated President, Nkrumah insisted that the coup had been a purely domestic affair.[32]

The demise of the CUT regime proved to be a watershed in more ways than one. In respect of the boundary equation, subsequent events underlined that rather more was at stake than the personalities of the respective heads of state. The leader of the new provisional government, Nicholas Grunitzky, had long been a political rival of Olympio and had indeed been exiled.[33] On the principle that an enemy's enemy was potentially a valuable friend, the Nkrumah regime sought to establish friendly relations with the incoming administration. However, unlike Olympio, Grunitzky had always subscribed to that body of opinion that was lukewarm about unification. Although he had every reason to desire a restoration of normal cross-border relations, Grunitzky was even less likely than his predecessor to agree to a surrender of political sovereignty. As it happened, the physical boundary very quickly became a source of friction between the two sides. Following a series of inter-governmental contacts, border restrictions were at first relaxed, and then in February 1963 the border was completely reopened. This restored liberty of passage, and permitted the free exchange of local produce and manufactured goods worth less than £10.[34] However, following an incident in June of that year, the border was closed once again. The refusal of the Togolese to raise their duties on imported spirits, which would have reduced the incentive to smuggle, meant that a supposedly temporary closure became a permanent fixture.[35]

Over the next two years, the Togolese engaged in repeated efforts to negotiate the reopening of the border, but met with Ghanaian intransigence. W. Scott Thompson has even suggested that the Nkrumah regime deliberately provoked a series of frontier incidents to create an excuse for keeping the border closed.[36] Quite what it expected to gain is difficult to gauge. The aim may have been to assist the campaign against smuggling, although this was hardly likely to be effective, given that the contraband was carried across myriad unofficial bush tracks. The logic might also have been more strictly political, in as much as militarization of the border zone could serve as a deterrent to dissidents living in Togo. Whatever the underlying motivations, the border remained sealed until July 1965 when the Nkrumah regime made fresh overtures and once again met with a favourable response. In the interim,

---

[30] Helen Kitchen, 'Filling the Togo vacuum', *Africa Report*, February 1963.

[31] Nkrumah claimed credit for dissuading Dahomey from sending in troops.

[32] Nkrumah himself was reported as saying of Olympio that 'He thought he was a bad man, but murder was never justified'. Telegram from Accra to Commonwealth Relations Office, 15 January 1963, PRO FO 371/167653.

[33] On a more personal level, Olympio was married to the sister of Grunitzky.

[34] Saffu, 'Nkrumah', p. 43.

[35] *Ibid.*, p. 44.

[36] Thompson, *Ghana's Foreign Policy*, pp. 368–9.

however, the Togolese signalled their long-term priorities by entering into new monetary and defence agreements with France. Finally, the border was closed yet again at the end of 1965, and remained that way until a couple of months after Nkrumah was himself toppled in a coup on 24 February 1966.

In sum, the hopes for a settlement that were expressed in 1958 had been killed off within a decade. Ultimately, the plans for political reunification failed to come to fruition because the political elites proved incapable of reaching an accommodation. Given his own declarations in 1947 and in subsequent years, it is deeply ironic that Sylvanus Olympio should have contributed to the entrenchment of the territorial partition. But when push came to shove, he retreated into a more exclusive Togolese nationalism, which he had hitherto decried when it had constituted the platform of the PTP. Although Nkrumah was still ostensibly pursuing a unificationist agenda, this looked suspiciously like Ghanaian expansionism. Furthermore, it was Nkrumah who proceeded to convert the cartographical boundary into a rigid line of demarcation, thereby effectively turning the clock back to the war years. By contrast, the Togolese authorities were all along concerned to minimize frontier restrictions. On both sides of the border, therefore, political elites ended up placing perceived 'national' interests above earlier appeals to a common Ewe ethnicity that transcended colonial boundaries.

The *cipipification* of British Togoland

While conflicting agendas were the fundamental impediment to closer association, the actions of the CPP regime within the TVT Region were a further irritant in the relationship between the two governments. In 1959, at a time when Nkrumah was supposedly still trying to convert Olympio to the merits of a political union, the CPP government proceeded to change the name to the Volta Region. The ostensible aim was to make a clean break with the past, by erasing the last symbolic reminder of the trusteeship period. But to the authorities in Lomé it was indicative of a failure to recognize that Togolanders bore an identity of their own. Moreover, the CPP made life difficult for *Ablode* supporters as it set about implementing a programme of *cipipification*. The latter involved a concerted drive to spread CPP structures both horizontally (across national space) and vertically (that is, from the seat of power down to the smallest village), which also implied a direct attack on opposition strongholds. The net effect was to drive a steady flow of refugees across the border. The willingness of Olympio, and later Grunitzky, to accommodate these refugees was a further affront to the Nkrumah regime.

The tensions between the desire for bureaucratic efficiency and the imperative of tighter party control have been examined in some detail by other writers on the CPP.[37] Here I am more narrowly concerned with the manner in which the CPP dealt with the perceived secessionist threat. In the period leading up to the 1956 plebiscite, there were clear indications that the leadership of the TC was prepared to moderate

---

[37] See, for example, Benjamin Amonoo, *Ghana 1957–1966: Politics of Institutional Dualism* (London: Allen & Unwin, 1981); and Richard Crook, 'Bureaucracy and politics in Ghana: a comparative perspective', in Peter Lyon and James Manor (eds), *Transfer and Transformation: Political Institutions in the New Commonwealth* (Leicester: Leicester University Press, 1983).

its stance on future relations with an independent Ghana. This was partly because the TC was allied to the National Liberation Movement (NLM) and the Northern People's Party (NPP) on a federalist platform.[38] However, the TC leaders also recognized that a complete divorce from the Gold Coast would be unattractive to many Togolanders who looked there for education and employment. During the plebiscite campaign, therefore, the TC had advised voters to choose separation in order that reunification with French Togoland could be accomplished, after which 'unified Togoland shall seek a relation with self-governing Gold Coast'.[39] Following the decision of the United Nations to endorse integration, the TC appeared to bow to the inevitable and concentrated on trying to extract some last-minute concessions. Hence, in the run-up to independence, senior chiefs from Buem, Akpini, Asogli, Gbi, Likpe, Lolobi and Akpafu despatched a series of petitions to the Secretary of State for the Colonies, in which they demanded at least a separate Regional Assembly for former Southern Togoland – that is, shorn of Gold Coast Eweland.[40] Although the government was forced to accept Regional Assemblies at the last minute, it was in no mood to contemplate the break-up of TVT. Furthermore, it had every intention of winding up the Regional Assemblies as soon as practicable after independence – and later did so.

The intransigence of the CPP led to frustration among the ranks of *Ablode* supporters who set out to signal their discontent in more explicit ways. In February, there were reports of armed gangs gathering in the bush who, in the words of Dennis Austin, 'marched up and down in ragged military formation, and practised with shotguns in the hope that they might thereby hasten the day of Togoland unification'.[41] The Police discovered a series of camps and caches of explosives in the vicinity of Alavanyo (west of Hohoe) and Hodzo (to the north-east of Ho). Whereas TC politicians claimed that these were nothing more sinister than hunters' hideouts, the government insisted that they had been built with military objectives in mind.[42] The discoveries led to the implementation of a Peace Preservation Ordinance, which was renewed in some areas through to 1959.[43] In the days leading up to and including independence day, there were violent clashes involving TC supporters in a number of locations, including Kpandu, Hohoe, Amedzofe, Abutia and Jasikan. These culminated in the destruction of a certain amount of property, five deaths and scores of

---

[38] There were also smaller parties, including the Anlo Youth Organisation. The TC relationship with the NPP was complicated because the latter campaigned for union at the plebiscite. Allman perhaps overplays her hand when she claims that the other parties either merged their identity with the NLM or 'realized nonetheless that their fate was inextricably tied to the NLM's'. Jean Marie Allman, *The Quills of the Porcupine: Asante Nationalism in an Emergent Ghana* (Madison: University of Wisconsin Press, 1993), p. 117. Because of the special status of Togoland, the TC could have chosen to do without the NLM – at least until 1956.

[39] Circular from the TC designed for voters, Trusteeship Council, *Report of the United Nations Plebiscite Commissioner for the Trust Territory of Togoland Under British Administration* (T/1258, 19 June 1956), annex IV.

[40] These petitions dating from February 1957 are to be found at GNAH RAO/C749.

[41] Austin, *Politics in Ghana*, p. 372.

[42] The police also believed that some militants had been sent to Ashanti for training, and possibly to acquire arms. Antor referred to links with Action Troopers (the CPP gangs), but presumably meant Action Groupers. Ghana, *Parliamentary Debates*, 1 May 1957, column 147. The allegation was repeated in Parliament by Krobo Edusei, *Parliamentary Debates*, 3 May 1957, columns 256–7.

[43] Statement by Ako Adjei, Minister of Interior, 1 May 1957, *Parliamentary Debates*, pp. 122–3.

serious injuries. Much of the violence surrounded the symbolic rituals associated with independence. Ever since British and German officers had first competed in distributing flags to chiefs, these emblems had been invested with a special significance. In the early days of March 1957, a series of clashes occurred when TC supporters either sought to dissuade chiefs from accepting the new flags or to prevent them from being hoisted, or when CPP activists insisted on TC sympathizers saluting the colours of the new nation.[44] In the wake of these incidents, the Ghana Regiment and the Police Reserve also exchanged gunfire with militants in Kpandu and in the vicinity of Hohoe. By the beginning of April, when they had managed to restore effective governmental control, a total of 5,198 firearms had been seized, 355 people had been arrested, and 158 had been convicted for breaches of the peace.[45]

In the wake of these developments, a vigorous debate ensued on whether the TC leadership had plotted a breakdown of order with a view to inducing the United Nations to intercede. The Minister of the Interior, Ako Adjei, referred to 'an organised design by subversive elements to disrupt the authority of the Government in the Region'.[46] On the other hand, S.G. Antor and Kodzo Ayeke denied that there was any such conspiracy, choosing instead to blame the violence on police harassment.[47] David Brown suggests that there was indeed a plan to seize control of the larger towns, in order to provoke a crisis that would command outside attention, but that this was foiled when the camps and arms caches were discovered.[48] *Ablode* supporters from outlying villages were reported to have converged on both Kpandu and Jasikan and to have been the main protagonists in the riots there.[49] Oral testimony from Likpe also supports the contention that this manoeuvre had been pre-planned. One informant from Likpe-Mate recalled an appeal to ex-servicemen – the precise origins of which are unclear – to convene at Jasikan, and in the clashes of 4 March, at least one man from Mate was seriously injured.[50] But while there was certainly an intention to flout governmental authority in order to make a point, it is doubtful that the *Ablode* militants envisaged a protracted campaign. The 'German scholars' who led the TC in places like Likpe-Mate were pillars of the local establishment and were not the kind of people who were likely to take up arms. And while there may have been some hotheads among the ranks of the ex-servicemen, it is doubtful that they ever

---

[44] TC supporters in Buem were later fined by the Omanhene for having urged him not to accept the flag, while in Ahamansu the head of the Tsevie community (French Togoland) was threatened with expulsion from his land unless he switched to the CPP and saluted the flag. These incidents are reported in Senior Superintendent of Police to Regional Officer, Ho (21 May 1957), GNAH RAO/C749 'Future of Togoland Under British Trusteeship'.

[45] Statement by Ako Adjei, Minister of Interior, 1 May 1957, Ghana, *Parliamentary Debates*, columns 127.

[46] Statement of 1 May 1957, *ibid.*

[47] Speech by S.G. Antor on 1 May and Kodzo Ayeke on 3 May 1957, Ghana, *Parliamentary Debates*, columns 144–56, 231–9. Antor and Ayeke were later brought to trial and given prison sentences of six years each, but were subsequently acquitted on appeal because of misdirections to the jury by the judge. Austin, *Politics in Ghana*, p. 381.

[48] David Brown, 'Politics in the Kpandu area of Ghana, 1925 to 1969: a study of the influence of central government and national politics upon local factional competition', unpublished Ph.D thesis, Birmingham University, 1977, p. 312.

[49] Ako Adjei in *Parliamentary Debates*, 1 May 1957, column 124. Brown, *ibid.*, pp. 314–16.

[50] Interview with Nicodemus Oloto, Likpe-Mate, 28 March 1986.

contemplated armed resistance. If they had, it would have made more sense to take to the hills along the border, which the authorities might have had real difficulty policing.[51] Although there was a small forest reserve in the vicinity of Alavanyo, this was hardly the ideal location in which to mount a sustained guerrilla insurgency.[52] On the whole, then, it is likely that the real objective was to register acute disaffection, and for that very reason *Ablode* activists may even have wanted the 'secret' camps to be discovered. Certainly, *Ablode* resistance was a far cry from the armed insurgency in Cameroun and the *shifta* operations of Somali separatists in the Northern Frontier District of Kenya at around the same time.[53] And while frequent allusions were made to Mau Mau precedents, the explosive mix of political alienation, landlessness and social deprivation was simply not present in former British Togoland.[54] Indeed, the wider context was one of unprecedented prosperity and opportunity.

Nevertheless, the spectre of violence did provide the CPP government with an excuse to move against its rivals. Kwame Nkrumah was inherently suspicious of political opposition, and was especially intolerant of regionalist movements that he regarded as a dangerous threat to national unity. Where regionalism verged on separatism, the imagined danger was further compounded. At the end of 1957, the government signalled its intention to push through a law that would outlaw political parties constituted on the basis of region, religion or ethnicity. This forced the TC to merge with five other opposition parties to form the United Party (UP).[55] Although *Ablode* supporters were now formally integrated into the political mainstream, the government continued to claim that they harboured separatist proclivities. In 1958, the CPP strongman from Ashanti, Krobo Edusei, was appointed the Acting Regional Commissioner (RC) in succession to C.H. Chapman, with a mandate to bring *Ablode* elements to heel by whatever means he deemed necessary. Before long opposition MPs were complaining about the indiscriminate arrest of their supporters and the harassment of chiefs who were sympathetic to their cause.[56] Edusei was succeeded by

---

[51] The contrast here with the successful guerrilla insurgency in the Matopos hills, which offered a comparable hideout, is instructive. See Terence Ranger, *Voices From the Rocks: Nature, Culture and History in the Matopos Hills of Zimbabwe* (Harare, Bloomington & Oxford: Baobab, Indiana University Press & James Currey, 1999), ch. 8.

[52] A forest reserve had been created in 1931. The fact that the people of Nkonya, whose CPP loyalties were well-known, disputed ownership of land of this area reduced any serious prospect of secrecy. Stool Land Boundaries Settlement Commission, Accra, File 7/79.

[53] In 1959, a secret police report stated that the UP no longer posed a security threat, although attendance at rallies in Togo were being monitored. GNAH secret unnumbered file, 'Ghana Police Internal Security Scheme, 1959 – Trans-Volta Togoland Region'. For comparisons, see Richard Joseph, *Radical Nationalism in Cameroun: Social Origins of the U.P.C. Rebellion* (Oxford: Clarendon Press, 1977), p. 342, who estimates the casualties of the UPC rebellion after 1956 as running into the thousands. On the Somalia case, see Catherine Hoskyns (ed.), *Case Studies in African Diplomacy: 2 – The Ethiopia, Somalia, Kenya Dispute* (London: Oxford University Press, 1969); Touval, *Boundary Politics*, pp. 101, 212–26.

[54] In Parliament, F.Y. Asare alluded to a threat from a cleric and TC activist, to unleash 'bloodshed, war anarchy and Mau Mau'. Speech of 3 May 1957, *Parliamentary Debates*, column 226. The possibilities of a Mau Mau scenario had previously been referred to by British officials in relation to the NLM. Allman, *Quills*, p. 105.

[55] These were the NLM, NPP, the Muslim Alliance Party, the Anlo Youth Organization and the Ga Shifimo Kpee. Austin, *Politics of Ghana*, p. 384.

[56] See the contributions of Antor and M.K. Apaloo to the debate on the Togoland (Assimilation of Law) Bill, *Parliamentary Debates*, First Series, Volume 12, 1958, columns 597–608.

other RCs like F.Y. Asare who proved no less assiduous in carrying *cipipification* through to its logical conclusion. The RCs were supported in their endeavours by District Commissioners (DCs), who were not civil servants but CPP appointees with a history of party activism behind them.[57] The latter were in no doubt that an essential part of their job was to advance the cause of the governing party.

Within the Volta Region, *cipipification* took place across three fronts that intersected at various points. First of all, the CPP manipulated the distribution of material resources in such a way as to reward political loyalty and to punish dissidence. David Brown has suggested that there was a basic incompatibility between the desire of the party leadership to win over opposition supporters and the determination of local activists to channel rewards to their loyal constituents while cutting out their long-standing opponents.[58] In practice, the divergence was not that great. At all levels of the CPP hierarchy, the expectation was that opposition supporters would need to make good their political mistakes before they could be considered eligible for equal treatment. In 1952, the CPP had managed to capture the majority of Local Councils, in part by co-opting councillors whose party affiliations were as yet unformed. This enabled the party to control the District Councils as well as the TVT Council, which presided over the £1 million special grant. In the 1958 elections, the CPP was able to consolidate its grip over the local government structure, and in subsequent years it proceeded to extend its control right down to level of the Village and Town Development Committees (V/TDCs).[59] When it came to the distribution of amenities, the Local Councils ensured that resources were channelled to communities that returned CPP candidates. In the Akpini Local Council area, for example, Brown notes that most amenities were located in Kpandu town, while the outlying *Ablode* villages were effectively bypassed.[60] Equally, jobs and perquisites were distributed in line with party affiliations. In Kpandu again, Brown has revealed how positions such as that of rate collector, council clerk and treasurer were parcelled out amongst the friends and family of the local party bosses. The latter reserved many of the juiciest pickings, such as Local Council contracts, for themselves.[61]

Although the Local Councils were expected to finance community development out of their own levies, central government was responsible for improvements to transport, education and medical infrastructure. Once again, investments were made the subject of straightforward political calculations, with particular communities being punished or rewarded according to their perceived loyalties. Hence in Likpe, Bakwa received a health centre; Kukurantumi was made the headquarters of a new cocoa district and received a tarred road that ran the length of the village; while Avedzeme received a water supply. By contrast, the perceived *Ablode* strongholds of Mate, Todome, Bala and Koforidua were snubbed. But there was no starker contrast than in the differential treatment accorded to Anfoega and Hohoe, respectively.

[57] After independence one of the leading CPP members in Kpandu, S.W. Kumah, was made DC for Ho District, while the equally vigorous Togbe S.T. Fleku became DC for Kpandu District. Brown, 'Politics in Kpandu', p. 317.

[58] *Ibid.*, pp. 225–6.

[59] Amonoo, *Ghana 1957–1966*, pp. 144–57.

[60] Brown, 'Politics in Kpandu', p. 294.

[61] *Ibid.*, p. 298.

Many believed that Hohoe would have been the logical choice for the regional capital by virtue of its size, central location and commercial importance. However, the Nkrumah government preferred Ho in order to punish Hohoe for providing a political home for S.G. Antor.[62] For the same reason, the main trunk road was tarred only as far as Ve-Golokwati, after which it reverted to laterite.[63] The economic wisdom of this policy was questionable, given that Hohoe lay at the heart of the cocoa trade. However, the intention was to make a political point, which would be underlined every time the citizens of Hohoe used their dusty (or alternatively waterlogged) roads, or travelled southwards. By comparison, the citizens of Anfoega benefited from the generous provision of infrastructure and amenities. The fact that their headchief, Togbe Tepre Hodo III, served for three terms as chairman of the TVT Council no doubt helped.[64] In the words of Ken Kwaku:

> By 1960, Anfoega had a Teacher Training College, a government supported Church hospital, a secondary school, local council offices, a tarred main street, post office and a police station... The roads leading into Hohoe were among the worst in the Region. The stretch from Golokwati to Hohoe was so gutted and dusty that the dust was popularly referred to as 'Antor atama' (Antor's snuff).[65]

Once again, there was a parallel in the distribution of spoils at the individual level. Brown includes jobs within the Cocoa Marketing Board (CMB) among his list of party placements, and this is borne out by testimony from Likpe. Hence, it was alleged that security officers appointed by the CMB to assist in the campaign against cocoa smuggling were recruited on a party basis.[66] Supporters of the UP were excluded from a share of the spoils, and those who were government employees ran the risk of being transferred, demoted or at worst losing their jobs altogether. Dissent, in other words, came at a personal price.

Secondly, *cipipification* took the form of direct government intervention in chieftaincy politics along the lines identified by Rathbone.[67] The Nkrumah regime was well aware of the fact that the TC leaned heavily upon the chiefs for its legitimacy and local organization. By placing a squeeze on the chiefs, the CPP hoped to disable the opposition at the grassroots level. Although the CPP posed as the party of the youngmen, it had already sought and won the adherence of a number of traditional rulers by 1956. Loyal chiefs like Togbe Tepre Hodo and the new Buem Paramount Chief, Nana Akpandja III, obliged by using all manner of 'traditional' sanctions against local UP activists in order to deter them from holding political meetings. Nevertheless, many leading chiefs remained firmly in the *Ablode* camp immediately after

---

[62] Frank Tsaku recalled that Nkrumah had wanted to choose Hohoe, but the feeling was that there was too much hostility to the CPP to make this a safe bet. He also claimed that the Hohoe people didn't want to be associated with anything that would be run by the CPP. Interview, Hohoe, 14 October 1986.

[63] S.W. Kumah claimed the credit for preventing the tarred road from reaching Hohoe. Brown, 'Politics in Kpandu', p. 294.

[64] Kwaku, 'Political economy of peripheral development', p. 190.

[65] *Ibid.*, pp. 190, 194

[66] Observation made by Mahama Tampurie, MP for South Mamprusi West, *Parliamentary Debates*, 14 June 1957, column 915.

[67] On this theme more generally, see Richard Rathbone, *Nkrumah and the Chiefs: The Politics of Chieftaincy in Ghana, 1951–60* (Oxford, Athens & Accra: James Currey, Ohio University Press & F. Reimmer, 2000).

independence. Some, like Togbe Gabusu IV of Gbi, had a long history of unificationist activity behind them – dating all the way back to the Togo Bund – and were
openly defiant towards the CPP. Unfortunately for them, there were potential
claimants to chiefly office at every level, which made it very easy for the government
to switch recognition from one faction to another. Where there were ongoing chieftaincy disputes, the government simply backed the faction that declared its support
for the CPP. The classic instance was in Ho, where there was a simmering dispute
between the Dome and Bankoe sections of the town. The stool had once resided with
Bankoe, but had been transferred to Dome by Captain Lilley, allegedly out of
personal pique.[68] Togbe Howusu had fluctuated in his sympathies, but by the time of
the plebiscite he was firmly aligned with Antor.[69] Predictably, the Bankoe section
gravitated towards the CPP as it intensified its campaign for restitution. Eventually,
the government appointed a commission of enquiry, which found in favour of
Bankoe, and by extension the CPP faction, in 1958. In Kpandu, the same result was
accomplished as early as 1955, when the Nyavor chiefly faction was passed over and
recognition was granted to the pro-CPP Howusu faction. Although Togbe Dagadu
V had no previous party loyalties, he was gazetted because of his willingness to come
out in favour of the governing party.

In Likpe, the death of Togbe Akototse in October 1955 was followed by a rerun of
the succession dispute that had broken out at the end of the 1920s. On this occasion,
both the Kalekato and the Kalelenti clans proposed candidates – Nicholas Soglo and
S.Q. Mantey, respectively – who were staunch supporters of the CPP. A vigorous
competition ensued as the two factions sought to outdo each other in protestations of
loyalty to the governing party, while raking up the *Ablode* histories of members on the
other side. In this case, after some intense lobbying by Nana Agya Mensah and the
personal intervention of F.Y. Asare, the government came down in favour of Nicholas
Soglo, who was duly gazetted in February 1958. And when the latter died in
mysterious circumstances in December 1960, the government controversially set
aside the rotatory principle and gazetted his brother, Victor, as Nana Soglo Allo III
the following year. The Kalelentis pulled every string to have this decision overturned, and Mantey even enrolled in the Ideological Institute in Winneba in order to
underline his party credentials. Nevertheless, the Nkrumah regime apparently felt
that Victor Soglo, a policeman and long-standing party member, stood the greatest
chance of restoring peace to Likpe. The secession of the Kalelentis to form a new
village at Abrani in August 1964 effectively brought the dispute to an end, by which
the point virtually the whole of Likpe had succumbed to *cipipification*. The
behaviour of the government over Likpe reflects a more general awareness of the
dangers associated with backing minority factions. The authorities preferred to
recognize chiefs who enjoyed popular support. Often the threat of backing an alternative candidate was sufficient to win an incumbent over to the CPP. But where the
chiefs proved intractable, the government did not flinch from replacing them with

---

[68] The Bankoe chief had refused to shake the left hand of Lilley who had lost his right hand in the First World
War. Barbara Callaway, 'Local politics in Ho and Aba', *Canadian Journal of African Studies*, 4, 1, 1970, p. 134.
However, the roots of the dispute about who was entitled to the stool go rather deeper.

[69] Trusteeship Council, *Report of the United Nations Plebiscite Commissioner for the Trust Territory of Togoland
Under British Administration* (T/1258, 19 June 1956), p. 64ff.

candidates who were considered more pliable. Hence in Hohoe Togbe Gabusu IV was forced into exile, destooled in his absence and replaced with a candidate who was more acceptable to the government. Another casualty was Togbe Atakora VI of Ala-vanyo, whose town had provided the focal point of the pre-independence crisis.

Finally, the CPP regime resorted to the expedient of political detention as a means of cutting the most stubborn knots of *Ablode* supporters. As we have already seen, a large number of TC activists were placed on trial and convicted for their part in the disturbances surrounding independence. In Likpe, the party chairman and secretary, G.K. Kumesi and Henry Kwashigah, received prison sentences of 18 and 6 months, respectively, for their part in these events.[70] In July 1958, the government passed the Preventive Detention Act, which made it possible to detain someone for a period of five years without any right of appeal to the courts. This piece of legislation was used unsparingly against leading UP politicians as well as activists at the local level. Imme-diately after passage of the Act, the first batch of *Ablode* supporters, including a number from Ho, was placed under detention. On the eve of Togolese independence, when the Nkrumah regime was at its most sensitive, a second sweep occurred. And in January 1960, government informers infiltrated a meeting at Yikpa, just across the border from Wli, at which it was alleged that plans for an 'underground army' were being discussed.[71] The government duly signed detention orders against another 26 individuals. Many of these chose to remain in exile in Togo, but others were caught in the net. The MP for Ho East, Rev. F.R. Ametowobla, was among the former. His seat was declared vacant and was duly captured for the CPP by E.Y. Attigah. The Kpandu North constituency was a harder nut to crack, being the fiefdom of S.G. Antor. In 1961, however, Antor was detained with a number of opposition politicians in the aftermath of the railway workers' strike. Once again, the seat was declared vacant and one of the hard core of CPP activists in Hohoe, Frank Tsaku, was elected unopposed to fill it. By this point, the UP saw little point in contesting the elections, since Ghana had become a *de facto* one-party state.

One effect of *cipipification* was to drive substantial numbers of people across the border in search of sanctuary. Many converged on Akposso, which, as we have seen, had a long-standing history of absorbing refugees. Some already owned cocoa farms in Akposso, while others were attracted by the prospect of renting land. Many others preferred Kpalimé, which, as a substantial commercial town, offered greater prospects for paid employment. In November 1961, British Embassy officials in Lomé estimated that there were some 50 refugees who were escaping specific deten-tion orders and another 5,600 who had simply judged it safer to leave Ghana.[72] In the middle of 1962, the United Nations High Commissioner for Refugees indicated that there were 1,500 refugees in the Kpalimé area, 800 in the Akposso-Badou area and another 1,200 scattered across the country.[73] Whereas the experience of exile may

---

[70] Interviews with Amatus Adela, son of G.K. Kumesi, Mate, 16 January 1986; and Emilson Kwashie, Mate, 15 February 1986.

[71] Saffu, 'Nkrumah', p. 42.

[72] Of these, it was claimed that 1,000 were located near Sansanne-Mango, 3,000 around Akposso and 2,000 around Kpalimé. J.W.S. Corbett to K.M. Wilford, Foreign Office (3 November 1961), PRO FO 371/155676.

[73] Reported in O. Kemp, British Embassy to Barbara Miller, Foreign Office (23 June 1962), PRO FO 371/155676.

sometimes heighten a sense of political grievance, in this case the refugees appear to have been deterred from maintaining an active interest in unification politics. The Togolese authorities did not wish to add credence to Ghanaian claims that they were encouraging subversion, and specifically informed them that they could stay only as long as they desisted from engaging in political activity.[74] It is easy to see that a highly politicized refugee population might also pose a threat to the power base of the Olympio regime itself. The fact that the exiles were widely dispersed across rural Togo posed a further barrier to regular interaction. For the majority of refugees, it appears that enforced exile was a rather solitary experience in which they sought to make ends meet, awaiting the day when they could return to their homes. In the words of one informant from Mate, who settled in Kpalimé and remained there as a farmer until 1967, 'Everybody was on his own. We only greeted each other. We had no meetings on Ghanaian affairs'.[75]

While those who had escaped to Togo ruminated over what had transpired, those that remained were considering whether it was advisable to persist in their opposition to the ruling party. After 1960, members of the older generation, who had played such an important leadership role, decided to withdraw from the fray or quite literally passed away. In Likpe, the political careers of Kwashigah and Kumesi, which dated back to the days of the Togo Bund, came to an abrupt end. The final demise of the 'German scholars' accentuated the shift in the balance of community influence towards younger and better educated men whose inclinations were towards the ruling party. In communities such as Kpandu, which had witnessed bitter factional struggles involving a mixture of chieftaincy and party politics, there was support for a new kind of consensus politics.[76] This made it possible for erstwhile *Ablode* supporters to switch to the CPP and for them to be accepted in good faith as genuine converts. Among those who made the switch in Kpandu itself were some of the leading TC stalwarts like Albert Simpson and Regina Asamany, both of whom became MPs during the 1960s.[77] In Likpe, former associates of Antor such as Nana J.Q. Sekyere became regular fixtures on CPP platforms.

This does raise the question of the extent to which there was anything more than a purely pragmatic attachment to the ruling party. In the case of the founding members, there can be no doubting the strength of identification. Genuine stalwarts, such as Emilson Kwashie from Likpe-Mate, have retained a sense of being CPP men down to the present day. It is difficult to believe that later arrivals felt quite the same sense of emotional attachment to the CPP, but it would be a mistake to underestimate the extent to which the CPP had won the political argument in the eyes of the local audience. During interviews, it proved extremely difficult to elicit from informants precisely what it was that made them change their minds. A recurrent observation was that the Togoland question had been conclusively settled in 1956 and ought not to be raised again. Since the fundamental rationale for the TC had evaporated – and indeed the party had ceased to exist – former unificationists

---

[74] Notes on a meeting between Commandant de Cercle and some 100 refugees at Badou on 30 March 1960, TNAL Atakpamé 2 APA/144.

[75] Interview with Matthew Kodjo Akorli, Abrani, 14 March 1986.

[76] Brown, 'Politics in Kpandu', ch. 13.

[77] *Ibid.*, p. 318.

apparently regarded a movement towards the CPP as the next logical step. The son of G.K. Kumesi, who was himself an engaged TC supporter, articulated a common view when he simply stated that: 'Even though he [Nkrumah] defeated our party, the way he started out development projects we saw he was going to do something for us'.[78] In one sense, this was an expression of pure instrumentalism, but at a more profound level it pointed to a belated acceptance of the CPP vision of modernity. This endorsement is perhaps surprising, given that the Nkrumah regime promised far more than it was able to deliver. Indeed, in some respects the ambitious plans of the CPP did more harm than good to the livelihood of peoples in the Volta Region. The Volta River Project led to the displacement of many riverain communities who were hastily resettled in villages that lacked electricity, running water or decent housing.[79] However, by a cruel irony – which some might have called just desserts – the greatest casualties were the very communities that had exhibited the clearest CPP sympathies during the 1950s: notably the peoples of Krachi and Nkonya and, to some extent, Kpandu. The communities that had backed Togoland unification enjoyed fewer rewards, but they also suffered fewer inconveniences.

The expansion of educational provision, in an area that had always been poorly served, made a particularly lasting impression on the peoples of the former Trust territory.[80] The Central Togo minorities were especially quick to seize on the opportunities that presented themselves. Remarkably, the 1960 population census revealed that the Central Togo groups had the highest rate of school attendance in the country for those over six years old – 71.2 per cent for males and a striking 44.8 per cent for females. This compared with 50.2 per cent and 21.2 per cent among the Akan, 50.6 per cent and 26.1 per cent among the Ga-Adangbe and 46.2 per cent and 20.2 per cent among the Ewe for males and females, respectively.[81] Needless to say, the ethnic categories are problematic. For example, it is not clear why the 'Akan' are lumped together and one suspects that there may have been significant variations within the Ewe category. Nevertheless, the figures are indicative of the very rapid educational strides made by the peoples of former Southern Togoland, probably including the northern Ewe. Although the expansion was greatest at the base, higher education was also opened up to the peoples of former British Togoland in a way that had never been possible before. For example, the first cohort of University graduates from Likpe began to emerge in the early 1960s, a list which included Ray Kakrabah-

---

[78] Interview with Amatus Adela, Mate, 16 January 1986.

[79] On the effects of the Volta River Project, see Leo Barrington, 'Migration and the growth of a resettlement community: Kete-Krachi, Ghana, 1962, and 1969', Ph.D. thesis, Boston University, 1972; R.M. Lawson, *The Changing Economy of the Lower Volta, 1954–67: A Study in the Dynamics of Rural Economic Growth* (London: Oxford University Press, 1972); Robert Chambers (ed.), *The Volta Resettlement Experience* (London: Pall Mall Press, 1970); and Kwaku Obosu-Mensah, *Ghana's Volta Resettlement Scheme: The Long-Term Consequences of Post-Colonial State Planning* (San Francisco, London & Bethesda: International Scholars Publications, 1996).

[80] This has to be seen in the context of the educational dearth of the period prior to 1951. Elementary schools were established in each village, while the number of secondary schools in the region had increased from zero to 12 in 1965, with seven training colleges. *Ghana Year Book 1965* (Accra: Daily Graphic), pp. 133–6, 144.

[81] Ghana Census Office, *1960 Population Census of Ghana: Special Report 'E' – Tribes of Ghana*, pp. lvii–lxv.

Quarshie, Dr Obed Asamoah and J.K. Kafe.[82] In subsequent years, the graduates came to exercise a profound influence over the political choices of their home communities. Crucially for our purposes, these were people who took their Ghanaian nationality very seriously, as did a growing cadre of government employees and school teachers. For the generation that increasingly wielded influence at the local level, the *Ablode* past was as much a foreign country as Togo itself was. In that sense, the sons and daughters of Togo Bunders had matured as model Ghanaians.

A double killing: the demise of the CPP and *Ablode*

The coup of 24 February 1966 represented as much of a rupture in the politics of the Volta Region as elsewhere. An unseemly rush to disown the CPP ensued, which only tended to confirm the impression that political loyalties had been essentially pragmatic. But once again, the element of cynicism should not be over-exaggerated. The atmosphere of intimidation in the wake of the coup was such that many people felt the need to participate in denunciation of the Nkrumah regime, even if they had their doubts. In Likpe, a letter from the office of Nana Soglo Allo III was circulated across Likpe, inviting the chiefs, people, local schools and the Border Guards to participate in a procession 'to tease Kwame Nkrumah alias Kofi Nwiah, the most wicked and corrupted Politician in Africa'.[83] An effigy of Nkrumah was paraded through Mate and then symbolically buried in the town cemetery.[84] A bonfire was also lit in the Post Office square, at which party cards and many records were publicly burned. However, this was a deliciously ambiguous exercise. Although it was supposed to signal rejection of everything the CPP stood for, local people were only too happy to participate in burning the very records that might incriminate them. Members of the branch executive nevertheless concealed certain party records at some personal risk to themselves, believing that the party would one day be revived.

However, a far more fundamental point is that the demise of the CPP did not really signal the rebirth of *Ablode* networks. Although some of the returnees set about rekindling former alliances, the environment was a very different one from which they had left behind. In Hohoe, the citizens of Bla, who had been made to suffer for their stubborn adherence to the TC, exacted their revenge on the CPP. They took

---

[82] Ray Kakrabah-Quarshie, who hailed from Likpe-Agbozome, entered the University of Ghana in 1958. Three years later, he became General Secretary of the National Union of Ghanaian Students. In subsequent years, he made a career for himself as a lawyer, journalist and founder member of the Progress Party. At one point, he tried to secure the parliamentary nomination for the CPP, but thereafter was squarely in the opposite camp. In 1996, he stood unsuccessfully for the New Patriotic Party in Hohoe-North constituency. On the latter, see Paul Nugent, *The Flight-Lieutenant Rides (To Power) Again: National Delusions, Local Fixations and the 1996 Ghanaian Elections* (Centre of African Studies, University of Edinburgh, Occasional Papers No. 76, 1998), pp. 53–70. J.K. Kafe, who came from the same village, also studied at Legon, and then proceeded to London University before returning to take up a position as Head Librarian at the University of Ghana. Obed Asamoah, who was from Bala, studied as a lawyer and received his Ph.D. at Columbia University. He returned to teach at the University of Ghana after the fall of Nkrumah, before entering politics. In subsequent years, he became Ghana's longest serving Secretary of Foreign Affairs under Flt-Lt Jerry Rawlings. His political activities at the centre can be traced through the pages of Paul Nugent, *Big Men, Small Boys and Politics in Ghana: Power, Ideology and the Burden of History* (London & New York: Frances Pinter, 1995).

[83] Circular letter from C.K. Broni, secretary to Nana Soglo Allo III, Mate, dated 15 March 1966.

[84] Interview with Emilson Kwashie, Mate, 25 March 1986.

delight in the incarceration of Frank Tsaku, and later erected a statue to General E.K. Kotoka when he was killed in a subsequent coup attempt. This statue, which stands on the road leading from Hohoe to Likpe and East-Buem, is still given a regular coat of paint. This should be interpreted less as a sign of Ewe ethnic solidarity (Kotoka being an Ewe) than a statement of eternal hostility towards the CPP. And yet, even in Hohoe there was no great desire to pick up the unification question where it had been left. Across the Volta Region, communities were apparently content to leave that phase behind them and to concentrate on making the most of the realities of independent Ghana. As the National Liberation Council prepared for a return to the barracks, former unificationist politicians did re-enter the political arena and took an active part in the debates about a future dispensation for Ghana.[85] But they too refrained from seeking to reopen the Togoland question, although they did insist that some acknowledgement should be accorded to the separate historical identity of former Southern Togoland. Within the Constituent Assembly, S.G. Antor and Alex Odame proposed an amendment that would have reinstituted the name of Trans-Volta Togoland. Odame hastily reassured his audience that there was no desire to push for secession, but merely a wish to reverse a change that had been imposed by the Nkrumah regime.[86] This amendment was, however, defeated by members of the Assembly who felt it would be wise 'to forget this colonial past'.[87] Among those who spoke against the proposed amendment was the Awoamefia, Togbe Adeladza II, who expressed his opposition to anything which might seek to drive a wedge between Anlo and the rest of the rgion.[88] In this brief debate, the issue of a separate status for the former Trust territory was finally laid to an anti-climactic rest.

As a return to civilian rule beckoned, formal political groupings began to germinate, eventually blossoming as fully fledged parties. Antor and his associates did not opt to organize purely around the Volta Region, but renewed their alliance with their former UP partners in the Progress Party (PP). Under the leadership of Kofi Busia, the PP was dedicated to the protection of the territorial integrity of Ghana. Its principal contender, the National Alliance of Liberals (NAL), was no less committed to this national project. This is hardly surprising given that NAL was headed by Komla Gbedemah who had campaigned vigorously against the breakaway of British Togoland during the 1950s. On the national question, as in much else, the two leading parties were in absolute agreement.[89] When it came to the choice of parliamentary candidates, however, there was an interesting and significant difference. In East Dayi, the PP fielded S.G. Antor, and in Buem Alex Odame contested substantially the same constituency where he had previously done battle against F.Y. Asare. Although Kofi Dumoga did not stand, he lent his support to the PP campaign. The NAL candidates, by contrast, stood out by virtue of their comparative youthfulness

---

[85] On the transition programme, see the various contributions to Dennis Austin and Robin Luckham (eds), *Politicians and Soldiers in Ghana 1966–72* (London: Frank Cass, 1975).

[86] Ghana, *Proceedings of the Constituent Assembly: Official Report*, 13 February 1969, column 798.

[87] The words of F.E. Boaten of the Senior Civil Servants Association, *Proceedings of the Constituent Assembly: Official Report*, 13 February 1969, column 798.

[88] *Proceedings of the Constituent Assembly: Official Report*, 13 February 1969, columns 800–1.

[89] Dr Obed Asamoah himself noted the similarities between the parties in 'Policy differences between government and opposition', *Legon Observer*, 5, 23, 1970, pp. 7–8.

and inexperience. Most of the candidates were in their thirties or early forties, which meant that had not been directly involved in the political struggles of the 1950s. They were also much more highly educated than the politicians of an earlier era. Out of 16 candidates, no fewer than six held foreign degrees: namely, Dr Obed Asamoah (Biakoye), C.K. Nayo (Buem), Frederick Segbefia (Avenor), Dr G.K. Agama (South Tongu), Sam Okudzeto (Tongu North) and Felix Adinyira (Ho West).[90] Another four held Ghanaian university degrees, namely, Richard Seglah (Anlo), J.Y.T. Dziwornu-Mensah (Some-Aflao), D.K. Avoke (East Dayi) and S.K. Osei-Nyame (Akan).[91] This was a significant departure from the pattern of the First Republic when a basic teaching qualification had represented the norm. But the most noticeable transformation lay in the fact that the educational gulf between the coast and the interior, which had underpinned the division between the AEC and TC leaderships, had been closed.[92] This, more than anything, demonstrated just how far the integrationist project had been implemented and must surely rank among the most important legacies of the Nkrumah regime.

Although the PP won the 1969 elections fairly comfortably, NAL captured all but two seats in the Volta Region (Krachi and Nkwanta) and lost even those by fairly narrow margins.[93] These results have been widely interpreted, not least by the political class itself, in straightforward ethnic terms. On this view, the voters shunned PP candidates because it was construed as predominantly an Akan party, whereas NAL could make play of its Ewe leadership. Although ethnicity may have been a motivating factor in other parts of Ghana, this interpretation begs more questions than it answers in respect of the Volta Region. Given that the TC had never suffered from its alliance with the NLM during the 1950s, it is necessary to explain why the association should have made a difference on this occasion. Moreover, the assumption that Komla Gbedemah could bank on Ewe solidarity is doubly fallacious. On the other hand, as we have seen, Ewe politics had traditionally been characterized by a fault line running north of Peki. There had previously been a pronounced aversion to Anlo leadership pretensions among the northern Ewe. If anything, this should have counted against Gbedemah, who had made himself deeply unpopular in the 1950s. On the other hand, the voters of the Volta Region included many peoples who were not Ewe at all and yet cast their votes for NAL candidates. A good case in point is the Akan constituency, in the Twi-speaking north of Buem, where a historically grounded sense of Akan identity did not deter voters from returning a NAL

---

[90] These details are mostly drawn from Moses Danquah, *The Birth of the Second Republic* (Accra: Editorial and Publishing Services, undated), pp. 107-10.

[91] Apart from Komla Gbedemah himself, who was not university educated, there were five other candidates for whom data is not available. It is possible that some of these were also graduates.

[92] The TC had counted two graduates among its leadership. Rev. F.R. Ametowobla and Anku Morny had studied at Edinburgh University and the London School of Economics, respectively. They were very much the exceptional cases.

[93] In Krachi B.K. Mensah won by 718 votes, while in Nkwanta R.K. Mensah won by 719 votes. The elections are sometimes wrongly depicted as a clean sweep for NAL, as in E.O. Akwetey, 'Ghana: violent ethno-political conflicts and the democratic challenge', in Adebayo O. Olukoshi and Liisa Laakso (eds), *Challenges to the Nation-State in Africa* (Uppsala & Helsinki: Nordiska Afrikainstitutet & Institute of Development Studies, 1996), p. 118.

candidate.[94] As I have already sought to prove in the previous chapter, ethnicity was a far more complex phenomenon than the politicians themselves were wont to pretend.

What appears to have happened in 1969 is that the voters spurned those candidates who epitomized the old guard – principally the former TC leadership – and embraced the new faces of NAL in the hope that they might bring a fresh start to regional politics. This helps to explain the dramatic reversal of fortunes of S.G. Antor, who received less than 20 per cent of the vote in a constituency much like the one he had dominated in the 1950s. Equally, Alex Odame managed to garner only 36 per cent of the vote in Buem. The rejection of these established leaders signalled a rejection of the separatist legacy and a desire to blend into the mainstream of Ghanaian politics. The cruel irony is that the results were interpreted in precisely the opposite fashion by the winning side: namely, as an affirmation of an exclusive Ewe identity.[95] Having voted for the wrong party once again, the peoples of the Volta Region found themselves on the receiving end of discriminatory treatment. Despite the emphasis placed upon rural development by the Busia regime, expenditure in the region actually declined. Hence, whereas government-financed community water projects virtually doubled during the Second Republic, the rate of construction fell by 30 per cent in the Volta Region. Equally, the length of new roads fell from 72 miles between 1967 and 1969 to 30 miles in 1969/70 and 1.5 miles in 1970/71.[96] Moreover, when the Busia regime embarked on a purge of the civil service and police in February 1970, a disproportionate number of the 586 employees slated for dismissal were reputed to be 'Ewes'.[97] It did not help matters that the Volta Region was totally unrepresented within the ranks of government ministers, although in fairness Busia only had two MPs to call on. As a result, expectations of a fresh start rapidly turned to disillusionment. When the armed forces intervened for a second time on 13 January 1972, the coup was greeted with genuine relief across the Volta Region.

The last gasp: the Secessionist scare of the 1970s

This is not the place to enter into a detailed examination of the politics of the successive military administrations presided over by Colonel (later General) I.K. Acheampong.[98] My aim is to sift out those developments that had a direct bearing on the border equation. Three in particular warrant closer attention: the surfacing of

---

[94] S.K. Osei-Nyame won almost twice as many votes as his PP rival.

[95] This has become a recurrent theme in interpretations of voting in the Volta Region. The opposition press and politicians made substantially the same observations in 1992 and in 1996 to explain the success of President Jerry Rawlings.

[96] D. Smock and A.C. Smock, *The Politics of Pluralism: A Comparative Study of Lebanon and Ghana* (New York: Elsevier, 1978), p. 248.

[97] Quite how this was computed, and whether 'Ewe' was taken to mean anyone from the Volta Region, is unclear. *Ibid.*, pp. 246–7.

[98] The National Redemption Council ruled until October 1975 when it was superseded by the Supreme Military Council (SMC). In July 1978, Acheampong was deposed by his fellow SMC members and Lt-General Fred Akuffo assumed the mantle until the coup of 4 June 1979. For details of this period, see Naomi Chazan, *An Anatomy of Ghanaian Politics: Managing Political Recession, 1969–1982* (Boulder: Westview, 1983), ch. 8; and Mike Oquaye, *Politics in Ghana, 1972–1979* (Accra: Tornado Publications, 1980).

The political economy of the Ghana–Togo border

alleged Ewe military conspiracies; the breakdown of relations with the Togolese regime; and the emergence of an overtly secessionist political organization.

Ironically, the National Redemption Council (NRC) made its pitch for popular legitimacy by attacking the ethnic particularism of the Busia regime. Although the NRC initially contained strong Ewe representation, a subsequent power struggle led to a purge of the ruling council and of the officer corps more generally. This was followed by government allegations about an Ewe conspiracy to seize power, which received extensive coverage during a show trial which dominated the state media over 1976.[99] Regardless of whether such a conspiracy actually existed, it seemed to have had a rather remote link to the border issue. To be sure, some of the protagonists, notably Captain Kojo Tsikata, fled into exile in Togo. However, a distinctive feature of the Ghanaian military was that the vast majority of Ewe soldiers came from areas that had formerly belonged to the Gold Coast – and more especially Anlo.[100] The only senior officer to hail from former British Togoland was E.K. Utuka (from Likpe) and he became a prominent member of the Acheampong regime.[101] Dissident Anlo officers may have wanted to effect a change of regime, but they and their civilian associates always took Ghana – within its existing boundaries – as their frame of reference. Whatever else they might have been, Kojo Tsikata and Kofi Awoonor were certainly not secessionists. Although rumours of an Ewe master-plan to transform the ethnic arithmetic of Ghana, by expanding its boundaries towards the Mono River, have continued to circulate, they are not backed up by a single shred of evidence.[102] Even if they had harboured a irredentist agenda, the dissidents were hardly likely to receive very much succour in Lomé, where the regime was sensitive to the dangers of Ghanaian expansionism, and no less worried about Ewe plots. For these reasons, it is not necessary to dwell on ethnic factionalism in the armed forces. Its relevance lies in helping to cement a siege mentality within the military regime which, as Brown has argued, intensified the search for scapegoats.[103]

A second development, namely the souring of inter-governmental relations, is of more immediate relevance to this discussion. Once again, the irony is that the Acheampong regime appeared to embark on the right foot. Relations between the Busia and Eyadema regimes had deteriorated after the passage of the Aliens

---

[99] It is not altogether clear whether such a plot actually existed. Kofi Awoonor denies the existence of any such plot, but provides abundance evidence that Ewe officers harboured serious grievances against Acheampong. At the trial, it was claimed that some of the accused were annoyed at their exclusion from positions of power despite their involvement in both the 1966 and 1972 coups. See the evidence given in the trial of Sowu and Von Backustein as reported in the *Daily Graphic*, 31 August 1976. This evidence is consistent with the tone of Awoonor's book. See *The Ghana Revolution: Background Account From a Personal Perspective* (New York: Oases Publishers, 1984).

[100] Major Agbo, who served on the original NRC was from Peki. His colleagues were from greater Anlo.

[101] Utuka was born in Mate in 1937, which meant that he was only 35 years old when Acheampong came to power. He had attended Sandhurst and had served with the Ghana Army during the Congo crisis. He was commissioned as a second lieutenant in 1961 and by the time of the coup had risen to the rank of Lt-Colonel in command of the Second Battalion at Takoradi. From there, he was transferred to the Teshie Military Academy. In 1973, he attended the Royal College of Defence Studies. At the start of 1975, he succeeded Akuffo as head of the Border Guards, which accounts for his elevation to the SMC.

[102] See, for example, Zaya Yeebo, *Ghana: The Struggle for Popular Power – Rawlings: Saviour or Demagogue* (London: New Beacon Books, 1991) p. 272.

[103] This is the underlying thesis in Brown, 'Sieges'.

Compliance Order in 1969.[104] The Eyadema regime had responded to what it regarded as discriminatory treatment by closing the border to non-Togolese citizens, while the Busia government introduced tighter frontier controls in an attempt to restrict the flow of imported goods. After the coup, Acheampong decided to seek a rapprochement with Eyadema, as one soldier to another. In March 1973, the two sides signed an agreement establishing a Permanent Joint Commission, which was mandated to harmonize policies with respect to 'political, scientific, legal, social and cultural affairs'.[105] The following month, a formal ceremony was held to mark the full reopening of the frontier post at Aflao.[106] Both sides evidently hoped to gain something from the freeing up of frontier restrictions. The Togolese, who maintained an open-door trade policy, expected to be able re-export a greater quantity of goods to Ghana. On the other hand, the Acheampong regime wished to exact greater Togolese co-operation in the eradication of smuggling. As a sign of goodwill, the Togolese authorities immediately cracked down on currency black-marketeers in Lomé.

However, as had happened before, the announcement of a fresh start in cross-border co-operation proved to be premature. On this occasion, the accords broke down as a result of the intrusion of the third development, namely, the resurgence of secessionist rumblings. In November 1972, an organization calling itself the National Liberation Movement for Western Togoland (TOLIMO) came to prominence when it despatched a petition to the OAU pointing to the broken promises of integration. In the words of David Brown, who has carried out the only detailed study of TOLIMO:

> The petitioners alleged that the Togoland Congress had been repressed by Nkrumah, and that the Volta River project had brought only flooded land and river blindness to British Togoland instead of the promised electricity and piped water. The impact of the border controls upon those living in the frontier areas was also stressed.[107]

When the UN Secretary-General, Kurt Waldheim, passed through Lomé in February 1974, he was greeted by TOLIMO members wielding placards and bearing a petition. The latter called on the UN to reopen the unification question, on the grounds that there had been irregularities in the conduct of the 1956 plebiscite and that the express wishes of the Ewe people had been ignored.[108] The Ghanaian authorities were taken aback at the resurrection of an issue that had apparently been laid to rest twenty years earlier. What was more worrying was other information garnered by Ghanaian intelligence sources. This indicated that TOLIMO was receiving direct assistance from the Eyadema regime, and was actively soliciting the support of chiefs on the Ghana side of the border. In January 1976, when relations had deteriorated sufficiently, Eyadema made his irredentist pitch more explicit. In an advertisement in *The Times*, the Togolese government urged Acheampong 'to show

---

[104] The Togolese figures suggested that 74,324 nationals were repatriated from Ghana. Brown, 'Sieges', p. 587.

[105] Reported in the *Daily Graphic*, 31 March 1973.

[106] Eyadema welcomed this initiative, somewhat implausibly, as the first step towards the effective removal of an artificial boundary. See the report in the *Daily Graphic*, 2 April 1973.

[107] Brown, 'Borderline politics', p. 584.

[108] See 'Livre blanc sur la réunification du Togo', *Revue Française d'Études Politiques Africaines*, no 121, Janvier 1976.

his statesmanship and restore Togo as she was before the Europeans got to work'.[109]

In a country as tightly regulated as Togo, TOLIMO could never have operated without at least the tacit endorsement of the Eyadema regime. However, Brown has suggested that the latter also began to provide financial assistance at the end of 1972. It was this material support that enabled TOLIMO leaders to engage in foreign travel and to invite prospective sympathizers to attend meetings on Togolese soil.[110] It would seem as if TOLIMO never ceased to be dependent upon this state patronage: it was, after all, a top-down and top-heavy organization. Among other things, this enabled the Togolese authorities to exercise a considerable measure of influence over its leadership and platform. Hence, when the Eyadema government decided to de-escalate the crisis in 1977, in response to increasingly bellicose threats issuing from Accra, TOLIMO was allowed to wither on the vine.[111] The Togolese authorities, it transpired, were able to turn the tap off as well as on.

Far from exhibiting the illegitimacy of colonial boundaries, the record of TOLIMO demonstrates the lack of any significant constituency for a secessionist alternative by the 1970s. The early leadership of TOLIMO could hardly be called obscure, including as it did Kofi Dumoga, S.G. Antor, Alex Odame, Gerald Awuma and Albert Simpson.[112] On the contrary, the problem was that these politicians were too well-known. Awuma and Simpson had once occupied prominent positions in the unification movement, but had subsequently defected to the integrationist camp in the 1950s. Antor, Odame and (less so) Dumoga had been consistent advocates of Togoland unification, but even they seemed to have backtracked by 1969. As we have already seen, the first two were decisively rejected in the elections of that year. Moreover, when Antor and Dumoga accepted ambassadorial postings from Busia, they associated themselves with a regime that was accused of acting with vindictiveness towards the Volta Region.[113] The Acheampong government was consequently able to make good mileage out of the inconsistent track record of the TOLIMO leadership. In fact, the Togolese government had already intervened to impose a new leadership on the organization in July 1975. The latter was substantially younger and more reflective of the diversity of the region. Although the new leaders did not carry the burden of past records, they were relatively unknown figures in the Volta Region. Finally, Brown points to the outbreak of a damaging schism within TOLIMO, along ethnic and generational lines, that followed the change of personnel at the top.[114]

In order to understand the historic failure of TOLIMO, it is not enough to concentrate on the deficiencies of its leadership – real as these undoubtedly were. One also has to take cognizance of the fact that there was not the kind of constituency that had helped to sustain the Togoland Congress during the pre-independence period.

---

[109] See *The Times* (London), 13 January 1976, p.13.

[110] Brown, 'Borderline politics', pp. 588–9.

[11] According to Brown, *ibid.*, p. 593, TOLIMO had planned to embark on guerrilla incursions, but was ordered to cease by the Togolese authorities. The latter were shaken by a coup attempt that seemed to enjoy Ghanaian backing.

[112] According to Brown, *ibid.*, p. 589, Dumoga was initially the dominant influence at a time when TOLIMO lacked formal structures.

[113] Antor and Dumoga were posted by the Busia regime to Togo and Dahomey, respectively.

[114] Brown, 'Borderline politics', pp. 590–1.

The TOLIMO leadership had learned one important lesson from the past, which was that it was crucial to win the backing of the chiefs. According to Brown, there had already been an increased level of cultural exchange between chiefs on either side of the border dating from 1969.[115] 'Traditional' gatherings provided an ideal opportunity for TOLIMO, and the Togolese authorities, to infiltrate a more overtly political message. According to Brown, around ten secret meetings were convened, mostly at Kpalimé, in the early 1970s. At one such meeting in March 1973, an estimated 100–200 chiefs from both sides of the border were in attendance.[116] However, these clandestine gatherings were easily infiltrated by Ghanaian informers, and on at least three occasions the participants were arrested at the border on their way back. The recollections of the chief of Akoefe-Achati suggest that many attended out of a combination of curiosity and some expectation of material reward.[117] This informant also recounted how events dissolved into farce on one particular occasion. As usual, the chiefs had been lavishly entertained, and left Kpalimé somewhat the worse for wear. When the car which was carrying Nana Akpandja III was stopped at the border, an inebriated Omanhene proclaimed to all and sundry that he and his colleagues were having nothing further to do with Ghana – at which point they were promptly placed under arrest. According to the same informant, Acheampong shortly afterwards summoned the senior chiefs to a meeting at which he promised them each a car if they would sever their links with TOLIMO.[118]

At the same time, the SMC made it clear that any further involvement would be considered tantamount to treason and would be severely punished. In March 1976, the SMC issued a decree that outlawed TOLIMO and prescribed a fine not exceeding ¢ 5,000, a prison sentence not exceeding five years or both for attending any of its meetings or even shouting its slogans.[119] As soon as it became clear that their activities were being monitored, most chiefs ceased to have any further association with TOLIMO. Indeed, the senior chiefs competed among themselves in their expressions of loyalty to the Ghanaian state and to the SMC regime. A number of paramount chiefs played an active part in 'Operation Counterpoint', which was an elaborate propaganda exercise directed at the twin threats of secessionism and smuggling. The leading players were the President of the Volta Region House of Chiefs, Osie Adja Tekpor VI of Avatime, and Togbe Adeladza II of Anlo. They were probably the instigators of a resolution passed at an emergency meeting of the House of Chiefs in March 1976, which criticized the activities of some chiefs and endorsed government actions to deal with the secessionist threat.[120] Adja Tekpor went even further in his association with the Acheampong regime by serving on the Ad Hoc Committee on Union Government, which was part of a grand strategy for perpetuating military rule. Most chiefs were not as directly implicated with the

---

[115] This arose out of a fresh attempt to revive a sense of Ewe cultural unity surrounding Nuatja (or Notsie) as the notional cradle of the Ewe people. Brown, *ibid.*, p. 598.

[116] Brown, *ibid.*, p. 599.

[117] Interview with Togbe Drake Tsigbe III, Akoefe-Achati, 30 March 1997. Brown notes that chiefs were given presents consisting of money and goods. *ibid.*, p. 599.

[118] Apparently, the cars never materialized.

[119] As reported in the *Daily Graphic*, 2 March 1976.

[120] For details, see *Daily Graphic*, 16 March 1976.

SMC, but a close examination of the files of Nana Soglo Allo III does suggest that regime leaned heavily upon the chiefs as political intermediaries.

Another reason why the traditional authorities rallied to the side of the regime was that there was a renewed debate concerning the legacies of the amalgamation policy.[121] Whereas the Togoland unification movement had once gained some mileage from associating itself with the cause of the unamalgamated divisions, on this occasion the dividends did not accrue to TOLIMO. In 1956 the Van Lare Commission had looked into chieftaincy in the Volta Region and had recommended the recognition of a number of paramountcies. The criterion was that a paramount chief should not have previously sworn an oath of allegiance to another stool. This helped to confirm the status of the heads of the former amalgamated states, but also rewarded the chiefdoms that had stubbornly resisted the amalgamation policy. Hence, the chiefs of Anfoega, Gbi, Likpe, Nkonya, Ve and Santrokofi were confirmed as Paramount Chiefs alongside the chiefs of Krachi, Peki, Anlo, Buem, Avatime, Ho and Kpandu. However, after the 1966 coup, the NLC passed Decree No. 112, which was intended to downgrade those stools that had been wrongfully elevated by Nkrumah. This led to the unamalgamated divisions being stripped of their paramount status. The waters were later muddied by a Legislative Instrument of 1974 which readmitted the latter as full members of the Regional House of Chiefs, but without restoring their paramount status.

By the mid-1970s, there was much restiveness surrounding chieftaincy in the region. Not surprisingly, the substantive Paramount Chiefs were only too happy to preserve the existing hierarchy. The chiefs who had been downgraded were intent on recovering their earlier status and argued that there was a need to revisit the issue. However, the greatest pressure seems to have come from the remaining chiefs who agitated for a reversion to the *status quo ante* the amalgamation policy on the grounds that they had been tricked into accepting a diminished status. The Acheampong regime found itself pulled in different directions by competing imperatives. On the one hand, it was likely to win more friends than it would lose by increasing the number of paramountcies. On the other hand, senior chiefs in the rest of Ghana would resent any inflation of chieftaincy titles in the Volta Region. The SMC resorted to the conventional expedient of a committee of enquiry, which sat under the chairmanship of Nana Agyeman Badu over 1975/76. At this point, chiefs from among the Central Togo minorities began to assert a claim to Guan origins. The Nkonya chiefs had long been playing the Guan card, but the suggestion that the Akpafu, Bowiri, Likpe, Logba, Lolobi, Nyangbo, Santrokofi and Tafi peoples were also Guans represented a complete innovation. It appears to have started in the Eastern Region where self-proclaimed Guan autochthons set themselves against supposed Akan hegemons.[122] In order to bolster their position, their leaders sought to

---

[121] On the chieftaincy politics of the Volta Region since independence, see Paul Nugent, 'An abandoned project? The nuances of chieftaincy, development and history in Ghana's Volta Region', *Journal of Legal Pluralism and Unofficial Law*, 37–8, 1996.

[122] The Guans were supposedly present in Ghana before the Akan arrived. The fascinating ethnic dimension to chieftaincy politics in Akuapem has been dealt with by Michelle Gilbert, '"No condition is permanent": ethnic construction and the uses of history in Akuapem', *Africa*, 67, 4, 1997. For a more recent example of the Guan project, which lays cultural claim to much of the Volta Region, see the contributions to *Guan Research*

associate the Central Togo minorities of the Volta Region with the Guan cultural project. Some chiefs responded positively to this reworking of history, recognizing that the claim to being ethnically distinct from the Ewe constituted a possible basis for claiming separate paramountcies.[123]

For our purposes, what is important is that a repackaged ethnic discourse under-lined the centrality of cultural and historic links to the west of the Volta, as opposed to the Ewe cradle of Notsie in Togo. This removed a crucial plank from an already creaking unificationist platform. At the end of its enquiry, the Agyeman Badu committee was unable to reconcile the principle of equity with the desire to limit the number of paramount chiefs, and its report was never published.[124] The decision to temporize once again ensured that chieftaincy remained in an unsettled state. However, this uncertainty also enabled the SMC to keep the chiefs on the political hook. With CPP precedents in mind, the traditional authorities were aware that they might forfeit their position within the pecking order if they continued to flirt with secessionism. Furthermore, they were conscious that for all the faults of the existing set-up, chiefs were accorded a measure of respect that was absent in Togo.[125]

The failure of TOLIMO was also reflected in its inability to win support among a new cohort of opinion leaders within the region. The erstwhile unification move-ment had depended upon the 'scholars', who looked to the precedent of German Togo, and upon school teachers, who railed against the dominance of the Anlo elite. By the 1970s, as we have seen, the northern half of the region could boast a university-educated intelligentsia to match that of the south. This latest cohort was an integral part of the Ghanaian intellectual establishment, and as such it displayed a conspicu-ous lack of interest in Togolese affairs. However, members of this intelligentsia shared at least one attribute with those who had blazed a trail in the inter-war period, namely, a concern with the upliftment of their home communities.[126] They were pro-foundly disturbed by the evidence that the region was lagging behind, but they believed that the remedy lay in gaining greater access to the corridors of power rather than seeking to separate from Ghana.

The NRC began its tenure by promising a fresh start in centre–local relations, in

---

[122 (cont.)] *Papers: Journal of the Guan Historical Society of Ghana*, Volume 1, parts I and II (undated).

[123] There was a complication, though, which was that the Guan spokesmen claimed to have had fetish priests rather than chiefs before the Akan arrived. This was not the best basis on which to claim a paramountcy. On this aspect, see Paul Nugent, *Myths of Origin and the Origin of Myth: Local Politics and the Uses of History in Ghana's Volta Region*, Working Papers on African Societies, No. 22, 1997 (Berlin: Das Arabische Buch), pp. 18-21.

[124] Nana Agyeman Badu made it clear at one point in the proceedings that the national norm was 28 members of the Regional Houses of Chiefs, and this would set limits on what was possible to recommend in the Volta Region. GNAA ADM 5/3/215 'Proceedings of the Enquiry into Volta Region Chieftaincy Affairs', 96th sitting, 5 August 1975, p. 27.

[125] As in most Francophone African states, Togolese chiefs were treated as functionaries. There is a certain sim-ilarity here with the contrast between the powers of traditional authorities on either side of the border between Nigeria and Niger. See William F.S. Miles, *Hausaland Divided: Colonialism and Independence in Nigeria and Niger* (Ithaca & London: Cornell University Press, 1994).

[126] Yaw Twumasi attributes the electibility of Dr Obed Asamoah in 1969 to his regular weekend visits to Likpe. This was a tradition he kept up throughout his lengthy tenure as Secretary of Foreign Affairs under Rawlings. Yaw Twumasi, 'The 1969 election', in Austin and Luckham, *Politicians and Soldiers*, p. 156.

an effort to draw the regional elite into a closer association with the state bureaucracy. As part of the new deal for the Volta Region, the NRC promised a tarred trunk road to run from Ve-Golokwati through Hohoe and Jasikan to Papase, which would eventually be extended to Bimbilla in the Northern Region. This was important because the northern half of the region beyond Hohoe had always suffered from inadequate infrastructure. A second road was to connect Asikuma and Kpeve through Peki, thereby bypassing the Togoland hills. Again, the NRC proposed that any town with a population of more than 2,000 people should be eligible to receive a piped water supply, while shallow wells with pumps would be provided for smaller settlements.[127] However, the military regime also made it clear that communities were expected to contribute their own energies, resources and ideas. In this context, regional power brokers perceived that the likelihood of bringing home the bacon would hinge on how skilfully they massaged the existing structures of power and influence. The activities of TOLIMO were regarded at best as a distraction, and at worst as a threat to the perceived long-term interests of the region.

The Volta Youth Association (VYA) had been formed in 1971 to campaign for the interests of the region. At that time, its leaders were comprised of teachers and traders in the Kadjebi area.[128] When a series of clandestine meetings was held in Kpalimé in 1973, VYA members were apparently present. The result was that the VYA came to be seen as a suspect organization, and Brown claims that the Acheampong regime set about sponsoring the Volta Region Development Association (VORDA) as a counterweight to it.[129] This does, however, accord undue significance to official machinations. During the transition to the Second Republic, a Development Association had already surfaced as part of a 'Third Force', which sought to steer a course independently of both Gbedemah and Busia.[130] Although it faded from view with the return to party politics, a precedent had been created. In July 1972, some 300 leading citizens gathered in the regional capital to discuss the formation of a new association to mobilize resources and to advise the administration on the development priorities of the region.[131] It was this initiative that culminated in the formal inauguration of VORDA in January 1973. The Regional Commissioner, Major Habadah, was only too happy to preside over the outdooring ceremony, but the initiative seems to have come from within the ranks of the elite. It is significant that the leadership of VORDA was made up of the same cast of characters who had made their mark in NAL – notably Dr G.K. Agama, Sam Okudzeto and Dr Obed Asamoah – none of whom could reasonably be described as stooges.

In view of the historic fault lines that have been traced through the pages of this book, it is telling that VORDA was unable to maintain a show of unity for long. In August 1973, the Volta Youth Association (VOYA) staged a breakaway with the apparent endorsement of the new Regional Commissioner, Colonel E.O. Nyante. An intense rivalry between the associations then ensued. Ken Kwaku suggests that the split followed occupational lines: that is, whereas professionals and intellectuals

---

[127] The population threshold was later increased to 4,000 people.
[128] Brown, 'Borderline politics', p. 602.
[129] *Ibid.*, p. 603, n. 3.
[130] Twumasi, '1969 election', p. 155.
[131] Kwaku, 'Political economy of peripheral development', p. 284.

predominated in VORDA, businessmen gravitated towards VOYA. He then relates this to the different emphases in their respective platforms: that is, whereas VOYA regarded private investment as the key to regional development, VORDA advocated long-term planning in association with the regional bureaucracy.[132] However, the division arguably reflected a more historic north–south divide. In a public advertisement in 1974, VORDA pointed out that while it had established a branch in Keta, VOYA maintained no presence in the north of the region.[133] In its own press statement, which protested too much, VOYA denied that it was a vehicle for southern hegemony.[134] In fact, it is likely that the occupational and intra-regional divisions reinforced one another. Whereas Anlo had spawned a substantial cadre of businessmen, the northern elite were a product of the educational expansion that had occurred in the 1950s. As a result, its members were disproportionately based in the professions, most notably law.[135]

These internal contradictions were never effectively reconciled. In December 1974, Brigadier Ashley-Lassen brokered a merger in the form of the Volta Development and Youth Association (VODYA). The incoming President, V.W.K. Agbodza, had a foot in both camps, being both a highly successful businessman and a native of Kpandu.[136] However, VODYA subsequently splintered and the regional elite remained at odds with itself for the remainder of the decade. For our purposes, what is important to stress is the lack of any significant engagement between TOLIMO and the leading protagonists in regional affairs. Although VOYA had allegedly asked the Eyadema regime for financial assistance in 1973, this is the only hint of a linkage.[137] When the rivalry between VORDA and VOYA was at its most intense, both sides went out of their way to distance themselves from secessionist demands. Hence, in a letter to the *Daily Graphic* in August 1973, L.K. Degbor set out to clarify the position of VOYA, stating that 'While we agree that the Volta Region has lagged behind in national development through no fault of the present regime we do not agree that secession can offer a solution to these problems'.[138] This stance was echoed by VODYA, which made a point of associating itself with the resolution of the House of Chiefs in March 1976. Although it would have been risky to have done otherwise, the consensus does appear to have been that secessionism was a blind alley.

During interviews in the mid-1980s, it proved surprisingly difficult to find people who could recall very much about TOLIMO despite its relatively recent demise.

---

[132] *Ibid.*, pp. 283–5.

[133] 'Press statement by the Volta Region Development Association (VORDA)', *Daily Graphic*, 18 September 1974.

[134] 'Full text of the press statement made by the Volta Youth Association (VOYA)', *Daily Graphic*, 3 September 1974.

[135] The legal profession was one of the great growth industries of post-independence Ghana. According to Robin Luckham, 'The Constitutional Commission 1966-69', in Austin and Luckham, *Politicians and Soldiers*, p. 63, the number of lawyers increased from about 60 in 1948 to over 600 in 1969. The lawyers have provided the bedrock of a Ghanaian elite that is truly national in complexion and outlook.

[136] Agbodza also became President of the Ghana Chamber of Commerce.

[137] Reported as an unsubstantiated claim in Brown, 'Borderline politics', p. 603, n. 3.

[138] Letter from L.K. Degbor, General Secretary of VOYA, to *Daily Graphic*, 31 August 1973. Like many of his ilk, Degbor served his time in office. At the time of fieldwork in the mid-1980s, he was the Deputy Regional Secretary.

Insofar as the name meant anything, it was associated with political developments internal to Togo. Although it is conceivable that people were wary about speaking openly about something as sensitive as secessionism, the same informants were often prepared to hold forth about Antor and *Ablode*. One former activist summed up a pervasive lack of interest in the entire subject of TOLIMO when he remarked that 'The two parties have fought and settled it [in 1956]. Why raise it again?'[139] In his view, and that of many other respondents, there really was nothing further to discuss.

Conclusion

The winding up of TOLIMO around 1977 signalled the final *coup de grâce* for the unificationist project. The politicians who had nurtured the Togoland unification movement in the 1940s and 1950s – men like Gerald Awuma, Kofi Dumoga and S.G. Antor – retired from active politics and subsequently died in relative obscurity. Insofar as they are still remembered, they have been incorporated into within the Busia/Danquah tradition's hall of fame of good Ghanaian nationalists.[140] Crucially, they had failed to pass the unificationist mantle to a new generation of political actors who might have articulated a vision of an alternative future. Some of the children of TOLIMO supporters continued to live in exile in Togo, but many of these returned at around the time of the 1992 elections with a view to taking up their options on Ghanaian nationality. Although relations between the Rawlings and Eyadema regimes remained fraught during the 1980s and early 1990s – as reflected in allegations of subversion and repeated border closures – secessionism has ceased to represent a challenge to the territorial integrity of Ghana. Equally, there has been little evidence of irredentist sentiment on either side of the border since the mid-1970s.

In this chapter, I have attempted to account for this outcome. I have emphasized the success with which the CPP uprooted *Ablode* networks at the local level. The result was a growing acceptance of the terms of integration that outlived the Nkrumah regime itself. TOLIMO enjoyed a brief moment of fame, but arguably its real claim to historical significance lies in its complete failure to mobilize a constituency behind demands for a revision of the international boundary. The generation of opinion leaders that came to prominence at the end of the 1960s, and the chiefs who continued to haggle over their status in the pecking order, were explicit in their identification with the Ghanaian nation. Ordinary 'Voltarians', who seldom received the opportunity to express themselves in the same way, nevertheless came to embrace this same sense of nationality and to live it in their daily existence. As far as the politics of unificationism is concerned, therefore, this really is the end of the story. But there remains some other unfinished business.

[139] Interview with Raphael Deku, Likpe-Todome, 14 February 1986.
[140] At the delegates' congress of the New Patriotic Party in September 2000, J.A. Kufuor mentioned S.G. Antor, Alex Odame and Reverend Ametowobla as those who had made a historic contribution.

7

'*Strangers Can Never See
All Corners of the Town*'[1]

Land, Contraband & the Boundary
Since Independence

The last two chapters have dwelt at some length on the high politics of the Ghana-Togo border. It is relatively easy to piece together this part of the story because political activists are in the business of leaving their statements of intent, as well as their justifications for past behaviour, on public record. The fact that the United Nations was both a good listener and an assiduous record keeper obviously helps. Equally, electoral statistics enable one to infer patterns of support with a measure of confidence. However, the problem with this kind of analysis – at least, when pursued in isolation – is that it tells us only a certain amount about how ordinary people worked around the realities that confronted them. Politicians are naturally inclined to believe that popular aspirations are channelled through the circuits for which they are the gatekeepers. If only this were true, then the sources identified above would come close to capturing the entire picture. But politics with a capital 'P' only ever occupies one corner within a much more extensive arena of collective activity and experience. Public spaces are shaped as much by the everyday activities of ordinary people, in ways that sometimes undergird but at other times may bypass the formal structures of politics – whether of the governmental or the oppositional variety. These practices are constitutive and not merely passive, and, in that sense, may be fairly described as political.

James C. Scott has used the term *infrapolitics* to delineate a realm of activities that lies outwith formal politics. In his words:

> If formal political organization is the realm of elites (for example, lawyers, politicians, revolutionaries, political bosses), of written records (for example, resolutions, declarations, news stories, petitions, lawsuits), and of public action, infrapolitics is, by contrast, the realm of informal leadership and nonelites, of conversation and oral discourse, and of surreptitious resistance.[2]

This statement would perfectly describe what this chapter is proposing, but for the

---

[1] This is an aphorism derived from Likpe, but is not unique to it.

[2] James C. Scott, *Domination and the Arts of Resistance: Hidden Transcripts* (New Haven & London: Yale University Press, 1990), p. 200.

231

last two words. Scott fully intends infrapolitics – involving a whole range of activities from poaching to squatting – to connote an aspect of resistance.[3] Now, the politics of everyday life – politics with a small 'p' – may embody an element of covert resistance, but to look for hidden transcripts at every turn is ironically to privilege the formal structures of power by referring everything to them. It may make sense when seeking to get to the bottom of closed and highly claustrophobic systems of power – for example, slavery – but it is unnecessarily restrictive in other contexts. Our concern is with activities that embody a logic and a dynamic that are not reducible to resistance, and that may even serve to reinforce certain aspects of state power. I prefer, therefore, to adopt a more open-ended framework of interpretation.

At the same time, it is necessary to distinguish my approach from two other positions with which it might easily be confused. The first assumes that the locality is often sufficiently detached from the centre to allow for a virtually autonomous local sphere. Such a view was advanced in respect of a number of crisis-ridden African countries during the 1980s, not least Ghana itself.[4] However, I wish to establish that even the most marginal border communities have been closely intertwined with the state. The idea of local autonomy is really a myth that derives from a certain model of politics rather than from evidence gathered in the field.[5] The second position is that everyday activities are unthinking and hence not really political at all. Again, I wish to argue that the practices of daily life have served to constitute power, by working upon state institutions, community relations and basic concepts of political space. I would also go as far as to argue that the acute political crisis that hit the country at the end of the 1970s owed many of its origins to the capillary effect of activities at the border. Rather than artificially separating the political from the personal – or the formal from the informal – I wish to demonstrate their interconnectedness.

It is my contention, therefore, that the perpetuation of the Ghana–Togo border cannot be understood purely as the outcome of a political contest between unificationists and integrationists that was decisively resolved in favour of the latter. In some respects, what was more decisive was the fact that border communities behaved in ways that helped to turn the paper partition into an enduring reality. This occurred for ostensibly different kinds of reasons. On the one hand, by seeking to take advantage of their unique location, border peoples were participating in a daily vote of confidence in favour of the status quo. On the other hand, regular interaction across the border, which might have been expected to work against the logic of national integration, actually tended to reinforce a sense of difference between those

[3] Hence Scott states that 'Each of the forms of disguised resistance, of infrapolitics, is the silent partner of a loud form of public resistance'. *Ibid.*, p. 199.

[4] See Naomi Chazan, 'Patterns of state–society incorporation and disengagement in Africa', in Donald Rothchild and Naomi Chazan (eds), *The Precarious Balance: State and Society in Africa* (Boulder & London: Westview Press, 1988). In respect of Ghana, Chazan argued that there had been a withdrawal from an unresponsive state into local theatres of activity where common values and agreed rules persisted. Naomi Chazan, *An Anatomy of Ghanaian Politics: Managing Political Recession, 1969–1982* (Boulder: Westview, 1983), chs 2 and 11; also Victor Azarya and Naomi Chazan, 'Disengagement from the state in Africa: reflections on the experience of Ghana and Guinea', *Comparative Studies in Society and History*, 19, 1987.

[5] I have argued in greater detail against this interpretation in my Ph.D thesis, entitled 'National integration and the vicissitudes of state power in Ghana: the political incorporation of Likpe, a border community, 1945–1986', University of London, 1991, ch. 6.

who now called themselves Ghanaian and Togolese.[6] There was an intriguing paradox at work: while the border defined a context that was out of the ordinary in all kinds of ways, in other respects it came to bear the stamp of national difference. It is this tension between the spatial singularity and national typicality of the border that provides the subject matter of this final chapter. My *modus operandi* is to begin by picking up the land question once more, and then to proceed to a more detailed consideration of the contraband trade.

The land question rephrased

As we have already seen in some detail in Chapter 2, the pursuit of land claims across the international boundary had generated considerable tension during the inter-war years. In the process, lives had been lost and substantial sums of money had been expended in legal fees. In most instances, the cases eventually came to court or were settled through arbitration. In the latter part of the 1930s, the heat seemed to go out of most of the disputes. However, this was less because the litigants were satisfied by the outcomes than for more practical considerations. The parties were financially exhausted, while cocoa – the source of most of the feverish competition for land – lost much of its allure with the outbreak of war. However, any hope that a definitive solution had been found proved to be overly optimistic. The litigants, it turned out, were merely catching their breath. As soon as cocoa prices began to rise again, there was a renewed scramble for prime forest land.

As had been true of the inter-war period, most of the land disputes were highly intricate affairs, turning as they did on virtually irreconcilable claims about history, colonial cartography and the ownership of cocoa trees. Some of the disputes involved *dukɔwo* from the same side of the border. In British Togoland, new life was breathed into a number of long-standing disputes, such as those between Asato and Apesokubi and between Nkonya and Alavanyo. Some new disputes also came to the fore, such as that between Ayoma and Likpe-Kukurantumi.[7] Similarly, in French Togoland there was a bitter tussle between the Adeles and their Akebu and Ntribu neighbours. Even where the contestants were from the same side of the border, the arguments tended to spill over it because disputed land was frequently sold to strangers or otherwise alienated through the *dibi* system. In French Togoland, it was migrant farmers from Anfoega who were often the casualties.

Other disputes straddled the border and presented renewed cause for official concern. These were messy affairs in which, as one French official astutely observed, issues of individual ownership became inextricably bound up – at least in the minds of the litigants themselves – with chieftaincy boundaries and the contours of the international frontier.[8] There were disputes along the full length of the boundary, but

---

[6] This phenomenon is, of course, instantly recognizable in terms of Barth's account of how ethnic boundaries typically arise out of conditions of similarity rather than difference. Frederik Barth, 'Introduction', in *Ethnic Groups and Boundaries: The Social Organization of Cultural Difference* (Boston: Little, Brown & Co., 1969).

[7] In 1986, I was fortunate in being able to examine the files for these disputes and some others at the Stool Lands Boundaries Settlement Commission, State House, Accra.

[8] P. Davy to Minister of Interior (8 August 1958), TNAL 2APA/449.

there were two particular trouble spots where matters threatened to escalate into open conflict. The first was at the meeting point between the Buem and their Ahlo and Akposso neighbours. In the south-eastern sector, the peoples of Baglo, Dzolu and New Ayoma accused their Ahlo counterparts of seeking to drive them off lands which had been deposited on the French side of the line. In 1958, the Secretary to the Regional Commissioner in Ghana wrote that:

> It appears that some Buem inhabitants of these towns who are Ghanaian citizens own cocoa farms which they purchased from the owners in French territory up to 20 years ago. These farms are now fully mature but the French Togoland farmer owners have taken to molesting the Ghanaian owners and their labourers when they go to visit their farms or to live in the farm hamlets.[9]

That was one interpretation of the facts. However, the chief of Baglo signalled that the issues went much deeper when he asserted that his lands had historically crossed the international border and extended from Ahlo right up to Kpete-Bena.[10] In support of this claim, he referred to the ever-controversial *Karte Von Togo* from 1905.

A second series of disputes involved the Buems and their Akposso neighbours. One area that was contested was a stretch of land to the west of Kute – called Olomavi after the river of that name – in the vicinity of boundary pillars 73 to 75 (see Map 2.2). A much older bone of contention was the land that had been contested between the Buems and the Akpossos during the 1930s. As we have already seen, the Privy Council judgment of 1939 had confirmed the partition of the disputed lands between the two parties. The Akpossos had been granted ownership of the land bounded to the north by the Odjindji River and to the west by the route linking Kadjebi and Ahamansu. For their part, the Buems had been awarded the disputed area to the north of the Odjindji River. In 1946, Thomas Agbo, acting on behalf of the Akposso stool, had requested a surveyor to physically demarcate the land. The Akpossos also demanded that they be placed in full possession of the land that had been awarded to them, which they took to mean the expulsion of the Buems still farming there. However, as the DC noted, the court had specifically ruled that the Buems who had bearing cocoa farms were to be left in possession thereof.[11] In 1949, Agbo went to the Buem Akan Native Court to demand title to the land bounded on the north by the Wawa River, on the south by the Menu River, on the east by the international boundary and on the west by the meeting point between the Menu and Wawa Rivers – only excluding the lands that had been specifically allocated to Buem in the earlier settlement. In effect, Agbo was staking a claim to a large chunk of northern Buem, covering an area which the Ahamansu and Papase chiefs regarded as their own.

The evolution of this particular dispute illustrates just how convoluted the links between chieftaincy politics and land could be. The efforts of Agbo to set himself up as a chief in his own right appears to have set him on a collision course with the Akposso regent in Badou. In 1952, Agbo took the latter to the Atakpamé tribunal to

---

[9] Minute by Secretary to Regional Commissioner (dated 11 November 1958), GNAH RAO C/854.
[10] Nana Yaw Buaku IV, chief of Baglo, to W. Henkel, DC, Buem-Krachi (12 December 1958), GNAH RAO C/854.
[11] T.A. Mead to CEP, 30 October 1946, GNAA ADM 39/1/1267.

demand recognition of his claim to the Akposso land located in British Togoland. The judgment went in favour of the regent who subsequently decided that it was time to clip the wings of the over-mighty Agbo. This he sought to achieve by establishing a working alliance with the Omanhene of Buem who had hitherto been regarded as the inveterate enemy of the Akpossos. When Agbo pursued his claims to the Wawa lands in the north, the regent withdrew his support and at least tacitly endorsed the assertion of ownership by the Ahamansu and Papase chiefs in that area. According to C.M. Weatherburn, he even went as far as to connive with the Omanhene against the chief of Kpete-Bena, who was presumably backing Agbo, in the struggle for control of the Olomavi lands.[12] Internal struggles within Akposso ranks had, therefore, produced a significant shifting of alliances.

The second important zone of contestation lay in the Krachi District and immediately across the border, at the meeting point between the Adjuati, the Adele and the Ntribu peoples. Whereas all the Adjuati had been brought together under the British flag, in exchange for western Akposso, the negotiations over the Adele had broken down in the early 1920s. They therefore remained on either side of the Togoland boundary. The tendency of the Adele people to move back and forth across the line created some uncertainty as to who was 'indigenous' and who was not. In 1931, a group of French Adeles from Ossingui crossed into British Togoland to escape French labour demands, and began planting cocoa and coffee farms. This brought them into dispute with the Adjuatis of Shiare, which was resolved in their favour through arbitration in 1936. Four years later, the Ossinguis decided that it was safe to return to French Togoland and settled at Dikpéléou. As far as they were concerned, they still retained ownership of the land in question, although they had largely ceased cultivating it after the move.[13] In 1951, the land issue resurfaced once more. The Ossinguis complained that while they were prepared to let Shiare farmers work the land, the latter had begun selling it off to strangers. The Shiares, on the other hand, continued to insist that the land was really their own, and responded that it was the Ossinguis who were attempting to sell their land. Some years later, the Ossinguis also started to lay claim to a more extensive area that had been planted with cocoa by Adjuati farmers. The Government Agent accused the Ossinguis of conducting 'a systematic plunder of Adjuati farms, carrying away cocoa and destroying crop farms and beating up any Adjuati people they encounter in the area'.[14] He pointed to a similar situation in the vicinity of Dadiase where there had been a number of violent incidents. The difference in this case was that both parties to the dispute were Adeles. The Dadiase chief complained that the international boundary had cut him off from part of his lands, and that French Adeles were now seeking to seize his possessions on the British side as well.[15] A third trouble spot was at Breniase where Ntribu farmers arrived from across the border at Degengue. The latter were already

[12] Report by C.M. Weatherburn, Government Agent (dated 17 April 1953), TNAL 2APA/449.

[13] This story is recounted in a letter from Robert Cornevin, le Chef de Subdivision, Atakpamé, to Commandant de Cercle de Centre (14 March 1952), TNAL 2APA/446. Cornevin later went on to become the leading historian of Togo.

[14] A.H. Brind, Government Agent, Jasikan to Secretary to Regional Commissioner (20 February 1958), GNAH RAO C/854.

[15] Kwasie Boafo, Dadiase, to Government Agent, Kete-Krachi (24 January 1956), GNAH RAO C/854.

engaged in a dispute with their Adele neighbours in French Togoland, and stood accused of selling land to all comers on both sides of the international boundary.

The timing of these various disputes, which came to a head between 1956 and 1958, was highly significant. They peaked not just at a time of a buoyant cocoa prices, but at the very moment when the future of British Togoland was up for grabs. The prospect of British Togoland becoming a part of Ghana was a source of anxiety for French Togolanders who farmed or claimed ownership of land there. Equally, there were British Togolanders who were worried about securing continued access to land on the other side. These fears were well-grounded in the sense that there was a concerted effort at the local level to play the national card in such a way as to nullify the claims of people from the other side. Many British Togolanders sought to stigmatize their neighbours as suspect foreigners, and perceived a certain advantage in supporting the integration option as a means of making a clean break between the territories. At the time of the 1956 plebiscite, the chief of Dadiase suggested that the movement of French Adeles across the border was part of a sinister plot to influence the vote in favour of unification.[16] In this way, land issues became thoroughly entangled with the plebiscite campaign. After the vote, long-standing Peki residents in Kpete-Maflo and Bena were attacked and had their belongings destroyed by a crowd that accused them of being CPP supporters who had supported integration.[17]

Litigants on either side of the border traded accusations that their rivals were engaged in routine acts of violence and the theft of crops, and requested their respective administrations to enforce the rule of law more rigorously. At the start of 1958, the Shiarewura wrapped himself in the new Ghanaian flag when he reminded the touring Regional Commissioner that 'Peace of mind and peaceful living are important to every Ghanaian' and repeated the accusation that French Togolanders were entering his lands and destroying crops.[18] These various attempt at co-opting the agents of the state enjoyed a certain amount of success at a time when official nationalism was running high. Hence administrators referred to 'infiltration' from French Togoland and were generally inclined to treat the farmers from across the border as the aggressors. Although there was a staggered transition from British to Ghanaian rule, it was nevertheless the case that the incoming DC and RCs often lacked a deep historical perspective on these disputes. One French administrator was surprised to discover that G.A. Boahene, the Government Agent, had no knowledge of the boundary map dating to the partition of Togoland, and actually had to provide him with a copy.[19] Individuals and communities who were threatened denied that they were strangers at all, as did the French Adeles, or sought to remind the authorities that the international boundary did not affect rights to land.

As before, administrators sought to resolve these difficulties by urging the complainants to have recourse to the courts. There was, however, a reluctance to do so because of the costs involved and the difficulty of serving summonses across the

---

[16] Kwasie Boafo to Government Agent (24 January 1956), GNAH RAO C/854.

[17] The petitioners claimed to have lived in these places for around 30 years. Humphrey Sakyi, Peki-Blengo and others to Sylvanus Olympio (7 June 1958), TNAL 2APA/513.

[18] Quoted in D.A. Anderson, Secretary to Regional Commissioner to Government Agent, Jasikan (23 January 1958), GNAH RAO C/854.

[19] P. Davy to Minister of Interior (8 August 1958), TNAL 2APA/449.

border.[20] Moreover, a court decision was only as good as the willingness of officials to enforce a judgment. And yet the authorities on either side were acutely aware that they lacked the manpower to provide effective policing along the disputed border areas. In the Krachi District, for example, the nearest Police station to the trouble spots was located in Kete-Krachi.[21] The authorities attempted to deal with a situation, which repeatedly threatened to get out of hand, by means of two expedients. The first was to convene meetings of chiefs and district officials from either side in an attempt to broker a peaceful settlement. The first such meeting was held at Akposso-Badou on 5 December 1958, and concentrated on the disputes between the Buem and Akposso. At this gathering, which was attended by around a thousand people, it was decided to establish a joint committee of four members to investigate complaints about victimization.[22] A week later, another meeting was convened at Nkwanta where the competing claims of the French Adeles and the Ghanaian communities concerned, including those of Shiare, Breniase and Dadiase, were addressed. On this occasion, the Ghanaian participants complained about the ransacking of their farms, while their rivals pointed out that they had been the same people before the international boundary was drawn and asserted that sections of their land had been placed on the wrong side of the border. Officials noted that both the Badou and the Nkwanta gatherings were carried out in a cordial atmosphere and allowed for a cathartic airing of grievances.

At the Nkwanta gathering, the Ghanaian chiefs had observed 'that the pillars demarcating the international boundary were few and far between and this situation tended to encourage the inhabitants from both sides of the boundary (who are mostly illiterate) to trespass on each other's rights'.[23] This point was taken on board by the authorities as a possible source of confusion. The second expedient, therefore, was to interpolate more boundary pillars in order to render the line more visible to the naked eye. This was actually a red herring because it implied that there ought to be some conformity between the international boundary and the line separating one chiefdom from the next. This was an assumption that had long since been abandoned, and its resurrection at this point merely added grist to the mill of those who wanted to push 'foreigners' off the land.

In September 1959, surveyors were sent to the border with a mandate to survey the border from Likpe-Bakwa as far as Menusu Preventive Station; to check the existing pillars and to interpolate new ones. Although this was supposed to be a purely technical exercise, it quickly became bogged down in competing claims and local anxieties. The survey party encountered resistance in the Olomavi area from the Akpossos. Chief Agbenyega Raphael from Kpete-Bena complained that cocoa trees were being destroyed by the party, but the real reason for the opposition appears to have been an apprehension that the Akpossos would lose access to farms that crossed

---

[20] The Shiares were allegedly reluctant to go to court for this reason. D. Thomas, Government Agent, Jasikan to Commandant de Cercle, Atakpamé (13 February 1957), TNAL 2APA/446.

[21] D.A. Anderson to Permanent Secretary, Ministry of External Affairs (3 April 1958), GNAH RAO C/854.

[22] 'Notes on meetings between the Ghana and French Togoland administrative authorities held on the 5th and 12th December to discuss frontier clashes between Ghanaian and French Togoland citizens', GNAH RAO C/854.

[23] Notes on Nkwanta meeting, GNAH RAO C/854.

the freshly demarcated border.[24] A crowd sought to persuade the survey party to deflect the boundary line and, when this failed, they physically threatened it in an attempt to bring the work to a halt. Here and in other locales, people from the Ghana side complained that the boundary pillars had been swiftly removed.[25] In the final analysis, it proved difficult to carry out the demarcation in a satisfactory manner because the parties to various local disputes believed that their land rights would be affected by the demarcation exercise. In what was effectively a rerun of the 1920s experience, the authorities only succeeded in rendering both the land disputes and the physical demarcation of the border more complicated by positing a possible link between them.

The difference on this occasion was that the two sets of district authorities found it increasingly difficult to negotiate directly with one another as relations between the national governments became more fraught. Arising out of the Badou meeting, both sides had agreed that it was desirable to create a Ghana/Togoland Joint Committee to mediate in cross-border disputes, but this was persistently frustrated at higher levels.[26] The French Togoland authorities advised their Ghanaian counterparts of their choice of committee members in March 1959, but the Accra government was reluctant to follow suit. The Cabinet formally decided in July that it was preferable to wait until Togolese independence before proceeding to the next stage.[27] The following year, the Commandant at Atakpamé warned that there was likely to be trouble with the onset of the 1960/61 cocoa season unless positive steps were taken. The Volta RC concurred and wrote to the Ministry of the Interior, urging that the committee be established without further delay. He referred to a narrowly averted riot near Hevi, which actually lay to the south of the most notorious trouble-spots, and pointed out that there was tension right along the length of the border.[28] His suggestion that 'the borders are not completely under control' created some alarm at the centre, but any sense of urgency was allayed by the Assistant Commissioner of Police who denied that there had been any serious incidents.[29] In November 1960, the RC was informed that while the Ministry of the Interior was in favour of the creation of such a cross-border body, the current state of inter-governmental relations militated against it:

> ... the Ministry of Foreign Affairs has replied to the effect that while agreeing in principle to the necessity of establishing a joint Ghana-Togo Commission to deal with border incidents, they do not consider that the time is opportune for an approach to be made to Mr. Olympio on this subject. The Ministry of Foreign Affairs has stated that this is confirmed by the Office of the President.[30]

[24] Chief Agbenyega Raphael, Kpete-Bena to Chief of Buem-Kute (7 May 1960), GNAH RAO C/854.

[25] J.R. Dabo, DC, Jasikan, to Secretary to Regional Commissioner (8 September 1960), GNAH RAO C/854.

[26] At the Badou meeting, it was agreed that complaints should be made to the respective administrations who would then refer them to the Joint Committee. The latter would carry out an on-the-spot inspection and make a report. Notes of meeting held at Badou, 5 December 1958, GNAH RAO C/854.

[27] G.B. Boahene, Government Agent, Jasikan, to Secretary to Regional Commissioner (20 August 1959), GNAH RAO C/854.

[28] G.L.K.M Markwei, Secretary to Regional Commissioner, to Principal Secretary, Ministry of the Interior (16 September 1960), GNAH RAO C/854.

[29] Assistant Commissioner of Police, Ho, to Secretary to Regional Commissioner (22 November 1960), GNAH RAO C/854.

[30] Acting Principal Secretary, Ministry of Interior, to Secretary to Regional Commissioner (8 November 1960), GNAH RAO C/854.

The context was one in which the Nkrumah government was seeking to place a squeeze on the Togolese by means of tighter border restrictions. In this context, the Olympio administration could hardly be expected to be co-operative. There is some evidence to suggest that local actors were acutely aware of this fact and manipulated events accordingly. Hence Togolese villagers were able to obstruct the work of the Ghanaian survey party in the knowledge that their own government was no longer prepared to play ball.

Although local officials continued to warn about the dangers of not taking decisive action, the promised formula for resolution of the land question never materialized. In 1971, the Busia regime signalled that the picture was as confused as ever when it sought to gather information from the chiefs about the 'irregular situation along the Ghana–Togo border in which some traditional areas are split into two, with one side in Ghana and the other in Togo'.[31] In subsequent years, there were periodic improvements in relations between the two governments, which produced renewed promises of closer co-operation to resolve the lingering difficulties. For example, as part of their rapprochement, the Acheampong and Eyadema regimes inaugurated a Ghana–Togo Border Committee in April 1973. However, this became defunct when the secessionist issue erupted. The pattern was repeated again in the mid-1980s when an alleged invasion of Togo from Ghanaian soil put paid to a fresh effort at rapprochement. The net result was that most of the border disputes that resurfaced during the 1950s were never definitively laid to rest.

This raises the intriguing question of precisely what happened on the ground. Unfortunately, there has been no detailed research on land use in the border areas, with the exception of R.A. Kotey's short study of cocoa and coffee cultivation in Kute.[32] One reason is that academic interest in the Ghana–Togo border has tended to revolve around high politics rather than the practical ramifications thereof. Another reason is that the very sensitivity of the border has militated against the conduct of detailed local research. Still, there is some evidence to suggest that land use has been brought into alignment with the international boundary line, mainly through the unilateral actions of border peoples themselves. Many communities have abandoned the attempt to maintain access to land across the line, while appropriating other land that has fallen on their side. In the process, there have been both winners and losers. The discourse of nationality, which has been promoted by both Ghanaian and Togolese regimes, has contributed to this state of affairs, but principally because it has made it possible for local players exploit the language of alterity. In Ghana, this discourse became most explicit with the passage of the Aliens Compliance Ordinance in 1969. The latter placed many people of Togolese extraction in an insecure position, even when they had lived in Ghana for many years.[33] Moreover, as successive Ghanaian governments became increasingly exercised about the evils of smuggling,

---

[31] K.A. Tamakloe, District Administrative Officer, Jasikan, to Clerks of Buem, Akan Wawa and Biakoye Local Councils (27 March 1971).

[32] R.A. Kotey, *Competition Between Cocoa and Coffee: A Case-Study*, Legon: Institute of Statistical, Social and Economic Research, University of Ghana, Technical Publications Series, no. 29, 1972.

[33] Under the Aliens Compliance Order, foreign nationals whose papers were not in order were given an ultimatum to leave. This stance was later softened, but many Togolese believed that their tenure in Ghana was unsafe.

it was easy to cast Togolese farmers in the role of villains. Their local detractors were able to play on the suspicion that Togolese nationals would be tempted to carry their cocoa and coffee crops back across the border rather than selling to the CMB as the law required. Equally, Ghanaian farmers with land across the border have at various times been accused of spying and lawlessness. Local pressures have therefore forced people on either side of the international border to abandon, sell or rent out lands that have been too difficult to farm. It is worth underlining that while state agencies have been accomplices in this process of land redistribution, it is border peoples themselves who have tended to dictate the terms. To start from the assumption that these are the hapless victims of the principle of the sanctity of colonial boundaries, is to obscure the reality that the boundary is very largely a local construction.[34]

Ironically, the net result in the longer term has been to inject a measure of stability into the land equation. This has in turn facilitated a level of renewed co-operation across the line in the recent past. The fact that cocoa has lost much of its allure, largely owing to the spread of diseases such as black pod, has also helped to reduce the intensity of competition for land. In Buem, the 1970s witnessed a reversal of the migration patterns of the last half-century as many effectively abandoned their ageing farms or switched to foodstuffs.[35] Although there have been periodic complaints about encroachments, the competition between claimants from Akposso and Buem has lost much of its intensity. Although it has not been possible to update the picture in this particular sector, two other case-studies illustrate both the potential for, and the limitations of, cross-border co-operation.

In the case of Likpe, scrutiny of the files of Nana Soglo Allo III has yielded a substantial body of correspondence, conducted mostly in Ewe, with his opposite numbers in Togo.[36] Interestingly, this personal contact between the chiefs has taken place largely beyond the purview of the state authorities. Like many other communities, the Bakpele claim that their lands historically stretched beyond the present international boundary on to the Danyi plateau.[37] With time, however, they have come to accept that this boundary should be taken as the effective line of demarcation with their eastern neighbours. As Nana Soglo explained to the Ministry of Foreign Affairs in 1988:

> We share a common boundary with the people of Danyi Dzidrame in the Republic of Togo on the Eastern border of Ghana. Our ancestral land extended far into places occupied by some

---

[34] By contrast, Jeffrey Herbst, *States and Power in Africa: Comparative Lessons in Authority and Control* (Princeton: Princeton University Press, 2000), ch. 8, emphasizes the role of the state in policing the boundaries of citizenship.

[35] One observer in the mid-1970s noted that 'The exodus of people for various reasons has resulted in the decay of some of the settlements. Most of the strangers' quarters in Kadjebi, Ahamansu and Papase (especially those inhabited by people of non-Ghanaian origin) are in complete disarray. Houses put up by some wealthy cocoa farmers for rental purposes are almost in ruins.' C. Dorm-Adzobu, 'The impact of migrant Ewe cocoa farmers in Buem, the Volta Region of Ghana', *Bulletin of the Ghana Geographical Association*, 16, 1974, p. 52. This picture is borne out by the 1984 population census, which demonstrated a fall in the population of Ahamansu from 3,222 in 1960 and 3,246 in 1970 to 2,929 in 1984. For Papase, the figures were 3,752 in 1960, 3,443 in 1970 and 3,319 in 1984. Republic of Ghana, *1984 Population Census of Ghana: Special Report on Localities by Local Authorities*, p. 98. Elsewhere the population was growing rapidly.

[36] I am grateful to Jacob Torddey for his translations of these letters.

[37] This is borne out by the *Karte Von Togo*.

towns of Togo, but because the international boundary pillars have been erected in our land in positions the British Government and the French Government agreed we have left the portions of our land in Togo to remain the property of the Togolese.[38]

Equally, the chief of the small Togolese village of Dzidrame, which lies just across the border from Mate, endorsed the principle that the international boundary should be taken as the benchmark for settling land claims. Despite this consensus on the rules of the game, there has nevertheless been a series of disputes since independence. In 1964, after repeated altercations over a piece of land on the border, the chief of Likpe-Todome complained to the RC about the behaviour of one Amudzi Agbedawu from Dzidrame. Because the land appeared to fall on the Ghana side of the line, the police were able to arrest and charge the latter with entering the country without authorization and for trespass, which led to a term of imprisonment for the unfortunate Agbedawu.[39] Quite apart from the vexed question of who the land had originally belonged to, this case concretely illustrates how the application of the principle of nationality might complicate access to farm land for Togolese nationals.

In 1986, there was a fresh dispute between one Sraku Kumodzi of Dzidrame and G.K. Kpatakpalu from Mate over a portion of land on the mountain overlooking Mate. This case became bound up with a wider set of complaints emanating from members of the two communities. Nana Soglo reported that Togolese farm labourers, who had been recruited to work on cocoa and coffee farms near the border, had begun to claim them as their own and were helping themselves to the crops.[40] On the other hand, the peoples of Dzidrame insisted that the disputed farms actually belonged to them, and complained in turn that cattle belonging to Mate people were destroying their crops. Once again, the litigants and the chiefs accepted the principle 'that the boundary should be pegged to the international boundary' and agreed that they would forgo any claim to land that was clearly demonstrated to lie on the other side of the line.[41] Nana Soglo Allo and his counterpart, Togbui Hini M.A. Gbedze X of Danyi Kakpa, resolved to settle the dispute among themselves without involving their respective governments, who might merely complicate matters. The arrangement was that both parties would meet at the border, identify the relevant boundary pillars and make a decision as to who owned which pieces of land. In practice, what should have been a purely technical exercise turned out to be rather more complicated. The ill-health of the two chiefs, and a long series of conflicting engagements, necessitated repeated postponements.[42] By the end of 1991, the two chiefs were still endeavouring to arrange a meeting between themselves, by which time the political crisis in Togo had thrown an additional spanner

---

[38] Nana Soglo Allo III to PNDC Secretary, Ministry of Foreign Affairs (5 February 1988), files of Nana Soglo Allo III. Coincidentally, the PNDC Secretary concerned was none other than Dr Obed Asamoah, who was from Likpe-Bala and so was well aware of the local situation.

[39] Assistant Commissioner of Police, Ho, to Secretary to Regional Commissioner (9 July 1964), GNAH VRG 1/7/2/1.

[40] Nana Soglo Allo III to Secretary of Foreign Affairs (5 February 1988), files of Nana Soglo Allo III.

[41] These are the words of Kpatakpalu in a letter to Nana Soglo Allo III (dated 26 February 1987). They echo an earlier letter from Kumodzi (dated 21 November 1986), files of Nana Soglo Allo III.

[42] Nana Soglo was extremely ill at this time and finally died in January 1995. His Danyi counterpart also had to move to Lomé for health reasons.

into the works.[43] More fundamentally, some of the boundary markers could not be identified. The fact that remnants of some pillars were to be found in the vicinity raised suspicions that they had been deliberately removed in order to assist the Dzidrame case. This led Nana Soglo to deviate from the ideal of seeking a purely local solution as early as 1988. He drew the attention of the Ghanaian authorities to the missing pillars and suggested that the case should be drawn to the attention of the Joint Boundary Commission.[44] However, a fresh bout of recriminations between the Rawlings and Eyadema regimes rendered a solution along these lines practically impossible. The Committees for the Defence of the Revolution (CDRs) did inspect the land to identify the missing pillars and made a report of their findings to the district administration, but that was as far as it went.[45]

In the early 1990s, there was evidence of renewed tension on the land as the Bakpele complained of further encroachments, of persistent harassment and the killing of their cattle. On the other side, the people of Dzidrame alleged that they were being maltreated by the People's Militia. This case demonstrates both the strengths and limitations of purely local initiatives. On the one hand, the chiefs and litigants were able to make some progress in sifting out the points in dispute without involving the slow-moving layers of government bureaucracy. After all, if a mutually satisfactory settlement was to be found, it would have to come through some meeting of minds at the local level. On the other hand, the proposed solution – which accepted the practical validity of the international boundary line – depended upon the existence of verifiable markers on the ground. When these turned out to be missing, the parties could not resist the temptation to appeal upwards to their respective authorities. The sensitivity of the latter to issues of territorial sovereignty was bound to prolong the dispute and was likely to complicate the search for a lasting solution. At the time of writing, this particular land issue had not been resolved.

By comparison, the Woamé-Honuta dispute appears to have developed in more promising directions. In Chapter 2, we left this case at the point in 1933 when the court, presided over by John Gutch, sought to effect a partition of the disputed land. The practical implication was that the Woamés were given possession of some land that fell within the boundaries of British Togoland. The Woamés were not satisfied with this judgment, however, and in 1945 the Honutas complained about fresh encroachments. Togbe Ayisa IV brought a case of trespass and, according to his successor, the legal proceedings dragged on until 1969 when judgement was finally given in favour of the plaintiff.[46] The following year, however, the Woamés appealed to the Supreme Court and the judgment went the other way. On this occasion, the court also ruled that the Gutch settlement had been *ultra vires*, which threw the entire land question into a state of confusion because there were now no agreed

---

[43] In the midst of the crisis, the Togolese banks were refusing to permit cash withdrawals, which made it difficult to secure the money to pay the surveyors. Secretary to Togbui Hini M.A. Gbedze X to Nana Soglo Allo III (4 August 1991), files of Nana Soglo Allo III.

[44] Nana Soglo Allo III to PNDC Secretary, Ministry of Foreign Affairs (5 February 1988), files of Nana Soglo Allo III.

[45] F.K. Onai, CDR Zonal Organizing Assistant to District Administrative Officer, Hohoe (19 December 1990), files of Nana Soglo Allo III.

[46] Interview with Togbe Ayisa V of Honuta, Ho, 31 March 1997.

arbitraments. This raised the prospect of a rash of fresh litigation that had already cost both sides, who had recruited the best legal counsel, an inordinate amount of money.[47] Togbe Ayisa V, who came to the Honuta stool in 1968, recalls that he was anxious to reach an amicable settlement, but that the late Togbe Atsridom of Kpedze sought to slow things down because he was unable to account for the proceeds during the period he had been acting as caretaker of the lands. Once this matter was resolved, the two communities were able to come to a settlement in 1972. It was agreed that stranger farmers would be allowed to work the land, and that the proceeds would be divided into two equal parts and paid to the two chiefs on behalf of their respective communities.

This local solution appears to have worked reasonably well for a time. But in the early 1980s, the Honutas began to accuse the Woamés of taking the cocoa and coffee for their own exclusive benefit. Togbe Ayisa therefore denounced the Woamés for complicity in smuggling.[48] This provided the pretext for the People's Defence Committees (PDCs) to take possession of the farms. At this point, the Woamés were cut out of their share, and all the proceeds were paid into community coffers in Honuta. From the Woamé perspective, this must have seemed like a land-grab, and it apparently created a great deal of ill-feeling there. Informants in Honuta recall that a fresh rapprochement was instigated in the mid-1980s.[49] One G.A. Anku, part of whose family was from Woamé, was elected 'youth leader' in Honuta and argued for a reconciliation on the grounds that the two communities had too many ties to warrant a prolongation of the dispute. His soundings were successful, and both communities agreed once more that the proceeds from the farms should be shared between them. The formula was that the farm workers would receive one-third of the money derived from the sale of the crops, while the remaining two-thirds would be divided equally between the two communities.

This arrangement was, however, viewed as a temporary expedient pending a final partition of the land. When interviewed in 1997, Togbe Ayisa indicated that he and the Woamé chief were meeting to discuss ways of fixing a straight line between their respective domains. Significantly, this initiative was being taken with minimal reference to the two governments. Because they were not depending on the international boundary line as their marker, unlike the peoples of Likpe and Dzidrame, it was easier to strike out independently. When asked about a possible government input, Togbe Ayisa was dismissive. He recalled that the Joint Boundary Commission had once come to the land, been fed and entertained, and had left again without making any meaningful contribution. From that point onwards, the two sides had concluded that there was little to be gained from involving their governments directly. Togbe Ayisa and other Honuta informants also noted that both communities recognized the crippling costs of continuing with the dispute and were keen to reach a solution that would be mutually acceptable. One suspects that the chances of reaching a lasting settlement will ultimately depend on abandoning all reference to the conflicting

[47] Honuta employed the services of the later Justice Apaloo, while the Woamés enlisted Justice Amaorin. Interview with Togbe Ayisa V, 31 March 1997.
[48] Because the disputed land lay in Ghana, any cocoa or coffee that was physically taken back to Togo counted as contraband.
[49] Interview with Regent, R.K. Adzudzor, and three others, Honuta, 30 March 1997.

German maps and resorting to a pragmatic partition of the disputed mountain areas. The fact that the Honutas continue to insist that there is already a perfectly workable boundary, which Dr Grüner had demarcated in 1912, may well mean that the disagreements about history will yet return to bedevil this local accord.[50]

Kalabule artists and armpit smugglers: the tar-baby effect revisited

Smuggling as public discourse

In *The Black Man's Burden*, Basil Davidson definitively abandons his earlier enthusiasm for successive variants on African nationalism and contends that the political elites who inherited power at independence made a cardinal error in buying into a model of the 'nation-state' that was not grounded in indigenous traditions of statecraft.[51] In the Ghanaian case, the two halves of the pairing – that is, nation and state – need to be delinked. As I have sought to demonstrate in earlier chapters, a sense of identification with a greater Gold Coast had become apparent in British Togoland by the early 1950s. Two decades later, the failure of secessionist appeals underlined the relative success of the national project even when so much else was clearly not going according to plan. Arguably, the political elite was not so much taken in by a false image of the new nation, but by other claims that were advanced in respect of the state.

During the inter-war years, the British had been only too happy to foster the illusion that the colonial state was both omniscient and capable of decisive intervention in the lives of its subjects. The very credibility of the colonial project, which always rested on somewhat fragile foundations, was predicated on the preservation of this grand illusion. The British did not let the leaders of the CPP into their little secret during the transition to independence. A simple reason is that even more ambitious claims for the state were being advanced at the time, as the twin discourses of development and decolonization were elaborated and fed off one another. When Nkrumah assured his audience that the CPP would bring electricity, roads, schools and other symbols of modernity to their doorsteps, he was not simply behaving as the consummate politician: he was also expressing a genuine faith in the capacity of the state to deliver. Of course, if the state was going to provide, it also needed to tax, as the National Liberation Movement (NLM) and its allies understood only too well. Over subsequent decades, the CMB functioned as a great suction pump, tapping resources from the cocoa sector and depositing them in the state exchequer. The CMB achieved this feat by maintaining a substantial gap between the world market price for cocoa and what was actually paid to the farmers.[52] In subsequent decades, a

---

[50] Ben K. Fred-Mensah, 'Bases of traditional conflict management among the Buems of the Ghana–Togo border', in I. William Zartman (ed.), *Traditional Cures for Modern Conflicts: African Conflict 'Medicine'* (Boulder & London: Lynne Rienner, 2000) highlights mechanisms for conflict management among the Buem, but their applicability across group boundaries is open to question.

[51] Basil Davidson, *The Black Man's Burden: Africa and the Curse of the Nation-State* (London: James Currey, 1992).

[52] For the role of the CMB in this regard, see G.R. Franco, 'The optimal producer price of cocoa in Ghana',

hidden tax also operated by virtue of the fact that the producer price was calculated at the official rate of exchange, which was increasingly out of alignment with the actual market rate.[53] In the 1960s, the state assumed the additional role of entrepreneur through substantial state investments in agriculture, manufacturing and the commercial sector. These investments were not merely expected to provide a stimulus to the national economy, but were also intended to yield financial returns for the state. The consensus is that the vast majority of these investments failed to deliver the goods – both literally and metaphorically.[54] As a result, the battery of state enterprises became a heavy drain on public funds, and failed to redress the shortages of essential commodities which became a recurrent feature of Ghanaian life from the last years of the First Republic down to the mid-1980s.

The response of successive governments was to resort to tighter regulation in an attempt to bridge the gap between the demand for, and supply of, scarce resources. Hence more restrictive import licensing was introduced by the CPP government to protect scarce foreign exchange reserves and to channel the distribution of goods coming from outside the country.[55] Moreover, an increasingly complex system of price controls was deployed in order to curb the inflationary effects of consumer shortages.[56] However, these efforts to square the circle were generally ineffective because substantial economic rents lay in the manipulation of scarcity. Rather than accept the reality of their limited means to remould social behaviour, successive regimes resorted to even more coercive expedients to achieve their objectives. During the 1970s, as traders both ignored price controls and hoarded essential

---

[52 (cont.)] *Journal of Development Economics*, 8, 1981; Jonathan Frimpong-Ansah, *The Vampire State in Africa: The Political Economy of Decline in Ghana* (London: James Currey, 1991), ch. 7; and V.K. Nyanteng, *The Declining Ghana Cocoa Industry: An Analysis of Some Fundamental Problems*, Legon: Institute of Statistical, Social and Economic Research, University of Ghana, Technical Publication Series, no. 40, 1980.

[53] The Ghanaian pound was fixed against the pound sterling until 1965. That year the cedi was introduced and fixed against the dollar at ¢1 to $1.17. The cedi was devalued in 1967 and again in December 1971. However, the NRC revalued the cedi so that ¢1 was exchanged officially at $0.78. Conversely, $1 traded for ¢1.28. Tony Killick, *Development Economics in Action: A Study of Economic Policies in Ghana* (London: Heinemann, 1978), p. 8. In 1973, the official rate was reduced slightly so that $1 was equivalent to ¢1.15, a rate which was maintained until 1978 despite the fact that the black-market exchange rate stood at ¢9.12 to the dollar in 1977. In 1978, the currency was devalued, but the new rate was pegged at ¢2.75 to the dollar despite the fact that the black-market was close to being ten times higher by 1981. The history of exchange rate policy reflects the extent to which a lack of realism prevailed at the centre.

[54] On the economic record of state entrepreneurship, see Elliot Berg, 'Structural change versus gradualism: recent economic development', in Philip Foster and Aristide Zolberg (eds), *Ghana and the Ivory Coast: Perspectives on Modernization* (Chicago & London: Chicago University Press, 1971); Killick, *Development Economics*, chs 4, 8 and 9.

[55] The Nkrumah regime initially perpetuated a fairly liberal system of open general licences. However, as foreign exchange reserves declined, there was a shift to specific licences with effect from 1962. Under the NLC and the Busia regime, there was a shift back towards open licensing system, but this precipitated a balance of payments crisis. The NRC responded by reinstituting specific licences in 1972, a system that remained in place until the liberalization drive of the 1980s. See Killick, *Development Economics*, pp. 264–86.

[56] The colonial regime had mooted the introduction of price controls in 1945, but met with local opposition. However, price control legislation was introduced in 1949 and remained in place until the passage of the much more comprehensive Control of Prices Act in 1962. See K. Ansa-Asare, 'Legislative history of the legal regime of price control in Ghana', *Journal of African Law*, 29, 1985, pp. 103–4; and Killick, *Development Economics*, pp. 286–91.

Table 7.1. *Financial incentives to smuggling, 1960/61–1982/83*

Year	Ghana producer price (cedis per tonne)	Togo price (cedis per tonne)
1960	220	291
1961	220	277
1962	220	169
1963	217	137
1964	198	154
1965	182	187
1966	152	351
1967	198	369
1968	248	498
1969	279	572
1970	294	523
1971	300	584
1972	361	588
1973	385	564
1974	484	676
1975	578	784
1976	679	1,056
1977	977	2,796
1978	1,601	4,632
1979	3,308	8,348
1980	3,936	17,232
1981	5,333	14,915
1982	12,133	30,204

Source: Ernesto May, *Exchange Controls and Parallel Market Economies in Sub-Saharan Africa: Focus on Ghana*, World Bank Staff Working Paper, no. 711, 1985, p. 129

commodities in expectation of price rises, soldiers were sent into the markets to enforce the law. When they seized hoarded or overpriced goods, traders responded by simply withholding commodities from the market. The net effect was simply to exacerbate the underlying shortages, thereby stoking the fires of inflation. Moreover, a dogged adherence to statist solutions eventually rebounded upon its advocates. In particular, the failure of the Supreme Military Council to stamp its authority over urban markets was crucial in hatching the crisis of legitimacy that came to a head in the mutiny of 4 June 1979.

This dialectic was especially pronounced along the borders. I have already demonstrated how the revenue imperative led the British to insist on the erection of a customs frontier between the two halves of Togoland in 1920. I have also underlined the sensitivity of the CPS to its limited capacity to carry out close border surveillance, which led it to lobby for government policies that would not create unnecessary inducements to smuggle. This simple precept that unenforceable laws exposed the authorities to ridicule was one of many which was mislaid in the course of decolonization. Part of the amnesia can be attributed to the wartime and immediate post-war crises that led the British to become markedly more dirigiste themselves. Many of the trade restrictions were lifted in response to the complaints of the Ewe and Togoland unification movements, but the final resting point still represented a less liberal regime than had prevailed in the interwar period.

The CPP embarked on its political apprenticeship in the early 1950s at a time when there were significant financial incentives to engage in smuggling. The fact that the CMB was holding back part of the world cocoa price meant that farmers living near the borders could often earn substantially more by trading their crops across them. Furthermore, ongoing consumer shortages in French territory ensured a ready market for commodities imported through the Gold Coast. Although the authorities were prepared to demonstrate some flexibility in relation to the trade in food crops, the Preventive Service was charged with upholding the statutory purchasing rights of the CMB and monitoring the flow of essential goods. With the limited resources at its disposal, the Preventive Service struggled to rein in the contraband trade. After independence, the economic nationalism of the CPP, which was modified only slightly by later governments, further increased the financial incentives to smuggle. For a time, there were fluctuations in the intensity of the trade in contraband cocoa (see Table 7.2).[57] But after the early 1960s, a long-term trend was established, as substantial quantities of Ghanaian cocoa, and some coffee, flowed in increasing quantities into Togo, while consumer goods were traded the other way. The creation of a free port at Lomé, located right on the border, enabled Togolese merchants to engage in the profitable re-export of consumer goods to Ghana. The contraband trade imparted considerable economic vitality not only to Lomé itself, but also to other frontier towns further north such as Kpalimé and Badou.[58] The Togolese state also reaped the revenue and foreign exchange accruing from the export of Ghanaian commodities.

From the standpoint of the authorities in Accra, the Togolese appeared to be feeding parasitically off the Ghanaian economy. From the early 1960s onwards, therefore, the smuggling issue became a serious irritant in inter-governmental relations. Indeed, the Ghanaians often preferred to leave the border closed altogether, so as to deter potential smugglers and to frustrate what they interpreted as Togolese scheming. Whereas the case for an open frontier had once been championed by CPP politicians, what emerged – at least on paper – was a relatively rigid boundary. From the early 1960s onwards, the border remained closed for years at a time, and even

---

[57] Ashok Kumar estimated that cocoa was smuggled from Togo towards Ghana in 1962/63, in the opposite direction in 1963/64 and then back again in 1964/65. See his 'Smuggling in Ghana: its magnitude and economic effects', *Universitas*, 2, 3, 1973, p. 127. By contrast, Franco, 'Optimal producer price', p. 86, suggests that there was some smuggling out of Ghana throughout the early 1960s. Kumar's methodology is somewhat problematic because it assumes a point zero from which variations in regional purchases can be pegged. It also assumes a single rate of growth for the sub-region. In its favour, the flow does roughly correspond with the price differentials.

[58] Gabriel Kwami Nyassogbo, 'Urban–rural interactions in sub-Saharan Africa: the case of Palimé and its hinterland in south-west Togo', in Jonathan Barker (ed.), *Rural–Urban Dynamics in Francophone Africa* (Uppsala: Nordic Institute of African Studies, 1997); and Frédéric Giraut, 'La constitution d'une petite ville en région de plantation frontalière: Badou (Togo)', *Cahiers d'Outre-Mer*, 47, 1994.

Table 7.2. *Estimate of Cocoa Smuggling to Togo (tonnes)*[59]

Year	Togolese Purchases*	Volta Region Purchases[t]	Estimate of Togolese Production	Estimate of Smuggling (column 3 less column 1)
1960/61	12,616	31,090	8,544	4,072
1961/62	11,460	28,956	8,631	2,829
1962/63	10,903	21,031	8,718	2,185
1963/64	13,834	28,651	8,805	5,029
1964/65	17,587	27,635	8,889	8,698
1965/66	14,807	20,117	8,976	5,831
1966/67	16,317	18,796	9,063	7,254
1967/68	18,337	24,282	9,150	9,187
1968/69	19,979	23,510	9,237	10,742
1969/70	23,188	20,930	9,321	13,867
1970/71	27,878	15,340	9,408	18,470
1971/72	29,361	10,260	9,435	19,926
1972/73	18,604	22,150	9,459	9,145
1973/74	16,000	14,350	9,480	6,500
1974/75	14,000	14,020	9,500	4,500
1975/76	18,000	13,610	9,520	8,480
1976/77	14,000	9,250	9,540	4,500
1977/78	17,000	7,520	9,560	7,440
1978/79	13,000	6,100	9,580	3,420
1979/80	16,000	4,880	9,600	6,400
1980/81	16,000	1,520	9,620	6,380
1981/82	11,000	1,730	9,640	1,360
1982/83	10,000	3,776	9,660	340
1983/84	17,000	2,656	9,680	7,320
1984/85	10,000	n.a.	9,700	300
1985/86	14,000	876	9,720	4,280
1986/87	13,000	n.a.	9,740	3,260
1987/88	11,000	n.a.	9,760	1,240

* Figures up to 1972/73 derived from David Bovet and Laurian Unnevehr, *Agricultural Pricing in Togo*, World Bank Staffing Paper, no. 467, July 1981; thereafter from Gill and Duffus, *Cocoa Statistics*.
† Figures derived from Cocoa Board, Accra.

[59] It is virtually impossible to calculate smuggling levels with any degree of precision, in the absence of reliable estimates for actual production and in the face of annual fluctuations in output. My method has been to try to calculate Togolese production and then to subtract estimated production from actual purchases. Togolese production levels are calculated by taking the estimate for the acreage under cocoa from Bovet and Unnevehr, *Agricultural Pricing in Togo*, p. 58 and then calculating on the basis of a yield of 6 loads per acre for half of the farms and 12 loads for the remaining farms (which would have been planted more recently). This takes me up to 1974/75, after which point I have assumed a slow increase in subsequent years. On the basis of other more impressionistic evidence, one suspects that Table 7.2 somewhat overestimates smuggling in the early 1960s and in the mid-1980s.

when it was open the authorities sought to restrict trade flows.[60] This represented the final culmination of the tar-baby effect, whereby different economic regimes necessitated tight controls at the geographical margins of the country. What Nkrumah and his successors had neglected to consider, however, was whether official restrictions could be implemented in practice. The tortuous history of border policing tells us that governments took a long time to draw the appropriate conclusions.

By the end of the 1950s, it was clear that the CPS had its work cut out in exercising surveillance. In order to lend it greater teeth, the Preventive Service was detached from the Customs Department and absorbed into the Police Service between 1960 and 1962.[61] In order to provide more personnel, members of the Field Agricultural Survey were absorbed into its ranks. However, this accretion of unqualified personnel merely seems to have had the effect of undermining the morale of serving officers.[62] At the time, the police were physically overstretched, but there were also reports that members of the service began to profit from their border postings. In January 1964, for example, one report reported that while the Togo border was officially sealed, policemen were bending the rules:

> … the border is still firmly closed and not even diplomatic cars have free passage It is believed that the police are not at all eager to have the border opened, owing to the loss of revenue they would suffer. For a 'consideration' it is quite possible to get one's car across the frontier either way – during dark hours.[63]

In subsequent reorganizations, the Preventive Service was hived off from the police and given a separate identity as the Border Guard Service, and then restored to police control. However, these interventions did not make much of a difference. The service was heavily criticized for presiding over a very marked increase in smuggling during the Busia years, when the greater part of the Volta Region cocoa crop ended up in Togo.

In 1972, the incoming Acheampong regime brought characteristic military zeal and naïveté to the question of border management. Its diagnosis of the problem was that the Border Guards lacked a proper sense of professional identity. The National Redemption Council (NRC) opted to militarize the Border Guards by absorbing them as the fourth wing of the armed forces. Henceforth the guards were to receive the same pay, conditions of service and facilities as the other armed services. To signal their new-found importance, the Border Guards were also placed under the control of a senior army officer while military personnel were transferred sideways to the three new battalions and three independent operational companies that were

---

[60] Tight border controls were in force between 1960 and 1963. After an easing of these controls, the border was then completely closed, with the exception of a brief interlude until 1966. Thereafter the border remained open, with greater or lesser restrictions until the PNDC era. The border was then fully or partially closed during 1982, 1983, 1986 and 1987.

[61] Joseph Anim-Asante, 'A descriptive list of the records of the Customs Department in the National Archives of Ghana, Accra, 1920–1950', dissertation for Diploma in Archives Administration, 1988, p. 44.

[62] K. Amissah-Koomson, 'The Border Guards: the case history of an amorphous organisation', *Focus on Customs*, 1, 2, December 1980, p. 11.

[63] 'Confidential report on Ghana, January 1964', West Africa Committee papers, Edinburgh University Library, Box 1.

created.[64] The first head of the revamped Border Guards was Colonel John Kaboré, and he was succeeded in turn by Brigadier F.W.K. Akuffo (who later became head of state), and Brigadier E.K. Utuka, who was appointed to the SMC on the strength of this position. In 1972, the guardsmen were specifically warned that they would be held accountable for any future failure to carry out their duties properly:

> All smuggled goods impounded will be traced to their source and their routes mapped out. When this has been done, all law enforcement agencies on these routes whose duty is to check the smuggling will also be severely and summarily dealt with. Action against the personnel of such law enforcement agencies will include instant dismissal.[65]

In tandem with these administrative reforms, successive regimes sought to bolster the penalties for would-be smugglers. The Cocoa Marketing Board Ordinance (No. 16) of 1947 already stipulated that it was illegal to sell cocoa to anyone who was not authorized to purchase on behalf of the CMB. A practical difficulty was that suspected cocoa smugglers often claimed that they were in the process of carrying their crops to the buying centres at the point when they were intercepted. To close this loophole, a new law was introduced in 1959, which created a presumption of smuggling when someone was shown to be carrying cocoa in the direction of the border. Six months after coming to power, the Acheampong regime passed a Subversion Decree, which prescribed the death sentence for trafficking in timber, gold and diamonds, and a prison sentence of not less than 15 and not more than 30 years for the smuggling of cocoa.[66] Cases that arose under the decree were to be tried by Special Military Tribunals set up in each region and their judgments were not subject to appeal. In border areas, Regional Commissioners threatened reprisals that went even further. At one point, the Brong-Ahafo Regional Commissioner threatened to evict the residents of 13 border villages, while his counterpart in the Volta Region – in apparent ignorance of the law – proclaimed that the government was willing to enforce the death penalty against anybody who was caught smuggling cocoa.[67]

During the early 1970s, official proclamations were positively dripping with military testosterone. However, beneath the uncompromising rhetoric one can detect a grudging realization that the authorities simply did not hold all the trump cards. In the first instance, smuggling was treated as a simple matter of illegality, and the authorities issued confident warnings that the culprits would be brought to book. However, this manifestly failed to happen on the required scale: between 1964 and 1970, the Preventive Service made between 1,277 and 2,011 seizures per annum across the various borders, while the number of persons convicted ranged from a low

[64] The Border Guards battalions were located at Ho, Dormaa-Ahenkro and Bolgatanga. *Ghana, 1977: An Official Handbook* (Accra: Information Services Department), p. 50.

[65] A release from the press secretary of the NRC, *Daily Graphic*, 26 February 1972.

[66] The decree was slightly amended in 1973. In respect of other goods, the Customs and Excise Decree (NRCD No. 114) of 1972, paragraph 49, stipulated a prison term of not less than five years and not exceeding ten years, or a fine of not less than five thousand cedis and not exceeding ten thousand cedis, or both. It also prescribed a penalty equal to treble the value of the goods or two thousand cedis (whichever was the greater), together with the seizure of the contraband goods.

[67] Reported in *Daily Graphic*, 2 September and 9 October 1972. In 1982, the PNDC did in fact extend the death sentence to other categories of smuggling.

of 1,117 in 1965 to a peak of 2,015 in 1970.[68] Given that several people might be tried together in any particular case, the number of instances of smuggling that were brought to book was a fraction of the figure for convictions. At the same time, there was a widespread perception within the country that both the incidence and range of smuggling activities were steadily increasing.

During the early 1970s, the authorities began to signal that there more was at stake than respect for the law. Ghanaians were informed that there was a greater moral issue, namely, whether individuals should be permitted to sacrifice the interests of the nation to their own selfish greed. Smuggling came to be depicted in almost pathological terms, especially in the government press. Consider, for example, the following editorial in the *Daily Graphic* in 1974:

> Nothing can justify smuggling: the impulse is generated by a perverted state of mind which sees money as an end in itself, just as it is with all dirty business deals. Smugglers are criminals pure and simple, and in view of the special situation of our country, their activities are wholly treasonable.... Short of the capital punishment it seems the best thing is to send all smugglers summarily into detention – lock them up and throw the keys away.[69]

The underlying message was that border people ought to think twice before smuggling, and to assist the Border Guards in the performance of their duties. The stakes were raised still further a couple of years later when the SMC made an explicit link between smuggling and secessionism. Hence, in 1977 Utuka asserted that smugglers were unwitting pawns in a Togolese power game:

> ... smuggling activities along the borders of Ghana and into and from Ghana is [*sic*] centrally organized, planned, co-ordinated, directed and financed by the Togo Government against Ghana. This is a fact. It is sad and unfortunate that some Ghanaians are being used as front men.[70]

In the Operation Counterpoint campaign of 1976, the issues of smuggling and secession were explicitly and repeatedly linked. Hence, at the launch in Ho in June of that year, the audience was photographed sitting beneath large banner that read 'Operation Counterpoint: Anti-Secession, Anti-Smuggling, Anti-Hoarding, Anti-Profiteering'.[71]

The danger of invoking appeals to a higher moral cause is that the latter could be used to judge the performance of the rulers themselves. In the latter half of the decade, the conduct of the SMC was subjected to close scrutiny and found sorely wanting. It was widely rumoured that senior members of the regime were deeply implicated in a range of *kalabule* activities, which included smuggling. In his capacity as head of the Border Guards, Utuka was reputed to have made a vast personal fortune in league with professional smugglers.[72] Indeed, it was this that led to his

---

[68] *Ghana: Statistical Yearbook, 1969–70* (Accra: Central Bureau of Statistics, 1973), p. 169.

[69] Editorial in *Daily Graphic*, 26 February 1974.

[70] 'Let's beat smugglers and saboteurs', *Daily Graphic*, part 2, 19 October 1977.

[71] A photograph of the rally was printed in the *Daily Graphic* 30 June 1976.

[72] Mike Oquaye provides some evidence of the questionable activities of Utuka, in the form of an incriminating signature, but this does not relate directly to smuggling. See his *Politics in Ghana, 1972–1979* (Accra: Tornado Publications, 1980), p. 23. In Likpe, there later developed a feeling that the claims were exaggerated. With the exception of a large property in Accra, which was taken over by Ghana Airways, Utuka did not seem to have

execution, along with other members of the government, in the wake of the first Rawlings coup of June 1979. During the brief tenure of the Third Republic that followed, it was publicly acknowledged that smuggling was rife. The debates in Parliament identified some of the fundamental reasons why this was the case. In 1980, the MP for Dormaa, while remaining true to the moralistic tone of public debate, identified clear economic rewards that permitted a tidy compact between smugglers and Border Guards:

> Both the smugglers and the guards have found smuggling a very lucrative enterprise. It is alleged that for every bag of cocoa which the guards get across the border, they collect something like ¢200 from the owner of the cocoa, that is the farmer, while the farmer earns not less than ¢1,000 which, of course, is far more than the ¢240 which he gets in Ghana, and which is not paid promptly by the Cocoa Marketing Board.[73]

During a debate on cocoa producer prices in November 1980, nine out of 10 MPs who spoke stressed the importance of making an immediate increase as a means of combating smuggling.[74] However, as the Dormaa MP had noted, the conduct of the Border Guards was also a factor in the equation. Because their official salaries were so paltry, there was inevitably a temptation for them to collude with the smugglers. The guardsmen were also posted to specific border locations in the expectation that they would gather local intelligence. But as the MP for Buem astutely observed, the guardsmen were dependent on the mercies of their local hosts:

> My observations are that there have not been proper accommodation arrangements for the Border Guards in some areas. They are left to stay with the rural folks, some of whom are themselves smugglers. I wonder how a Border Guard can arrest and efficiently prosecute his landlord or any member of his landlord's extended family.[75]

Although the MP had put her finger on a real dilemma, the thoroughly demoralized Border Guards remained the butt of public criticism. The Constitution provided for the creation of an integrated Customs and Preventive Service, but this was never given legislative effect, and a policy of drift continued.[76]

The overthrow of the Limann regime in the coup of 31 December 1981, and the proclamation of a revolution, brought with it a renewed effort to convert the campaign against smuggling into a genuinely popular cause.[77] In the rhetoric of the time, smugglers were not simply branded as cynical nation-wreckers, but stood accused of being counter-revolutionaries to boot. The regime insisted that those who profited from smuggling were primarily members of the dominant class who lived parasitically off various forms of *kalabule* rather than engaging in productive activity. For that

---

[72] (cont.) accrued very much. For Bakpele perceptions of their local son, see Paul Nugent, 'National integration and the vicissitudes of state power in Ghana: the political incorporation of Likpe, a border community, 1945–1986', unpublished Ph.D thesis, University of London, 1991, pp. 211–14.

[73] D.A. Manson, PFP Member for Dormaa in *Parliamentary Debates*, 26 November 1980. The Limann regime dithered at the time, but tripled the producer prices a year later.

[74] For the debate, see *Parliamentary Debates*, 11 November 1980.

[75] Monica Atenka, PNP Member for Buem in *Parliamentary Debates*, 1 December 1979.

[76] Amissah-Koomson, 'The Border Guards', p. 11.

[77] I have written about the ideological contours of the revolution in Paul Nugent, *Big Men, Small Boys and Politics in Ghana: Power, Ideology and the Burden of History* (London & New York: Frances Pinter, 1995), ch. 2.

reason, the campaign against smuggling was imbued with deep political meaning. In a visit to the Volta Region in September 1982, Flt-Lt Rawlings promised 'drastic revolutionary measures' to deal with smuggling.[78] His problem was, however, that the Border Guards were a notoriously unreliable instrument. Their head pleaded, with some justification, that it was virtually impossible for 3,000 officers to police such lengthy stretches of frontier.[79] The response of the government was to despatch sections of the police and army to assist them. At the same time, the regime sought to involve border peoples directly in anti-smuggling operations through the People's Defence Committees (PDCs). The calculation was that the PDCs were likely to be privy to local information in a way that the Border Guards could never be. Moreover, there was a hope that the PDCs would not be tainted by the ethos of corruption that had become deeply engrained within the Border Guards.

The first set of PDC Guidelines specifically stated that:

> The PDCs are to expose all smugglers, black marketeers, hoarders and profiteers, and criminals of all shades and categories, and organise the people to deal with such saboteurs, with revolutionary discipline.[80]

This was a significant departure from the statist approach to border policing that had hitherto held sway. It is true that Utuka had mooted a plan for 'people's anti-smuggling teams' as early as 1976 and that the Limann regime had advocated the use of vigilante squads.[81] However, there is no evidence that these earlier statements of intent had ever been acted upon. By contrast, every border village boasted its PDC by the first few months of 1982, and its members were constantly reminded that their most important responsibility lay in monitoring activity along the frontier. The desire to break the mould was also evident in the announcement towards the end of 1982 that 'People's Tribunals' would be established in every border town in order to expedite the punishment of offenders. As finally constituted in 1983, the Public Tribunals were composed of laymen rather than people who had a proper legal training, in an explicit attempt to avoid the perceived class bias of the formal judicial system.[82]

However, the decision to appeal directly to the 'people' did culminate in a number of practical inconsistencies. The personnel of the Border Guards, police and army – whether corrupt or committed in the performance of their duties – resented the intrusion, as they saw it, of untrained civilians into their professional domain. During 1982, there was a series of unseemly incidents in the Volta Region, involving PDCs and service personnel. At one point, the Deputy Volta Regional Secretary and a group of students were beaten up by Border Guards at Aflao, and when this was followed by a police assault on PDCs at a roadblock in September, there was a full-

---

[78] Reported in the *Daily Graphic*, 4 September 1982.

[79] Quoted in *Daily Graphic*, 30 July 1982.

[80] 'Guidelines for the proper functioning and effectiveness of the People's Defence Committees, released by the Interim Co-ordinating Committee for People's Defence Committees', published as a supplement to the *Legon Observer*, April 1982, p. iv.

[81] Utuka saw these squads as a possible check on the Border Guards. Reported in *Daily Graphic*, 29 June 1976.

[82] Only the presiding member was expected to have an intimate legal knowledge, despite the fact that the Tribunals were empowered to pass the death sentence in respect of smuggling and other offences. Nugent, *Big Men*, p. 57.

blown political crisis in Ho.[83] Another fundamental problem was that the PDCs were being asked to perform an impossible balancing act. They were supposed to nurture popular support for the revolution, but anti-smuggling campaigns were distinctly unpopular in border areas. The PDCs were left with a choice between turning a blind eye towards smuggling or taking a stand and alienating much of their local constituency. In either event, their ability to carry out the government agenda was bound to be compromised. And finally, the infrastructure of the Public Tribunal system never became sufficiently well developed for it to be able to function at the community level. Smuggling cases were normally referred to the Regional Public Tribunal in Ho whose members were not drawn from the communities concerned, but were appointed from the centre. In that sense, the tribunals never administered the 'popular justice' that had been touted as a radical break with the past.

After 1983, the Rawlings regime resorted to yet more reforms in an attempt to resolve the problems that had been thrown up in the heat of the revolution. Following perennial complaints about deep-seated corruption and obstructionism, the Border Guards Service was formally disbanded towards the end of 1985. Some of its personnel were absorbed into the army, which henceforth assumed direct responsibility for border duties.[84] This restructuring, which completed the militarization of border management, presented two perceived advantages from the point of view of the regime. One was that all of the intelligence resources of the regular army could be drawn upon for anti-smuggling operations. Another was that the soldiers could be rotated between border and other military duties, thereby minimizing the likelihood that they would become drawn into lasting relationships with smugglers.

The second substantive reform was the formation of a People's Militia in 1984. The militia was recruited from among local youth, but was not strictly accountable to local communities in the sense that the PDCs, and later the Committees for the Defence of the Revolution (CDRs), were supposed to be.[85] The expectation was that the militiamen would be deployed across a given district, which meant that while they would possess some understanding of local conditions, they would be less likely to succumb to pressure from immediate kin. They were also to be directly rewarded for their efforts according to a formula that divided the proceeds from the sale of contraband between individual militiamen who had made a seizure and the district secretariat. The underlying intention was to render participation in anti-smuggling operations a paying proposition in the same way that smuggling itself was. Given that the militiamen were likely to be drawn from broadly the same constituency as the smugglers, this represented a shrewd mechanism for converting potential law-breakers into servants of the state. At the same time, the PNDC sought to allay military concerns by placing the militia under the wing of a newly created Civil Defence Organization (CDO), which was headed by an army officer, Brigadier Tehn-Addy. Retired military personnel were also recruited for the regional and district

---

[83] The attempt by the Deputy Regional Secretary, Kwasi Kamasa, and the Regional Co-ordinating Committee of PDCs to depose the Assistant Commissioner of Police and to take control of other government departments led to a purge of so-called 'ultra-leftists'. For details, see Nugent, *ibid.*, pp. 70–2.

[84] In the case of the Volta Region, it was the Mortar Regiment at Ho that was vested with the task of carrying out border policing.

[85] The CDRs replaced the PDCs in 1984.

secretariats, whose job was to impart a modicum of military discipline and to furnish the militiamen with some basic weapons training. Hence the People's Militia always embodied a fundamental tension: while it was drawn from the border communities, it was not really of them.

The element of selective continuity with the revolution was also apparent in respect of the Public Tribunals, which were subjected to limited reform after 1983. The tribunals were preserved as an instrument of PNDC power, in structural tension with the formal legal system, because they permitted the regime to short-circuit the procedural niceties of the courts. It was considered vitally important to bring smugglers to justice with the least possible delay. No less importantly, the tribunals were intended to dispense justice in the full view of the public in a way that the courts generally did not. Whereas the main court buildings in Ho were physically set back from the road and exuded an air of formality, the Regional Public Tribunal was located on one of the busiest streets in Ho and its doors were literally thrown open to the public. During the mid-1980s, tribunal hearings typically attracted very large audiences consisting not just of family members of the accused, but also curious passers-by. In this way, the ability of the regime to punish smugglers was constantly brought to the attention of the general public. The fact that the tribunal was dealing with cases that might well involve the death sentence lent added drama to the proceedings, and further underlined the dangers of flouting the law.

An anatomy of smuggling

Thus far, I have demonstrated how official discourse and practical implementation twisted and turned as successive governments struggled to exact compliance from border peoples. At this point, I wish to leave the state on one side and to subject the phenomenon of smuggling itself to closer scrutiny. The questions I wish to consider are: what was the nature of the contraband; who were the smugglers and how did they operate; and how best might their actions be interpreted?

The smugglers and the smuggled

Since the mid-1960s, the range of goods that have been smuggled in either direction has been an impressive one. The principal commodities which have been drawn towards Togo fall into three groups. First, there are crops that emanate from the Volta Region itself. The list includes cocoa and coffee, but also a variety of agricultural goods such as maize, rice, yam, cassava and palm-nuts. The second group consists of consumer goods that have been subsidized by the Ghanaian state and that have consequently attracted higher prices in Togo. Although cocoa has been the most valuable item of contraband, there has also been a very substantial trade in petrol and kerosene, at least when these items have been available.[86] Thirdly, there has been a

---

[86] Vehicle operators and chainsaw operators from Likpe received coupons which allowed them to purchase a limited quantity of petrol in Hohoe. However, the former often sought to establish a relationship with filling station attendants, who would agree to sell additional jerry cans of petrol under the counter. These were then conveyed to border villages and entrusted to local carriers who would ferry them across the border by night. In 1986, a lorry also visited the Likpe villages in order to sell kerosene directly to the people. In Mate, the owner of a set of storage tanks managed to persuade the drivers to sell everything to himself. Having cornered the supply, he could then sell at a mark-up to people who made a living in the smuggling of kerosene to Togo.

trade in precious metals from other parts of Ghana. The list includes diamonds and gold, but the records of the Regional Public Tribunal in the early 1980s also point to some traffic in other metals such as copper wire and brass.[87]

The list of goods that have been smuggled the other way is an even longer one, reflecting not merely price differentials but also chronic consumer shortages. In 1974, one newspaper itemized the following: wigs, soap, sugar, refrigerators, television sets, radiograms, vehicle spare parts, textiles, suiting materials, footwear, cosmetics, sardines, corned beef, drinkables, perfumes and cigarettes.[88] In early 1986, when I was able to carry out a small census of my own, people who crossed from Likpe-Mate to Dzidrame on market days were typically returning with consumer items like clothing, blankets, sugar, metal pans and cigarettes.[89] And in my own spot-check of a village store in Likpe-Mate in September of that year, I also identified tinned fish, batteries, razor blades, soft drinks, cigarettes, talcum power, pomade, cocoa butter, cubed and granulated sugar, pens and tinned tomatoes as being of Togolese provenance. Iron roofing sheets, beer and basic drugs were also regularly purchased from Togo. Of all these illicit imports, textiles and clothing were probably the most important in terms of their commercial value. By the end of the 1970s, textile factories in Ghana were operating at a fraction of capacity, and it was widely rumoured that their finished products failed to reach the Ghanaian public because management was in the habit of smuggling them into Togo. In order to acquire cloth for everyday use and for occasions such as funerals, it was necessary for consumers in the Volta Region to look towards Togo. The venerable 'Nana Benz' – the female textile merchants of Lomé – prospered on the strength of their sales to the Ghanaian market.[90] Some cloth was also traded in the opposite direction. The expert weavers of Agotime were, for example, in the habit of smuggling their highly valued product to Togo in exchange for hard currency. Ironically, it is likely that much of the Agotime cloth eventually found its way back into Ghana, such was the level of consumer demand.

A profile of the smugglers themselves can also be constructed on the basis of tribunal records, the testimony of informants and local observation. At a basic level, it is helpful to distinguish between the owners of contraband goods, the financiers of the trade and the actual smugglers. The first category refers chiefly to cocoa farmers who took advantage of the prices being offered by itinerant smugglers and agreed to sell part of their crop to them. It also refers to traders on the Togo side of the border

---

[86 (cont.)] Crucially, he also insisted that the smugglers pay him in CFA francs, which he then used to purchase other Togolese goods for sale.

[87] Togo exported CFA 137.1 million worth of diamonds in 1978 despite the fact that the country had no mines. For these statistics, see Samuel Decalo, *Historical Dictionary of Ghana* (2nd edn), (Metuchen & London: Scarecrow Press, 1987), p. xviii. See also 'Togo: local Wall Street', *West Africa*, 26 March–1 April 1990, pp. 505–6.

[88] 'Smuggling: the base of Ghana's economy', *Daily Graphic*, 24 July 1974.

[89] This involved sitting on the main mountain path leading from Dzidrame to Mate on successive market days and seeking to establish what people were carrying in either direction. In most cases, people seemed happy enough to disclose the contents of their loads, although it is more than possible that people co-operated because they believed I was soliciting information for official purposes.

[90] On the cloth traders of Lomé, whose networks extended further afield, see Rita Cordonnier, *Femmes Africaines et commerce: les revendeuses de tissu de la ville de Lomé* (Paris: L'Harmattan, 1987).

who supplied goods to traffickers. In either case, these people were complicit in smuggling activity, but not directly involved in it. The second category refers to the individuals who actually financed the smuggling operations. The wealthier they were, the less likely they were to be involved in the actual haulage of the contraband. The third category refers to those people who ensured that the goods were physically moved from one side of the border to the other. They might be engaged in the smuggling of their own items, but equally they might be in the employ of those who capitalized a given smuggling operation. The attraction of strangers to the border zone, which became established during the inter-war period, was if anything accentuated after independence. Border towns and villages became remarkably cosmopolitan places, sucking in settlers from as far afield as Nigeria and Mali as well as Togo itself. In Kpedze, the Muslim (and hence non-local) population was large enough to warrant the construction of a substantial mosque, which was allegedly paid for by one extremely wealthy smuggler who had taken up residence there. These outsiders were often employed as cocoa labourers and caretakers. Indeed, the majority of cocoa workers in the region were Togolese – principally people of Kabré and Kotokoli origin. However, farm workers might also have a second form of employment consisting of their participation in the contraband trade.

This categorization also contains within it an implicit distinction between the scale of smuggling operations and hence the calculations underlying them. At one end of the spectrum were the activities of whose who one retired Border Guard referred to as 'armpit smugglers'.[91] This term is extremely felicitous because it encapsulates ideas about both size (evidently extremely small) and motivation (bodily need). The 'armpit smugglers' were people who crossed the border with small quantities of goods on an *ad hoc* basis. In Likpe during the mid-1980s, it was common practice for people to cross over to Dzidrame to purchase particular items – such as drugs or sugar – as and when they needed them. To be able to buy these items with CFA francs, they needed to carry other commodities that they could sell on the other side. On market days, one could witness individuals carrying small quantities of cocoa, coffee and palm nuts in order to make their purchases. It was generally understood that it might be necessary to pay border officials something small if they happened to be lying in wait on the route, because they were technically in breach of the law.[92] Even individuals who regarded themselves as staunchly law-abiding, most notably the chiefs, perceived no contradiction in sending someone to make a few essential purchases on the other side, even if this was officially reckoned as smuggling and involved some petty bribery along the way.

At the other end of the spectrum were the *kalabule* merchants who financed very large smuggling operations. The symbol of their trade was not the 'armpit', but the articulated lorry, which trundled through official entry points bearing cargoes of contraband goods. This kind of business, in which very large sums of money were put at risk in every expedition, rested upon developing good working relations with the upper echelons of the police and Border Guards. The latter were paid

---

[91] Interview with Victor Mantey, former staff sergeant of Border Guards at Leklebi-Dafo, Abrani, 14 September 1992.

[92] The sale of cocoa and coffee to anyone other than an accredited CMB buyer was illegal. Quantities of other agricultural goods could be taken over the border in non-commercial quantities.

handsomely for their complicity in seeing the lorries through, and sometimes this co-operation went even further. The assault which precipitated the crisis in Ho in September 1982 apparently started when the Kpedze smuggling magnate, mentioned above, requested the Assistant Commissioner of Police to remove a PDC roadblock which was impeding his operations.

In between these extremes were substantial numbers of people for whom smuggling constituted a profit-making exercise, but who were working on fairly narrow profit margins. They generally lacked the degree of personal contact with senior state officials. Equally, because they could not afford to pay off too many officials, their preference was for a strategy of avoidance. When the turnover of border officials was rapid, these committed smugglers could play the game of evasion successfully. Whereas the *kalabule* merchants drove their goods across the border by daylight, members of this intermediate layer normally preferred to ferry their goods across under cover of darkness. There were some exceptions to this general rule. Some lorry owners built secret compartments for smuggled goods. Others apparently contented themselves with carrying passengers, but actually made money from emptying their petrol tanks on the other side. Equally, border officials became alert to the subterfuge of apparently pregnant or corpulent female passengers wrapping as many cloths as they could around their midriffs. For the most part, though, the primary goal of avoiding detection meant crossing the border in a covert fashion. In areas where smuggling was rife, people often travelled in teams and carried firearms so as to deter border officials who might be tempted to interfere.

In line with successive reforms of border policing, officials were sometimes appointed to an area for long periods in order to enable them to develop an awareness of local conditions. After some time, border officials would tend to find out who was making money through contraband and might then demand protection money. Professional smugglers were sometimes forced to strike a deal with a middle-ranking officer who could secure the compliance of subordinates. For this reason, the policy of turning border officials over very slowly had the effect of entrenching corruption rather than discouraging smuggling. Even then, there were many smugglers who chose not to strike a deal, preferring instead to take the risk. If they were caught, they might need to pay off the relevant officials at that point. This could be a risky and expensive business as one case, which reached the Public Tribunal in September 1983, demonstrates. It transpired from the evidence in court that the defendant, one Felicia Serwaah, had been asked by a Border Guard to assist in the carriage of some goods from Togo. After three successful operations in the vicinity of Dzindzisu, the local police got wind of the deal. Serwaah was forced to pay three police officers off and to cut one of them in on future operations. This backfired when his own son was arrested, and the sergeant and Serwaah both found themselves indicted for smuggling. She was then advised to meet the Chief Inspector in Krachi who demanded ¢10,000 and two bottles of schnapps, and then passed her on to another police officer who extracted another ¢40,000 in return for an agreement to rewrite the witness statements. Subsequently, Serwaah claimed, a PDC official had demanded a further sum of money, and when she could not pay she was forced to grant the sexual services of her daughter in lieu. The fact that she still ended up being arraigned before the Tribunal exemplifies the uncertainties associated with trying to strike a bargain after the event. All along the frontier, smugglers calculated the gains and risks associated with making deals. The fact that smuggling proliferated as it did is a clear sign that, on balance, it paid well enough for the majority of participants.

For heuristic purposes, the range of smuggling phenomena can be summed up in terms of a series of dualisms: daylight and night-time; headload and lorry-load; path and road. In each case, one of these terms corresponds to a particular model of smuggling activity. For the 'armpit smuggler', headloads were typically carried across bush paths by day. For intermediate smugglers, headloads were also carried across bush paths, but more typically by night. Finally, *kalabule* merchants were not afraid of moving their goods by truck during daylight hours, which was when the border posts were open to traffic. Moreover, there is also a sense in which the different levels of corruption among officialdom corresponds to these three models. There was a practical difference between what was paid by 'armpit smugglers' to local border officials, which went into their own pockets; the rather greater share that was paid to middle-level functionaries, some of which percolated upwards and filtered downwards; and the substantial deals that were cut between senior functionaries and the big-time smugglers in which the principal benefits were top-heavy. It is because of these differences that local officials drew a further distinction between their own petty peculation, which enabled them to subsist, and the *kalabule*, which Utuka and his associates were implicated in. Indeed, the 1979 coup was born out of precisely this kind of conceptual distinction between grand corruption and the survival imperative.

Public and local discourses of morality

I have already indicated that the adoption of a moralistic public discourse amounted to a tacit admission of the limits to state power, and that the shifting contours thereof spoke of an ongoing failure to find a formula that actually worked. What remains is to consider in greater detail how these appeals were received on the border itself. This is not the kind of question that can easily be answered because there is a seldom a local voice that responds directly to the official rhetoric. I am reliant on the response solicited from informants during fieldwork carried out in the mid-1980s and early 1990s, on the correspondence of Nana Soglo Allo III and on inferences from observed behaviour.

In his 1990 study, James C. Scott argues that the official transcript of power relations seldom elicits explicit challenges from subordinated groups, except during moments of systemic crisis when the mask may finally be permitted to drop.[93] At other times, when the structures of power are secure, the response of the subordinate is to circulate their own knowing and hidden transcript among themselves, traces of which may seep into the public arena and thus destabilize the official version. If Scott is correct, one should not merely look for open gestures of defiance, but also keep an eye out for alternative constructions of reality embedded in the words and the deeds of ordinary people. In the course of fieldwork in Likpe, it was certainly rare to encounter an outright defence of smuggling. The one noteworthy exception to the rule emanated from none other than Nana Agya Mensah who responded to questioning in typically pugnacious style:

[93] Scott, *Domination and the Art of Resistance: Hidden Transcripts, passim.*

I would say that the name [of smuggling] is wrongly applied. You blackmail a man to charge him. Farmers aren't given their due price. Last year the price was 16 per cent of the world price. When I produce anything I have the right to send it to any market. But you force me to send it over there [to the Cocoa Board]. This is legalized robbery of the farmers. You give me a name to blackmail me because you don't give me my rights.[94]

One other informant acknowledged that he was technically a smuggler, but repeated the point that it really came down to a matter of definition: 'Smuggling is a two-way process. It's called smuggling, but it's an exchange of goods over the boundary.'[95] Given that the state has historically arrogated to itself the right to distinguish legitimate from illegal activity, this kind of statement may be fairly interpreted as a rejection of government presumptions. However, these were rare moments of frankness in fieldwork interviews. For the most part, the opinions that were expressed were more nuanced and stand in need of some decoding.

When state officials broached the issue of smuggling directly, or when the matter was discussed during interviews, two broad patterns of response emerged. Within the first, the general tendency was to deny that there was a significant problem along this stretch of boundary. Viewed from the government perspective, the area around Likpe was a hotbed of smuggling activity and had been for some time. In the words of the CDO Commander in Hohoe:

Likpe is noted to be full of very hardened smugglers since time immemorial, because of the geographical position. It would be very difficult to set up a border station there because of the mountain, so they're taking advantage of that.[96]

In Likpe, this assessment was frequently contested on two grounds. The first was that declining cocoa purchases did not so much reflect an increased level of smuggling as the ravages of black pod disease. As recently as 1968, one expert had felt able to proclaim that fungal diseases were a minor hazard.[97] However, within a couple of years there were reports of a serious outbreak of black pod in the Dodo-Amanfrom area.[98] Over the course of the next decade, the disease swept across the region and had become endemic in the Likpe-Kukurantumi cocoa district by the early 1980s.[99] On many farms, there was hardly a pod that had not been blackened and rendered useless. For that reason, the contention that government consistently overestimated the scale of smuggling would seem to be well-founded. There was also a perception that the state was partly responsible for the problem in the first place. Whereas the Cocoa Services Division (CSD) blamed the farmers for not maintaining their farms properly, local informants were convinced that the construction of the Volta Lake

---

[94] Interview with Nana Agya Mensah III, Likpe-Avedzeme, 19 February 1986. Shortly afterwards, Agya Mensah resigned the Avedzeme stool, thus ending a colourful chiefly career.

[95] Interview with T.O., Bakwa, 28 January 1986.

[96] Interview with Lawrence Akoto, CDO District Commander, Hohoe, 6 October 1986.

[97] Extracts of a paper by Dr J.A. Asomaning to International Conference on Agricultural Research Priorities for Economic Development in Africa, April 1968, contained in Ministry of Agriculture files, Ho, 'Cocoa–General Correspondence'.

[98] Report by Senior Agricultural Officer, Jasikan zone, dated 24 August 1971, 'Cocoa–General Correspondence'.

[99] Between 1977/78 and 1981/82, cocoa purchases fell from 2,175 tonnes to 192 tonnes.

had affected the water table and/or increased the overall levels of humidity.[100] Local informants insisted that they received very little cocoa from their farms and that whatever crossed the border conformed mostly to the model of 'armpit smuggling'. A second contention was that most smugglers passed through Likpe en route to Togo and hence were not really local offenders at all.[101] Nana Soglo Allo III was among those who repeatedly insisted that the stigma was unfairly attached to the Bakpele. Both of these responses conceded something to official discourse. Each appeared to accept that, in principle, smuggling was wrong: they simply questioned whether smuggling was happening on any significant scale, or they ascribed the blame to others.

The second broad pattern of responses conceded less to the official version of events. It drew attention to the underlying factors that encouraged people to engage in smuggling. With respect to cocoa, the question of prices was one that was repeatedly raised. Nana Agya Mensah was not the only informant who explicitly identified the yawning gap between the world market price and what was paid to the cocoa farmers. As one farmer neatly put it: 'The world price of cocoa is universal. So why is it that in Ghana prices are lower? That has discouraged many of us'.[102] Although the price issue loomed large, it was not the only source of grievance. Almost as important was the failure of the CMB to pay the farmers on time. When the buying centres ran out of cash, they were often issued with chits and so needed to make several return journeys to secure payment. In 1982, the PNDC sought to resolve this and other problems by introducing the *akuafo* cheque.[103] This had its own drawbacks, though, because the cocoa farmer still needed to travel to a bank to cash the cheque. Although Rural Banks were founded, including one at Likpe-Kukurantumi, these were not always easily accessible. Moreover, the Rural Banks sought to impede farmers from immediately withdrawing money from their accounts in order to remain financially afloat.

One farmer, who had worked as a buyer for the UAC and G.B. Ollivant before the war, drew an unfavourable comparison between the colonial and post-independence arrangements:

> I hate the chit and cheque system because the small-scale cocoa farmer has to travel for a few cedis whilst in the colonial days you were paid on the spot in cash and could buy your needs even their from their own stores. Or during the off-season, you could credit the goods or ask for a cash advancement so that the cocoa farmer was at no time in need. Where are those facilities today when the Secretary Receivers have either tightened or loosened the weighing scales to cheat the poor cocoa farmer of a few kilograms for their personal benefit?[104]

---

[100] Interviews with Nana Afrim, Ahamansu, 19 September 1992; and Okyeame Kwame Gyapong, Kadjebi, 19 September 1992.

[101] For example, in 1972 the Bakwa chief wrote to his counterparts in Lolobi and Wli to complain that their citizens were buying up cocoa in the area, 'thus shifting the blame on my people'. Circular letter from Nana W.K. Amoah V (19 September 1972), files of Nana Soglo.

[102] Interview with Godfried Kofi Akorli, Abrani, 14 March 1986. After the revolution, the PNDC had sought to avoid increasing the producer price.

[103] The *akuafo* cheque was also introduced in order to mop up excessive liquidity, which had nothing to do with the concerns of farmers.

[104] Interview with Daniel Kosi Agyeman, Agbozome, 11 August 1986.

As this quotation suggests, the issue of prices was closely bound up in local perceptions with access to items of consumption. The shortages of most essential goods
were, if anything, seen as a more pressing issue than that of cocoa prices.[105] In 1982,
the government had tried to promote the idea of People's Shops, but these had failed
to resolve the fundamental problem of supply. In order to be able to live as they were
accustomed to, local people felt that they could not do without consumer items such
as cloth and sugar. In the words of another informant: 'If I need farm inputs or cloth
I will have to go and sell over there. I only *need* Togo currency because of a lack of
goods here.'[106] It is here that one can detect the operation of an alternative moral
discourse, which still partially accepted the terms of the official discourse – in the
sense that smuggling was still cast as undesirable – but accounted for the contraband
trade in terms of sheer necessity. In the perception of Bakpele informants, smuggling
was not a matter of financial aggrandizement, but an issue of basic subsistence.
Hence, the Bakpele saw themselves as the quintessential 'armpit smugglers' – as
reluctant lawbreakers rather than as 'nation-wreckers'. This opened up some space
for the official discourse to breathe, in that it raised doubts about the status of
professional smuggling.

Perhaps because there was a degree of alignment between the two discursive
fields, the state was actually able to exact a measure of local compliance in its anti-
smuggling campaigns. Within border communities, there were a number of arenas of
disputation that led local actors to invoke official versions of reality. One, as we have
seen, concerned the ownership of land. In places along the border where there were
conflicting claims, as in the vicinity of Honuta, it was tempting to insinuate that
Togolese farmers were inherently disposed towards smuggling because of their need
to remit resources homewards. This struck a chord with government, which was
already inclined to blame economic crime on foreign nationals. In the mid-1980s the
Volta Regional administration even stepped in to redeem pledged cocoa farms on the
grounds that they would otherwise fall into Togolese hands, and thereby add to the
stock of smuggled goods.[107]

A second, and related, arena of disagreement concerned the relationship between
cocoa farmers and their labourers. In a survey of the Jasikan area in 1956, McGlade
discovered that the *kotokunu* labour system was by far the most common.[108] Under

---

[105] This was the finding of a survey of 281 informants that I conducted in 1986. A total of 122 respondents, or
43.2%, cited the lack of goods as the main reason for cocoa smuggling, as opposed to 52 respondents (18.4%)
who cited prices. See Paul Nugent, 'National integration', p. 174,

[106] Interview with Ralph Kofi-Asare, Bakwa, 28 January 1986.

[107] According to the Jasikan District Secretary: 'Most pledged farms on the border. No farmer would walk one
mile to the buying centre on the Ghanaian side to get a lower price when he can walk 200 yards over the border
into Ghana and then back to Togo where he can get a better price'. Interview with U.S. Clarke, 29 September
1986. The same month, the Regional and District Secretaries passed a resolution purporting to abrogate all
pledging agreements with immediate effect. The farms concerned were handed over to 'mobisquads' who
were instructed to rehabilitate the farms in return for a one-third share of the proceeds. Once the creditors
were paid off, the farms were supposed to revert to the original owners.

[108] This is excluding the *dibi* system. C. McGlade, *An Economic Survey of Cocoa Farmers in the Jasikan Area of
Trans-Volta/Togoland*, Economics Research Division, University of Ghana, Cocoa Research Series, 1957, p. 5.
This is borne out by a wealthy cocoa farmer from Asato who used to employ 50 cocoa labourers, of whom 11
were on *abusa* contracts. Interview with Henry Yao Gyambibby, chief farmer of Asato, 19 September 1992.

this system, the labourers received a fixed price per load, which typically amounted to less than the one-third share that prevailed under the *abusa* system. Her assessment was that this was a historical relic that persisted in the Volta Region because of its proximity to the comparatively abundant supply of labour in Togo.[109] This advantage was, however, undercut by the passage of the Aliens Compliance Order which, according to the Togolese government, led to the return of 100,000 nationals.[110] As labour became more scarce in the region, so the remaining labourers began to demand more favourable terms. Whereas a *kotokunu* labourer had received about 13 per cent of the producer price in the mid-1950s, this had risen to 20 per cent thirty years later.[111] Moreover, the farmers were forced to offer additional inducement such as gifts, loans and access to oil-palms from which they could tap palm-wine on a share-crop basis. However, these concessions could not detract from the fact that the labourers were experiencing a decline in real income as a result of the combined effects of black pod disease and falling producer prices. Their response was to reduce their inputs of labour. Thus, whereas labourers had once weeded the farms twice a year, they were reluctant to do so without additional remuneration at the start of the 1980s. It was this which the CSD was inclined to blame for the spread of the black pod disease. The farmers may not have shared this assessment of the root causes, but they did perceive the labourers as failing to fulfil their obligations. Hence in 1982/83, the Chief Farmers of Likpe and Lolobi began to meet in order to try fix a standard rate of remuneration in return for the performance of a minimum of tasks.[112]

These efforts to impose greater discipline over the labourers do not seem to have gone down well. With increasing frequency, the workers resorted to under-declaring the harvest, and then smuggling the balance themselves or selling it on to professional smugglers. As early as 1972, a chief in the Jasikan District described how a Togolese national living in the Dodo-Amanfrom area was in the business of buying stolen cocoa beans, drying them and then recruiting Kotokoli youths to headload them to Togo.[113] In Likpe itself, many informants claimed that they had been forced to dismiss their labourers for theft – and, by implication, smuggling. Hence when government took up the contraband theme, it met with a receptive reaction in some quarters. Where labour relations were particularly strained, the farm owners sometimes denounced their own labourers as smugglers. However, the threat was more commonly resorted to than the practice. One wealthy farmer at Asato, who had caught some of his labourers stealing cocoa, explained that he could not take any action against them because labour was scarce: 'If I do that, they will run away'.[114]

---

[109] McGlade, *Economic Survey*, p. 11.

[110] *Africa Contemporary Record 1969–70* (London: Rex Collings), p. B473.

[111] McGlade, *Economic Survey*, pp. 7–8.; interview with C.K. Agblobi, Mate, 13 September 1992. In 1992, when the producer price was ¢7,520 per load, Henry Gyambibby reported that he was paying his *kotokunu* labourers ¢1,500 per load, which amounted to a one-fifth share. Interview with Henry Gyambibby, 19 September 1992.

[112] Up until this point, the absence of a norm allowed the labour terms to drift in a direction favourable to the workers. The Chief Farmers sought to establish some uniformity in order to protect the interests of the farm owners. They agreed that the labourers should receive a one-fifth share, unless they weeded twice annually, in which case they would be entitled to a one-third share. This was in itself a concession of sorts. Interview with C.K. Agblobi, Mate, 14 September 1986.

[113] Reported in the *Daily Graphic*, 6 October 1972.

[114] Interview with Henry Yao Gyambibby, 19 September 1992.

A third arena of contestation turned on underlying generational conflict. During interviews in Likpe, older informants proudly recounted the years during which they had planted particular cocoa farms. As we have seen, cocoa cultivation had historically been associated with more expansive patterns of consumption, which were justified with reference to enterprise and hard work. By the mid-1980s, the cocoa industry was in crisis for reasons already identified. In addition, there was a lack of forest land on which to plant new trees, which precluded the youth from following the example of their parents and grandparents. The route to wealth increasingly turned on other alternatives. Some of the younger generation turned to food farming, especially rice, and even looked upon the 1983 bushfires as a blessing in disguise, in that they freed up more land.[115] However, the market for foodstuffs was limited and at particular times, most notably in 1984, it was actually glutted.[116] However, far more important was the money that could be made through smuggling other goods, such as cocoa, petrol and kerosene. The money thus earned was used for basic subsistence, but some of it also went into displays of conspicuous consumption, including the drinking of alcohol. This led to some disquiet within the ranks of the older generation, who grumbled that the youth did not understand the meaning of hard work. In the words of one informant, 'The youngsters have refused to do any yam farming out of laziness. And if we, the old ones, make yam farms, the young ones will steal'.[117] The youth who returned from Nigeria in 1983 were regarded as especially reluctant to earn money through legitimate means. Theft and smuggling were regarded as natural bedfellows, and for that reason community leaders were inclined to treat the second as a potential threat to social order.

Of course, not all smugglers were youthful and some of the same accusations were also levelled at others who flaunted their wealth. A case in point was Kofi Kuma of Likpe-Todome. The latter had started his career as a driver and purchased his first vehicle in 1961. By 1977, he owned five lorries, which were used as passenger vehicles on the Likpe–Hohoe route, as well as his own personal car.[118] At this time, Kuma was actively involved in smuggling and, by all accounts, doing extremely well out of it. A number of informants recalled that Kuma became arrogant, especially in his dealings with the chiefs, because he felt that his wealth should confer greater respect upon him. From the point of the chiefs, however, Kuma was an upstart and not even a proper son of the soil.[119] In 1977, Kuma was arrested by the Border Guards. As he recalls:

> They suspected me of smuggling. Nana Soglo Allo III sent a letter to the late Utuka saying now that I get money I don't respect. Utuka showed the letter to me.

The case against Kuma was that he could not have bought so many vehicles without

---

[115] Many women farmers also rented land in the Hohoe area in order to grow rice. On the rice boom in the 1980s, see Nugent, 'National integration', pp. 258–63.

[116] For this reason, some of the food crops were sold across the border to Togo. Interview with T.O., Bakwa, 28 January 1986.

[117] Interview with Emmanuel Osibo, Mate, 9 March 1986.

[118] Interview with Kofi Kuma (I have adopted a pseudonym here to protect the identity of my informant), Todome, 20 September 1992.

[119] His family were apparently of Togolese origin, a fact that was often used against him.

engaging in smuggling. He was held at the Border Guards headquarters for two weeks, was then transferred to the custody of Military Intelligence at Burma Camp and then to the Airforce Annex, before finally ending up at the Nsawam Medium Security Prison. After a year in detention, his family and Nana Soglo interceded with Utuka for his release, on the grounds that he had learned his lesson.[120] In February 1978, a special executive instrument was passed and a chastened Kuma finally re-emerged from prison.[121] Although he seems to have resumed smuggling, he had learned that it was wise to be circumspect because there were people who would resent the display of wealth.[122] On his release he immediately sold all but one of his vehicles and invested the proceeds in some property in Hohoe, which would attract less attention. Kuma remained in the transport business with the one remaining vehicle and was regarded by the other drivers as their leader during the 1980s. The Kuma case is significant, because it reveals some of the moral ambiguity that could attach to smuggling.

Smuggling as resistance

As I have already argued, seductive as the Scott model undoubtedly is, its weakness is that it invites one to read resistance into just about every response. In the specific context of the border, one also has to ask the question: resistance to what? It is problematic to interpret smuggling as resistance to the existence of the border when the benefits associated with the one could not exist without the other. An instructive comparison is with the findings of Donna Flynn with respect to the Nigeria–Benin border. In a fascinating article, she shows how communities have been extremely adept at moulding the border into something that benefits them – not just through direct participation in smuggling, but also by taxing other traders passing through. Having alluded to the efforts of communities to encourage the opening of border posts in their midst, she concludes that:

> Shabe border identity illustrates how borderlanders can be empowered by their positioning on boundaries and crossroads. Far from being invisible, they claim to embody the border.[123]

This sense of 'deep placement within the borderland' is very much shared by communities living along the Ghana–Togo frontier. The lack of interest in the redrawing of border lines speaks volumes about what these have meant in practical terms. In response, it might be countered that communities have not so much benefited from the boundary as derived a limited kind of compensation from its existence. Hence, if cocoa prices had been higher and if there had been an abundance of consumer goods in Ghana, there would have been no need for 'armpit smugglers' to cross the border at all – and hence no real gain would have accrued from smuggling. However,

---

[120] Utuka did his best, but it took some time for the case against him to be dropped. Major-General E.K. Utuka to Ministry of Defence, Burma Camp (23 December 1977), files of Nana Soglo Allo III.

[121] Kuma had been held under the Preventive Custody (Amendment) Decree of 1974 (NRCD 246). He showed me a copy of Executive Instrument (EI 20) of 16 February 1978. which had been passed specifically for him.

[122] In 1996, I coincidentally met a driver in the Togolese town of Adeta who had helped Kuma in his later smuggling operations.

[123] Donna Flynn, '"We are the border": identity, exchange and the state along the Bénin–Nigeria border', *American Ethnologist*, 24, 2, 1997, p. 326.

specialist smugglers evidently derived a substantial economic rent from exploiting consumer shortages and price differentials. Equally, the legion of carriers and scouts were able to earn an income in advance of what they could expect to make from farming.

Intuitively, it might be thought that the proliferation of trading networks across the borderline would pose a challenge to the state's own conception of a territorially bounded community. Flynn's own assessment is that a sense of 'being the border' was held in common by peoples on either side of the line.[124] In the case of the Ghana–Togo border, the picture is a rather more ambiguous. In many ways, the impact of smuggling on the shaping of identities was counter-intuitive. Those who had to cross the border to purchase their wants were given a constant reminder of what made them different from their Togolese neighbours. Their sense of unease was reflected in dismissive comments to the effect that the Togolese were virtual paupers who only managed to make a living because Ghanaians chose to trade with them. Of course, unlike the 'armpit smugglers', the specialists needed to cultivate close ties with purchasers of cocoa and suppliers of goods in Togo. But even these relationships were often infused with a measure of mistrust. It is striking how widespread and deeply entrenched the negative stereotypes of the Togolese have become. As with most stereotypes, the images are complex and sometimes contradictory, but they are also highly revealing. At one level, the Togolese are regarded as overly deferential to authority. At another, they are viewed as being more prone to 'anti-social' behaviour such as theft and deception. A recurrent theme in interviews with smugglers in Likpe was the fear of being double-crossed by their Togolese partners. For example, somebody who purchased goods from a Togolese supplier might be arrested by gendarmes working on a tip-off. The contraband would then be seized and returned to the original owner in return for a bribe. Another scam was for Togolese purchasers of cocoa to claim that they had no money to hand and to ask the Ghanaian smuggler to return at a later date. When the latter came back, the purchaser denied all knowledge of the transaction and threatened to denounce the smuggler to the gendarmes if he/she made a fuss. For these reasons, some smugglers in Likpe preferred to let the Togolese come to them, rather than risk being cheated in this manner.[125] Still, the financial returns on smuggling were related to the degree of risk involved, and for this reason there remained a brisk trade across this border during the mid-1980s.

If it is difficult to identify opposition to the border as such, it is still conceivable that border peoples were resistant to the local embodiments of state power. Once again, the picture is more murky than might at first appear. Border officials certainly constituted a nuisance if they insisted on seeking to enforce border controls.[126] Even when they were blatantly corrupt, their exactions could eat into profit margins. However, in the final analysis, there were normally ways and means of blunting the practical impact of border policing. From the 1970s, the attempt to saturate border spaces with Border Guards required smugglers to become more creative in their

---

[124] *Ibid.*, p. 319.

[125] Interview with T.O., Bakwa, 28 January 1986.

[126] Smugglers worked in large groups, and made a point of arming themselves in order to deter over-zealous officials. One former Border Guard claimed that smuggling gangs might contain as many as 200 people. Interview with Victor Mantey, 14 September 1992.

dealings. The provision of lodgings was one means by which relations of affection could be established. Equally, the bonds which developed between Border Guards and local women helped to induct the former into village life. Because border officials could be domesticated in this fashion, outright resistance was generally unnecessary. During the mid-1980s, the soldiers who were posted to Likpe were certainly regarded with a certain amount of suspicion. On the one hand, their demands for bribes in return for safe passage constituted a daily annoyance, especially for the 'armpit smugglers'. On the other hand, their willingness to condone smuggling activity meant that they did not pose a genuine threat to the contraband trade. The wife of the sergeant in charge of the Army post in Mate was herself a regular smuggler of petroleum products, and many of his soldiers patently did very well out of the business. Kofi Kuma recalled how one soldier was able to return to Ashanti with 25 bundles of iron sheets, two chainsaw machines, two refrigerators and some sewing machines – all on the strength of his illegal earnings.[127] Although local eyebrows were raised, these soldiers were also in the habit of spending a lot of money on consumer goods such as bottled beer, which put some additional business the way of local traders.

Whereas the army presence was tolerated as an unavoidable nuisance, assessments of the People's Militia were generally much more damning. The fact that the militiamen were recruited from among these very communities did not make them any more acceptable. On the contrary, the fact that the Rawlings government was putting guns in the hands of 'small boys' (and girls) was deeply resented. By the mid-1980s, the militiamen had made a noticeable impact in Likpe. They engaged enthusiastically in anti-smuggling patrols, primarily because they received half of the value of the contraband as their reward. In 1986, the financial arithmetic seemed to favour playing by the official rules: hence a group of five Militiamen who seized a load of cocoa and sent it to the Cocoa Board would have received ¢233 a head, whereas if they had accepted the standard bribe of CFA 1,000 or ¢500 they would only have received ¢100 each.[128] In one case that came before the Regional Public Tribunal in 1988, the evidence confirmed that the militiamen were motivated by the expectation of sharing the rewards among themselves. The tribunal was deeply troubled by this phenomenon, noting that:

> The leadership at least in the region has not been able to firmly take control of the operations of the militias and has in most cases contributed to the wrong notion that their boys have that the CDO is an organ which 'Creates and Shares'. The evidence which came out during the trial is that the militias seize items and only take it to the District Commanders who distribute them without recourse to either the court or the tribunal or any other appropriate authority. This is wrong and cannot be accepted.[129]

The Tribunal went on to acknowledge that the militiamen were motivated by the financial incentive and recommended instituting a system of regular remuneration instead. This arguably misconstrued the whole reason for the creation of the militia

---

[127] Interview with Kofi Kuma, 20 September 1992.

[128] These calculations are based on evidence from Mate at the time.

[129] Observation by the chairman in 'The People versus Bukari Haruna and nine others', Volta Region Public Tribunal, 17 August 1988.

in the first place, which was to wean local youth off smuggling. By 1986, militia activities had introduced a destabilizing element into the smuggling equation, forcing at least one local storekeeper to start buying his beer supplies from Hohoe rather than Togo. This development was not to the liking of the smugglers or the soldiers, who regarded the militia as a threat to the local compact.

Critics of the militia, however, tended to place the accent elsewhere. They asserted that the militiamen were drawn from the least trustworthy sections of the community, with the result that they were inclined to connive with the smugglers. The comments of Nana Soglo Allo III are instructive in this regard:

> ... since the Militia have no pay, it's an extortion unit. I think they get 50 per cent. What I see of the CDR question is that it is becoming a problem because we don't get decent people joining the CDRs or the Militia. Its the riffraff who join the Militia. Any new organization like that starts with the ruffians and the unemployed.[130]

On this issue, at least, he was of one mind with Nana Mantey Akototse of Abrani.[131] That this was not a purely local perception was also borne out by interviews in Buem. Henry Gyambibby, a very substantial cocoa farmer, followed up his assertion that shiftless youth were more interested in smuggling than cocoa farming with the observation that the very same elements tended to join the militia: 'Many of them rushed to the militia, but they are all thieves. I have told my children none of them should enter the militia group'.[132] Kofi Kuma equally claimed to have uncovered evidence of Militia complicity in corruption. Because of his past record, Kuma became a target for the state security agencies. At one point, he was called in by the Bureau of National Investigation and told that if he wanted to clear his name he would have to co-operate as an informant.[133] One day, Kuma helped to intercept some women who had been waved through a militia barrier despite being in possession of contraband alcohol. It transpired that the militiamen were acting on the say-so of their commander in Hohoe. The latter, who was reported by Kuma, had actually been appointed in succession to the first CDO commander, who had himself been dismissed on the basis of his alleged participation in smuggling.[134] Such cases allowed critics of the militia to argue that it was no less tainted by corruption than the army.

It is not difficult to detect an element of generational bias in some of the most negative statements about the militia. However, the hostility of local youths was, if anything, even more pronounced. During the second half of the 1980s, there were a number of violent incidents in Likpe. The Abrani chief recounted an episode in mid-1986 when militiamen assaulted a young man from the village, and were besieged by local youths intent on exacting their revenge. On this occasion, it was only the intervention of the chief that saved them from a serious beating.[135] In another instance, a young man from Agbozome was shot at a militia checkpoint in an altercation over a football. An even more serious incident occurred in the vicinity of Todome in 1989

---

[130] Interview with Nana Soglo Allo III, Mate, 20 August 1986.
[131] Interview with Nana Mantey Akototse IV, Abrani, 3 October 1986.
[132] Interview with Henry Gyambibby, 19 September 1992.
[133] By comparison with the British period, the use of informants was comparatively limited.
[134] Interview with Kofi Kuma, 20 September 1992.
[135] Interview with Nana Mantey Akototse IV, Abrani, 3 October 1986.

when a very popular young man was shot and killed by the militia. Kofi Kuma claims that the militiamen, who had to seek police protection, fabricated evidence to prove that he had been smuggling at the time. The failure of the authorities to deal swiftly with this case generated a great deal of resentment at what was perceived as a cover-up.

Towards the end of the 1980s, the Rawlings regime was starting to have its own doubts about the militia. One reason was the mounting evidence of collusion in corrupt practices. Ironically, the declining performance of the militia appears to have been a direct consequence of its earlier success: that is, when smuggling was rife, there was some financial incentive to engage in anti-smuggling activity, but this tailed off as the volume of cross-border trade declined. The straitened circumstances of the militiamen tempted many to engage in acts of extortion, which further diminished their local credibility. The fact that tensions were threatening to boil over also engendered a change of heart at the centre. Although the militia were not formally disbanded, they were accorded a lower profile in the early 1990s. In sum, therefore, there certainly was opposition to the militia, which came from active smugglers as well as from pillars of the local establishment. The fact that the militiamen were ordinary young men and women only made them a greater target of hostility. Local pride was also a factor when militiamen sought to intervene in the affairs of communities that were not their own. In all of this, however, what is striking is not so much the phenomenon of resistance to the state, but the playing out of tensions and rivalries at the local level. The Scott model does not seem particularly helpful in making sense of this kind of phenomenon.

Reinventing the wheel

As has been widely documented, the Rawlings regime embarked on a substantive change of policy direction in 1983, which gathered pace as the decade progressed.[136] The economic orthodoxies of the Economic Recovery Programme (ERP) had a direct bearing on border management. Indeed, it was the failure of earlier regimes to find a solution to the smuggling quandary that contributed to the policy shift in the first place. The broad thrust of the ERP was in the direction of economic liberalization, which was intended to kill two birds with one stone: unimpeded market signals would restore incentives to productive activity, while obviating the need for the kind of regulation that had tended to encourage rent-seeking rather than a more rational allocation of resources.

This *volte face* facilitated a significant retreat from three decades of ineffective border management. First of all, while the shift towards floating exchange rates was not without its drawbacks, it did help to squeeze the currency black market, which had always been a major contributing factor to smuggling. Secondly, the PNDC sought to increase the real cocoa producer price in a bid to encourage the farmers to properly maintain old farms, plant new ones and sell what they did produce to the Cocoa Board. Thirdly, the government calculated that a loosening of import

---

[136] The literature on the ERP is very substantial. I have sketched the broad contours of these policies in *Big Men*, pp. 129–36, 167–74. See also 'Educating Rawlings: the evolution of government strategy towards smuggling', in Donald Rothchild (ed.), *Ghana: The Political Economy of Recovery* (Boulder & London: Lynne Rienner, 1991), pp. 74–82.

controls and a revival of domestic manufacturing would resolve the problem of consumer shortages and thereby reduce the allure of neighbouring markets. In all three respects, the ERP was broadly successful in meeting the stated objectives. In the 1990s, informants in Likpe and Buem agreed that there had ceased to be much of a financial incentive to engage in smuggling.[137] Indeed, so significant was the turnabout that cocoa prices were sometimes higher than those in Togo, leading to a modest flow of crops in the opposite direction. Furthermore, there was no longer any real need to shop in Togo as consumer goods could be brought in from Hohoe instead.

At the same time as the Rawlings regime was seeking to 'get the prices right', it instituted a fundamental reform of the structures of border policing. The army reverted to strictly military duties, while its preventive functions were reunited with the revenue arm of the Customs Department to form an integrated Customs, Excise and Preventive Service (CEPS) in 1986.[138] This went together with a conscious effort to rebuild a sense of professional ethos. The importance of a flashy new uniform and symbols of office in instilling pride in the service should not be underestimated.[139] The authorities initially failed to follow through in introducing badges of rank, allegedly after complaints from the army that this was encroaching on military symbols. But in other respects the PNDC demonstrated its commitment to construct an effective instrument of border management. A small example of the shift in approach was the publication a quarterly staff magazine, *Customs News*, which sought to instil a fresh sense of professional pride and collegiality. This publication covered a range of issues affecting employees, such as promotions, but also paid a good deal of attention to sporting and social activities held under CEPS auspices. The magazine even provided a forum for budding poets and creative writers. Most of their literary contributions were not work-related, but some did deal with the experience of being posted to remote frontier locations inhabited by snakes and mosquitoes. In fact, there was a noteworthy shift in policy with respect to the posting of personnel. CEPS abandoned the strategy of maintaining a regular presence in every border community, and contented itself with manning official border posts (like Wli), and targeting particular trouble spots. In villages like Likpe-Mate, CEPS officers were rarely seen. The fact that the overall level of smuggling had declined provided an additional justification for pursuing a less interventionist approach to border policing.

[137] In the words of Kofi Kuma, who knew more about the subject than most: 'This time smuggling has stopped. The cocoa price is the same, so you don't need to worry yourself', interview on 20 September 1992. In fact, there was still a slight difference in 1992 when the Togo price was equivalent to ¢9,000 per load as against the COCOBOD price of ¢7,520. But this was still not enough to make most people bother to make the journey. Towards the end of 2000, however, smuggling of petroleum products increased markedly when the Togolese withdrew their subsidies while the Rawlings regime felt unable to increase prices in an election year.

[138] This was effected under the Customs, Excise and Preventive Services Law (PNDC Law 144) of March 1986. The duties of the service and the penalties for smuggling were subsequently consolidated under the Customs, Excise and Preventive Service (Management) Law (PNDC Law 330) of 1993. The changes are summarized in Gilbert Adjei-Darko, 'From a department to a service', *Customs News*, 5, 11, June 1987. I am grateful to Mohammed Abukari of CEPS for enabling me to lay hands on the relevant pieces of legislation.

[139] According to officers in the personnel department, the uniform was mentioned by a number of applicants as one of the reasons why they wished to join CEPS.

Although it was never explicitly commented upon, the Rawlings regime was effectively seeking to return to the inter-war model of border management. The Comptrollers of the erstwhile CPS would undoubtedly have approved of the effort to combine a sensitivity to price differentials with flexible responses. As they had explicitly argued, and as the experience of post-independence Ghana has subsequently confirmed, the state could call upon limited coercive means, and for that reason there was a need to work with the grain of local expectations.

Conclusion

In this chapter, I have revisited land disputes and the contraband trade as contributing factors in the entrenchment of the Ghana–Togo boundary. Whereas each of these dimensions might be taken as confirmation of the problematic character of the boundary, I have sought to place a rather different construction on the evidence. I have set out to show that they have together provided the raw material with which border peoples have moulded the border to suit their own convenience. In the early independence period, litigants were extremely adept at deploying the state discourse of nationality so as to nullify competing claims from the other side of the border. Ironically, as a *de facto* partition ensued, neighbouring communities later found it easier to consult one another over the fine tuning. In some cases, as in the Likpe–Dzidrame example, the parties have been content to follow the contours of the international boundary line. In others, as in the Honuta–Woamé example, the ideal of finding an alternative line of demarcation remains on the agenda.

As for smuggling, it has provided many peoples with a vested interest in the maintenance of the international boundary line. The fact that strangers have gravitated towards the border zone is a clear indication that it has come to be associated with opportunity. Moreover, in the course of shuttling back and forth across the line, local smugglers have emerged with a clearer sense of what makes them different from the Togolese. The emergence of this foil goes some way towards accounting for the absence of a popular constituency for secessionism within the Volta Region. Contrary to the assertions of the Acheampong regime, therefore, there has been no necessary contradiction between participation in smuggling and the harbouring of national sentiment. On the contrary, the two are more likely to be mutually reinforcing. Finally, it is worth noting that a sense of Ghanaian identity has grown inwards from the geographical margins at least as much as it has been disseminated from the centre. An appreciation of this dialectic is of cardinal importance in making sense of the post-independence experience of Ghana as a whole. At a more general level, I hope to have demonstrated that communities that are marginal in the geographical sense are not necessarily peripheral in other respects.

Conclusion

In his fascinating history of the making of the Franco–Spanish border, Peter Sahlins highlights some of the ambiguous meanings attached to this construct by the Cerdan population. He writes that the Cerdans participate in a 'shared myth' about the artificiality of the border, but that 'the national boundary remains accepted and uncontested, and the Cerdans deny their own role in the making of France and Spain'.[1] Although Sahlins is dealing with a line of demarcation that dates back to the mid-seventeenth century, and one which was never colonial in origin, precisely the same general observations apply to the Ghana–Togo border. At one level, the practical absurdities of the partition are a stock in trade of local discourse. A visitor is likely to be regaled with stories about people who have their houses in one country and their latrines or kitchens in another. Some of these represent the border equivalent of the urban myth. Nevertheless, the bizarre contours of the partition are also clearly visible in places, and nowhere more so than to the south of Batome junction where it is only a road surface that separates Ghana from Togo. One informant told of how, at the height of the revolution, members of the People's Defence Committees (PDCs) sought to participate in a wake-keeping that had to be moved to the Togolese village of Wodome because of the curfew in Ghana. They could not cross the road for fear of being arrested by the Togolese authorities, but they were able to take part from the other side of the road. They shouted their orders for cigarettes across and paid by rolling their money up in a piece of paper, attaching it to a stone and lobbing it across to the vendor. Like the Cerdans, the peoples of the Ghana–Togo borderlands are often inclined to attribute these peculiar configurations to the interventions of outsiders. And yet, as I have sought to demonstrate throughout this study, these same people have been active and knowing participants in the construction of this boundary that divides them at different levels. In the Wodome case, the PDC members were themselves engaged in a campaign to effectively eliminate cross-border trade in the Batome area. It is this paradox that has been central to this study.

---

[1] Peter Sahlins, *Boundaries: The Making of France and Spain in the Pyrenees* (Berkeley: University of California Press, 1989), p. 298.

Conclusion

It is not my intention to rehearse all the arguments that have been advanced, as summaries may be found at the end of each chapter. However, it may be helpful to restate the principal findings and to relate these to existing bodies of knowledge. These findings may be simply stated:

1   The boundary lines drawn by the various colonial powers – British, German and French – were never arbitrary in any simple sense. They embodied a certain logic by virtue of being superimposed upon a long-standing pre-colonial frontier zone. Moreover, when it came to the demarcation of the final boundary line, there was a genuine effort to iron out the obvious anomalies arising in the Milner– Simon agreement even if the final results were less than dramatic. This is not an entirely fresh discovery, since previous work by Anene and Thom has already drawn attention to the ways in which the colonial partition was shaped by pre-colonial realities.[2] Nevertheless, in the light of the claims repeated by Wole Soyinka and others, it is a point which is still worth underscoring.

2   The boundaries which were drawn by the European powers created local sets of vested interests that added significantly to the balance of forces favouring the maintenance of the status quo. Whereas Jeffrey Herbst is justified in insisting on the strength rather than the weakness of boundaries in Africa, he falls into the trap of construing them purely as the creation of state actors.[3] Without wishing to deny that political elites have exploited international boundaries, this neglects the role of much larger constituencies living along the borders themselves. I have considered the land question in a certain amount of detail, something that I believe has not been attempted in a systematic fashion before. The evidence clearly points to the important role played by litigants in giving practical effect to the paper partition in the pre-independence period. Since that time, land owner-ship and the border have been brought into *de facto* alignment. Ironically, this has contributed to a lessening of tensions and, as I demonstrated in Chapter 7, has even facilitated a degree of cross-border co-operation at the local level. I have also devoted a considerable amount of space to the question of smuggling. Apart from seeking to lay bare the mechanics thereof, I have argued that the opportunities for smuggling have turned the border zone into a theatre of opportunity. For that reason, it has served as a powerful magnet for stranger populations. Whereas the land question has received relatively scant attention in African boundary studies, smuggling is a hardy perennial. However, much of the research has been absorbed with smuggling as a form of evasion or resistance, and has tended to under-estimate its contribution towards stabilizing border areas. Nevertheless, an excellent recent article on the Nigeria–Bénin border confirms the findings of this study in a striking manner.[4]

---

[2] J.C. Anene, *The International Boundaries of Nigeria 1885–1960* (London: Longman, 1970); and D.J. Thom, *The Nigeria–Niger Boundary. 1890–1906: A Study of Ethnic Frontiers and a Colonial Boundary*, Africa Series, 23, Athens, Ohio University Centre for International Studies, 1975.

[3] Jeffrey Herbst, *States and Power in Africa: Comparative Lessons in Authority and Control* (Princeton: Princeton University Press, 2000), pp. 252–3.

[4] Donna Flynn, '"We are the border": identity, exchange and the state along the Bénin–Nigeria border, *American Ethnologist*, 24, 2, 1997.

Conclusion

3 The fact that the boundary has divided a putative ethnic group or 'culture area' has not been sufficient to override the forces conspiring towards maintenance of the border. I have followed in the footsteps of many other studies of African ethnicity in questioning whether ethnic groups – in this case the Ewe – can be treated as an ahistorical given, existing prior to the partition. In fact, expressions of Ewe cultural and political nationalism were evidently a response to European rule. I have sought to demonstrate that expressions of ethnicity were a refraction of identity politics at other levels. I have also invoked the currently unfashionable opinion that territorial identification has proved more powerful than ethnicity in the long run. Anybody feeling disposed to doubt this reading of history would need to account for the singular failure of the Ewe unification movement in the 1940s and of the secessionist movement in the 1970s. As Miles has proposed in the case of partitioned Hausaland, divergent value systems may arise on either side of a colonial border and become deeply entrenched with time.[5] What is true of the Hausa holds equally well for the Ewe. Much the same phenomenon is also apparent in the political differences between Tigrina-speaking political elites on either side of the Eritrea–Ethiopia border.[6]

4 Border communities have neither been divorced from the state, nor especially resistant to it. On the contrary, they have invoked state power when it has been to their advantage, and have successfully domesticated the local agents of state power when they have been placed in their midst. *Contra* James C. Scott, I have argued that the paradigm of the 'powerful' and the 'powerless' is unhelpful, and that the relationship between the state and border communities has been altogether more complex. I have revealed how the Customs Preventive Service was acutely aware of the limits to its powers of surveillance and coercion, and tailored its actions accordingly. I have also contended that this fundamental insight was lost sight of at the moment of independence and had to be relearned the hard way. By the end of the 1980s, the Rawlings regime, which had once been highly dirigiste, had been forced to revert to a strategy of working with the grain of society. The remarkable upshot was that the structures of the state were remoulded to accommodate the predilections of border populations who could not be coerced into compliance. This accommodation between the state and border society, which avoided the rupture which has characterized much of the rest of the continent, has implications that transcend the immediate context.

At the turn of the millennium, when a full-scale war raged along the Eritrean–Ethiopian border and another engulfed the eastern marches of the Congo, African boundaries found themselves very much back at the centre of academic and journalistic debate. But while there is evidence of a renewed interest in the meaning and legacy attached to inherited borders in Africa, it is questionable whether the

---

[5] William F.S. Miles, *Hausaland Divided: Colonialism and Independence in Nigeria and Niger* (Ithaca & London: Cornell University Press, 1994).

[6] For an effort to account for this reality, see Alemseged Abbay, *Identity Jilted or Re-Imagining Identity? The Divergent Paths of the Eritrean and Tigrayan Nationalist Struggles* (Lawrenceville & Asmara: Red Sea Press, 1998).

appropriate tools of analysis are to hand. Arguably, there is much intellectual baggage that needs to be shed and possibilities that need to be seriously entertained. This study has suggested some ways in which the question of boundaries might better be approached. What is sorely needed are further studies that are properly grounded in local-level research.

Bibliography

Primary Sources

Archival Sources

1 *Public Record Office [PRO]*
Note: the classification system changed in the course of doing the research. The file numbers are those which were current at the time. The problematic cases are signalled with an asterix*. In the first series of Colonial Office files for Togoland, the same file number corresponds to more than one file name.

CO 96/681/8 'Spirit Licence Ordinance'
CO 96/685/2 'Liquor Traffic'
CO 96/691/10 'Control of Migration Between Togoland and the Gold Coast'
CO 96/691/6541*
CO 96/692/6 'Liquor Traffic'
CO 96/697/6 'Liquor Traffic'
CO 96/710/6 'Disturbances at Lomé, French Togoland and Petition of Togoland Natives Resident in the Gold Coast'
CO 96/711/9 'Petition of Chief and Inhabitants of Woamé, French Togoland, Regarding Ground Belonging to Petitioners Situated in British Togoland'
CO 96/715/10 'Liquor Traffic'
CO 96/719/3 'Togoland: Petitions to League of Nations from the "Bund der Deutsch Togolander"'
CO 96/751/8 'Togoland: Petition to the League of Nations From the "Bund der Deutsch Togolander"'
CO 96/776/31467*
CO 96/780/31458*
CO 96/780 file 31458/6*
CO 96/809/31614*
CO 554/1032 'Togoland Administration'
CO 554/1033 'Togoland Administration'

Bibliography

CO 554/1035 'Togoland Administration'
CO 724/1 'Division of Togoland'
CO 724/1 'Division of Togoland: Free Labour for Diversion of Railway from Nuatja to Anecho'
CO 724/1 'Division: Position of British Merchants in French Zone'
CO 724/1 'Handing Over to the French'
CO 724/1 'Religious Liberty for Natives in French Togoland'
CO 724/1 'Togoland Mandate'
CO 724/2 'Actions of French in their Sphere of Togoland'
CO 724/2 'British Mandated Sphere of Togoland'
CO 724/2 'Import Duties Between British and French Spheres of Togoland'
CO 724/2 'Taxation of Natives in French Togoland'
CO 724/3 'Annual Report for 1923'
FO 371/138171 'Political Relations Between Ghana and Togoland'
FO 371/138270 'Foreign Policy in Togoland'
FO 371/147612 'Togo – Internal Political Situation'
FO 371/147613 'Togo: Foreign Policy'
FO 371/155656 'Togo: Foreign Policy'
FO 371/155676 'Refugees from Ghana'
FO 371/167653 'Togo Political Relations – Ghana'

2 *Ghana National Archives, Accra [GNAA]*

ADM 5/3/215 'Proceedings of the Enquiry into Volta Region Chieftaincy Affairs'
ADM 11/1/433 'Cocoa Trade – Report on'
ADM 11/1/1620 'Togoland Secret and Confidential Papers'
ADM 11/1/1622 'Notes on Statements taken before SNA in Togoland and Enclaves'
ADM 29/1/52 'Judgements of W.A.C.A'
ADM 29/4/27 'Appeals Record Book (Togoland)'
ADM 29/4/28 'Appeal Record Book (Togoland)'
ADM 39/1/93 'Federation of Divisions in Togoland Under United Kingdom Trusteeship'
ADM 39/1/95 'Anfoega Division (Southern Togoland) Native Affairs'
ADM 39/1/123 'Buem Strangers Union'
ADM 39/1/171 'Joint Council for Togoland Affairs – Views Expressed on Announcement Released 16/6/53'
ADM 39/1/190 'Transfer of Native Lands'
ADM 39/1/199 'Togoland, Partition of Between British and French'
ADM 39/1/205 'Roads – Ho and Kpandu District'
ADM 39/1/212 'Buem Division Native Affairs General'
ADM 39/1/214 'Mandated Area Togoland – Trade of'
ADM 39/1/216 'Kpandu Native Affairs'
ADM 39/1/228 'Anglo-French (Togoland) Frontier Incidents'
ADM 39/1/229 'Togoland Roads General'
ADM 39/1/235 'History of Avatime Division'
ADM 39/1/267 'Fiaga Egblomese of Akposso v. Nana Akpandja, Omanhene of Buem'
ADM 39/1/284 'Cocoa Card System'
ADM 39/1/295 'Ewe Community'
ADM 39/1/305 'Quarterly Reports – Kpandu District'
ADM 39/1/312 'Food Control'
ADM 39/1/339 'Unification of Ewe Speaking Peoples'

ADM 39/1/441 'Scholarships - Request for Establishment of a Central Fund for the Four States of Togoland'

ADM 39/1/456 'Handing Over Reports'

ADM 39/1/495 'Representation of Togoland on the Legislature'

ADM 39/1/515 'Amalgamation of Divisions in Togoland Under British Mandate'

ADM 39/1/517 'Rural Development'

ADM 39/1/545 'Amalgamation of Divisions in Togoland Under British Mandate'

ADM 39/1/567 'Buem State Native Affairs'

ADM 39/1/570 'Buem Strangers Union'

ADM 39/1/572 'Native Affairs Buem State'

ADM 39/1/574 'Alienation of Land in Togoland'

ADM 39/1/646 'Buem State Native Affairs'

ADM 39/1/652 'Togoland Youth Movement'

ADM 39/1/665 'Ho-Kpandu District Education Committee'

ADM 39/1/675 'All Ewe Conference'

ADM 39/1/676 'Standing Consultative Commission for Togoland'

ADM 39/1/1267 'Fiaga Egblomese of Akposo v. Nana Akpandja, Omanhene of Buem'

ADM 39/4/3 'Civil Record Book (Ho)'

ADM 39/4/4 'District Record Book (Ho)'

ADM 39/4/5 'Civil Record Book (Ho)'

ADM 39/4/7 'Civil Record Book (Ho)'

ADM 39/4/8 'Civil Record Book (Ho)'

ADM 39/4/9 'Civil Record Book (Ho)'

ADM 39/5/73 'District Record Book'

ADM 39/5/79 'Preventive Service'

ADM 39/5/81 'Customs Dues on Boundary Between British and French Zones'

ADM 43/4/16 'Civil Record Book'

ADM 43/4/18 'Criminal Record Book (Kpandu District)'

ADM 43/5/1 'District Patrol Book'

CSO 6/5/14 'Delegation of Powers to Officers in Charge of Frontier Stations'

CSO 6/5/21 'Smuggling and Seizures in the Southern Section, Eastern Frontier Preventive Station'

SCT 2/4/127 'Judicial Records: High Court, Accra'

3 *Ghana National Archives, Ho [GNAH]*

DA/C31 'Cocoa Industry'

DA/D78 'Handing Over Notes'

DA/D113 'Togo Union'

DA/D313 'Likpe Native Affairs'

DA/D314 'Likpe Native Affairs'

DA/240 'Local Government'

DA/D309 'Buem State Native Affairs'

KE/C27 'Smuggling General'

KE/C146 'Customs Preventive'

RAO/C705 'Congress of British Togoland'

RAO/C749 'Future of Togoland Under British Trusteeship'

RAO C/854 'Ghana/French Togoland Land Border Incidents'

RAO C1236/TA66/4 'Likpe Traditional Affairs'

Bibliography

RAO/C2073, 'Togoland: A History of the Tribal Divisions of the District of Misahuhe and of the Sub-Districts of Ho and Kpandu'

TA/31 'Complaints by Togo Congress Against Acts of Oppression'

VRG 1/7/2/1 'Land Dispute on Ghana–Togo Border Between Gyasehene of Likpe and Amudzi Agbedawu of Danyi'

Secret unnumbered file 'Ghana Police Internal Security Scheme, 1959 – Trans-Volta Togoland Region'

4 *Ministry of Agriculture, Ho*

Unnumbered file, 'Cocoa - General Correspondence'

5 *Padmore Library, Accra*

Bureau of African Affairs files No. 915 'Togoland'

6 *Stool Archives of Nana Soglo Allo III, Likpe-Mate*

Individual correspondence cited in the text

7 **Stool Lands Boundaries Settlement Commission, State House, Accra**

File 6/76 'Boundary Dispute Between Asato and Apesokubi'

File 7/79, 'Nkonya and Alavanyo Stool'

8 *Togo National Archives, Lomé [TNAL]*

2APA/446 'Service de domain: litiges fonciers entre les Akebous et les Adeles'

2APA/449 'Service de domain: litiges fonciers au sujet cacaoyers situés au Territoire Britannique'

2APA/513 'Justice indigène: diverses plaintes addressés au Commandant de Cercle'

8 APA/171 'Correspondances du Gouverneur-Générale de l'AOF par interim à l'Administrateur Supérieur du Togo'

8APA/101 'Rapport sur l'extension systematique de l'excitation anti-Allemande'

Atakpamé 2 APA/2 'Rapport sur le voyage du Lieutenant Plehn (allemand) dans la région d'Atakpamé, Akposso et Kpessi, 4 mars–17 avril 1896'

Atakpamé 2 APA/144 'Administration générale et politique'

Douanes 7D/22 'Harmonisation des taux de taxation douanière'

Douanes 7D/68 'Rapport sur un incident survenant à la frontière de la Gold Coast'

Klouto 2/APA 2 'Administration générale avec les colonies voisines'

Klouto 2 APA/2 'Administration générale et politique: relations avec les colonies voisines, correspondences avec l'Anglaise en Gold Coast'

Klouto/70 'Correspondances (en Anglais) au sujet d'Hitler chez un ressortisant de la Gold Coast'

9 *Edinburgh University Library, Special Collections*

West Africa Committee papers

10 *Rhodes House Library, Oxford*

Captain Dann papers at Mss. Afr. S.141 f 203-218

A.J. Beckley Papers, Mss. Afr. 2932

Muchmore papers, Mss. Afr. s.414

Howard Ross papers, Mss. Afr. S.469–475

John Holt Papers, Mss. Afr.536

John Holt Papers, Mss. Afr. S.825-826

'Transcript of interview with Sir George Sinclair', Mss. Afr.s.1622

Bibliography

Printed Materials

Colonial Office. *Togoland Annual Reports*, 1926–1945

Foreign Office, *Togoland* (handbook no. 17) (London: 1919)

Gill and Dufus, *Cocoa Statistics* (London)

Gold Coast. 'The Customs Ordinance of 1923 (No. 8)'

Gold Coast. H.M. Customs, *Preventive Service Instructions* (1935)

Gold Coast. *The Gold Coast Census of Population, 1948: Report and Tables*

Republic of Ghana. Census Office, *1960 Population Census of Ghana: Special Report 'E' – Tribes of Ghana*

Republic of Ghana. Census Office, *1984 Population Census of Ghana: Special Report on Localities by Local Authorities*

Republic of Ghana. *Ghana, 1977: An Official Handbook*

Republic of Ghana. *Ghana: Statistical Yearbook, 1969–70*

Republic of Ghana. *Parliamentary Debates*

Republic of Ghana. *Proceedings of the Constituent Assembly: Official Report* (1969)

Republic of Ghana. *Report of the (Jiagge) Commission into the Assets of Specified Persons*, 1969

United Nations Trusteeship Council. *Official Records*, 1947–1956

United Nations Trusteeship Council. *Reports of the United Nations Visiting Mission to Trust Territories in West Africa, Official Records of the Seventh Session of the Trusteeship Council (1 June–21 July 1950)*, Supplement No. 2 (T/798), 1951

United Nations Trusteeship Council. *United Nations Visiting Mission to Trust Territories in West Africa, 1952: Special Report on the Ewe and Togoland Unification Problem, Official Records: Eleventh Session (Second Part) (19 November–3 December 1952)*, Supplement No. 2

United Nations Trusteeship Council. *United Nations Visiting Mission to Trust Territories in West Africa, 1952: Report on Togoland Under United Kingdom Administration, Official Records: Thirteenth Session (28 January–25 March 1954)*, Supplement No. 2, 1954

United Nations Trusteeship Council. *Reports of the United Nations Visiting Mission to Trust Territories of Togoland Under British Administration and Togoland Under French Administration, 1955: Report on Togoland Under British Administration, Official Records, Eighteenth Session (7 June–14 August 1956)*, Supplement No. 2, 1956

United Nations Trusteeship Council. *Report of the United Nations Plebiscite Commissioner for the Trust Territory of Togoland Under British Administration* (T/1258, 19 June 1956)

Newspapers and Magazines

African Morning Post

Ashanti Pioneer

Customs News

Evening News

Ewe News-Letter

Focus on Customs

Gold Coast Express

Gold Coast Spectator

Legon Observer

(People's) Daily Graphic

West Africa

Bibliography
Secondary Sources
Articles

Adjei-Darko, Gilbert, 'From a department to a service', *Customs News*, 5, 11, June 1987

Ajayi, J.F.A., 'Colonialism: an episode in African history', in L.H. Gann and Peter Duignan (eds), *Colonialism in Africa 1870–1960 – Volume 1: The History and Politics of Colonialism 1870–1914*, Cambridge: Cambridge University Press, 1969

Akwetey, E.O., 'Ghana: violent ethno-political conflicts and the democratic challenge', in Adebayo O. Olukoshi and Liisa Laakso (eds), *Challenges to the Nation-State in Africa*, Uppsala & Helsinki: Nordiska Afrikainstitutet & Institute of Development Studies, 1996

Amenumey, D.E.K., 'The extension of British rule to Anlo (south-east Ghana), 1850–1890', *Journal of African History*, IX, 1, 1968

—— 'The pre-1947 background to the Ewe unification movement', *Transactions of the Historical Society of Ghana*, X, 1969

—— 'The general elections in the 'Autonomous Republic of Togo', April 1958: background and interpretation', *Transactions of the Historical Society of Ghana*, 15, 2, 1974

Amissah-Koomson, K., 'The Border Guards: the case history of an amorphous organisation', *Focus on Customs*, 1, 2, December 1980

Anon., 'Livre blanc sur la réunification du Togo', *Revue Française d'Études Politiques Africaines*, no. 121, Janvier 1976

Ansa-Asare, K., 'Legislative history of the legal regime of price control in Ghana', *Journal of African Law*, 29, 1985

Arhin, Kwame, 'The Ghana Cocoa Marketing Board and the cocoa farmer', in Kwame Arhin, Paul Hesp and Laurens van der Laan (eds), *Marketing Boards in Tropical Africa*, London & Boston: Kegan Paul International, 1985

Asiwaju, A.I., 'Migrations as revolt: the example of the Ivory Coast and the Upper Volta before 1945', *Journal of African History*, 17, 4, 1976

—— 'Partitioned culture areas: a checklist', in A.I. Asiwaju (ed.), *Partitioned Africans: Ethnic Relations Across Africa's International Boundaries 1884–1984*, London & Lagos: Christopher Hurst and University of Lagos Press, 1984

—— 'Law in African borderlands: the lived experience of the Yoruba astride the Nigeria–Dahomey border', in Kristin Mann and Richard Roberts (eds), *Law in Colonial Africa* , 1991

—— 'Borderlands in Africa: a comparative research perspective with particular reference to Western Europe', in Paul Nugent and A.I. Asiwaju (eds), *African Boundaries: Barriers, Conduits and Opportunities*, London & New York: Francis Pinter, 1996

Austin, Gareth, 'The emergence of capitalist relations in south Asante cocoa farming', *Journal of African History*, 28, 1987

—— 'Capitalists and chiefs in the cocoa hold-ups in south Asante, 1927-1938', *International Journal of African Historical Studies*, 21, 1, 1988

—— 'Human pawning in Asante 1800–1950: markets and coercion, gender and cocoa', in T. Falola and P. Lovejoy (eds), *Pawnship in Africa*, Boulder: Westview, 1994

—— 'Mode of production or mode of cultivation: explaining the failure of European cocoa planters in competition with African farmers in colonial Ghana', in William Gervase Clarence-Smith (ed.), *Cocoa Pioneer Fronts Since 1800: The Role of Smallholders, Planters and Merchants*, Houndmills & London: Macmillan, 1996

—— '"No elders were present": commoners and private ownership in Asante, 1807–96', *Journal of African History*, 37, 1, 1996

Bibliography

Azarya, Victor and Chazan, Naomi, 'Disengagement from the state in Africa: reflections on the experience of Ghana and Guinea', *Comparative Studies in Society and History*, 19, 1987

Barkindo, Bawuro, 'The Mandara astride the Nigeria-Cameroon boundary', in A.I. Asiwaju (ed.), *Partitioned Africans: Ethnic Relations Across Africa's International Boundaries 1884–1984*, London & Lagos: Christopher Hurst and University of Lagos Press, 1984

Barth, Frederik, 'Introduction', in *Ethnic Groups and Boundaries: The Social Organization of Cultural Difference*, Boston: Little, Brown & Co., 1969

Berg, Elliot, 'Structural change versus gradualism: recent economic development', in Philip Foster and Aristide Zolberg (eds), *Ghana and the Ivory Coast: Perspectives on Modernization*, Chicago & London: Chicago University Press, 1971

Brown, David, 'Anglo-German rivalry and Krepi politics, 1886-1894', *Transactions of the Historical Society of Ghana*, XV, ii, 1974

—— 'Borderline politics in Ghana: the National Liberation Movement of Western Togoland', *The Journal of Modern African Studies*, 18, 4, 1980

—— 'Who are the tribalists? social pluralism and political ideology in Ghana', *African Affairs*, 81, 322, 1982

—— 'Sieges and scapegoats: the politics of pluralism in Ghana and Togo', *The Journal of Modern African Studies*, 21, 34, 1983

Brydon, Lynne, 'Rice, yams and chiefs in Avatime: speculations on the development of a social order', *Africa*, 51, 2, 1981

—— 'Women, chiefs and power in the Volta Region of Ghana', *Journal of Legal Pluralism and Unofficial Law*, 37–38, 1996

Callaway, Barbara, 'Local politics in Ho and Aba', *Canadian Journal of African Studies*, 4, 1, 1970

Chazan, Naomi, 'Patterns of state-society incorporation and disengagement in Africa', in Donald Rothchild and Naomi Chazan (eds), *The Precarious Balance: State and Society in Africa*, Boulder & London: Westview Press, 1988

Clapham, Christopher, 'Boundaries and states in the new African order', in Daniel Bach (ed.), *Regionalisation in Africa: Integration and Disintegration*, Indianapolis & Oxford: Indiana University Press & James Currey, 1999

Collins, David, 'Partitioned culture areas and smuggling: The Hausa and groundnut trade across the Nigeria-Niger boundary up to the 1970s', in A.I. Asiwaju (ed.), *Partitioned Africans: Ethnic Relations Across Africa's International Boundaries 1884–1984*, London & Lagos: Christopher Hurst and University of Lagos Press, 1984

Crook, Richard, 'Bureaucracy and politics in Ghana: a comparative perspective', in Peter Lyon and James Manor (eds), *Transfer and Transformation: Political Institutions in the New Commonwealth*, Leicester: Leicester University Press, 1983

Darkoh, M.B.K., 'A note on the peopling of the forest hills of the Volta Region of Ghana', *Ghana Notes and Queries*, 11, June 1970

Dei, George J.S., 'Coping with the effects of the 1982–83 drought in Ghana: the view from the village', *Africa Development*, 13, 1, 1988

Dorm-Adzobu, C., 'The impact of migrant cocoa farmers in Buem, the Volta Region of Ghana', *Bulletin of the Ghana Geographical Association*, 16, 1974

Dowse, Robert, 'Military and police rule' in Dennis Austin and Robin Luckham (eds), *Politicians and Soldiers in Ghana 1966–72*, London: Frank Cass, 1975

Dumett, Raymond and Johnson, Marion, 'Britain and the suppression of slavery in the Gold Coast Colony, Ashanti and the Northern Territories', in Suzanne Miers and Richard Roberts (eds), *The End of Slavery in Africa*, Madison: University of Wisconsin Press, 1988

Fanso, Verkijika G., 'Traditional and colonial African boundaries: concepts and functions in inter-

Bibliography

group relations', *Présence Africaine*, 137/138, 1986

Flynn, Donna, '"We are the border": identity, exchange and the state along the Bénin-Nigeria border', *American Ethnologist*, 24, 2, 1997

Franco, G.R., 'The optimal producer price of cocoa in Ghana', *Journal of Development Economics*, 8, 1981

Fred-Mensah, Ben K., 'Bases of traditional conflict management among the Buems of the Ghana-Togo border', in I. William Zartman (ed.), *Traditional Cures for Modern Conflicts: African Conflict 'Medicine'*, Boulder & London: Lynne Rienner, 2000

Gayibor, N.L., 'Le remodelage des traditions historiques: la legende d'Agokoli, roi de Notse', in Claude-Helène Perrot (ed.) *Sources orales de l'histoire de l'Afrique*, Paris: CNRS, 1989

Gayibor, Nicoué, 'Agokoli et la dispersion de Notsé', in François de Medeiros (ed.), *Peuples du Golfe du Bénin*, Paris: Karthala, 1984

Gilbert, Michelle, '"No condition is permanent": ethnic construction and the uses of history in Akuapem', *Africa*, 67, 4, 1997

Giraut, Frédéric, 'La constitution d'une petite ville en région de plantation frontalière: Badou (Togo)', *Cahiers d'Outre-Mer*, 47, 1994

Griffiths, Ieuan, 'Permeable boundaries in Africa', in Paul Nugent and A.I. Asiwaju (eds) *African Boundaries: Barriers, Conduits and Opportunities*, London & New York: Frances Pinter, 1996

Herbst, Jeffrey, *States and Power in Africa: Comparative Lessons in Authority and Control*, Princeton: Princeton University Press, 2000

Hinjari, Wilberforce L., 'The impact of an international boundary on the political, social and economic relations of border communities: a case study of the Kano/Katsina states of Nigeria and Niger Republic', in A.I. Asiwaju and B.M. Barkindo (eds), *The Nigeria-Niger Transborder Cooperation*, Lagos & Oxford: Malthouse Press, 1993

Hodder, B.W., 'The Ewe problem: a reassessment', in C.A. Fisher (ed.), *Essays in Political Geography*, London: Methuen, 1968

Howard, Rhoda, 'Differential class participation in an African protest movement: the Ghana cocoa boycott of 1937–38', *Canadian Journal of African Studies*, 10, 3, 1976

Hughes, David McDermott, 'Refugees and squatters: immigration and the politics of territory on the Zimbabwe-Mozambique border', *Journal of Southern African Studies*, 25, 4, 1999

Johnson, Marion, 'Ashanti east of the Volta', *Transactions of the Historical Society of Ghana* VIII, 1965

Joseph, Richard, 'The German question in French Cameroun, 1919–1939', *Comparative Studies in Society and History*, 17, 1, 1975

Kea, R.A., 'Akwamu-Anlo relations', *Transactions of the Historical Society of Ghana*, X, 1969

Killingray, David, 'Military and labour policies in the Gold Coast during the First World War', in Melvin Page (ed.), *Africa and the First World War*, London: Macmillan, 1987

—— 'Guarding the extending frontier: policing the Gold Coast, 1865–1913', in David Anderson and David Killingray (eds), *Policing the Empire: Government, Authority and Control, 1830-1940*, Manchester: Manchester University Press, 1991

Kirk-Greene, A.H.M., 'The thin white line: the size of the British colonial service in Africa', *African Affairs*, 79, 1980

Kitchen, Helen, 'Filling the Togo vacuum', *Africa Report*, February 1963

Kopytoff, Igor, 'The internal African frontier: the making of African political culture', in Igor Kopytoff (ed.), *The African Frontier: The Reproduction of Traditional African Societies*, Bloomington & Indianapolis: Indiana University Press, 1987

Kopytoff, Igor and Miers, Suzanne, 'African 'slavery' as an institution of marginality', in Suzanne Miers and Igor Kopytoff (eds), *Slavery in Africa: Historical and Anthropological Perspectives*,

Bibliography

Madison: University of Wisconsin Press, 1977

Kropp-Dakubu, M.E. and Ford, K.C., 'The Central-Togo languages', in M.E. Kropp-Dakubu (eds), *The Languages of Ghana*, London: Kegan Paul International/International Africa Institute, 1988

Kumar, Ashok, 'Smuggling in Ghana: its magnitude and economic effects', *Universitas* 2, 3, 1973

Lasisi, R.O. , 'Liquor traffic in Africa under the League of Nations 1919–1945: French Togo as an example', *Nordic Journal of African Studies*, 5, 1, 1996

Law, Robin, 'Constructing "a real national history": a comparison of Edward Blyden and Samuel Johnson', in P.F. de Moraes Farias and Karin Barber (eds), *Self-Assertion and Brokerage: Early Cultural Nationalism in West Africa*, University of Birmingham: Centre of West African Studies 1990

—— 'Dahomey and the north-west', in Claude-Helène Perrot (ed.), *Cahiers du CRA no. 8: Spécial Togo–Bénin*, Paris: Afera Editions, 1994

Lentz, Carola, '"Tribalism" and ethnicity in Africa: a review of four decades of Anglophone research', *Cahiers des Sciences Humaines*, 31, 2, 1995

Lilley, C.C., 'A short history of the Nkonya division', *Gold Coast Review*, 1, 1925

Lonsdale, John, 'Wealth, poverty and civic virtue in Kikuyu political thought', in Bruce Berman and John Lonsdale (eds), *Unhappy Valley: Conflict in Kenya and Africa , Book Two: Violence and Ethnicity*, London: James Currey, 1992

Luckham, Robin, 'The Constitutional Commission 1966-69', in Dennis Austin and Robin Luckham (eds), *Politicians and Soldiers in Ghana 1966-72*, London: Frank Cass, 1975

Lyons, Maryinez, 'Foreign bodies: the history of labour migration as threat to public health in Uganda', in Paul Nugent and A.I. Asiwaju (eds), *African Boundaries: Barriers, Conduits and Opportunities*, London: Frances Pinter, 1996

Maier, Donna, 'Slave labor and wage labor in German Togo, 1885-1914', in Arthur Knoll and Lewis Gann (eds), *Germans in the Tropics: Essays in German Colonial History*, Westport: Greenwood, 1987

—— 'Military acquisition of slaves in Asante', in David Henige and T.C. McCaskie (eds), *West African Economic and Social History: Studies in Memory of Marion Johnson*, Wisconsin: Wisconsin University African Studies Program, 1990

Miles, John, 'Rural protest in the Gold Coast: the cocoa hold-ups, 1908-1938', in Clive Dewey and A.G. Hopkins (eds), *The Imperial Impact: Studies in the Economic History of Africa and India*, London: Athlone Press, 1978

Miller, Joe, 'Lineages, ideology and the history of slavery in Western Central Africa', in Paul Lovejoy (ed.), *The Ideology of Slavery in Africa*, Beverly Hills: Sage, 1981

Nugent, Paul, 'Educating Rawlings: the evolution of government strategy towards smuggling', in Donald Rothchild (ed.), *Ghana: The Political Economy of Recovery*, Boulder & London: Lynne Rienner, 1991

—— 'An abandoned project? The nuances of chieftaincy, development and history in Ghana's Volta Region', *Journal of Legal Pluralism and Unofficial Law*, 37–38, 1996

—— 'Arbitrary lines and the people's minds: a dissenting view on colonial boundaries in West Africa', in Paul Nugent and A.I. Asiwaju (eds), *African Boundaries: Barriers, Conduits and Opportunities*, London & New York: Frances Pinter, 1996

—— 'Power versus knowledge: smugglers and the state along Ghana's eastern frontier, 1920–1992', in M. Rösler and Tobias Wendl (eds), *Frontiers and Borderlands: Anthropological Perspectives*, Frankfurt, Berlin & New York: Peter Lang, 1999

—— '"A few lesser peoples": the Central Togo minorities and their Ewe neighbours', in Carola Lentz and Paul Nugent (eds), *Ethnicity in Ghana: The Limits of Invention*, London & New York:

Bibliography

Macmillan & St Martin's Press, 2000

—— 'The art of dissimulation: smugglers, informers and the Preventive Service along the Ghana–Togo frontier, 1920–1939', in C. Dubois, M. Michel and P. Soumille (eds), *Frontières plurielles frontières en Afrique subsaharienne*, Paris & Montréal: L'Harmattan, 2000

Nyassagbo, Gabriel Kwami, 'Urban–rural interactions in sub-Saharan Africa: the case of Palimé and its hinterland in south-west Togo', in Jonathan Barker (ed.), *Rural–Urban Dynamics in Francophone Africa*, Uppsala: Nordic Institute of African Studies, 1997

Owusu, Maxwell, 'Politics without parties: reflections on the Union Government debate', *African Studies Review*, 22, 2, 1979

Patterson, K. David, 'The influenza pandemic of 1918–19 in the Gold Coast', *Transactions of the Historical Society of Ghana*, XVI, 2 (also New Series No. 1), 1995

Pauvert, J.C., 'L'évolution politique des Ewe', *Cahiers d'Etudes Africaines*, 2, 1960

Phiri, S.H., 'National integration, rural development and frontier communities: the case of the Chewa and the Ngoni astride Zambian boundaries with Malawi and Mozambique', in A.I. Asiwaju (ed.) *Partitioned Africans: Ethnic Relations Across Africa's International Boundaries 1884–1984*, London & Lagos: Christopher Hurst and University of Lagos Press, 1984

Ranger, Terence, 'The invention of tradition in colonial Africa', in E. Hobsbawm and T. Ranger (eds), *The Invention of Tradition*, Cambridge: Cambridge University Press, 1983

—— 'Missionaries, migrants and the Manyika: the invention of ethnicity in Zimbabwe', in Leroy Vail (ed.), *The Creation of Tribalism in Southern Africa*, London: James Currey, 1989

—— 'The invention of tradition revisited: the case of colonial Africa', in Terence Ranger and Olufemi Vaughan (eds), *Legitimacy and the State in Twentieth-Century Africa*, London: Macmillan, 1993

Rathbone, Richard, 'Defining Akyemfo: the construction of citizenship in Akyem Abuakwa, Ghana, 1700–1939', *Africa*, 66, 4, 1996

Rhodie, Sam, 'The Gold Coast cocoa hold-up of 1930–31' *Transactions of the Historical Society of Ghana* 9, 1968

Saffu, E.O., 'Nkrumah and the Togoland question', *Economic Bulletin of Ghana*, 12, 2/3, 1968

Schober, Reinold, 'Native co-operation in Togoland', *Africa*, 9, 1936

Thompson, Vincent B., 'The phenomenon of shifting frontiers: the Kenya–Somalia case in the Horn of Africa', *Journal of Asian and African Studies*, 30, 1–2, 1995

Toulabor, Comi, 'Jeu de mots, jeu de vilains: lexique de la dérision politique au Togo', in J-F. Bayart, A. Mbembe and C. Toulabor (eds), *La politique par la bas en Afrique noire: contributions à une problématique de la démocratie*, Paris: Karthala, 1992

—— 'Political satire past and present in Togo', *Critique of Anthropology*, 14, 1, 1994

Twumasi, Yaw, 'Prelude to the rise of mass nationalism in Ghana, 1920–49: nationalists and voluntary associations', *Ghana Social Science Journal*, 3, 1, 1976

—— 'The 1969 election', in Dennis Austin and Robin Luckham (eds), *Politicians and Soldiers in Ghana 1966–1972*, London: Frank Cass, 1975

Vail, Leroy, 'Introduction: ethnicity in Southern African history', in Leroy Vail (ed.), *The Creation of Tribalism in Southern Africa*, London: James Currey, 1989

Van Allen, Judith, '"Aba riots" or Igbo "women's war"? Ideology, stratification and the invisibility of women', in Nancy Hafkin and Edna Bay (eds), *Women in Africa: Studies in Social and Economic Change*, Stanford: Stanford University Press, 1976

Ward, Barbara, 'Some notes on migration from Togoland', *African Affairs*, 49, 1950

Yearwood, Peter J., 'Great Britain and the repartition of Africa, 1914–19', *Journal of Imperial and Commonwealth History*, XVIII, 3, 1990

—— '"In a casual way with a blue pencil": British policy and the partition of Kamerun,

Bibliography

1914–1919', *Canadian Journal of African Studies*, 27, 2, 1993
—— 'From lines on maps to national boundaries: the case of Northern Nigeria and Cameroun', in J. Stone (ed.), *Maps and Africa: Proceedings of a Colloquium at the University of Aberdeen April 1993*, Aberdeen: Aberdeen University African Studies Group, 1994

Monographs

Adam, L., *Het Eeenheidsstreven Der Ewe*, Leiden: Afrika-Instituut, 1952
Addae, Stephen, *Evolution of Modern Medicine in a Developing Country: Ghana, 1880–1960*, Durham: Durham Academic Press, 1997
Afigbo, E.A., *The Warrant Chiefs: Indirect Rule in South-Eastern Nigeria, 1891–1929*, London: Longman, 1972
Agbanon II, Fio, *Histoire de Petit-Popo et du royaume Guin*, Lomé & Paris: Editions Haho & Karthala, 1991
Agyemang, Fred, *Amu The African: A Study in Vision and Courage*, Accra: Asempa, 1988
Akakpo, Amouzouvi, *Les frontières Togolaises: les modifications de 1927–1929*, Lomé: Université du Benin, 1979
Akyeampong, Emmanuel, *Drink, Power and Cultural Change: A Social History of Alcohol in Ghana c. 1800 to Recent Times*, Oxford: James Currey, 1996
Alemseged Abbay, *Identity Jilted or Re-Imagining Identity? The Divergent Paths of the Eritrean and Tigrayan Nationalist Struggles*, Lawrenceville & Asmara: Red Sea Press, 1998
Allman, Jean, *Quills of the Porcupine: Asante Nationalism in an Emergent Ghana*, Madison: University of Wisconsin Press, 1993
Amenumey, D.E.K., *The Ewe in Pre-Colonial Times*, Accra: Sedco, 1986
—— *The Ewe Unification Movement: A Political History*, Accra: Ghana Universities Press, 1989
Amonoo, Benjamin, *Ghana 1957–1966: Politics of Institutional Dualism*, London: Allen and Unwin, 1981
Anderson, Benedict, *Imagined Communities: Reflections on the Origin and Spread of Nationalism*, London and New York: Verso, 1983
Anene, J.C., *The International Boundaries of Nigeria 1885-1960*, London: Longman, 1970
Anon., *'Most Secret' Politics in Togoland: The British Government's Attempt to Annex Togoland to the Gold Coast*, New York: Contemporary Press, 1953
Asiwaju, A.I., *Western Yorubaland Under European Rule: A Comparative Analysis of French and British Colonialism*, London: Longman, 1976
Austin, Dennis, *Politics in Ghana, 1946-60*, Oxford: Oxford University Press, 1970
Austin, Dennis and Luckham, Robin (eds), *Politicians and Soldiers in Ghana*, London: Frank Cass, 1975
Awoonor, Kofi, *The Ghana Revolution: Background Account From a Personal Perspective*, New York: Oases Publishers, 1984
Baynham, Simon, *The Military and Politics in Nkrumah's Ghana*, Boulder & London: Westview, 1988
Beckman, Bjorn, *Organising the Farmers: Cocoa Politics and National Development in Ghana*, Uppsala: Scandinavian Institute of African Studies, 1976
Black, Jeremy, *Maps and History: Constructing Images of the Past*, New Haven & London: Yale University Press, 1997
Bosman, William, *A New and Accurate Description of the Coast of Guinea*, first published in 1704, London: Frank Cass, 4th English edn, 1967
Bovet, David and Unnevehr, Laurian, *Agricultural Pricing in Togo*, World Bank Staffing Paper, No. 467, July 1981

Bibliography

Bowdich, T.E., *Mission From Cape Coast Castle to Ashantee*, first published 1819, London: Frank Cass, 3rd edn, 1966

Brownlie, Ian, *African Boundaries: A Legal and Diplomatic Encyclopaedia*, London: Christopher Hurst/Royal Institute of International Affairs, 1979

Burke, Timothy, *Lifebuoy Men, Lux Women: Commodification, Consumption and Cleanliness in Modern Zimbabwe*, London: Leicester University Press, 1996

Callahan, Michael D., *Mandates and Empire: The League of Nations and Africa, 1914–1931*, Brighton & Portland: Sussex Academic Press, 1999

Cary, Joyce, *Mister Johnson*, London: Penguin edn, 1985

Chabal, Patrick and Daloz, Jean-Pascal, *Africa Works: Disorder as Political Instrument*, Oxford, Bloomington & Indianapolis: James Currey & Indiana University Press, 1999

Chambers, Robert (ed.), *The Volta Resettlement Experience*, London: Pall Mall Press, 1970

Chatterjee, Partha, *The Nation and its Fragments: Colonial and Postcolonial Histories*, Princeton: Princeton University Press, 1993

Chazan, Naomi, *An Anatomy of Ghanaian Politics: Managing Political Recession, 1969–1982*, Boulder: Westview, 1983

Coleman, J.S., 'Togoland', *International Conciliation*, No. 509, 1956

Comaroff, Jean and Comaroff, John, *Of Revelation and Revolution: Christianity, Colonialism and Consciousness in South Africa, Volume One*, Chicago & London: University of Chicago Press, 1991

Comaroff, John L. and Comaroff, Jean, *Of Revelation and Revolution: The Dialectics of Modernity on a South African Frontier, Volume Two*, Chicago & London: University of Chicago Press, 1997

Cordonnier, Rita, *Femmes Africaines et commerce: les revendeuses de tissu de la ville de Lomé*, Paris: L'Harmattan, 1987

Crowder, Michael *West Africa Under Colonial Rule*, London: Hutchinson, 1968

Crozier, Andrew, *Appeasement and Germany's Last Bid For Colonies*, Houndmills: Macmillan, 1988

D'Almeida-Ékué, Silivi, *La révolte des Loméennes 24–25 Janvier 1933*, Lomé: Les Nouvelles Éditions Africaines du Togo, 1992

D'Almeida, Silivi K. and Gbedemah, Seti Y., *Le Gouverneur Bonnecarrère au Togo*, Lomé: Les Nouvelles Éditions Africaines, 1982

Danquah, Moses, *The Birth of the Second Republic*, Accra: Editorial and Publishing Services, undated

Davidson, Basil, *The Black Man's Burden: Africa and the Curse of the Nation State*, London: James Currey, 1992

Debrunner, Hans, *A Church Between Colonial Powers: A Study of the Church in Togo*, London: Lutterworth Press, 1965

Decalo, Samuel (ed.), *Coups and Army Rule in Africa; Studies in Military Style*, New Haven & London: Yale University Press, 1976

—— *Historical Dictionary of Togo*, 2nd edn, Metuchen & London: Scarecrow Press, 1987

Donnan, Hastings and Wilson, Thomas M., *Borders: Frontiers of Nation and State*, Oxford & New York: Berg, 1999

Edney, Matthew, *Mapping an Empire: The Geographical Construction of British India 1765–1843*, Chicago: University of Chicago Press, 1990

Ellis, A.B., *A History of the Gold Coast of West Africa*, first published 1893, London & Dublin: Curzon Press, 1971

Farwell, Byron, *The Great War in Africa, 1914–1918*, Harmondsworth: Viking, 1987

Firmin-Sellers, Kathryn, *The Transformation of Property Rights in the Gold Coast: An Empirical Analysis Applying Rational Choice Theory*, Cambridge: Cambridge University Press, 1996

Foucault, Michel, *The History of Sexuality: An Introduction*, London: Penguin, 1978

Bibliography

—— *Discipline and Punish: The Birth of the Prison*, Harmondsworth: Penguin, 1979

Forbes, Frederick, *Dahomey and the Dahomans*, Vol. 1, reprint edn by Frank Cass, London, 1851

Frimpong-Ansah, Jonathan, *The Vampire State in Africa: The Political Economy of Decline in Ghana*, London: James Currey, 1991

Gayibor, Nicoué Lodjou, *Le Genyi: un royaume oublie de la côte de Guinee au tempe de la traite des noirs*, Lomé & Paris: Editions Haho & Karthala, 1990

—— (ed.), *Histoire des Togolais, Volume I: des origines à 1884*, Lomé: Presses de l'Université de Bénin, 1997

Genoud, Roger, *Nationalism and Economic Development in Ghana*, New York: Praeger, 1969

Greene, Sandra, E., *Gender, Ethnicity and Social Change on the Upper Slave Coast: A History of the Anlo-Ewe*, London: James Currey, 1996

Herbst, Jeffrey, *States and Power in Africa: Comparative Lessons in Authority and Control*, Princeton: Princeton University Press, 2000

Herslet, E., *The Map of Africa By Treaty, Volume I*, London: Frank Cass reprint edn, 1967

Hill, Polly, *The Gold Coast Cocoa Farmer: A Preliminary Survey*, Oxford: Oxford University Press, 1956

—— *Migrant Cocoa-Farmers of Southern Ghana*, Cambridge: Cambridge University Press, 1963

—— *Studies in Rural Capitalism in West Africa*, Cambridge: Cambridge University Press, 1970

Hoskyns, Catherine (ed.), *Case Studies in African Diplomacy: 2 - The Ethiopia, Somalia, Kenya Dispute*, London: Oxford University Press, 1969

Howard, Rhoda, *Colonialism and Underdevelopment in Ghana*, London: Croom Helm, 1978

Hyden, Goran, *Beyond Ujamaa in Tanzania: Underdevelopment and an Uncaptured Peasantry*, London: Heinemann, 1980

—— *No Shortcuts to Progress: African Development Management in Perspective*, London: Heinemann, 1983

Johnson, Samuel, *The History of the Yorubas*, Lagos: C.M.S. Bookshop, 1921

Jones, Trevor, *Ghana's First Republic, 1960-1966*, London: Methuen, 1976

Joseph, Richard, *Radical Nationalism in Cameroun: Social Origins of the U.P.C. Rebellion*, Oxford: Clarendon Press, 1977

Kay, G.B., *The Political Economy of Colonialism in Ghana: A Collection of Documents and Statistics, 1900–1960*, Cambridge: Cambridge University Press, 1972

Kent, John, *The Internationalization of Colonialism*, Oxford: Clarendon Press, 1992

Killick, Tony, *Development Economics in Action: A Study of Economic Policies in Ghana*, London: Heinemann, 1978

Kimble, David, *A Political History of Ghana, 1850–1928*, Oxford: Clarendon Press, 1963

Klose, Heinrich, *Le Togo sous drapeau Allemand (1894–1897)*, translation by Philippe David, Lomé: Edns Haho & Karthala, 1992

Knoll, Arthur J., *Togo Under Imperial Germany, 1884–1914: A Case Study in Colonial Rule*, Stanford: Hoover Institution Press, 1978

Knoll, Arthur and Gann, Lewis (eds), *Germans in the Tropics: Essays in German Colonial History*, New York & London: Greenwood, 1987

Kotey, R.A., *Competition Between Cocoa and Coffee: A Case Study*, Legon: Institute of Statistical, Social and Economic Research, University of Ghana, 1972

Kotey, R.A., Okali, C., and Rourke, B.E. (eds) *Economics of Cocoa Production and Marketing*, Legon: Institute of Statistical, Social and Economic Research, University of Ghana, 1974

Ladouceur, Paul, *Chiefs and Politicians: The Politics of Regionalism in Northern Ghana*, London: Longman, 1979

Law, Robin *The Slave Coast of West Africa, 1550–1750: The Impact of the Atlantic Slave Trade on an*

Bibliography

African Society, Oxford: Clarendon Press, 1991

Lawson, R.M., *The Changing Economy of the Lower Volta, 1954–67: A Study in the Dynamics of Rural Economic Growth*, London: Oxford University Press, 1972

Lentz, Carola and Nugent, Paul (eds), *Ethnicity in Ghana: The Limits of Invention*, London & New York: Macmillan & St. Martin's Press, 1999

Lovejoy, Paul and Hogendorn, Jan, *Slow Death For Slavery: The Course of Abolition in Northern Nigeria, 1897–1936*, Cambridge: Cambridge University Press, 1993

Louis, Wm Roger, *Great Britain and Germany's Lost Colonies, 1914–1919*, Oxford: Clarendon Press, 1967

Lyons, Maryinez, *The Colonial Disease: A Social History of Sleeping Sickness in Northern Zaire, 1900–1940*, Cambridge: Cambridge University Press, 1992

MacGaffey, Janet, *The Real Economy of Zaire: The Contribution of Smuggling to National Wealth*, London: James Currey, 1991

Maier, D.J.E., *Priests and Power: The Case of the Dente Shrine in Nineteenth-Century Ghana*, Bloomington: Indiana University Press, 1983

Mamdani, Mahmood, *Citizen and Subject: Contemporary Africa and the Legacy of Late Colonialism*, Kampala, Cape Town & London: Fountain, David Philip & James Currey, 1996

Manoukian, Madeline, *The Ewe-Speaking People of Togoland and the Gold Coast*, London: International Africa Institute, 1952

Marguerat, Yves, *Lomé: une brève histoire de la capitale du Togo*, Lomé & Paris: Edns Haho & Karthala, 1992

—— (ed.) *Dynamique urbaine: jeunesse et histoire au Togo*, Lome: Les Presses de l'Université du Bénin, 1993

Maroix, Général, *Le Togo pays d'influence française*, Paris: Larose-Editeurs, 1938

May, Ernesto, *Exchange Controls and Parallel Market Economics in Sub-Saharan Africa: Focus on Ghana*, World Bank Staff Working Paper, No. 711, Washington DC: World Bank, 1985

Mazrui, Ali, *The Africans: A Triple Heritage*, London: BBC Publications, 1986

McEwen, A.C., *International Boundaries of East Africa*, Oxford: Oxford University Press, 1971

McGlade, C., *An Economic Survey of Cocoa Farmers in the Jasikan Area of Trans-Volta / Togoland*, Economics Research Division, University of Ghana, Cocoa Research Series, 1957

Meyer, Birgit, *Translating the Devil: Religion and Modernity Among the Ewe in Ghana*, Edinburgh & London: Edinburgh University Press/International Africa Institute, 1999

Miers, Suzanne and Roberts, Richard (eds) *The End of Slavery in Africa*, Madison: University of Wisconsin Press, 1988

Mikell, Gwendolyn, *Cocoa and Chaos in Ghana*, New York: Paragon House, 1989

Miles, William F.S., *Hausaland Divided: Colonialism and Independence in Nigeria and Niger*, Ithaca & London: Cornell University Press, 1994

Moberly, F.J., *Military Operations: Togoland and the Cameroons*, London: His Majesty's Stationery Office, 1931

Nugent, Paul, *Big Men, Small Boys and Politics in Ghana: Power, Ideology and the Burden of History*, London & New York: Frances Pinter, 1995

—— *Myths of Origin and the Origin of Myth: Local Politics and the Uses of History in Ghana's Volta Region*, Working Papers on African Societies, no. 22, Berlin: Das Arabische Buch, 1997

—— *The Flight-Lieutenant Rides (to Power) Again: National Delusions, Local Fixations and the 1996 Ghanaian Elections*, Occasional Paper, Centre of African Studies, University of Edinburgh, 1998

Nukunya, G.K., *Kinship and Marriage Among the Anlo Ewe*, London: Athlone Press, 1999

Nyanteng, V.K., *The Declining Ghana Cocoa Industry: An Analysis of Some Fundamental Problems*, Legos: Institute of Statistical, Social and Economic Research, University of Ghana, Technical

Bibliography

Publication Series, no. 40, 1980

Obosu-Mensah, Kwaku, *Ghana's Volta Resettlement Scheme: The Long-Term Consequences of Post-Colonial State Planning*, San Francisco, London & Bethesda: International Scholars Publications, 1996

Okali, Christine *Cocoa and Kinship in Ghana: The Matrilineal Akan of Ghana*, London: Kegan Paul, 1983

Oquaye, Mike, *Politics in Ghana, 1972–1979*, Accra: Tornado Publications, 1980

Owusu, Maxwell, *Uses and Abuses of Political Power: A Case Study of Continuity and Change in the Politics of Ghana*, Chicago & London: University of Chicago Press, 1970

Pan, Lynn, *Alcohol in Colonial Africa*, Helsinki & Uppsala: Finnish Foundation for Alcohol Studies & Scandinavian Institute of African Studies, 1975

Peel, J.D.Y., *Ijeshas and Nigerians: The Incorporation of a Yoruba Kingdom, 1890s–1970s*, Cambridge: Cambridge University Press, 1983

Petrides, S. Pierre, *The Boundary Question Between Ethiopia and Somalia: A Legal and Diplomatic Survey with 20 Maps*, New Delhi: People's Publishing House, undated

Phillips, Anne, *The Enigma of Colonialism: British Policy in West Africa*, London: James Currey, 1989

Prescott, J.R.V., *Political Boundaries and Frontiers*, London: Allen & Unwin, 1987

Quaison-Sackey, Alex, *Africa Unbound: Reflections of an African Statesman*, New York: Praeger, 1963

Ranger, Terence, *Voices From the Rocks: Nature, Culture and History in the Matopos Hills of Zimbabwe*, Harare, Bloomington & Oxford: Baobab, Indiana University Press & James Currey, 1999

Rathbone, Richard (ed.), *British Documents on the End of Empire, Series B Volume 1: Ghana, Part II 1952–1957*, London: HMSO, 1992

—— *Nkrumah and the Chiefs: The Politics of Chieftaincy in Ghana, 1951–60*, Oxford, Athens & Accra: James Currey, Ohio University Press & F. Reimmer, 2000

Rodney, Walter in *How Europe Underdeveloped Africa*, Nairobi: East African Educational Publishers, 1972

Rothwell, Victor, *British War Aims and Peace Diplomacy, 1914–1918*, Oxford: Clarendon Press, 1971

Sahlins, Peter, *Boundaries: The Making of France and Spain in the Pyrenees*, Berkeley: University of California Press, 1989

Scott, James C., *Weapons of the Weak: Everyday Forms of Peasant Resistance*, New Haven & London: Yale University Press, 1985

—— *Domination and the Arts of Resistance: Hidden Transcripts*, New Haven & London: Yale University Press, 1990

Sharp, Alan, *The Versailles Settlement: Peacemaking in Paris, 1919*, Basingstoke: Macmillan, 1991

Sherwood, Marika, *Kwame Nkrumah: The Years Abroad, 1935–1947*, Legon: Freedom Publications, 1996

Smock, D. and Smock, A.C., *The Politics of Pluralism: A Comparative Study of Lebanon and Ghana*, New York: Elsevier, 1978

Spear, Thomas, *Mountain Farmers; Moral Economies of Land and Agricultural Development in Arusha and Meru*, Oxford: James Currey, 1997

Spieth, Jakob, *Die Ewe-Stämme: Material zur Kunde des Ewe-Volkes in Deutsch-Togo*, Berlin: Dietrich Reimer, 1906

Staniland, Martin, *The Lions of Dagbon: Political Change in Northern Ghana*, Cambridge: Cambridge University Press, 1975

Stone, Jeffrey C., *A Short History of the Cartography of Africa*, Lewiston, Queenston & Lampeter: Edwin Mellen Press, 1995

Thom, D.J., *The Nigeria-Niger Boundary, 1890-1906: A Study of Ethnic Frontiers and a Colonial*

Bibliography

Boundary, Athens: Ohio University Centre for International Studies, 1975

Thompson, W. Scott, *Ghana's Foreign Policy, 1957–1966: Diplomacy, Ideology, and the New State*, Princeton: Princeton University Press, 1969

Throup, David, *Economic and Social Origins of Mau Mau, 1945-53*, London: James Currey, 1987

Touval, Saadia, *The Boundary Politics of Independent Africa*, Cambridge, Mass.: Harvard University Press, 1972

Vail, Leroy, *The Creation of Tribalism in Southern Africa*, London: James Currey, 1989

Vaughan, Megan, *Curing Their Ills: Colonial Power and African Illness*, Cambridge: Polity Press, 1991

Verdon, Michel, *The Abutia Ewe of West Africa: A Chiefdom That Never Was*, Berlin, New York & Amsterdam: Mouton, 1983

Welch, Claude, *Dream of Unity: Pan-Africanism and Political Unification in West Africa*, Ithaca: Cornell University Press, 1966

Welman, C.W. *The Native States of the Gold Coast Part I: Peki*, London: Dawson reprint edn, 1969

Wesseling, H.L., *Divide and Rule: The Partition of Africa, 1880–1914*, translated by Arnold J. Pomerans, Westport & London: Praeger, 1996

Widstrand, Carl Gösta (ed.) *African Boundary Problems*, Uppsala: Scandinavian Institute of African Studies, 1969

Wilks, Ivor, *Asante in the Nineteenth Century*, Cambridge: Cambridge University Press, 1975

—— *Forests of Gold: Essays on the Akan and the Kingdom of Asante*, Athens: Ohio University Press, 1993

Yeebo, Zaya, *Ghana: The Struggle for Popular Power – Rawlings: Saviour or Demagogue*, London: New Beacon Books, 1991

Young, Crawford, *The African State in Comparative Perspective*, New Haven & London: Yale University Press, 1994

Theses and Unpublished Sources

Aligwekwe, I.E., 'The Ewe and Togoland problem: a case-study in the paradoxes and problems of political transition in West Africa', unpublished Ph.D thesis, Ohio State University, 1960

Anim-Asante, Joseph, 'A descriptive list of the records of the Customs Department in the National Archives of Ghana, Accra, 1920–1950', dissertation for Diploma in Archives Administration, 1988

Austin, G.M., 'Colonialism and economic development in southern British Togoland, 1921-1945', B.A. dissertation, University of Cambridge, 1978

Barrington, Leo, 'Migration and the growth of a resettlement community: Kete-Krachi, Ghana, 1962 and 1969', Ph.D thesis, Boston University, 1972

Brown, David, 'Politics in the Kpandu area of Ghana, 1925–1969: a study of the influence of central government and national politics upon local factional competition', unpublished Ph.D thesis, Birmingham University, 1977

Brydon, Lynne, 'Status ambiguity in Amedzofe Avatime: women and men in a changing patrilineal society', unpublished Ph.D thesis, Cambridge University, 1976

Buhler, Peter, 'The Volta Region of Ghana: economic change in Togoland, 1850–1914', Ph.D thesis, University of California, 1975

Coby, Paul, 'The development of the cocoa industry in Southern British Togoland', B.A. dissertation, University of Cambridge, 1978

Darkoh, M.B.K., 'An historical geography of the Ho-Kpandu-Buem area of the Volta Region of Ghana: 1884–1956' unpublished M.A. thesis, University of Ghana, 1966

Grau, Eugene E., 'The Evangelical Presbyterian Church (Ghana and Togo), 1914–1946: a study of

Bibliography

European mission relations affecting the beginning of an indigenous church', Ph.D thesis, Hartford Seminary Foundation, 1964, Ann Arbor: University Microfilms

Kouassi, Edouard Kwam, 'Les échanges frontaliers entre le Togo et le Ghana', memoire pour le diplôme de l'Institut d'Etudes Politiques du Paris, 1969

Kwaku, Ken, 'The political economy of peripheral development: a case-study of the Volta Region (Ghana) since 1920', Ph.D thesis, University of Toronto, 1975

Nugent, Paul, 'National integration and the vicissitudes of state power in Ghana: the political incorporation of Likpe, a border community, 1945–1986', Ph.D thesis, University of London, 1991

Osibo, Emmanuel, 'A short history of the Bakpeles (Likpes)', typescript, undated

Index

Index

Index

Index

Index

Index

Index

Index